NEW YORK & THE MID-ATLANTIC'S

BEST TRIPS

27 AMAZING ROAD TRIPS

This edition written and researched by

Michael Grosberg, Adam Karlin

SYMBOLS IN THIS BOOK

✓ Top Tips	📖 History & Culture	📷 Essential Photo
🔗 Link Your Trips	👪 Family	🏃 Walking Tour
💬 Tips from Locals	🍷 Food & Drink	🍴 Eating
↪ Trip Detour	🌳 Outdoors	🛏 Sleeping

📞 Telephone Number	@ Internet Access	📋 English-Language Menu
🕐 Opening Hours	🔊 Wi-Fi Access	👶 Family-Friendly
P Parking	🥗 Vegetarian Selection	🐾 Pet-Friendly
🚭 Nonsmoking	🏊 Swimming Pool	
❄ Air-Conditioning		

MAP LEGEND

Routes
- ▬▬▬ Trip Route
- ▬▬▬ Trip Detour
- ▬▬▬ Linked Trip
- ▬▬▬ Walk Route
- ▬▬▬ Tollway
- ▬▬▬ Freeway
- ▬▬▬ Primary
- ▬▬▬ Secondary
- ▬▬▬ Tertiary
- ▬▬▬ Lane
- ▬▬▬ Unsealed Road
- ✕✕✕ Plaza/Mall
- ▥▥▥ Steps
-)==(Tunnel
- ▬▬▬ Pedestrian Overpass
- --- Walk Track/Path

Boundaries
- --- International
- ---- State/Province
- ▬▬▬ Cliff

Population
- ✪ Capital (National)
- ◉ Capital (State/Province)
- ● City/Large Town
- ◦ Town/Village

Transport
- ✈ Airport
- ⊕ Cable Car/Funicular
- P Parking
- ⊕ Train/Railway
- ⊕ Tram
- Ⓜ Underground Train Station

Trips
- 1 Trip Numbers
- 9 Trip Stop
- 🏃 Walking tour
- ↪ Trip Detour

Highway Route Markers
- 97 US National Hwy
- 5 US Interstate Hwy
- 44 State Hwy

Hydrography
- River/Creek
- Intermittent River
- Swamp/Mangrove
- Canal
- Water
- Dry/Salt/Intermittent Lake
- Glacier

Areas
- Beach
- Cemetery (Christian)
- Cemetery (Other)
- Park
- Forest
- Reservation
- Urban Area
- Sportsground

PLAN YOUR TRIP

ON THE ROAD

CONTENTS

New York State
p31

New Jersey & Pennsylvania
p103

Washington DC, Maryland & Delaware
p181

Virginia
p251

Contents cont.

Classic Trips

Look out for the Classic Trips stamp on our favorite routes in this book.

Saranac Lake Tranquil waters in Adirondack Park (Trip 5)

WELCOME TO
NEW YORK &
THE MID-ATLANTIC

Backcountry wilds are a short drive from iconic skylines. This region, the heart of the East Coast, stretches along hundreds of miles of Atlantic Ocean and inland to remote mountains. And to take in all its variety, the physical and cultural landscape behind those peculiar accents and the local delicacies, you have to get in your car and drive.

These 27 road trips take you through Virginian backwoods to Chinatown alleyways. Up the Hudson Valley and down the Skyline Drive. They traverse the Adirondacks and the Appalachians and visit Niagara Falls and Chesapeake Bay. New Yorkers, Philadelphians and Washingtonians might be unaware of the rushing rivers only a half a tank of gas away, but we're not.

Explore colonial-era America and follow the route of Civil War armies. Make a pilgrimage to architectural and artistic icons. Escape to the beach or to far-off hiking trails. And if you've only got time for one trip, make it one of our eight Classic Trips, which take you to the very best of New York & the Mid-Atlantic states. Turn the page for more.

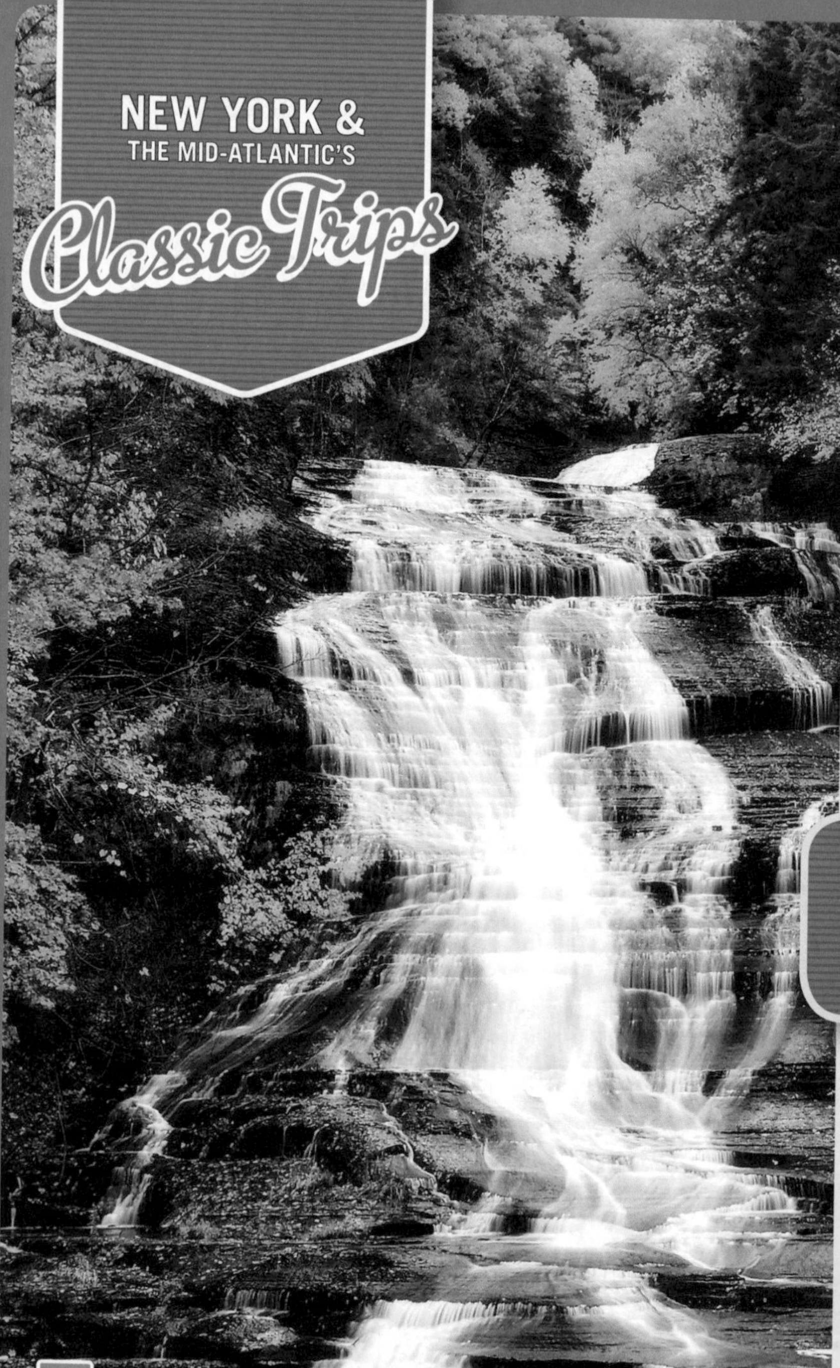
NEW YORK &
THE MID-ATLANTIC'S
Classic Trips

What is a Classic Trip

All the trips in this book show you the best of New York and the Mid-Atlantic states, but we've chosen eight as our all-time favorites. These are our Classic Trips – the ones that lead you to the best of the iconic sights, the top activities and unique experiences. Turn the page to see the map, and look out for the Classic Trip stamp throughout the book.

4 Finger Lakes Loop
Hike, fish or just admire the spectacular scenery at Buttermilk Falls State Park.

12 Pennsylvania Dutch Country Lancaster's bucolic farmland offers a taste of the quiet life.

23 The Civil War Tour
Discover the places where America forged her identity.

NODEROG/GETTY IMAGES ©

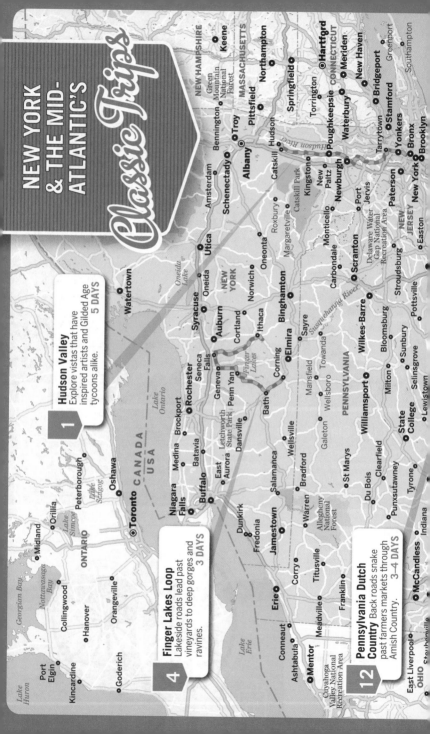

NEW YORK & THE MID-ATLANTIC'S

Classic Trips

1 Hudson Valley
Explore vistas that have inspired artists and Gilded Age tycoons alike.   **5 DAYS**

4 Finger Lakes Loop
Lakeside roads lead past vineyards to deep gorges and ravines.   **3 DAYS**

12 Pennsylvania Dutch Country Back roads snake past farmers markets through Amish Country.   **3–4 DAYS**

8 **The Jersey Shore**
Boardwalks and beaches galore line the Atlantic for classic summertime fun. **3–7 DAYS**

17 **Maritime Maryland**
Seaside towns, miles of marsh and sweaty Chesapeake crab shacks. **4 DAYS**

23 **The Civil War Tour**
Preserved battlefields, 19th-century countryside and Southern small towns. **3 DAYS**

25 **Blue Ridge Parkway**
College towns, back-road hamlets and miles of woolly wilderness trails. **4 DAYS**

21 **Skyline Drive**
Cross the Commonwealth's high-altitude spine in the green Shenandoah Valley. **3 DAYS**

ATLANTIC OCEAN

100 miles
200 km

New York & the Mid-Atlantic's best sights and experiences, and the road trips that will take you there.

NEW YORK &
THE MID-ATLANTIC'S
HIGHLIGHTS

National Mall

The Mall serves a number of roles. It is the great public green of America, hosting her seat of government (OK, the White House is technically a few blocks away), plus hundreds of protests, rallies and assorted demonstrations of mass democracy. On **Trip 15: Maryland's National Historic Road**, see how it serves as a space of shared memory via the Smithsonian Institution's museums, monuments and memorials to the nation's heroes.

TRIP 15

National Mall Washington Monument

Niagara Falls View of the falls from New York

Niagara Falls

The most jaded traveler will be impressed by the thundering spectacle of Niagara Falls on **Trip 6: Niagara Falls & Around**. The falls, a gushing tribute to nature's power, have inspired hundreds to take a leap – either a daredevil jump in a barrel, or into a wedding chapel. Sure, there are tacky shops nearby, but the falls are undeniably dramatic and become more impressive the closer and wetter you get.

TRIP 6

Wine Regions

Your search for the perfect vino will take you to beautiful beaches, verdant mountains and small lakeside towns. See vines cooled by salty Atlantic breezes on **Trip 2: Long Island**, or take in the mineral-filled land of upstate New York on **Trip 4: Finger Lakes Loop**. Sip your way through **Trip 26: Peninsula to the Piedmont**, then head for scenic mountains on **Trip 25: Blue Ridge Parkway**.

TRIPS 2 4 25 26

Civil War Sites

The legacy of the nation's great internecine conflict is imprinted on the landscape, especially on battlegrounds such as Antietam, Manassas and Gettysburg. See them on **Trip 23: The Civil War Tour**. A drive across Virginia from Petersburg to Appomattox traverses miles of split rail fences and green hills, and such museums as the American Civil War Experience in Richmond thoroughly examine the war.

TRIPS 12 23

Pennsylvania Dutch Country Amish boys driving a horse-drawn bugg

BEST BEACH BOARDWALKS

Ocean City Bad behavior, tacky T-shirts, lots of neon and odd art galleries. **Trip** 19

Rehoboth Beach Catering to families and the LGBT community. Try the saltwater taffy. **Trip** 19

Wildwood The Grand Daddy of Jersey Shore boardwalks with rides to rival most amusement parks. **Trip** 8

Atlantic City Massive casinos on one side, beach and amusements on the other. **Trip** 11

Coney Island An old-fashioned roller coaster and famous hot dogs anchor NYC's classic boardwalk. **Trip** 2

Pennsylvania Dutch Country

As you'll see on **Trip 12: Pennsylvania Dutch Country**, the Amish really do drive buggies and plow their fields by hand. In Dutch Country – where small roads wind their way through postcard-perfect farmland – the pace is slower. This is no costume reenactment. While 21st-century commercialism and suburbia are close at hand, here picturesque windmills are still a power source.

TRIP 12

15

Blue Ridge Parkway Linn Cove Viaduct winds around forested mountains

Blue Ridge Parkway

The backbone of Virginia is the Blue Ridge Mountain range: the beginning of wild America, a forested spine that was our nation's first frontier. **Trip 25: Blue Ridge Parkway** snakes across these summits. On either side of the mountains lies a unique culture that blends fiercely conservative small-town values and artsy, progressive collegiate havens.

TRIP 25

BEST SCENIC ROADS

US 13 This road runs through an isolated, unique wetland and cultural enclave. **Trip** 20

Rte 6 Rugged stretch of mountains includes gushing creeks and wildlife. **Trip** 14

Old Mine Rd One of the country's oldest roads offers beautiful river vistas. **Trip** 10

Platte Clove Rd/Rte 16 A hair-raising vertiginous mountain road through forested Catskills. **Trip** 3

Skyline Drive Follow the peaks and valleys of a forested former frontier. **Trip** 21

17

Central Park New York City overlooks this vast green space

Beaches Rehoboth Beach boardwalk (Trip 19)

Central Park

One of the world's most renowned green spaces, Central Park has 843 acres of rolling meadows, elm-lined walkways and manicured gardens, a lake, a reservoir, an outdoor theater, a zoo, an idyllic waterside eatery and one very famous statue of Alice in Wonderland. New Yorkers sunbathe, picnic, stroll, bike and run in what is essentially their backyard. Join them on **Trip 2: Long Island**.

TRIP 2

Historic Architecture

From the Gilded Age mansions on **Trip 1: Hudson Valley** to the townhouses of Richmond, VA, the region's role in the nation's history is writ large. Check out historic architecture in Frederick, MD, on **Trip 15: Maryland's National Historic Road**, or see Colonial Williamsburg on **Trip 26: Peninsula to the Piedmont**.

TRIPS 1 9 11 15
17 23 26

Beaches

As you may realize on **Trip 8: The Jersey Shore** or **Trip 19: Delmarva**, all of the New Jersey coastline and southern Delaware is basically one big beach, including artsy enclaves and quiet refuges. **Trip 17: Maritime Maryland** offers cheesy boardwalk fun, while those searching for the anti-boardwalk experience should head to Sandbridge Beach on Assateague Island.

TRIPS 2 8 17
19 27

Appalachian Trail

Cutting through the Mid-Atlantic's mountain ranges, the Appalachian Trail is about 2200 miles long – and you're meant to walk it. You may not have that kind of time, but many of the trips we have created – especially **Trip 22: Across the Appalachian Trail** – allow you to pop on and off the trail, savoring its immense natural beauty and the unique cultural folkways that have grown around it.

TRIP

Small Towns

This is a region of small towns and stunning scenery, where city dwellers seek a slower pace and artists retreat for inspiration. Experience the bohemian vibes of Catskill hamlets on **Trip 3: Tranquil Catskills** or visit college towns such as Lexington, VA. See Maryland's crab-picking waterman's villages on **Trip 20: Eastern Shore Odyssey** or journey along the Delaware River – it's lined with small towns.

TRIPS

(left) **Appalachian Trail** New River Gorge, Fayetteville (Trip 22);
(below) **St Lawrence Seaway** Small towns line this route

St Lawrence Seaway

Virtually unknown to downstate New Yorkers, in part because of its relative inaccessibility, this region of more than 1800 islands is a scenic wonderland separating the US from Canada. **Trip 7: St Lawrence Seaway** passes through small towns and fishing villages backed by the vivid blues of Lake Ontario and the St Lawrence River.

TRIP 7

BEST FOOD

Red Roost All-you-can-eat steamed crabs in an old chicken coop. **Trip** 17

AVA Restaurant & Wine Bar Fine dining for all, including vegans. **Trip** 25

Blue Hill at Stone Barns A farm-fresh feast that's always exceptional. **Trip** 1

Hazelnut Kitchen Inventive food in the heart of Finger Lakes wine country. **Trip** 4

Brewer's Alley Go for the beer, stay for the food...and another beer. **Trip** 27

IF YOU LIKE ...

Pennsylvania Let the kids horse around (Trip 12)

Outdoor Activities

Explore mountain forests, deep river gorges and glacial lakes, not to mention windswept beaches and sandy dunes.

21 Skyline Drive Numerous hikes, wildlife campouts and cavern systems are on offer.

5 Adirondack Peaks & Valleys Backcountry paths turn into cross-country trails in winter.

17 Maritime Maryland Explore the transition space between salt and freshwater, including stunning marsh and wetland biomes.

14 Through the Wilds Along Route 6 Combine stargazing with backcountry trails to canyon floors.

16 Along the C&O Canal This forested track lays on the banks of the Potomac River and in the shadow of the Appalachian Mountains.

Art & Architecture

Every taste is satisfied, whether you're a devotee of Frank Lloyd Wright or a fan of stately pre-revolutionary row houses, world class museums or massive open-air sculpture parks.

13 Pittsburgh & the Laurel Highlands Stunning architectural masterpieces in the country and top flight museums in the city.

20 Eastern Shore Odyssey The cute red brick of Dover contrasts nicely with the palatial grounds nearby.

1 Hudson Valley Modern art at the Dia:Beacon, spectacular mansions and the valley's own school of painting.

16 Along the C&O Canal Georgetown and Harpers Ferry both have a plethora of lovely Federal-style architecture.

Urban Adventures

Big, cosmopolitan NYC is a world unto itself but don't forget about Philly, DC, Baltimore and Pittsburgh, each with their own distinctive personalities.

2 Long Island Begin the trip in NYC, the nation's most exciting metropolis of kaleidoscopic variety and dizzying proportions.

11 Brandywine Valley to Atlantic City Philly's historic cobblestone streets are alive with contemporary culture.

15 Maryland's National Historic Road Explore Baltimore, one of the oldest, saltiest, and most eccentric ports in North America.

23 The Civil War Tour Richmond was once capital of the Confederacy; now it has a small, vibrant food and nightlife scene.

Harpers Ferry Take a boat ride along the Potomac River to this quaint town (Trip 16)

Family Fun

Child-friendly destinations abound, from boardwalk amusement parks to natural wonders and living history museums.

12 Pennsylvania Dutch Country Ride a horse and buggy carriage or an old steam engine through picturesque farmland.

20 Eastern Shore Odyssey Friendly towns like Berlin and Snow Hill, plus Ocean City's beaches, are nice family retreats.

19 Delmarva Bethany Beach is a family-friendly seaside retreat and kids love the ponies on Assateague Island.

26 Peninsula to the Piedmont Much of Virginia Beach is family friendly, as are colonial Williamsburg, Yorktown and Jamestown.

6 Niagara Falls & Around Get wet from a close-up perspective of mesmerizing Niagara Falls.

History

Much of the young nation's fortunes were determined by events in this region. Visit significant sites of the French and Indian War, Revolutionary War and Civil War not to mention Philly's role as the country's first capital.

23 The Civil War Tour Learn about the nation's most important conflict while visiting some of its most sacred battlefields.

9 Bucks County & Around See where George Washington strode and the founding fathers hashed things out.

15 Maryland's National Historic Road Maryland, one of the most diverse states in America, has a history that's both progressive and painful.

18 Southern Maryland Triangle Explore an area that somehow blended advocacy for religious freedom with enforced slavery.

Natural Vistas

Stunning landscapes are all over this region's map, but it's not only the mountains that provide spectacular views. Lakeside vineyards, sandy dunes and river valleys also provide dramatic panoramas.

25 Blue Ridge Parkway Sunsets in western Virginia turn the Blue Ridge that particular shade of cobalt that is simply stunning.

10 Down the Delaware Get out on the river for continually changing wide-open perspectives on the valley all around you.

21 Skyline Drive The name isn't an exaggeration: rolling on this road makes you feel like you're skimming atop the Shenandoahs.

5 Adirondack Peaks & Valleys Ride the Whiteface Mountain gondola for a bird's-eye perspective of the mountains.

NEED ^{TO} KNOW

CELLPHONES

The only foreign phones that work in the USA are GSM multiband models. Network coverage is poor in mountainous and rural regions.

INTERNET ACCESS

Free wi-fi is found in hotels, cafes and several fast food chains in the region, though the smaller the town, the more likely you'll only have access in hotel lobbies.

FUEL

Gas stations, open late or 24 hours, are ubiquitous in areas surrounding large urban centers but infrequent and with more limited hours in rural parts of the region. Plan ahead. Not found on Blue Ridge and Skyline Drive. Average cost per gallon is $3.50.

RENTAL CARS

Avis (www.avis.com)

Dollar (www.dollar.com)

Rent-A-Wreck (www.rentawreck.com)

IMPORTANT NUMBERS

AAA (☎800-222-4357)

Directory Assistance (☎411)

Emergency (☎911)

Climate

Warm to hot summers, cold winters
Warm to hot summers, mild winters

● **Lake Placid**
GO Dec–Mar

● **New York City**
GO Sep–Dec

● **Pittsburgh**
GO May–Sep

● **Ocean City**
GO Jun–Sep

● **Richmond**
GO Apr–May

When to Go

High Season (Jun–Aug)

» The weather can be extremely hot and humid; mountains offer relief.

» Storms (including hurricanes) occur at this time.

» Many festivals and outdoor concerts.

Shoulder Season (Mar–May & Sep–Nov)

» This is high season for DC due to the Cherry Blossom festival.

» Some hotels open in beach towns if the weather is warm.

» Most temperate time of year. But March, October and November are wet.

Low Season (Dec–Feb)

» Cold weather, rainy conditions (snow in the mountains so peak time there for winter sports).

» Attractions open fewer days and shorter hours.

» Most businesses in beach towns shut during this period.

Daily Costs

Budget: Less than $100
» Camping: $20–$30

» Meals in roadside diners: $5–$15

» State parks, walking tours: free

Midrange: $100–$250
» Double room in midrange hotel or B&B: $75–$120

» Meals at midrange restaurants: $20–$40

» Museum admission: $10–$20

Top End: More than $250
» Swanky B&B or hotel: $200 and up

» Meals in top-end restaurants: $50 and up

Eating

Roadside Diners Wide-ranging menus of classic American food.

Farmers Markets Regional-specific freshly harvested produce and locally produced goods.

Restaurants The more rural the area, the less likely you'll find healthy choices.

Vegetarian Selections available at most restaurants and cafes.

Eating price indicators represent the cost of a main dish:

$	less than $10
$$	$11–$19
$$$	more than $20

Sleeping

B&Bs Often evoking a homespun atmosphere, and usually including breakfast.

Camping Tent sites and sometimes cabins available at most state parks; facilities range from 'primitive' to 'developed'.

Motels Affordable roadside accommodations commonly clustered around interstate exits and main routes into town.

Resorts Typically all-inclusive affairs with activities on offer.

Sleeping price indicators represent the cost of a double room with private bathroom:

$	less than $100
$$	$100–$200
$$$	more than $200

Arriving in New York & the Mid-Atlantic

John F Kennedy International Airport

Rental Cars Take the AirTrain to the Federal Circle stop for car rental companies.

Taxis To Manhattan: $52 plus tolls and tip.

Subway Airtrain to Jamaica Station for the LIRR ($17 total) into Penn Station or to Howard Beach for A train ($7.50 total) into city.

Shuttles Door-to-door from $20.

Newark International Airport

Rental Cars Take the AirTrain Newark (free) to stations P2 and P3 for car rental company offices.

Taxis To west side of midtown Manhattan: $55 plus tolls and tip.

Train Air train ($5.50) connects to Jersey Transit rail service and PATH trains into city.

Shuttles Door-to-door from $20.

Reagan National Airport

Rental Cars Agencies are a 10-minute walk/free shuttle ride away in parking garage A.

Taxis Around $12 to $20 to downtown Washington DC.

Shuttles Door-to-door $14 to $25.

Metro Reagan National Airport metrorail station is attached to the airport.

Money

ATMs widely available. Credit cards accepted at most hotels and restaurants.

Tipping

Standard is 15% to 20% for waiters and bartenders and 10% to 20% for taxi drivers.

Opening Hours

Opening hours are reduced in January and February.

Bars ⏰5pm–midnight, to 2am or later in large cities.

Restaurants ⏰Breakfast 7am–11am, lunch midday–3pm, dinner 5pm–11pm.

Shops ⏰10am–7pm, some closed on Sunday.

Useful Websites

National Parks Service (www.nps.gov/parks) Fast facts about national parks, recreation areas and historic sites.

Civil War Trails (www.civilwartrails.org) The most exhaustive resource for Civil War Trail tourists.

Lonely Planet (www.lonelyplanet.com/USA) Travel tips, accommodation, travelers' forum and more.

For more, see Driving in New York & the Mid-Atlantic (p334

CITY GUIDE

NEW YORK CITY

Loud, fast and pulsing with energy, New York City is symphonic, exhausting and constantly reinventing itself. Fashion, theater, food, music, publishing and the arts all thrive here and almost every country in the world has its own enclave somewhere in the five boroughs.

Getting Around

City driving is an adventure, nay a survival course. Take the subway, though service changes can confuse. Buses go slowly but provide views. Hundreds of miles of cycling lanes have been added and a new bike-share program was initiated in June 2013.

Parking

Street signage can cause confusion. Ticket-giving transit cops roam in force. Ask a passerby for advice. Private garages, in Manhattan especially, charge extortionate rates. The further away from the center of the city's grid, the more likely you are to find a spot. Some hotels provide valet parking for $40 to $65 for 24hrs.

New York City Brooklyn Bridge

Where to Eat

Nearly 20,000 restaurants means food is everywhere. The highest concentration of good food is downtown, south of 14th St. Head to Chinatown for delicious hole-in-the-wall eateries, the East Village for an enormous variety of affordable ethnic restaurants and the Lower East Side and West Village for more upscale trendy dining.

Where to Stay

Unsurprisingly, hotels are clustered in and around the tourist mecca of Times Square and midtown in general. For less frenzy try a B&B in the East or West Village or a boutique hotel in lower Manhattan.

Useful Websites

Gothamist (www.gothamist.com) Blog with insider notes about all the goings-on in the city.

New York Magazine (www.nymag.com) News, culture and latest happenings.

NYC & Company (www.nycgo.com) City's official tourism site with loads of information.

Lonely Planet (www.lonelyplanet.com//usa/new-york-city) Tips from your trusted travel source.

Trips through New York City

For more, check out our city and country guides. www.lonelyplanet.com

Philadelphia Old City and Independence National Historic Park

PHILADELPHIA

Dubbed 'America's most historic square mile,' Philly's fascinating colonial past is on display at Independence National Historic Park. Wander beyond the cobblestone alleyways to explore the city's independent-minded restaurant scene, its copious riverfront parks, unique museums and evolving neighborhoods where ethnic pride mixes with contemporary boho culture.

Getting Around

Downtown distances are short enough to let you see most places on foot, and a train, bus or taxi can get you to places further out relatively easily.

Parking

You can pay with a card rather than hunt for quarters at parking kiosks. Signs, however, can be tricky. For insider tips check out www.visitphilly. com/parking. Most hotels offer a parking service, usually $20 to $45 per day.

Where to Eat

Reading Terminal, the 9th St Market and cheesesteaks all deservedly come to mind. But the city's culinary diversity is on par with almost any other East Coast city and an expanding homegrown, slow-food, neighborhood-centric restaurant culture threatens to overshadow the old-school classics.

Where to Stay

Though the majority of places are found in and around Center City, alternatives are sprinkled throughout other neighborhoods. There's certainly no shortage of places to stay, but it's primarily national chains or B&Bs.

Useful Websites

Visit Philly (www.visitphilly. com) Well-organized site of the city's official tourism bureau.

Foobooz (www.foobooz.com) An up-to-date guide to drinking and eating in the city.

Hidden City Philadelphia (www.hiddencityphila.org) Blog covering lesser-known aspects and happenings in the city.

Trips through Philadelphia `9` `11`

WASHINGTON, DC

The nation's capital is best known to tourists for its superlative monuments and museums, but there's so much more to DC. A staggering amount of the young, ambitious and talented are drawn here, and a burgeoning food, arts and nightlife scene grows every day to accommodate this demographic.

Getting Around

The DC metro (subway) system is the easiest way around town. Five lines – green, red, yellow, orange and blue – connect across town, and fare is based on the distance traveled between stations. The metro is open until midnight on weekdays and 3am on Friday and Saturday nights.

Parking

Garages are expensive and street parking is a hassle. Numerous restrictions mean it's hard to park longer than two hours anywhere, and many streets are too crowded with cars for parking anyway. Some hotels provide parking for a fee.

Where to Eat

There are great restaurants, generally mid-range to high-end (DC has few budget eateries) within easy walking distance of the following metro stops: Gallery Place-Chinatown; U-Street/African-Amer Civil War Memorial/Cardozo; Columbia Heights; Eastern Market; Capitol South; Dupont Circle; Woodley Park-Zoo and Cleveland Park. Georgetown, which is off the metro, is also a good bet.

Where to Stay

Hotels are sprinkled across town, especially near the following metro stops: Metro Center, Farragut West, Georgetown, Gallery Place-Chinatown, Dupont Circle and Capitol South, as well as Georgetown, off the metro. Try Arlington and Alexandria for cheaper chain-hotel options.

Useful Websites

Washington Metropolitan Area Transit Authority (www.wmata.com) Guide to the DC metro.

Washington Post Going Out Guide (www.washingtonpost.com/gog) A run-down on events, dining and entertainment.

The Washingtonian (www.washingtonian.com) Covers all elements of DC's cultural scene.

Trips through Washington, DC `16` `23`

New York
Trips

UPSTATE AND DOWNSTATE, FROM THE GREAT LAKES TO LONG ISLAND, New York covers a vast range of territory. It's most famous for its eponymous city, but beyond the borders of Manhattan are deep mountain ravines, swiftly moving rivers and quaint villages evolving into weekend arts retreats. Upstate New York is a living canvas of lush forests, crystal-clear lakes and stormy dark hills.

Generations of artists have immersed themselves in the solitude of the Catskills, the fragrant vineyards of the Finger Lakes, the soaring heights of the Adirondack Mountains and the roaring thunder of Niagara Falls, which flows into the island-studded St Lawrence River. Anchoring these delights is New York City, the always-changing cosmopolitan colossus.

Hudson Valley
JUNE MARIE SOBRITO/GETTY IMAGES ©

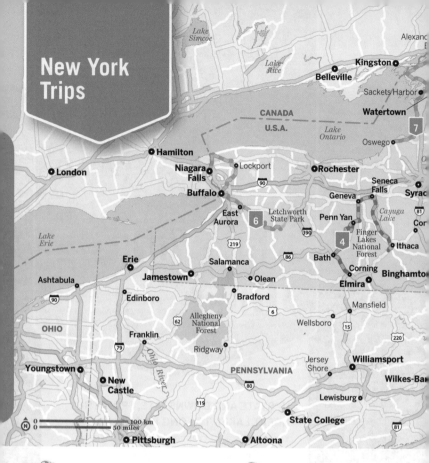

New York Trips

Classic Trip

1 Hudson Valley 5 Days
Explore vistas that have inspired artists and Gilded Age tycoons alike. (p35)

2 Long Island 4 Days
Follow this route to wide ocean beaches, vineyards and the luxurious Hamptons. (p47)

3 Tranquil Catskills 3–4 Days
See small rural towns in a bucolic region of undulating, forest-covered mountains. (p57)

Classic Trip

4 Finger Lakes Loop 3 Days
Lakeside roads lead past dozens of vineyards to deep gorges and ravines for hiking. (p65)

5 Adirondack Peaks & Valleys 7 Days
This enormous, majestic region is dotted with lakes, rivers and high mountain peaks. (p75)

6 Niagara Falls & Around 3–4 Days
Mesmerising falls get you started on a trip to architectural and historic sites in western New York. (p85)

7 **St Lawrence Seaway 2–3 Days**
Head down this island-studded stretch
of small towns and fishing villages on the
waterlogged Canadian border. (p93)

DON'T MISS

Roxbury Motel

Spend a few nights in
one of the whimsically
designed rooms
inspired by movies and
TV shows from the '70s
and '80s on Trip **3**

Wild Center

Animals and scratch-
and-sniff exhibits make
this natural history
museum anything but
stuffy. Journey here on
Trip **5**

Boldt Castle

Surrounded by water,
this iconic fairy-tale-
like home inspires the
imagination. Hop on a
boat to take you here on
Trip **7**

Sagamore Hill

A nature trail behind
the museum leads to a
picturesque little sandy
beach. Take a break
from the museum here
on Trip **2**

Bear Mountain State Park

Enjoy great views of
the Manhattan skyline
from the top of this
park's peak, only 40
miles from New York
City. See it on Trip **1**

Hudson An attractive town with a hip community

Classic Trip

Hudson Valley

1

Painters, presidents and captains of industry were beguiled by the breathtaking river views this drive affords. The mansions still stand, as do forested parks, museums and a military academy.

TRIP HIGHLIGHTS

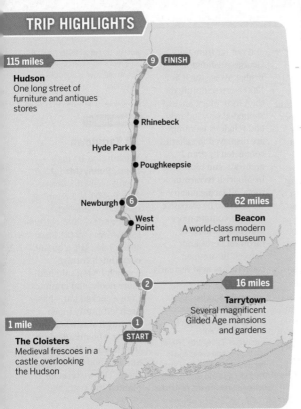

115 miles ⑨ **FINISH**

Hudson
One long street of furniture and antiques stores

● **Rhinebeck**

Hyde Park ●
● **Poughkeepsie**

Newburgh ● ⑥ **62 miles**

West Point ●
Beacon
A world-class modern art museum

② **16 miles**

Tarrytown
Several magnificent Gilded Age mansions and gardens

1 mile ① **16 miles**
START

The Cloisters
Medieval frescoes in a castle overlooking the Hudson

5 DAYS
115 MILES / 185KM

GREAT FOR ...

BEST TIME TO GO
Grounds of historic estates open mid-May through September.

 ESSENTIAL PHOTO

Valley view from Olana for classic panorama.

 BEST FOR FOODIES

It's worth making a pilgrimage to Blue Hill at Stone Barns.

1 Hudson Valley

Immediately north of New York City, green becomes the dominant color and the vistas of the Hudson River and the mountains breathe life into your urban-weary body. The history of the region, home to the Hudson River School of painting in the 19th century and a retreat for Gilded Age industrialists, is preserved in the many grand estates, flowering gardens and picturesque villages.

TRIP HIGHLIGHT

1 The Cloisters

This trip along the Hudson begins at one of New York City's most magnificent riverside locations. Gaze at medieval tapestries, frescoes, carvings and gold treasures, including a St John the Evangelist plaque dating from the 9th century, inside the **Cloisters Museum & Gardens** (www.metmuseum. org/cloisters; Fort Tryon Park; suggested donation adult/child $25/free; ⊙9:30am-4:45pm Tue-Sun Nov-Feb, to 5:15pm Mar-Oct). This magnificent Metropolitan Museum annex, built to look like an old castle, is set in Fort Tryon Park overlooking the Hudson River, near the northern tip of Manhattan

and not far from the George Washington Bridge. Works such as a 1290 ivory sculpture of the Virgin Mary, ancient stained-glass windows and religious paintings are displayed in galleries connected by grand archways and topped by Moorish terracotta roofs, all facing an airy courtyard. The extensive grounds contain more than 250 varieties of medieval herbs and flowers. In summer, concerts are held regularly.

The Drive » Rte 9A north crosses the Spuyten Duyvil Creek, marking the boundary between Manhattan (p44) and the Bronx with some nice river views. Taking Rte 9 North is a slow option compared to hopping on I-87, the New York Thruway, and you pass through some run-down parts of Yonkers,

but you do get a feel for several nice residential communities. The whole drive is about 18.5 miles long.

TRIP HIGHLIGHT

2 Tarrytown

Washington Irving's home, **Sunnyside** (♪Sat & Sun 914-591-8763, Mon-Fri 914-631-8200; 89 W Sunnyside Lane, Sleepy Hollow; adult/ senior/child $12/10/6; ⊙10am-5pm Wed-Mon Apr-Oct, 10am-4pm Nov-Dec; ♿), a quaint, cozy Dutch cottage – which Irving said had more nooks and crannies than a cocked hat – has been left pretty much the way it was when the author who dreamed up the Headless Horseman and Ichabod Crane lived there. The wisteria he planted 100 years ago

still climbs the walls, and the spindly piano inside still carries a tune.

Not far north on Rte 9 is **Philipsburg Manor** (☎Mon-Fri 914-631-8200, Sat & Sun 914-631-3992; www.historichudsonvalley.com; 381 N Broadway, Sleepy Hollow; adult/senior/child $12/10/6; ☺10am-5pm Wed-Mon Apr-Oct, 10am-4pm Nov-Dec;), a working farm in 17th-century Dutch style. Wealthy Dutchman Frederick Philips brought his family here around 1680 and meticulously built his new farm. Inside the rough-hewn clapboard barns and three-story, whitewashed fieldstone manor, it's all sighs and clanks as old fireplaces and strained beams do their work.

From Philipsburg Manor, grab a shuttle to the sprawling splendor of **Kykuit** (☎914-631-9491; Pocantico Hills, Tarrytown; adult/senior/

S LINK YOUR TRIP

3 **Tranquil Catskills**
Head into forested mountain roads from Rte 9W near Kingston or off I-87 at New Paltz.

5 **Adirondack Peaks & Valleys**
For true wilderness, follow the Hudson River to its source by taking I-87 north to Lake George.

child $22/20/18; ⊙ tours 9:45am, 1:45pm & 3pm), the Rockefeller family's old European-style estate perched on a bluff high atop the Hudson River. The exterior is stately neoclassical revival while inside it's more fine art gallery than summer home. Outside, the carefully sculpted gardens, dotted with modern art installations from the likes of Giacometti and Picasso, are a delight to wander through.

 p44

The Drive ⟫ Start this 32-mile drive by crossing over the Hudson River at one of its widest points on the 3-mile long Tappan Zee Bridge to South Nyack. (It's the state's longest bridge, and although experts question its current structural soundness, it's still safe to drive on. Construction of a new span, costing more than $4 billion, is to begin in 2013 and will take six years.) Take the Palisades Pkwy north from here.

③ Bear Mountain & Harriman State Parks

Shockingly, only 40 miles north of New York City is a pristine forest with miles of hiking trails, swimming and wilderness camping. The 72 sq miles of **Harriman State Park** (☎845-786-5003; http://nysparks.state.ny.us/parks) were donated to the state in 1910 by the widow of railroad magnate Edward Henry Harriman, director of the transcontinental Union Pacifica Railroad and frequent target of Teddy Roosevelt's trustbusters. Adjacent **Bear Mountain State Park** (☎845-786-2701; http://nysparks.state.ny.us/parks; ⊙8am-dusk) offers great views from its 1305ft peak, with the Manhattan skyline looming beyond the river and surrounding greenery, and there's a restaurant and lodging at the inn on Hessian Lake. In both parks there are several scenic roads that snake past mountain-fed streams and secluded lakes with gorgeous vistas; you'll spot shy, white-tailed deer, stately blue herons and – in the remotest regions – even a big cat or two.

Head to **Fort Montgomery State Historic Site** (www.nysparks.state.ny.us; Rte 9W; museum $2; ⊙9am-5pm Wed-Sun mid-Apr – Oct 31) in Bear Mountain for picture-perfect views from its cliffside perch overlooking the Hudson. The pastoral site was host to a fierce skirmish with the British on October 6, 1777. American soldiers hunkered behind fortresses while they tried to hold off the enemy; the ruins are still visible in the red earth. A museum at the entrance has artifacts and more details on the bloody battle.

> **DETOUR:**
> ## ARTHUR AVE

Start: ① The Cloisters

For some authentic Italian food and an old-school vibe, head to Arthur Ave (aka Belmont), the Bronx's answer to Little Italy. Tracksuited Albanians, well-dressed old timers and nostalgic Italian families (likely now living elsewhere in the city or Jersey) sip espressos and browse the bakeries for traditional favorites. Stop in the enclosed **Arthur Avenue Market** (2344 Arthur Ave; ⊙8am-6pm Mon-Sat) for a sandwich or cannoli. Just off Arthur Ave, **Roberto Restaurant** (☎718-733-9503; 603 Crescent Ave btwn Arthur & Hughes Aves; ⊙lunch Mon-Fri, dinner Mon-Sat) has a great reputation; its fans swear, with frightening passion, that it's New York's – not just Belmont's – best Italian restaurant.

The best way to get here is to head south from the Cloisters and take I-95 Cross Bronx Expwy to Webster Ave.

The Drive » It's only 14 miles to West Point – take Rte 9W to the town of Highland Falls and continue on Main St until you reach the parking entrance for West Point Visitors Center on the right.

4 West Point

Occupying one of the most breathtaking bends in the river is West Point US Military Academy. Prior to 1802, it was a strategic fort with a commanding position over a narrow stretch of the Hudson. **West Point Guided Tours** (📞845-446-4724; www.westpointtours.com; adult/child $12/9) offers one- and two-hour combo walking and bus tours of the stately campus; try to go when school is in session since the cadets' presence livens things up. Guides move swiftly through the academy's history, noting illustrious graduates such as Robert E Lee, Ulysses S Grant, 'Buzz' Aldrin and Norman Schwarzkopf, as well as famous drop-outs (Edgar Allen Poe for one). Guides will also explain the rigorous admissions criteria for parents hoping to land a spot for their kids. At least as interesting is the highly regimented daily collegiate life they lead.

Next to the Visitors Center is a fascinating **museum** (10:30am-4:15pm; free admission) – even for the pacifists among us – that traces the role of war and the military throughout human history. Displays of weapons from Stone Age clubs to artillery pieces highlight technology's role in the evolution of warfare, and elaborate miniature dioramas of important moments like the siege of Avaricum (52 BC) and the Battle of Austerlitz (1805) will mesmerize anyone who played with toy soldiers as a kid. Give yourself enough time to take in the substantial exhibits and when you've had enough of fighting check out the collection of paintings, prints and drawings by Hudson River School artists.

The Drive » On this 11.5-mile drive, take NY-218 north leaving Highland Falls and connect to Rte 9W (not Storm King Hwy which NY-218 becomes). Exit on Quaker Ave, right on NY-32 and left on Orrs Mills Rd. You can see Storm King from the New York State Thruway (and vice versa) but there's no convenient exit.

5 Storm King Art Center

Storm King Art Center (📞845-534-3115; www.stormking.org; Old Pleasant Hill Rd; admission $10; ☺Apr-Nov) in Mountainville (p44), on the west side of the Hudson River, is a giant open-air museum on 500 acres, part sculpture garden and part sculpture landscape. The spot was founded in 1960 as a museum for painters, but it soon began to acquire larger installations and monumental works that were placed outside in natural 'rooms' created by the land's indigenous breaks and curves. There's a small museum on site, formerly a 1935 residence designed like a Norman chateau, and plenty of picnic sites that visitors are encouraged to use (besides vending machines, there's no food sold here).

Across the expanse of meadow is the *Storm King Wall*, artist Andy Goldsworthy's famously sinuous structure that starts with rocks, crescendos up and across some hills, encompasses a tree, then dips down into a pond, slithering out the other side and eventually disappearing into the woods. Other permanent pieces were created by Alexander Calder, Henry Moore, Richard Serra and Alice Aycock, to name a few.

The Drive » NY-32 takes you past the down-on-its luck riverside town of Newburgh. If you have time, turn right on Washington St. Near the river is a small building and museum marking General George's longest lasting Revolutionary War base. Otherwise, head over the Newburgh-Beacon bridge ($1 toll).

TRIP HIGHLIGHT

6 Beacon

This formerly scruffy town is now on the map of art world cognoscenti because of the **Dia:**

WHY THIS IS A CLASSIC TRIP
MICHAEL GROSBERG, AUTHOR

I love the fact that only a short drive north of the city you can be wilderness camping in Harriman State Park. A seven-plus mile section of the Appalachian Trail runs through here and it's not uncommon to see grizzled hikers with walking sticks, loaded down with packs, alongside the highway or peeking out from the forest like creatures from a secret world.

Top: Bear Mountain Bridge
Left: Vanderbilt Mansion
Right: Cloisters Museum

PHIL HABER/GETTY IMAGES ©

BARRY WINIKER/GETTY IMAGES ©

Beacon (📞845-440-0100; www.diaart.org; 3 Beekman Street; adult $10; 🕑11am-6pm Thu-Mon mid-April–mid-Oct, 11am-4pm Fri-Mon mid-Oct–mid-Apr), a former factory, now a major museum. Inside are big names on a big scale, including an entire room of Andy Warhol's shadow paintings, and a hangar-sized space to house Richard Serra's *Torqued Ellipses*.

Main St has a few cafes, restaurants and galleries and **Hudson Beach Glass** (www.hudsonbeachglass.com; 162 Main St), a boutique-gallery where you can buy artfully designed, hand-crafted pieces or sign up for a class to learn how to do it yourself.

The Drive » Strip mall-lined Rte 9 north passes through Poughkeepsie (puh-kip-see), the largest city on the east bank and home to Vassar and Marist colleges. During this 22-mile drive, stop (exit on Marist Dr/Rte 9G north and then left on Parker Ave) for a stroll and incomparable river views on a converted railroad bridge, now a state park known as the Walkway Over the Hudson.

- - - - - - - - - - -

7 Hyde Park

Hyde Park, just north of Poughkeepsie, has long been associated with the Roosevelts, a prominent family since the 19th century. The estate of 1520 acres, formerly a farm, includes the **Franklin D Roosevelt Library & Museum** (📞845-229-8114; www.

41

fdrlibrary.marist.edu; 511 Albany Post Rd/Rte 9, admission museum $7, museum & house $14; ⊙9am-5pm), which details achievements in FDR's presidency; a visit usually includes a guided tour of **Springwood** (⌖800-967-2283; Albany Post Rd; admission $14; ⊙9am-5pm), FDR's lifelong home. Intimate details have been preserved, including his desk – left as it was the day before he died – and the hand-pulled elevator he used to hoist his polio-stricken body to the 2nd floor.

Two miles to the east is First Lady Eleanor Roosevelt's peaceful cottage, **Val-Kill** (⌖845-229-9115; www.nps.gov/elro; Albany Post Rd; admission $8; ⊙9am-5pm daily May-Oct, Thu-Mon Nov-Apr), her retreat from Hyde Park and FDR himself. Many dignitaries and heads of state were hosted here.

Just north of here is the 54-room **Vanderbilt Mansion** (⌖877-444-6777; www.nps.gov/vama; Rte 9; adult/child $8/free; ⊙9am-5pm), a Gilded Age spectacle of lavish beaux-arts design built by the fabulously wealthy Frederick Vanderbilt, grandson of Cornelius, once a Staten Island farmer who made millions buying up railroads. Nearly all of the original furnishings imported from European castles and villas remain in this country house – the smallest of any of the Vanderbilt family's! Hudson River views are best from the gardens and the Bard Rock trail on the property.

Further north is Staatsburg, a hot spot for antiquing. If you prefer to look rather than buy, duck into the 100-year-old **Staatsburg State Historic Site** (⌖845-889-8851; www.nysparks.state.ny.us; Old Post Rd, Staatsburg; admission free; ⊙10am-5pm Wed-Sat, noon-5pm Sun Apr-Sep; ♿), a beaux-arts mansion boasting 79

luxurious rooms filled with brocaded Flemish tapestries, gilded plaster-work, period paintings and Oriental art.

✕ ⊨ p44

The Drive » It's only 10 miles north on Rte 9 to Rhinebeck.

- - - - - - - - - - -

❽ Rhinebeck

Just 3 miles north of the charming small town of Rhinebeck is the **Aerodrome Museum** (⌖845-752-3200; www.oldrhinebeck.org; 9 Norton Rd; adult/child Sat & Sun $20/5, Mon-Fri $10/3; ⊙10am-5pm mid-Jun–mid-Oct) with a collection of pre-1930s planes and automobiles. There are air shows on weekends in the summer; the vintage aircrafts that take off at 2pm on Saturday and Sunday are reserved for a highly choreographed period dog-fight. If vicarious thrills aren't enough you can don helmets and goggles and take an open-cockpit 15-minute flight (per person $75) in a 1929 New Standard D-25 four-passenger biplane.

In a large red barn out the back of the Beekman Arms (6387 Mill St), widely considered the longest continually operating hotel in the US, is the **Beekman Arms Antique Market** (open 11am-5pm daily), where 30 local antiques dealers offer up their best Americana.

⊨ p45

✓ TOP TIP: SUMMERTIME THEATER

Across the river from West Point and Storm King Art Center, near the town of Cold Spring, the **Hudson Valley Shakespeare Festival** (⌖845-265-9575; www.hvshakespeare.org) takes place between mid-June and early September, staging impressive open-air productions at the magnificent Boscobel estate.

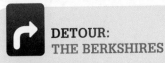

DETOUR:
THE BERKSHIRES

Start: ❾ Hudson

Head east to the Berkshire Mountains in Massachusetts, another region of bucolic scenery, quaint towns and vibrant arts scenes. Choose one of the following ways to access the area depending on two recommended stops on your way out of New York.

If you head east out of Hudson on Rte 23, you eventually come to Hillsdale and the **Catamount Aerial Adventure Park** (📞518-325-3200; catamounttrees.com; 2962 Hwy 23, Hillsdale; ⏰9am-5:30pm daily Jun 17-Sep 2, Sat & Sun May 11-Jun 16 & Sep 7-Oct 27). This is no ordinary zip line or ropes course but easily the most exciting and challenging one we've tried. No matter your strength or your capacity for tolerating heights, there's a route earmarked for you (plus there's skiing in the winter). From Catamount, it's only an 8-mile drive along MA-23 to Great Barrington in the Berkshires.

Taking NY-66 north for 14 miles from Hudson, you come to the small town of Chatham, where in the summer months, Golden Age Broadway musicals are performed by professional actors at the theatre-in-the-round **Mac-Haydn Theatre** (📞518-392-9292; www.machaydntheatre.org; 1925 Rte 203, Chatham, NY; adult/child $30/12; ⏰May 23 – Sep 15). While productions like *Brigadoon* tend to border on cheesy, the cast is usually energized and the generally older, pastel-clad crowd appreciative. Definitely stick around for the solo acts in the old-fashioned cafe-cum-cabaret room where you can enjoy show tunes while chowing down on a slice of pie. From here, you can carry on to Stockbridge or Great Barrington.

The Drive 》 Rte 9G north is a better choice than Rte 9 north for this 25-mile drive; it's more rural and every once in a while opens up to views of the Catskill Mountains on the other side of the river in the distance. Also across the river is Saugerties (p45), worth a visit – cross the Kingston-Rhinecliff Bridge and take Rte 9W north – if you have time.

- - - - - - - - - -

TRIP HIGHLIGHT

❾ Hudson

Hudson is an attractive town with a hip, gay-friendly community of artists, writers and performers who fled the city in the hope of creating more 'sustainable' lives. Warren St, the main roadway through town, is lined with antique shops, high-end furniture stores, galleries, restaurants and several cafes. Most of these urban refugees are happy to share their stories and chat – there's a welcoming vibe despite the high sticker price for some of the goods. Be warned: overnight street parking rules are extremely poorly signposted.

Just a few miles south of town is **Olana,** (📞518-828-0135; www.olana.org; Rte 9G, Hudson; tour adult/child $12/free; ⏰grounds 8am-sunset daily, tours 10am-5pm Tue-Sun) the fish-out-of-water looking Moorish-style home of Frederic Church, one of the primary artists of the Hudson River School of Painting. Church actually designed the 250-acre property, creating a lake, planting trees, orchards, etc with his idealized version of a landscape in mind so that the grounds became a complementary part of the natural views across the valley with the eastern escarpment of the Catskills looming overhead. On a house tour you can appreciate the totality of Church's aesthetic vision, as well as view paintings from his own collection.

🍴 🛏 p45

Eating & Sleeping

Manhattan

✖ Red Rooster — Modern American $$

(www.redroosterharlem.com; 310 Malcolm X Blvd btwn 125th & 126th Sts, Harlem; dinner mains $16-35; ⏱11:30am-10:30pm Mon-Fri, 10am-11pm Sat & Sun) This hot spot is run by Ethiopian-Swedish chef Marcus Samuelsson, who laces upscale comfort food with a world of flavors. Grilled salmon is garnished with peanuts while 'dirty rice' features aged basmati. Best of all are the Swedish meatballs, served with potatoes and lingonberries. The menu is largely the same and significantly cheaper at lunch and on Sundays when it hosts a popular gospel brunch.

⬛ Country Inn the City — Historic Inn $$$

(☎212-580-4183; www.countryinnthecity.com; 270 W 77th St btwn Broadway & West End Aves; apt $220-350; ✴🖵) Country Inn, a landmark 1891 limestone brownstone on a tree-lined block, has four roomy, self-contained apartments, each of which comes with sparkling wood floors, four-poster beds and other decorative bits, conveying a late 19th-century feel. Each unit comes with private bath and kitchenette. There's a three-night minimum. Winter rates drop considerably.

⬛ Jazz on the Park Hostel — Hostel $

(☎212-932-1600; www.jazzhostels.com; 36 W 106th St btwn Central Park West & Manhattan Ave; dm/r $35-45/$85-115; 🖵) This flophouse-turned-hostel right off of Central Park is generally a good bet, with clean dorms sporting four to 12 bunks in co-ed and single-sex configurations. Public spaces include a cafe/TV lounge, three terrace sitting areas and a basement lounge. The snack bar serves hamburgers-and-hot-dog fare.

Tarrytown ❷

✖ Blue Hill at Stone Barns — $$$

(☎914-366-9600; www.bluehillfarm.com; 630 Bedford Rd, Pocantico Hills; 5-course meal $108, 8-courses $148; ⏱5-10pm Wed-Thu, to 11pm Fri & Sat, 1-10pm Sun) A pillar of the farm-to-table movement, this elegant country restaurant sits atop the Rockefeller estate that is also home to Stone Barns Center for Food and Agriculture, a non-profit educational center and farm that provides much of the restaurant's bounty. Instead of a traditional menu, expect a multi-course farmer's feast based on the day's harvest. Meals often include a flourish of little bites leading up to the main dish, as teams of waiters present each course by lifting silver cloches off each plate in synchronized service to reveal a locavore's dream. Make a day of your visit and explore the surrounding fields and pastures.

Mountainville

⬛ Storm King Lodge — Hotel $$

(☎845-534-9421; www.stormkinglodge.com; 100 Pleasant Hill Rd, Mountainville; r $160-195) Once a carriage home for a large farming estate, the charming Storm King Lodge is a stately structure from the 1800s that's filled to the brim with tasteful furnishings like cozy quilts, deep leather parlor chairs, shiny wooden floors and fresh flowers.

Hyde Park ❼

✖ Culinary Institute of America — International $–$$$

(☎845-471-6608; www.ciarestaurants.com; Hyde Park; ⏱most restaurants 11:30am-1pm & 6-8pm) The chefs might all be students, but they know what they're doing, and you can judge their efforts at any of the CIA restaurants: American Bounty for an experiment in local, organic cooking; Ristorante Caterina de' Medici for sophisticated Italian; Bocuse for contemporary French dining (the old-fashioned Escoffier has closed); St Andrew's Café for so *au courant* farm-to-table fare; and the Apple Pie Bakery Café (7:30am-5pm Mon-Fri) for elaborately prepared pastries, the only place where no reservations are needed. Outside of the hours listed above, the restaurants have a number of irregular closures so be sure to double-check before planning on a visit.

🛏 Journey Inn   Inn $$

(📞845-229-8972; www.journeyinn.com; 1 Sherwood Pl, Poughkeepsie; r $130-190) Tuck in for a good night's sleep at Journey Inn, a six-room B&B – including a Roosevelt Room, of course – right in the middle of Hyde Park's big estates.

Rhinebeck ⑧

🛏 Olde Rhinebeck Inn   Inn $$$

(📞845-871-1745; www.rhinebeckinn.com; 340 Wurtemberg Rd, Rhinebeck; r $275-295) Built by German settlers three decades before the Revolutionary War, this beautifully restored oak-beamed, cozy inn oozes comfort and authenticity.

Saugerties

🛏 Saugerties Lighthouse   Guesthouse $$$

(📞845-247-0656; www.saugertieslighthouse. com; 168 Lighthouse Dr, Saugerties; r incl breakfast $225; ⏰Thu-Sun, closed Feb) For a truly romantic and unique place to lay your head, head to the town of Saugerties on the west side of the Hudson. The picturesque 1869 landmark sits on a small island in the Esopus Creek, accessible by boat or more commonly by a half-mile-long trail from the parking lot. Rooms are booked months in advance so a stay here requires substantial advance planning. If you can't overnight here, a walk to the lighthouse is highly recommended.

Hudson ⑨

✗ Helsinki   Modern American $$

(📞518-828-4800; www.helsinkihudson.com; 405 Columbia St, Hudson) This popular music venue and adjacent restaurant, transplanted from the Berkshires, showcases rock, jazz, and indie performers – and big-name acts such as Suzanne Vega and Nick Lowe – while the kitchen dishes out locally sourced cuisine such as garlicky kale salad and applewood smoked chicken. With dark wood accents and soaring ceilings, the large restored carriage house now serves as a hub for the valley's working artists.

🛏 Front St Guesthouse   Guesthouse $$

(📞518-828-1635; www.frontstreetguesthouse. com; 20 S Front St, Hudson; r from $140; ❄🛜) At the riverside end of town, this guesthouse's all-white color scheme, polished wood floors and high-end bedding create a cozy and affordable retreat. There's no lobby or on-site staff presence per se, but the friendly and accommodating owner will quickly meet any guests' needs.

Montauk Point Lighthouse This historic
lighthouse overlooks beautiful beaches

Long Island

2

Discover windswept dunes and magnificent beaches, important historic sites, renowned vineyards and of course the Hamptons, in all their luxuriously sunbaked glory.

TRIP HIGHLIGHTS

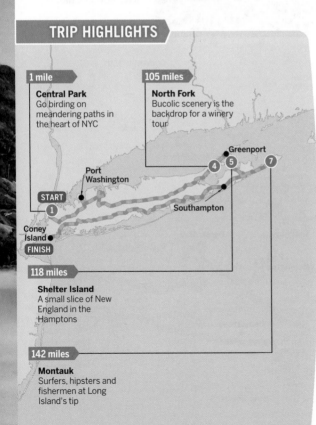

1 mile

Central Park
Go birding on meandering paths in the heart of NYC

105 miles

North Fork
Bucolic scenery is the backdrop for a winery tour

118 miles

Shelter Island
A small slice of New England in the Hamptons

142 miles

Montauk
Surfers, hipsters and fishermen at Long Island's tip

4 DAYS
267 MILES / 429KM

GREAT FOR ...

BEST TIME TO GO

Early September when crowds have dissipated but water temperatures are OK.

 ESSENTIAL PHOTO

Sunset from Montauk Lighthouse.

 BEST FOR FAMILIES

Riding the rickety Cyclone roller-coaster in Coney Island.

2 Long Island

Once the site of small European whaling and fishing ports from as early as 1640, today's Long Island evokes a complicated menagerie of images: cookie-cutter suburbia, nightmare commutes, private-school blazers and moneyed decadence. But visions of suburban dystopia aside – this Long Island loop, which begins and ends in New York City, has wide ocean and bay beaches, renowned vineyards, mega mansions and important historic sites.

TRIP HIGHLIGHT

1 Central Park

Central Park (www.centralparknyc.org; 59th & 110th Sts btwn Central Park West & Fifth Ave; ⏰6am-1am; 🚻), the rectangular patch of green that occupies Manhattan's heart, began life in the mid-19th century as a swampy piece of land that was carefully bulldozed into the idyllic landscapes you see today with more than 24,000 trees, 136 acres of woodland, 21

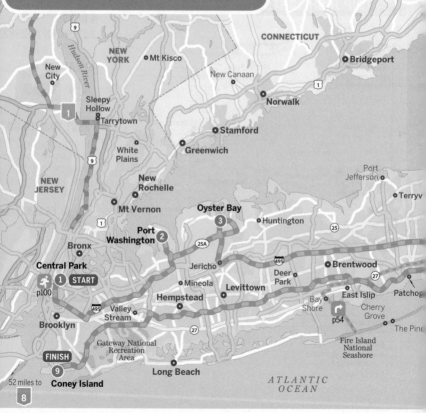

playgrounds and seven bodies of water.

The **Great Lawn** is a massive emerald carpet at the center of the park – between 79th and 86th Sts – and is surrounded by ball fields and London plane trees. Immediately to the southeast is **Delacorte Theater**, home to an annual Shakespeare in the Park festival, as well as **Belvedere Castle**, a lookout. Further south, between 72nd and 79th Sts, is the leafy **Ramble**, a popular birding destination. On the

southeastern end is the **Loeb Boathouse**, home to a waterside restaurant that offers rowboat and bicycle rentals.

The arched walkways of **Bethesda Terrace**, crowned by the magnificent Bethesda

Fountain (at the level of 72nd St), have long been a gathering area for New Yorkers. To the south is the **Mall**, a promenade shrouded in mature North American elms. The southern stretch, known as Literary Walk,

LINK YOUR TRIP

1 Hudson Valley
Head to the Cloisters in upper Manhattan to begin a trip to culturally rich towns along the Hudson.

8 The Jersey Shore
Leave NYC via the Holland Tunnel, take I-95 S to the Garden State Pkwy to explore endless beaches and boardwalks.

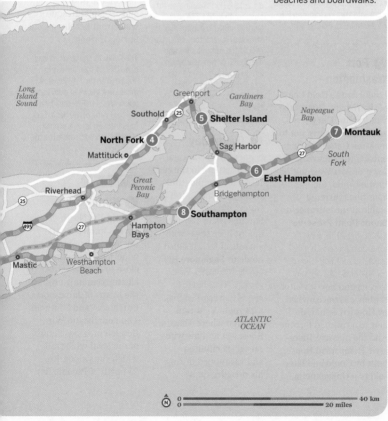

is flanked by statues of famous authors.

Strawberry Fields is a simple mosaic memorial that pays tribute to John Lennon, who was killed across the street outside the Dakota Building. Funded by Yoko Ono, its name is inspired by the Beatles song 'Strawberry Fields Forever.'

 p55

The Drive >> Getting out of Manhattan can be a slog. Cross the East River on the Queensboro Bridge (aka the 59th St Bridge) and follow signs for I-495 east, aka the Long Island Expway or LIE. This too can be a nightmare. Get off at exit 36 to Searingtown Rd which turns into Port Washington Rd; it's 4.5 miles to Sands Point.

- - - - - - - - - - - - - -

❷ Port Washington

Long Island's Gold Coast of the roaring '20s, of the Vanderbilts, Chryslers and Guggenheims, not to mention Gatsby, begins outside the suburban town of Port Washington. Castle Gould, the enormous turreted stable at the entrance to **Sands Point Preserve** (☎516-571-7900; www. sandspointpreserve.org; 127 Middleneck Rd; admission per car/walk-in $5/$2; ☺9am-4:30pm) and now a visitor center, was once owned by Howard Gould, the heir to a railroad fortune. And the massive Tudor-style Hempstead House, built by Gould and later sold to a Guggenheim,

stands nearby; it's mostly unfurnished and used for events but you can usually peek in to get a sense of its dimensions and scale. However, the 1923 Norman-style **Falaise** (admission $10; ☺Thu-Sun May 1 – Oct 31) is intact and furnished and open to guided tours (hourly from noon to 3pm). Sands Point includes forested nature trails and a beautiful sandy bayfront beach that's worth a stroll; you can even look into the picture windows of several massive modernist beachfront homes.

The Drive >> On this 13-mile drive, take Port Washington Rd back south to Rte 25A east/ Northern Blvd, a commercial strip with several tony suburban residential communities and a golf club or two nearby. Go left on Cove Rd; when it turns into Cove Neck Rd it offers very idyllic views of Oyster Bay Harbor.

- - - - - - - - - - - - - -

❸ Oyster Bay

Named by the original Dutch settlers in the early 1600s for the plentiful shellfish found in the waters of Long Island Sound, Oyster Bay is a quaint little town with a nautical feel. It's also home to **Sagamore Hill** (☎516-922-4788; www.nps. gov/sahi; adult/child $5/ free; ☺9am-5pm Wed-Sun), a 23-room Victorian mansion where Theodore Roosevelt and his wife raised six children and vacationed during his presidency; it's

preserved with the books, furnishings and exotic artifacts, such as animal heads, that Roosevelt acquired on his travels. He passed away here and is buried in the nearby Youngs Memorial Cemetery. Spring and summer months mean long waits for guided tours (however, as of the summer of 2013, guided tours of the home were suspended until a renovation and rehabilitation project is completed). A nature trail leading from behind the excellent **museum** (admission free) that's also on the property ends at a picturesque waterfront beach on Cold Spring Harbor.

The Drive >> The quickest way to do this 58-mile drive is to hop back on the I-495 east; 42 miles later, get off at exit 71 and follow NY-24 to Riverhead, really the beginning of the North Fork. Pass through town and onto Main Rd or NY-25 where the trip picks up.

- - - - - - - - - - - - - -

TRIP HIGHLIGHT

❹ North Fork

Mainly, the North Fork is known for its unspoiled farmland and wineries – there are close to 30 vineyards, clustered mainly around the towns of Jamesport, Cutchogue and Southold. The Long Island Wine Council provides details of the local wine trail, which runs along Rte 25 north of Peconic Bay.

The Hamptons Beach houses on Shinnecock Bay

One of the nicer outdoor settings for a tasting is the **Peconic Bay Winery** (☎631-734-7361; www.peconicbaywinery.com; 31320 Main Rd, Cutchogue); this also means it's popular with bus- and limo-loads of party-goers.

The main North Fork town and the place for **ferries** (☎631-749-0139; www.northferry.com) to Shelter Island, **Greenport** is a charming laid-back place lined with restaurants and cafes, including family-owned **Claudio's Clam Bar** (www.claudios.com; 111 Main St; mains $15; ⊙11:30am-9pm, closed Wed) with a wraparound deck perched over the marina. Or grab a sandwich for a picnic at the Harbor Front Park where you can take a spin on the historic carousel.

The Drive » The Shelter Island ferry (one-way vehicle and driver $10) leaves just a couple blocks from Main St in Greenport. This could involve something of a wait – open your windows and take the 10 minutes to breathe in the fresh air.

- - - - - - - - - - -

TRIP HIGHLIGHT

⑤ Shelter Island

Between the North and South Forks, Shelter Island is a low-key microcosm of beautiful Hamptons real estate with more of a traditional maritime New England atmosphere. This mellow refuge was once sold by Manhanset Native Americans to a group of prosperous sugar merchants from Barbados who intended to harvest the island's oak trees in order to build barrels to transport their precious cargo. In the 1870s, a group of Methodist clergy and laymen bought property on the heights to establish a religious retreat. Some of these buildings, a variety of colonial revival, Victorian and Queen Anne, make up the island's 'historic district.' The **Mashomack Nature Preserve** (☎631-749-1001; www.nature.org; Rte 114; ⊙9am-5pm Mar-Sep, to 4pm Oct-Feb) covers more than 2000 acres of the southern part of the island and is a great spot for hiking or kayaking (no cycling) – the Hamptons' glamour and excess feel very far away.

🛏 p55

The Drive » The ferry (one-way vehicle/passenger $14/$1) to North Haven on the South Fork leaves from southern Shelter Island on NY-114. Continue on NY-114 to Sag Harbor (p55). Check out its Whaling & Historical Museum, or stroll up and down its narrow, Cape Cod–like streets. NY-114 continues for seven miles to East Hampton.

- - - - - - - - - - -

⑥ East Hampton

Don't be fooled by the oh-so-casual-looking summer attire, heavy on pastels and sweaters tied around the neck – the sunglasses alone are probably equal to

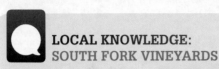

LOCAL KNOWLEDGE:
SOUTH FORK VINEYARDS

Most people associate Long Island wineries with the North Fork but the South Fork has a handful of good ones as well. You'll know you've arrived at **Duck Walk Vineyards** (☎631-726-7555; www.duckwalk.com; 231 Montauk Hwy, Water Mill), the first stop on this mini tour, when you spot a reddish-brick, Normandy-style château, fronted by spiky blue spruce trees and backed by row upon row of neatly clipped grapevine shoots clinging tightly to the sandy soil. Explore the 130 acres of the Damiano family estate and you'll get an up-close look at the startling variety of libations produced here: Merlot, Sauvignon, a late-harvest Gewurztraminer, Pinot Grigio, blush wines, two kinds of port and even boysenberry wine.

Just down the road are the 30 acres of vine trellises and grape plants of **Channing Daughters Vineyard** (☎631-537-7224; www.channingdaughters.com; 1927 Scuttlehole Rd, Bridgehampton). Step across the wide stone patio dotted with plush chaise lounges that look out on the property, and keep your eyes peeled for the Alice-in-Wonderland-like sculptures of owner Walter Channing – his works pop up everywhere, staring down at you from the end posts of vineyard rows and emerging in the shape of towering inverted trees against the horizon.

Further east, past the village of Bridgehampton, is the graceful Tuscan-villa-style tasting room of **Wolffer Estates** (☎631-537-5106; www.wolffer.com; 139 Sagg Rd, Sagaponack). Sun-faded ochre walls, bright Grecian-blue window shutters and massive wooden beams set the scene for sampling the crisp whites and earthy reds Wolffer is renowned for. Experiment with some of the vineyard's more unusual offerings, including an apple wine, rose wines and sweet dessert drinks.

a month's rent. Some of the highest-profile celebrities have homes here and a drive down its tony lanes can evoke nauseatingly intense real estate envy. However, it's worth swallowing your pride and trying to glimpse what are undoubtedly some of the priciest properties in the country. Examples of fabulous residential architecture (as well as cookie-cutter gaudy McMansions) are concealed behind towering hedgerows and gates. For a chance to rub shoulders with the locals, you can catch readings, theater and art exhibits at **Guild Hall** (☎631-324-0806; www.guildhall.org; 158 Main St).

 p55

The Drive » Join the parade of cars leaving town on Montauk Hwy, which becomes hilly and more beautiful the further east you go on this 25-mile drive.

- - - - - - - - - -

TRIP HIGHLIGHT

⑦ Montauk

Once a sleepy and humble stepsister to the Hamptons – though more working-class Jersey, less Cote d'Azur royalty – these days Montauk, at the far-eastern end of Long Island, continues to draw a fashionable, younger crowd and even a hipster subset to its beautiful beaches. Longtime residents, fishermen and territorial surfers round out a motley mix that makes the dining and bar scene louder and a little more democratic compared to other Hamptons villages.

At the very eastern, wind-whipped tip of the South Fork is Montauk Point State Park, with its impressive, 1796 **Montauk Point Lighthouse** (☎631-668-2544; www.montauklighthouse.com;

adult/child $9/4; ☺10:30am-5:30pm, hours vary), the fourth oldest still-active lighthouse in the US. You can camp a few miles west of town at the dune-swept **Hither Hills State Park** (☏631-668-2554; www.nysparks.com; 164 Old Montauk Hwy), right on the beach; just reserve early during summer months. Several miles to the north is the Montauk harbor, with dockside restaurants and hundreds of boats in the marinas.

 p55

The Drive » Backtrack the way you came on the Montauk Hwy through East Hampton, Bridgehampton and Water Mill.

- - - - - - - - - - - - -

⑧ Southampton

The village of Southampton appears blemish-free, as if it has been Botoxed. At nighttime, when clubgoers dressed in their most glamorous beach chic let their hair down, it can feel as if the plastic-surgery-free are visitors in a foreign land. However, before wine-making and catering to the celebrity crowd became the area's two most dominant industries, it was a whaling and seafaring community. Its colonial roots are evident at Halsey House, the oldest residence in the Hamptons, and the nearby **Southampton Historical**

Museum (☏631-283-2494; www.southamptonhistoricalmuseum.org; 17 Meeting House Ln; adult/child $4/free; ☺11am-4pm Tue-Sat), a perfect place to learn more about the region's former seafaring ways. It has a homey collection of local relics displayed in an 1843 sea-captain's house, plus Rogers Mansion, an old sea-captain's residence full of whaling lore.

To learn about an even earlier age of Long Island's history, head to the **Shinnecock Nation Cultural Center & Museum** (☏631-287-4923; www.shinnecock.com; 100 Montauk Hwy, Southampton; adult/child under 5 $10/free; ☺11am-5pm Thu-Sun) at the edge of the village. Run by the Native American group who live on an 800-acre peninsula that juts into the bay, the recently opened site allows Shinnecock members and visitors alike to experience a recreated Wikun (village) c 1640–1750 with guided tours, singing, dancing and demonstrations of traditional skills.

Its beaches – only Coopers Beach (per day $40) and Road D (free) offer parking to non-residents from May 31 to Sep 15 – are sweeping and gorgeous, and the **Parrish Art Museum** (☏631-283-2118; www.parrishart.org; 279 Montauk Hwy, Water Mill; adult/child $10/free; ☺11am-6pm

Wed-Mon, to 8pm Fri) is an impressive regional institution. Its quality exhibitions feature great local artists and there's a cute gift shop stacked with glossy posters of famous Long Island landscapes.

 p55

The Drive » The 95-mile drive back to the city needs to be timed properly – never during rush hour or anytime on a Sunday in the summer. Either take I-495 west back towards the city or Montauk Hwy to the Southern Pkwy to the Belt Pkwy.

- - - - - - - - - - - - -

⑨ Coney Island

This is about as far from the Hamptons as you can get, not geographically but, well, in every other way, and still be on Long Island. Coney Island became known as 'Sodom by the Sea' by the end of the 19th century, when it was infamous as a den for gamblers, hard drinkers and other cheery sorts you wouldn't want to introduce to Mom.

In the early 1900s, the family era kicked in as amusement parks were built. Its most famous, Luna Park, opened in 1903 – a dreamworld with live camels and elephants and 'rides to the moon'.

By the 1960s, Coney Island's pull had slipped and it became a sad, crime-ridden reminder of past glories. A slow, enduring comeback has meant the emergence

DETOUR:
FIRE ISLAND

Start: ❽ Southampton

On a long barrier island running parallel to Long Island, just off the southern shore, are Fire Island's 32 miles of virtually car-free white sand beaches, shrub-filled forests and hiking trails as well as 15 hamlets and two villages. The Fire Island Pines and Cherry Grove (both car-free) comprise a historic, gay bacchanalia that attracts men and women in droves from New York City, while villages on the west end cater to straight singles and families. At the western end of Fire Island, Robert Moses State Park is the only spot accessible by car; check out the lighthouse here which holds a small museum with a tiny section dedicated to nude sunbathing. If you want to skip the scene altogether and just get back to nature, enjoy a hike through the 300-year-old Sunken Forest, where crazily twisted trees have been misshapen by constant salt-spray and sea breezes. It's 'sunken' because its 40 acres are below sea level; it has its own ferry stop (called Sailor's Haven).

There are limited places to stay, and booking in advance is strongly advised (check www.fireisland.com for accommodations information). **Madison Fire Island** (☎597-6061; www.themadisonfi.com; The Pines; r $200-775; ❄️📶🏊), the first and only boutique hotel here, rivals anything Manhattan has to offer in terms of amenities, and also has killer views from a rooftop deck and a gorgeous pool. At the eastern end of the island, the 1300-acre preserve of Otis Pike Fire Island Wilderness is a protected oasis of sand dunes that includes beach camping at Watch Hill, though mosquitoes can be fierce and reservations far in advance are a must.

Fire Island Ferries (☎631-665-3600; www.fireislandferries.com; adult/child round-trip $17/7.50) runs services to Fire Island beaches and the national seashore (May to November); the terminals are close to LIRR stations at Bay Shore, Sayville and Patchogue.

To reach Fire Island from Southampton, head west on NY-27 (aka the Sunrise Hwy) for 46 miles until exit 44 for Bay Shore. Take Brentwood Rd a mile south, turn right onto E Main St and after close to another mile make a left onto Maple Ave. The ferry terminal is on your left about a half mile further on.

---

of the wild Mermaid Parade (held on the third Saturday in June), a newer, more upscale, slightly more generic **Luna Park** (www.lunaparknyc.com; Surf Ave & 10th St; ⏰late Mar-Oct; 🚻), an aquarium and a minor-league baseball team. The Cyclone is its most legendary ride: a wooden roller-coaster that reaches speeds of 60mph and makes near-vertical drops.

The hot dog was invented in Coney Island in 1867, which means that eating a frankfurter at **Nathan's Famous** (1310 Surf Ave cnr Stillwell Ave, Coney Island; hot dog $4; ⏰breakfast, lunch & dinner till late), which has been around since 1916, is practically obligatory. The hot dogs are the real deal and its clam bar is tops in summer. If you're around in the winter, consider taking a dip in the frigid Atlantic Ocean with the Coney Island Polar Bears Club. It's best known for its New Year's Day Swim, when hundreds of hungover New Yorkers take the plunge.

Eating & Sleeping

Manhattan ❶

✖ Danji   Korean $$

(www.danjinyc.com; 346 W 52nd St, Midtown West; plates $7-20; ⊙noon-10:30pm Mon-Thu, to 11:30pm Fri, 5:30-11:30pm Sat) Chef Hooni Kim has captured tastebuds with his Michelin-starred Korean 'tapas.' Served in a modern space, the celebrity dish is the sliders, a duo of *bulgogi* beef and spiced pork belly. Go early or prepare to wait.

🛏 Dylan   Boutique Hotel $$$

(☎866-553-9526; www.dylanhotel.com; 52 E 41st St btwn Madison & Park Aves; r $219-550) This 108-room luxury hotel was once home to the Chemists Club. There's somber lighting in cushy rooms, full-marble bathrooms and cube-like armchairs. Best is the Alchemy Suite, created in the 1930s as a mock medieval lab.

Sag Harbor

🛏 American Hotel   Hotel $$$

(☎725-3535; www.theamericanhotel.com; Main St; r low season $200-300, high season $300-400) An old-world hotel that's still excellent and modern, with a downstairs restaurant and bar that continues to be a center of the social scene. An ideal choice for lovers of European elegance.

Shelter Island ❺

🛏 Pridwin Beach Hotel
& Cottages   Hotel $$

(☎631-749-0476; www.pridwin.com; 81 Shore Rd; r & cottages from $165-315; ✳🤶) Surrounded by woods and fronting a small beach and the bay, Pridwin has standard hotel rooms as well as private water-view cottages.

East Hampton ❻

✖ Living Room   Modern American $$$

(☎631-324-5440; 207 Main St; mains $30; ⊙8-10:30am, noon-2:30pm & 5:30-10:30pm) This long-standing restaurant is housed in the pricey Maidstone Inn, featuring haute design as well as haute cuisine – basically thoughtfully conceived American with a Swedish influence, and sourced from local growers when possible.

✖ Nick & Toni's   Mediterranean $$$

(☎631-324-3550; 136 North Main St; mains $22-38; ⊙6-11pm Fri & Sat, to 10pm Mon-Thu, to 9pm Sun) Celebrating its 25th year in 2013, this Hamptons institution serves finely prepared Italian specialties using locally sourced ingredients. Despite attracting celebrity regulars, non-famous names are also treated well.

✖ Townline BBQ   Barbecue $

(www.townlinebbq.com; 3593 Montauk Hwy; mains $9; ⊙11:30am-10pm) East of town on the way to Bridgehampton is this down-to-earth roadside restaurant churning out smoky ribs and barbecue sandwiches.

Montauk ❼

✖ Lobster Roll   Seafood $$

(☎631-267-3740; 1980 Montauk Hwy; mains $10-12; ⊙11:30am-10pm summer) On Rte 27, between the towns of Amagansett and Montauk, a few roadside fish shacks like this one pop up. The Lobster Roll serves the namesake sandwich as well as fresh steamers and fried clams.

🛏 Surf Lodge   Motel $$$

(☎631-483-5037; www.thesurflodge.com; 183 Edgemere St; r from $300; ✳🤶) Set on Fort Pond a half-mile north of the beach, this hipster haven has been at the forefront of Montauk's transformation. Its casual chic design includes private decks and cooking stoves. The bar and restaurant, called Byron, does organic cuisine and seafood with an Australian surfer-town vibe.

Southampton ❽

🛏 1708 House   Inn $$$

(☎631-287-1708; www.1708house.com; 126 Main St; r incl $195-495; ✳🤶) History buffs might gravitate toward this local standout. It's in central Southampton and prides itself on its turn-of-the-century charm.

Mohonk Mountain House
A castle straight out of a fairytale

Tranquil Catskills

3

A handful of unspoiled, rustic towns still embrace the free-wheeling and art-focused lifestyle that put this section of upstate New York on the map and inspired a generation.

TRIP HIGHLIGHTS

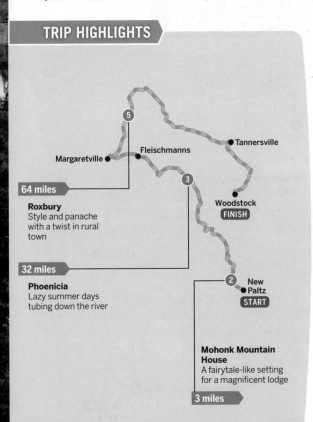

64 miles

Roxbury
Style and panache with a twist in rural town

32 miles

Phoenicia
Lazy summer days tubing down the river

3 miles

Mohonk Mountain House
A fairytale-like setting for a magnificent lodge

3–4 DAYS
115 MILES / 185KM

GREAT FOR...

BEST TIME TO GO
April to November for comfortable outdoor temperatures.

ESSENTIAL PHOTO
Views from Skytop Tower near Mohonk Mountain House.

BEST FOR FAMILIES
Tubing down Esopus Creek near Phoenicia.

Tranquil Catskills

American painters discovered this mountainous region rising west of the Hudson Valley in the mid-19th century. They celebrated its hidden mossy gorges and waterfalls as examples of sublime wilderness rivaling the Alps in Europe. And while the height and profile of its rounded peaks might have been exaggerated and romanticized, while traveling through the Catskills it's still possible to glimpse the landscapes that beguiled these artists and inspires others today.

❶ New Paltz

On the western side of the Hudson is New Paltz, home of a campus of the State University of New York, natural food stores and a liberal ecofriendly vibe. A few blocks north of the center are several homes of the original French Huguenot settlers of New Paltz (c 1677) on **Historic Huguenot Street** (☑845-255-1660; www. huguenotstreet.org; 88 Huguenot St; guided tours adult/child $16/10; ⊘closed Tue & Wed, otherwise check for hours), the oldest in the US. **Water**

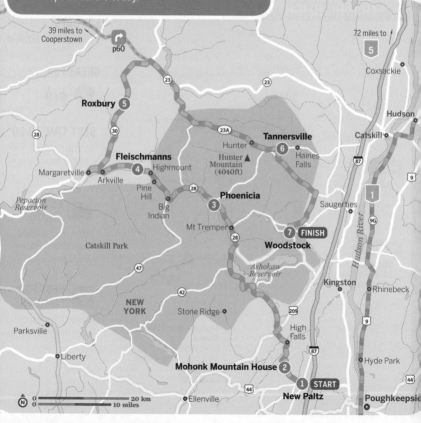

Street Market at the western edge of town on the Wallkill River (access the river walking path here) is an admittedly artificial but pleasant collection of shops, antique stores and cafes with a ski-village vibe.

In the distance behind the town the ridge of the **Shawangunk** (Shongum or just the 'Gunks') mountains rises more than 2000ft above sea level. More than two dozen miles of nature trails and some of the best rock climbing in the Eastern US is found in the **Mohonk Mountain Preserve**. Contact **Alpine Endeavors** (☏877-486-5769; www.alpineendeavors.com) for climbing instruction and equipment. Nearby Minnewaska State Park Preserve has 12,000 acres of wild landscape, the centerpiece of which

LINK YOUR TRIP

1 **Hudson Valley**
Hop on any east-bound road until you hit the Hudson River to begin touring the valley's mansions and gardens.

5 **Adirondack Peaks & Valleys**
Get on I-87 N for Lake George, the gateway to a trip through this mountainous wilderness.

is two usually ice-cold mountain lakes, Lake Minnewaska and Lake Awosting.

The Drive ≫ Once you cross the small bridge over the Wallkill River at the western edge of town, the view is of lush farmland and the 'Gunks' in the distance. Mountain Rest Rd then climbs and winds the 4 miles northwest to Mohonk Mountain House.

- - - - - - - - -

TRIP HIGHLIGHT

2 Mohonk Mountain House

The iconic **Mohonk Mountain House** (☏845-255-1000; www.mohonk.com; 1000 Mountain Rest Rd; r $320-2500; ❄️🛜🏊) looks like it's straight out of a fairytale: a rustic castle perched magnificently over a dark lake. It's an all-inclusive resort where guests can gorge on elaborate five-course meals, stroll through gardens, hike miles of trails, canoe, swim, go ice-skating, etc. A luxury spa center is there to work out the kinks. Only suites in the Victorian towers have TVs plus restored antique claw-footed tubs; it's a place to get outdoors or gather with friends and family in rocking chairs set up on a porch and deck overlooking the lake – it feels about as close to the classic mountain lodges in the great parks out west as you can get. Non-overnight guests can visit the grounds

(adult/child per day $25/20) by paying cash at the entrance gate – easily worth the price of admission – and you can hike between here and the Minnewaska State Park. Another recommended hike is the two-mile one-way scramble up the Lemon Squeeze and Labyrinth (closed in winter) to the Skytop Tower.

The Drive ≫ This pleasant 31-mile leg begins with a scenic drive north on Mohonk Rd to the hamlet of High Falls – the river and falls are on your left as you drive through town. Turn left on Rte 213, also signposted 'Scenic Byway S1', and carry on to the Ashokan Reservoir; pull into the lot for views or a walk. Then take Rte 28 to Phoenicia, passing Mt Tremper – home to a recommended resort (p63) and the world's largest kaleidoscope – on the way.

- - - - - - - - -

TRIP HIGHLIGHT

3 Phoenicia

Downtown Phoenicia, all three blocks of it, is the place to go for a day's jaunt – **Town Tinker Tube Rental** (☏845-688-5553; www.towntinker.com; 10 Bridge St; tubes per day $15; 🚻) offers beginner tube rentals, an expert trail for those who like it rough, and even kayaks if an old tire's too low-tech for you. No walking required; you'll be picked up at day's end and driven back to your car. A lazy day inner-tubing down Esopus Creek is the perfect way to stay cool on hot summer days. If you prefer a more placid surface you can head around 11 miles west on Rte 28 to swim in Pine Hill Lake at **Belleayre Beach** (📞845-254-5202; per person/car $2/10; ⏱10am-6pm Mon-Fri, to 7pm Sat & Sun Jun 14-Sep), which has outdoor concerts in the summer; Belleayre Mountain has skiing in the winter.

📖 p63

The Drive » Mountains are on either side of Rte 28 for the 15 miles west to Fleischmanns. About halfway there on your left is Rte 47 which climbs through the heart of Catskill Park proper and its highest peaks. The road is narrow and somewhat rough in places though it's a scenic way to connect with Sullivan County to the south.

---

❹ Fleischmanns

The once well-known town of Fleischmanns was home to the famous yeast company of the same name as well as dozens of lodging houses that brought summer vacationers in the late 1800s and early 1900s. Now little more than a tiny main street surrounded by the second homes of wealthy New Yorkers in the hills, Fleischmanns is an offbeat location for lunch. In the summer months it fills up with Orthodox Jewish families who've adopted it as their weekend retreat. On Saturday evenings after

Sabbath the families stroll the streets, not doffing their customary clothes or hats even in August heat.

You can get a glimpse of early railroad life nearby in Arkville at the Empire State Railway Museum, housed in the historic **Delaware & Ulster Station** (📞845-688-7501; www.esrm.com; 43510 State Hwy 28, Arkville; ⏱11am-4pm Sat & Sun; 🚼) that was built around 1899. Displays detail how the old train tracks turned this corner of the Catskills into a tourist center. You can also travel the 24 miles between Arkville and Roxbury in a steam locomotive (adult/child $12/7; check website for schedule) past rural if unspectacular scenery.

The Drive » Head west to the town of Margaretville where you then turn north on Rte 30; about 5 miles up is Pakatakan Farmers Market (9am-2pm Sat mid-May to mid-Oct), one of the best in the area, housed in the distinctive-looking round barn. Roxbury is another 10 miles further along.

TRIP HIGHLIGHT

❺ Roxbury

Bringing style and panache to this rural region and a destination into and of itself, the **Roxbury Motel** (📞607-326-7200; www.theroxburymotel. com; 2258 County Hwy 41; r incl breakfast wkday Jun-Oct $100-300; ❄🏵) is a fabulous

---

↱ DETOUR: COOPERSTOWN

Start: ❺ **Roxbury**

For sports fans, Cooperstown, 50 miles west of Albany, is instantly recognized as the home of the shrine for the national sport (baseball). But the small-town atmosphere and stunning views of the countryside around beautiful Ostego Lake make it worth visiting even for those who don't know the difference between ERA and RBI.

The **National Baseball Hall of Fame & Museum** (📞888-425-5633; www.baseballhalloffame.org; 25 Main St; adult/child $19.50/7; ⏱9am-5pm, to 9pm summer) has exhibits, a theater, a library and an interactive statistical database. The old stone **Fenimore Art Museum** (📞607-547-1400; www.fenimoreartmuseum.org; 5798 Lake Rd; adult/child $11/5; ⏱10am-4pm Tue-Sun) has an outstanding collection of Americana.

To reach Cooperstown, leave Roxbury on Rte 30 north and after 6 miles turn onto Rte 23 west. After 28 miles, hook up with Rte 28 north for another 16 miles.

PANORAMIC IMAGES/GETTY IMAGES ©

Tannersville Kaaterskill Falls

and welcoming retreat. From the outside, it looks like an immaculate, if conventional, whitewashed motel. Initially planned as a tribute to the heyday of the Catskills and mid-century modern style, it soon turned into a project guided by inspiration from '70s and '80s films and TV shows – think *The Jetsons*, *The Addams Family*, *The Wiz*, *Saturday Night Fever* etc. The decor features items sourced from estate sales and online vendors around the world, and with contributions from artist friends and local craftspeople, owners Greg and Joseph have brought an obsessive attention to detail and aesthetics to each of the 28 rooms and suites. Worth a quick tour if unoccupied is the 'The Archeologist's Digs' cottage (sleeps six, wkdays $475-650), easily the most lavish of Roxbury's offerings. A few details worth mentioning: ibis-shaped bedside lamps in Cleopatra's bedroom; a Murphy bed concealed behind a mural of a Mayan deity; a 'secret' mineshaft cave with a lantern, pictographs and peekaboo hole onto the living room; a bathroom aquarium…

Wintertime (lower room rates) means huddling around the fire pit whereas warm-weather stays involve sunbathing and lounging near the gazebo and small stream that runs along the property; at any time of year it's worth relaxing at the full-service spa split between rooms in the two wings.

The Drive » On this 32-mile route, continue north on Rte 30 to the one-stoplight town of Grand Gorge (the trailhead for the beautiful and highly recommended Mine Kill Falls Overlook is a few miles north) and make a right onto Rte 23 which turns into Rte 23A after the Schoharie Reservoir. You pass Hunter Mountain Ski Resort a few miles west of Tannersville.

6 Tannersville

The highest falls in New York (260ft compared to Niagara's 167ft), gorgeous **Kaaterskill Falls** are only a few miles from the small town of Tannersville, which primarily services nearby Hunter Mountain. Popular paintings by Thomas Cole, who settled in nearby Catskill, Asher Durand (check out his painting *Kindred Spirits*) and other artists in the mid-1800s elevated this two-tier cascade to iconic status. Soon, however, wealthy tourists followed and most artists could no longer afford to stay in the Mountain Top area where the falls are found. The most traveled trail starts near a horseshoe curve in Rte 23A. Park the car in a turnout just up the road, cross to the other side and walk back down behind a guardrail. What you see from here is only Bastion Falls; it's a not very strenuous hike, a little more than 3/4 mile up to the lower falls.

Other delights are a bit more off the beaten track: consider hiking to Devil's Kitchen Falls, or trekking up the overlooked Kaaterskill High Peak trail. It's lonely, but you'll be rewarded with up-close views of Wildcat, Buttermilk and Santa Cruz waterfalls. Skiers head to nearby Hunter Mountain in the winter.

 p63

The Drive ›› About 7 of the miles south to Woodstock involve white-knuckle driving on Platte Clove Rd/Rte 16 (also signposted as 'Plattecove Mtn Rd') through a narrow and steep valley (sometimes no guardrail; no trucks or buses allowed; closed Nov-Apr). You're mostly descending 1200ft in this direction. Eventually, make a right onto W Saugerties/ Woodstock Rd.

- - - - - - - - - - -

❼ Woodstock

Famous for the 1969 concert that didn't actually happen here but in Bethel, the town's two main walkable thoroughfares – Tinker St and Mill Rd – are lined with cafes and shops. The **Woodstock Artists Association Gallery** (📞845-679-2940; www. woodstockart.org; 28 Tinker St; ⏰noon-5pm Thu-Mon; 🚻) is where you're most likely to bump into a local creative type or a visiting Byrdcliffe Arts Colony resident hanging their latest work. The permanent collection features a wide range of Woodstock artists in all sorts of mediums.

If you feel a frisson upon entering the **Woodstock Center for Photography** (📞845-679-9957; www.cpw.org; 59 Tinker St; ⏰noon-5pm Wed-Sun; 🚻), that's because it was formerly the Espresso Café, hallowed ground for counter-culture types. Bob Dylan once had a writing studio above the now-defunct Espresso – that's where he typed up the liner notes for *Another Side of Bob Dylan* in 1964 – and Janis Joplin was a regular performer. Now the space is hung with photography exhibits that cover far-flung global events as well as nature shots of the rugged Catskills.

Spend time in the afternoon exploring **Opus 40** (📞246-3400; www. opus40.org; 50 Fite Rd; adult/ child $10/$3; ⏰11:30am-5pm Fri-Sun), a startling collection of pathways, pools and obelisks spread over 6.5 acres of a former quarry. Creator Harvey Fite, who painstakingly carved and set all the bluestone pieces, thought it would take him 40 years to complete: it took his entire life.

Get in touch with your spiritual side at **Karma Triyana Dharmachakra** (📞845-679-5906; www.kagyu. org; 335 Meads Mountain Rd), a Buddhist monastery in the Catskill Mountains, about 3 miles from Woodstock. Inside the shrine room is a giant golden Buddha statue; take off your shoes and meditate with him.

 p63

LOCAL KNOWLEDGE: KALEIDOSCOPIC VIEWS

Attached to the Emerson Resort (see p63) and housed in a pitch-black, 60ft silo is the world's largest kaleidoscope. The gigantic optical instrument spins its bright colors in mesmerizing, hypnotizing patterns, inducing sleep in the road-weary. A boutique sells incredibly designed hand-crafted kaleidoscopes, really pieces of art or sculpture, that range from $20 to thousands of dollars.

Eating & Sleeping

Mt Tremper

🛏 Emerson Resort & Spa   Resort $$$

(📞877-688-2828; www.emersonplace.com;
5340 Rte 28; s/d from $190/220; ❄🌐) A full-
service base for year-round Catskills adventures
with both luxurious Asian-inspired suites
and rustic-chic rooms in the log-cabin-style
lodge. The Phoenix restaurant (mains $15 to
$30) is probably the best in the region and the
Catamount, popular with locals, has pub fare
(mains $10) including burgers and BBQ ribs and
live music and dancing Monday night.

🛏 Kate's Lazy Meadow Motel   Motel $$

(📞845-688-7200; www.lazymeadow.com; 5191
Rte 28; r from wkdays/wkends $175/200; ❄🌐)
A kitschy, upbeat and comfortable mountain
motel with 1950s-style decor and mini-
kitchenettes (owned and run by Kate Pierson
of B-52s fame). Plus, there's an outside fire pit
for toasting marshmallows while gazing across
babbling Esopus Creek.

Phoenicia ❸

🛏 Phoenicia Lodge   Motel $

(📞845-688-7772; www.phoenicialodge.com;
Rte 28; r from $80, ste from $130; ❄🌐📺)
Less than a mile west of town, this classic
and affordable roadside motel has simple and
unpretentious rooms with wood-paneling and
a touch of mid-century modern decor. Groups
should try a cottage or suite.

Tannersville ❻

🍴 Last Chance Cheese   American $$

(6009 Main St, Tannersville; mains $9-20;
🕙11am-midnight Fri-Sun) This independent-
minded eclectically furnished Tannersville
institution has an overstuffed counter displaying
gourmet cheeses, chocolates, candies and 300
varieties of beer. The menu runs the gamut from
big salads to lasagna to steaks and hearty chili,
not to mention fondue and s'mores. Live music
Friday and Saturday nights.

🛏 Hotel Mountain Brook   Hotel $$

(📞518-589-6740; www.hotelmountainbrook.
com; 57 Hill St; r wkdays/wkends with breakfast
from $150/200; ❄🌐📺) If not for the parking
lot of the middle school across the street, the
Mountain Brook, which is set on a hill with
forested mountain views, would evoke an
Adirondack 'great camp.' Rooms are furnished
in stylistically rustic decor with luxurious
bedding and breakfast is a gourmet feast. With
a sofa in front of a fireplace, room 7, on the 2nd
floor of the main cabin, is especially cozy.

Woodstock ❼

🍴 Taco Juan's   Mexican $

(Tinker St; mains $8-15) There's no missing this
popular Mexican organic eatery, thanks to the
vivid yellow and blue facade and flamboyant
window art.

🛏 Village Green B&B   B&B $$

(📞845-679-0313; www.villagegreenbb.com;
12 Tinker St; r incl breakfast $135; ❄🌐)
Overlooking Woodstock's town square, in front
of the bus stop, is this three-story Victorian with
comfortable, homey rooms.

🛏 Woodstock Inn on the
Millstream   Inn $$

(📞845-679-8211; www.woodstock-inn-ny.com;
48 Tannery Brook Rd, Woodstock; r $140-250;
❄🌐) Beautifully decorated rooms with flat-
screen TVs, quiet pastels and electric fireplaces.
Also has serene, flower-filled grounds.

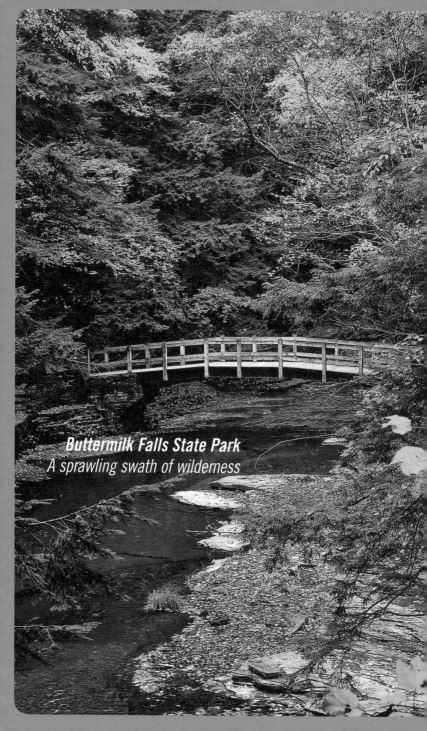

Buttermilk Falls State Park
A sprawling swath of wilderness

Finger Lakes Loop

4

'Ithaca is Gorges' T-shirts don't lie. Cornell's Ivy League campus has them, but there are dozens more in the area with gorgeous waterfalls, plus lakeside vineyards producing top wines.

TRIP HIGHLIGHTS

**3 DAYS
144 MILES / 231KM**

92 miles

Rte 54, Keuka Lake
Picturesque vineyards on bluffs overlooking the lake

1 mile

Ithaca
Dramatic gorges run through college town's campus

Seneca Falls

Geneva

Cuyuga Lake

Seneca Lake

6

Keuka Lake

Hammondsport

1 START
2

8 FINISH

Corning
One of the world's finest collections of glass

144 miles

Buttermilk Falls & Robert H Treman State Parks
A dazzling variety of falls and swimming holes

5 miles

GREAT FOR...

BEST TIME TO GO

May to October for farmers markets and glorious sunny vistas.

 ESSENTIAL PHOTO

The full height of Taughannock Falls.

✓ **BEST FOR OENOPHILES**

With more than 65 vineyards, a designated driver is needed.

Classic Trip

4 Finger Lakes Loop

A bird's-eye view of this region of rolling hills and 11 long narrow lakes – the eponymous fingers – reveals an outdoor paradise stretching all the way from Albany to far-western New York. Of course there's boating, fishing, cycling, hiking and cross-country skiing, but this is also the state's premier wine-growing region, with enough variety for the most discerning oenophile and palate-cleansing whites and reds available just about every few miles.

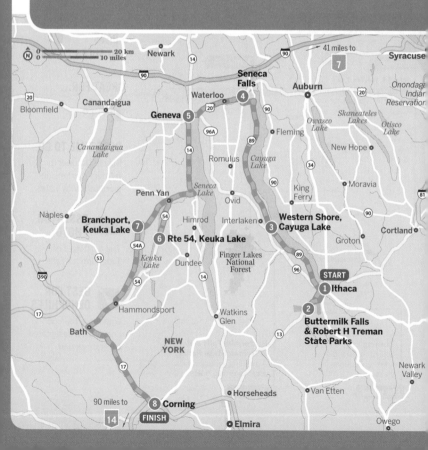

TRIP HIGHLIGHT

1 Ithaca

An idyllic home for college students and older hippies who cherish elements of the traditional collegiate lifestyle – laid-back vibe, cafe poetry readings, arthouse cinemas, good eats – Ithaca is perched above Cayuga Lake.

Founded in 1865, Cornell University boasts a lovely campus, mixing traditional and contemporary architecture. The modern **Johnson Museum of Art** (607-255-6464; www. museum.cornell.edu; University Ave; 10am-5pm Tue- Sun) **FREE**, designed by IM Pei, has a major Asian collection, plus pre-

Columbian, American and European exhibits. Just east of the center of the campus is **Cornell Plantations** (607-255-2400; www.cornellplantations. org; Plantations Rd; 10am-5pm, closed Mon) **FREE**, an expertly curated herb and flower garden and arboretum. Kids can go interactive-wild at **Sciencenter** (607-272-0600; www.sciencenter.org; 601 First St; adult/child $8/6; 10am-5pm Tue-Sat, from noon Sun;).

The area around Ithaca is known for its waterfalls, gorges and gorgeous parks. However, downtown has its very own, **Cascadilla Gorge**, starting several blocks from Ithaca Commons and ending, after a steep and stunning vertical climb, at the Performing Arts Center of Cornell.

✕ ⌂ p72

The Drive » It's only 2 miles south on Rte 13 to Buttermilk Falls State Park.

TRIP HIGHLIGHT

2 Buttermilk Falls & Robert H Treman State Parks

A sprawling swath of wilderness, **Buttermilk Falls State Park** (607-273-5761; Rte 13) has something for everyone – a beach, cabins, fishing, hiking, recreational fields and camping. The big draw, however, is the waterfalls. There's more

than 10, with some sending water tumbling as far as 500ft below into clear pools. Hikers like the raggedy Gorge Trail that brings them up to all the best cliffs. It parallels Buttermilk Creek, winding up about 500ft. On the other side of the falls is the equally popular Rim Trail, a loop of about 1.5 miles around the waterfalls from a different vantage point. Both feed into Bear Trail, which will take you to neighboring Treman Falls.

It's a trek of about 3 miles to Treman, or you can pop back in the car and drive the 3 miles south to **Robert H Treman State Park** (607-273-3440; 105 Enfield Falls Rd), still on bucolic Rte 13. Also renowned for cascading falls, Treman's gorge trail passes a stunning 12 waterfalls in under 3 miles. The two biggies you don't want to miss are Devil's Kitchen and Lucifer Falls, a multi-tiered wonder that spills Enfield Creek over rocks for about 100ft. At the bottom of yet another watery gorge – Lower Falls – there's a natural swimming hole; it's a deep, dark, refreshing pool of river water that's impossible to resist on hot summer days.

The Drive » Take Rte 13 back into Ithaca to connect with Rte 89, which hugs Cayuga Lake shore for 10 miles. The entrance to Taughannock Falls State Park is just after crossing the river gorge.

LINK YOUR TRIP

7 St Lawrence Seaway

Drive north from any of the eastern lakes to hook up with this trip along a Great Lake – Lake Ontario – and river islands.

14 Through the Wilds Along Route 6

From Corning, it's less than an hour on Rte 15 south to Wellsboro and a trip filled with gorges and wild forests.

Classic Trip

❸ Western Shore, Cayuga Lake

Trumansburg, a one-street town about 15 miles north of Ithaca, is the gateway to **Taughannock Falls State Park** (☑607-387-6739; www. nysparks.com; 2221 Taughannock Rd, Trumansburg). At 215ft, the falls of the same name are 30ft higher than Niagara Falls. There are 5 miles of hiking trails, most of which wind their way around the slippery parts to bring you safely to the lookout spots at the top. One trail follows the stream bed to the falls.

A little further along on Rte 89, near the village of Interlaken, is the **Creamery** (☺11am-8pm), a roadside restaurant that, in addition to ice-cream sundaes, serves buzz-inducing wine-infused sorbets. Just past here is **Lucas Vineyards** (☑607-532-4825; www. lucasvineyards.com; 3862 County Rd 150, Interlaken; ☺10:30am-5:30pm), one of the pioneers of Cayuga wineries. A little further north, by the lake shore and a small community of modest but charming summer homes, is **Sheldrake Point Winery** (☑607-532-9401; www. sheldrakepoint.com; 7448 County Rd; ☺11am-5pm Fri-Mon Jan-Mar, 10am-5:30pm daily Apr-Dec), which has stunning views and award-winning whites. **Knapp Winery & Restaurant** (☑607-869-9271; www.knappwine.com; 2770 Ernsberger Rd, Romulus; ☺10am-5:30pm Apr-Nov, 11am-5pm Dec-Mar) has a wide lawn surrounded by gnarly roots and rioting wildflowers; you can look out over the trellis-covered vineyards while sampling homemade wines, grappas and limoncellos.

✕ 🛏 p72

TOP TIP:
SAPSUCKER WOODS SANCTUARY

Only a few miles northeast of Ithaca is Cornell University's **Sapsucker Woods** (☑800-843-2473; www. birds.cornell.edu; 159 Sapsucker Woods Rd), a bird-feeding garden and 10-acre pond full of ducks, geese and other wildlife. The 4 miles of trails, open from dawn to dusk, are teeming with birds and butterflies. Also look out for *Stone Egg*, a huge cairn built from local stone by internationally acclaimed environmental artist Andy Goldsworthy and students from Cornell.

The Drive » Rte 89 continues along the lake shore and passes Cayuga Lake State Park, which has beach access and picnic tables, a few miles before you turn left onto County Rd 116 east.

---

❹ Seneca Falls

This small, sleepy town is where the country's organized women's rights movement was born. After being excluded from an anti-slavery meeting, Elizabeth Cady Stanton and her friends drafted an 1848 declaration asserting that 'all men and women are created equal.' The inspirational **Women's Rights National Historical Park** (☑315-568-2991; www.nps.gov/ wori; 136 Fall St; ☺9am-5pm) **FREE** has a small but impressive museum with an informative film, plus a visitor center offering tours of Cady Stanton's house. The surprisingly tiny **National Women's Hall of Fame** (☑315-568-8060; www.greatwomen.org; 76 Fall St; adult/child $3/free; ☺10am-4pm Wed-Sat year round, from noon Sun Jun-Aug) honors American women such as First Lady Abigail Adams, American Red Cross founder Clara Barton and civil-rights activist Rosa Parks.

🛏 p72

The Drive » The 10 miles on NY-20 west to Geneva passes through strip mall-lined Waterloo; Mac's Drive-In, a classic 1950s-style burger joint, is worth a stop.

❺ Geneva

Geneva, one of the larger towns on this route, has interesting, historic architecture and a lively vibe with both Hobart and William Smith colleges calling it home. South Main St is lined with turn-of-the-century Italianate, Federal and Greek Revival homes in immaculate condition, products of its former status as the region's commercial hub. The restored 1894 **Smith Opera House** (☎315-781-5483; www.thesmith.org; 82 Seneca St) is the place to go for theater, concerts and performing arts in the area. Stop by **Microclimate** (38 Linden St, Geneva; ⊗6pm-midnight Mon, 4:30pm-1am Thu-Sun), a cool little wine bar offering wine flights where you can compare locally produced varietals with their international counterparts.

🛏 p73

The Drive » On your way south on Rte 14 you pass Red Tail Ridge winery, a gold Leadership in Energy & Environmental Design (LEED) certified place on Seneca Lake. Then turn right on Rte 54 to Penn Yan.

TRIP HIGHLIGHT

❻ Route 54, Keuka Lake

Y-shaped Keuka is about 20 miles long and in some parts up to 2 miles wide, its lush vegetation uninterrupted except for neat patches of vineyards. Keuka is surrounded on both sides by two small state parks that keep it relatively pristine. One of its old canals has been converted into a rustic bike path, and it's a favorite lake for trout fishers.

Just south of Penn Yan, the largest village on Keuka Lake's shores, you come to **Keuka Spring Vineyards** (☎315-536-3147; www.keukaspringwinery.com; 54 E Lake Rd, Penn Yan; ⊗10am-5pm Mon-Sat, from 11am Sun summer, weekends other months) and then **Rooster Hill Vineyards** (☎315-536-4773; www.roosterhill.com; 489 Rte 54, Penn Yan; ⊗10am-5pm Mon-Sat, from 11am Sun) – two local favorites that offer tastings and tours. Keuka Spring has won many awards for its oaky Cabernet Franc and Rooster Hill's fine whites spark a buzz among wine aficionados. A few miles further south along Rte 54 brings you to **Barrington Cellars** (☎315-536-9686; www.barringtoncellars.com; 2690 Gray Rd, Penn Yan; ⊗10:30am-5pm Mon-Sat, from noon Sun summer, Fri-Sun spring, Sat winter), flush with Labrusca and Vinifera wines made from local grapes. Barrington's deck is a favorite place to stop for a drink.

On Saturdays in summer everyone flocks to the **Windmill Farm &**

Craft Market (⊗8am-4:30pm) just outside Penn Yan. Check out Amish and Mennonite goods, from hand-carved wooden rockers to homegrown veggies and flowers.

The Drive » After about 5.5 miles on Rte 54A take a detour south onto Skyline Dr, which runs down the middle of 800ft Bluff Point, for outstanding views. Backtrack to Rte 54A and Branchport is only a few miles further along.

❼ Branchport, Keuka Lake

As you pass through the tiny village of Branchport at the tip of Keuka's left fork in its Y, keep an eye out for **Hunt Country Vineyards** (☎315-595-2812; www.huntwine.com; 4021 County Rd 32, Branchport; ⊗10am-6pm Mon-Sat, from 11am Sun summer) and **Stever Hill Vineyards** (☎315-595-2230; 3962 Stever Hill Rd, Branchport; ⊗11am-6pm daily summer), the latter of which has its tasting room in a restored old barn. Both wineries are family run and edging into their sixth generation. On top of tastings there are tours of the grape-growing facilities and snacks from the vineyards' own kitchens.

✕ 🛏 p73

The Drive » Rte 54A along the west branch of Keuka passes by the Taylor Wine Museum just north of Hammondsport. Carry on to Bath where you connect with I-86 east/NY-17 east for another 19 miles to Corning.

Classic Trip

LOCAL KNOWLEDGE
DAVE BREEDEN,
WINEMAKER,
SHELDRAKE POINT

There's a burgeoning new food and wine economy. New distilleries, microbreweries, bakeries, cheese shops and community-supported agriculture ventures. And everyone is collegial, we borrow things when needed and of course taste each others' wines. If you come in the spring you'll likely be able to interact more with winemakers while harvest time in the autumn is beautiful because of the fall foliage.

Top: Buttermilk Falls State Park
Left: Vineyard, Lake Keuka
Right: Cornell University, Ithaca

GLENN VAN DER KNIJFF/GETTY IMAGES ©

TRIP HIGHLIGHT

8 Corning

The massive **Corning Museum of Glass** (☎800-732-6845; www.cmog.org; 1 Museum Way; adult/child $15/free; ◷9am-5pm, to 8pm Memorial Day-Labor Day; 👪) is home to fascinating exhibits on glassmaking arts, with demonstrations and interactive items for kids and adults. It's possibly the world's finest collection, both in terms of its historic breadth – which spans 35 centuries – and its sculptural pieces. Also stop by **Vitrix Hot Glass Studio** (www.vitrixhotglass.com; 77 W Market St; ◷9am-8pm Mon-Fri, from 10am Sat, noon-5pm Sun) to take a gander at museum-quality glass pieces ranging from functional bowls to organic-shaped sculptures.

Housed in the former City Hall, a Romanesque Revival building c 1893, the **Rockwell Museum of Western Art** (☎607-937-5386; www.rockwellmuseum.org; 111 Cedar St; adult/child $8/free; ◷9am-5pm, to 8pm summer; 👪) has the largest collection of art of the American West including great works by Albert Bierstadt, Charles M Russell and Frederic Remington. Native American arts and crafts are also well represented and there's a room designed and decorated like a great western lodge.

✕ p73

Eating & Sleeping

Ithaca ❶

✕ Glenwood Pines   Burgers $

(1213 Taughannock Blvd; burgers $6; ⏰11am-10pm) According to locals in the know this modest roadside restaurant, overlooking Lake Cayuga on Rte 89 and 4 miles north of Ithaca, serves the best burgers.

✕ Moosewood Restaurant   Vegetarian $

(www.moosewoodcooks.com; 215 N Cayuga St; mains $8-18; ⏰11:30am-8:30pm Mon-Sat, 5:30-9pm Sun; 🖉) Famous for its creative and constantly changing vegetarian menu and recipe books by founder Mollie Katzen. Meat eaters should be able to find something to their liking, such as fish or Szechuan eggplant.

✕ Yerba Maté Factor Café & Juice Bar   Sandwiches $

(143 The Commons; mains $8; ⏰9am-9pm Mon-Thu, to 3pm Fri, from noon Sun) Run by members of a fairly obscure religious organization, this large restaurant, housed in a converted historic building on the Ithaca commons, is good for Belgian waffles, sandwiches and coffee.

🛏 Inn on Columbia   Inn $$

(☎607-272-0204; www.columbiabb.com; 228 Columbia St, Ithaca; r incl breakfast $175-225; ❄🛜🐾) This modern, contemporary inn on a quiet residential street is the kind of place that appeals to those who have fantasies of living as a tenured professor. Restored by its architect-owner, the inn is suffused with light and sophistication.

🛏 William Henry Miller Inn   B&B $$

(☎607-256-4553; www.millerinn.com; 303 N Aurora St, Ithaca; r incl breakfast $115-215;

❄🛜🐾) Gracious, grand and only a few steps from the commons, this completely restored historic home features luxuriously designed rooms – three have Jacuzzis – and gourmet breakfasts.

Cayuga Lake ❸

✕ Hazelnut Kitchen   Modern American $$

(☎607-387-4433; 53 East Main St, Trumansburg; mains $14-23; ⏰5-9pm Thu-Mon) The new owners, a young couple from Chicago interested in collaborating with area farmers, have maintained Hazelnut's status as arguably the finest restaurant in the region. Local ingredients of course, seasonally inspired menu and au courant interesting meat dishes like pig face torchon.

🛏 Buttonwood Grove Winery   Cabin $$

(☎607-869-9760; www.buttonwoodgrove.com; 5986 Rte 89; r $135; 🐾) Has four fully furnished log cabins nestled in the hills above Lake Cayuga (open April to December); free wine tasting included.

Seneca Falls ❹

🛏 Hotel Clarence   Boutique Hotel $$

(☎315-712-4000; www.hotelclarence.com; 108 Fall St, Seneca Falls; r $140; ❄🛜🐾) Originally a 1920s-era hotel, the downtown building housing the Clarence has undergone a stylish renovation with a nod to the past – the mahogany bar comes from an old Seneca Falls saloon and there's a projection of Frank Capra's film *It's a Wonderful Life* on the lobby wall. The standard rooms are small but the Kitchen, an upscale restaurant, is the best in town.

Geneva ⑤

🛏 Belhurst Castle   Inn $$

(📞315-781-0201; www.belhurst.com; 4069 Rte 14 S, Geneva; ❄️🛜) Even if you're not planning a wedding, this fairy tale castle overlooking Lake Seneca might inspire you to take the plunge. The huge back lawn is so picturesque it feels cinematic. Check out the three separate properties with a variety of room types. There's also two restaurants: the casual Stone Cutters, with live music on weekends, and the more formal Edgar's.

Keuka Lake ⑥

🍴 Switz Inn   American/Seafood $$

(www.theswitz.com; 14109 Keuka Village Rd; mains $8-16; 🕙11am-10pm) A rowdy, outdoorsy burger joint that also serves up all-you-can-eat crab legs and a weekend fish fry. On hot days you can dive off the dock into the lake.

🛏 Gone with the Wind B&B   B&B $$

(📞607-868-4603; www.gonewiththewindon keukalake.com; 14905 West Lake Rd, Branchport; r incl breakfast $110-200; ❄️) This lakeside B&B is every bit as beautiful as Tara and has a sweeping deck with great views. There are two accommodation choices – the original stone mansion and a log lodge annex – though both have generally homey furnishings.

Corning ⑧

🍴 Gaffer Grill & Tap Room   Steakhouse $$

(www.gaffergrillandtaproom.com; 58 W Market St; mains $10-35; 🕙11:30am-10:30pm Mon-Thu, from 4:30pm Sat & Sun) An old-school steakhouse with a contemporary dedication to sourcing meat only from local organic farms. The biggies like New York strip, Delmonico and ribs are on the menu as are brisket sandwiches and pasta, fish and chicken dishes. An inn is attached.

Lake George *A peaceful gateway to Adirondack Park*

Adirondack Peaks & Valleys

5

New York's wide, northern territory is dominated by an untamed wilderness of craggy peaks with bushy tufts of spruce trees that loom over a series of idyllic, mirror-like lakes.

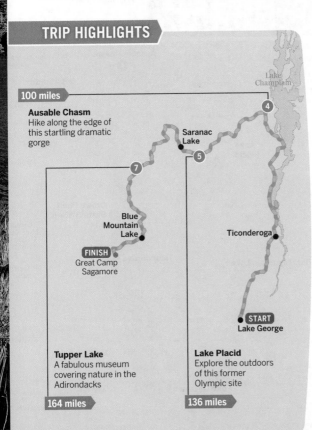

TRIP HIGHLIGHTS

100 miles

Ausable Chasm
Hike along the edge of this startling dramatic gorge

Saranac Lake

Blue Mountain Lake

Ticonderoga

FINISH
Great Camp Sagamore

START
Lake George

Tupper Lake
A fabulous museum covering nature in the Adirondacks
164 miles

Lake Placid
Explore the outdoors of this former Olympic site
136 miles

Lake Champlain

7 DAYS
237 MILES /
381KM

GREAT FOR...

BEST TIME TO GO
Backcountry trails and sights open June to September.

 ESSENTIAL PHOTO
Heart Lake from the summit of Mt Jo.

 BEST FOR ADRENALIN SEEKERS
Bobsled down an Olympic track.

Adirondack Peaks & Valleys

Majestic and wild, the Adirondacks, a mountain range with 42 peaks over 4000ft high, rival any of the nation's wilderness areas for sheer awe-inspiring beauty. The 9375 sq miles of protected parklands and forest preserve that climb from central New York State to the Canadian border include towns, mountains, glacial lakes, rivers and more than 2000 miles of hiking trails.

1 Lake George

The southern gateway to the Adirondack Park is a kitschy little village – think T-shirt shops, a wax museum and a Polynesian-themed hotel – on the shores of the eponymously named 32-mile long lake. On windy days, it froths with whitecaps; on sunny days it shines like the placid blue sky.

Not far from the water is the reconstructed **Fort William Henry Museum** (☎518-668-5471; www.fwhmuseum.com;

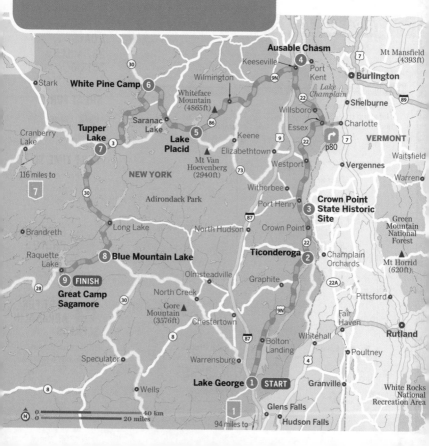

48 Canada St; adult/senior/child $17/14/8; ☺9am-7pm summer, to 5pm rest of yr;); the fort was built by the British during the French and Indian War (1754–63) as a staging ground for attacks against the garrison that would later become Fort Ticonderoga, and its fall would become the focus of James Fenimore Cooper's epic novel, *The Last of the Mohicans*. Guides dressed in Revolutionary garb muster visitors along, with stops for battle reenactments that include firing period muskets and cannons.

Lake George Steamboat Co's three boats – including the *Minnie Ha-ha,* a paddle wheeler – depart from Steel Pier on downtown Beach Rd in the summer months on one-hour jaunts (adult/child from $13/7) and half- or full-day trips.

If you have time for a short detour, take an afternoon visit to **Glens Falls**, about 10 miles south of Lake George along Rte 9. Its chief attraction is the **Hyde Collection** (☎518-792-1761; www.hydecollection. org; 161 Warren St; adult/under-12 $8/free; ☺10am-5pm Tue-Sat, noon-5pm Sun), a remarkable gathering of art amassed by local newspaper heiress Charlotte Pryun Hyde. In her rambling Florentine Renaissance mansion you'll stumble across Rembrandts, Rubens, Matisses and Eakins, as well as tapestries, sculptures and turn-of-the-century furnishings.

✕ ⌖ p83

The Drive » Rte 9N hugs the lake shore on this 40-mile stretch, passing dozens of old-school motels before coming to the prosperous village of Bolton Landing, a good place to stop for a bite to eat. Along the way, peek through the trees to glimpse forested islets and stately waterfront homes once known as 'Millionaires' Row'. Rte 9N veers inland and becomes more commercial approaching Ticonderoga.

- - - - - - - - - - - - -

❷ Ticonderoga

The small town of Ticonderoga is known essentially for two things: the No 2 pencil factory that's long since shut down, and its iconic fort. Since it was taken from the British in 1775 by the 'Green Mountain Boys' (a group of independence-loving hotheads from Vermont led by Ethan Allen and Benedict Arnold, a colonel at the time and pre-betrayal), **Fort Ticonderoga** (☎518-585-2821; www.fortticonderoga. org; 100 Fort Ti Rd; adult/child $17.50/8; ☺9:30am-5pm May 17-Oct 20) has been synonymous with the American Revolution. Nowadays its buckling stone walls and rickety wooden outposts, affording stellar views of the surrounding lakes, can barely sustain their own weight, let alone that of a 300lb cannon. But every summer the carefully preserved fort opens its museum and grounds for tours and reenactments.

The Drive » It's a good idea to fuel up on gas before leaving Ticonderoga for this 18-mile drive. Each turn of Rte 22 brings a new view of Lake Champlain's sculpted shores, pushed up against the foothills of the Green Mountains. On the other side, it's all wavy-gold meadows and carefully sculpted fields.

- - - - - - - - - - - - -

❸ Crown Point State Historic Site

The remains of two major 18th-century forts, the British Crown Point and the French St Frederic, sit on a once strategic promontory where Lake

LINK YOUR TRIP

7 **St Lawrence Seaway**

Head west from Saranac Lake to Alexandria Bay to descend to the waters of the St Lawrence for a bucolic riverside drive.

1 **Hudson Valley**

Take I-87 south to the town of Catskill for local roads to the small towns and historic sites along the river.

Champlain narrows between New York and Vermont. The British, after several failed attempts to wrest control of the commanding overlook, finally succeeded in 1759 after it was abandoned by the French. Today, the **Crown Point State Historic Site** (📞518-597-4666; www.nysparks.com; 21 Grandview Dr, Crown Point; ⊕grounds 9am-6pm) ruins look like they're in the midst of an archaeological dig. Still, views of the mountains and lake are beautiful and it's interesting to imagine the numerous forks history could have taken when the French first built the stone citadel in the 1600s. Check out the exhibits in the small museum (adult/child $4/3) to understand the area's role in the quest for empire.

The Drive » On this 50-mile drive, Rte 22 north passes through beautiful countryside, alongside shore line train tracks and the Boquet River; note the falls in tiny Wadhams. Just before the historic village of Essex (c 1775) and its highly recommended inn (p83), you pass by Essex farm, made famous in Kristin Kimball's book *The Dirty Life: A Memoir of Farming, Food & Love*.

TRIP HIGHLIGHT

④ Ausable Chasm

One of the country's oldest natural attractions, the dramatically beautiful **Ausable Chasm** (📞518-834-9990; www.ausablechasm.com; 2144 Rte 9; adult/child $17/10; ⊕9am-5pm summer, to 4pm rest of yr; 🚻) is a 2-mile long fissure formed by a gushing river that over thousands of years carved its way through deep layers of sandstone, creating 200ft cliffs, waterfalls and rapids. The privately owned sight, in danger of shutting its gates for good after the devastating floods of Tropical Storm Irene in 2011, has rebuilt its walkways and connecting bridges and added a rappelling course for those seeking an alternative to the riverside trail. In the wintertime, strap on microspikes to see majestic icicles that complement the unique rock formations. When the weather warms, lazily slide downriver in a raft, rented kayak or inner tube, gazing at the birds and butterflies that fill the light-drenched gorge.

Along with a large cafe there's a small museum, primarily about the life and work of the naturalist, writer and photographer Seneca Ray Stoddard, whose guidebooks, photos and maps of the region were instrumental in the formation of the Adirondack Park in 1892 – unregulated logging was threatening

Lake Placid A scenic drive near the lake

DETOUR: VERMONT

Start: ❸ Crown Point Historic Site

Neighboring Vermont is within your reach – at Essex just jump onto **Lake Champlain Ferries** (📞802-864-6830; www.ferries.com; driver & vehicle one-way $9.50, additional passenger $3.75; 🕑open May-Dec) and in 20 minutes you'll be in **Charlotte**, VT, a quaint hamlet established in 1792 and dedicated to farming and rustic pursuits like making maple syrup and maple syrup candy (other ferries are at Port Kent to Burlington and Plattsburgh to Grand Isle further north). Or take the Lake Champlain Bridge at Crown Point State Historic Site to the college town of **Middlebury** only a half hour away.

to destroy much of the region's forests.

The Drive ⟫ With passport in hand, consider a detour to Montreal, a straight shot north less than an hour and a half away. If not, make tracks on 9N which follows the Ausable River to Rte 86 – views of Whiteface Mountain grow more distinct as you make your way about 30 miles southwest to Lake Placid.

- - - - - - - - - - - - -

TRIP HIGHLIGHT

❺ Lake Placid

While the town of Lake Placid, set on beautiful Mirror Lake, is a fairly typical commercial strip, its winter Olympic legacy (1932 and 1980) remains vital. The official **Olympic Center** (📞518-302-5326; www.whiteface.com; 2634 Main St; adult/child $7/5; 🕑10am-5pm; 👶) is on Main St, a large white building where the inside temperatures are kept bone-chillingly

cold, thanks to the four large skating rinks where athletes come to train. Hockey fans will recognize this complex as the location of the 1980 'Miracle on Ice' when the upstart US hockey team managed to defeat the seemingly unstoppable Soviets and go on to win Olympic gold. The Lake Placid Winter Olympics Museum inside the center has a fairly unexceptional display of memorabilia.

Not far from town on Rte 73 is the **Mackenzie-Intervale Ski Jumping Complex** (📞518-523-2202; www.whiteface.com; 5486 Cascade Rd; adult/child $11/8; 🕑hours vary seasonally), an all-weather training facility for ski jump teams; non-acrophobic visitors can take the 20-story elevator ride to the top for impressive views (there's snow

tubing on a nearby hill in winter). A 7-mile scenic drive south brings you to **Mt Van Hoevenberg** (📞518-523-4436; 8 John Brown Rd, Rte 73, Lake Placid; adult/child $10/8, bobsled rides $30; 🕑hours vary seasonally; 👶), home to Olympic 'sliding sports' where you can sign up for a bone-rattling, adrenalin-pumping ride on a bobsled, skeleton or luge during certain times of the year.

A large network of back country hiking and cross-country trails start from the ADK Loj (p83) on Heart Lake.

🍴 🛏 p83

The Drive ⟫ It's only 9 miles west on Rte 86 to the somewhat dreary town of Saranac Lake; stock up on groceries here or stay in a recommended lodge (p83). Continue north on Rte 86 past small farms (look for roadside markets in warm months) with mountain views until the turnoff for White Pine Camp.

- - - - - - - - - - - - -

❻ White Pine Camp

About 14 miles north of the town of Saranac Lake (which was once a center for tuberculosis treatments), you'll find **White Pine Camp** (📞518-327-3030; www.whitepinecamp.com; 432 White Pine Rd, Paul Smiths; two-person cottage from $105 end Oct – end Jun; weekly from $1085 mid-May – end Oct), one of the few remaining Adirondack 'great camps' where you can spend a night. Great camps were usually grand lakeside compounds built by the very wealthy, usually all from wood, in the latter half of the 19th century in the Adirondacks. White Pine, however, is far from ostentatious; rather, it's a collection of rustically cozy cabins set amid pine forests, wetlands and scenic Osgood Pond – a boardwalk leads out to an island tea house and an antique all-wood bowling alley. The fact that President Calvin Coolidge spent a few summer months here in 1926 is an interesting historical footnote but the camp's charm comes through in its modest luxuries like claw-footed tubs and wood-burning fireplaces. Naturalist walking tours are open to non-guests on select days from mid-June to September.

Because White Pine feels so remote, the campus of **Paul Smith's College**, only a few miles away, feels disconcertingly modern. While the majority attend the school for degrees in forestry and wildlife-related sciences, it's worth visiting for lunch or dinner at the **St Regis Cafe** (☏518-327-6355; www. paulsmiths.edu; Rte 30, Paul Smiths; ☺11:30am-12:30pm Mon-Fri, 5:30-6:30pm Wed). It overlooks Lower St Regis Lake and is staffed by culinary students when school is in session – a

three-course meal will cost you $10. Call for reservations.

The college also maintains a system of interpretive and backcountry trails with cross-country skiing in the winter.

The Drive » From Paul Smith's, Rte 30 winds its way south and east past several beautiful lakes, ponds and wetland areas including Lake Clear and Upper Saranac Lake. The final 5 ½ mile stretch on Rte 3 is more mundane.

– – – – – – – – – – –

TRIP HIGHLIGHT

⑦ Tupper Lake

Only a few miles east of this otherwise nondescript town is the **Wild Center** (☏518-

3597800; www.wildcenter. org; 45 Museum Dr, Tupper Lake; adult/child $17/10, under 3 free; ☺10am-6pm daily end May-early Sep, 10am-5pm Fri-Sun Sep-Mar, closed Apr; ⊞), a jewel of a museum dedicated to the ecology and conservation of the Adirondacks. Interactive exhibits include a digitally rendered spherical Earth which visually displays thousands of science-related issues like sea surface temperatures or the history of volcanic activity (there are only about 100 of these in use worldwide). River otters perform acrobatics in an aquarium; walking trails lead to an oxbow overlook and the Raquette River

WILDLIFE FUN FACTS

» Stay clear of rattlesnakes when hiking – the nearest hospital with a vial of anti-venom is in the Lake George area.

» Saliva from a water-snake bite contains an anticoagulant; though not poisonous, you might bleed profusely.

» The vomit of a turkey vulture – they do this when nervous – is an assault on your olfactory senses. Don't make them nervous.

» Ravens, considered one of the smartest bird species, can imitate other birds and even human speech.

» Eastern coyotes found in the Adirondacks are larger than other subspecies because they contain added DNA from wolves out west.

» Swarms of black flies and other biting pests typically emerge from streams and rivers from late May through early September.

SNOWBOUND IN THE DEEP WOODS

The North Creek area of the Adirondacks feels more remote than spots further north and east. For dozens of miles of backwoods hiking and cross-country trails head to **Garnet Hill Lodge** (☎518-251-2444; www.garnet-hill.com; s/d from $115/150) overlooking Thirteenth Lake. It has the homespun vibe and log cabin aesthetics of an earlier era and new owners committed to the business. Nearby **Gore Mountain** (☎518-251-2411; www.goremountain.com; 793 Peaceful Valley Rd) has some of the best downhill skiing in the area.

The easiest way to access North Creek is from Lake George or, for a more scenic route, from Bolton Landing – on Rte NY8 you cross over the Hudson River (yep, the very same that runs down to New York City) and follow it further along on Rte 28. You might spot an eagle or two on the way.

(snowshoes provided *gratis* in winter months); watch Stickley the porcupine's slow motion feeding; catch one of several naturalist films; and don't miss the 'back of the house' tour where you'll see the nuts and bolts of the operation, such as freezers full of dead mice to feed the center's snakes, owls, skunks and other animals. Give yourself three to four hours here minimum.

The Drive » Scenic Rte 30 south takes you past several lakes and ponds on this 33-mile leg. You'll pass through the town of Long Lake, originally settled as a mill town in the 1830s and today a vacation center that swells with visitors in the summer (float planes ferry in hikers and hunters); there's a little public beach on Rte 30 just over the bridge and across from the Adirondack Hotel.

8 Blue Mountain Lake

A wonderful pairing with the Wild Center, the **Adirondack Museum** (☎518-352-7311; www.adkmuseum.org; 9097 Rte 30; adult/child $18/6; ☉10am-5pm May 24-Oct 14; 🖼) tells the other, human-centered story of the mountains. This large, ambitious and fascinating complex with two dozen separate buildings occupies a 30-acre compound overlooking Blue Mountain Lake. The history of mining, logging and boat building are explored, as is the role of 19th- century tourism in the region's development. Lots of hands-on exhibits and activities for kids including a bouldering wall and snowshoeing even in summertime.

The Drive » It's another half hour south on Rte 28 past several beautiful lakes to Great Camp Sagamore.

9 Great Camp Sagamore

On the shores of Raquette Lake, **Great Camp Sagamore** (☎315-354-5311; www.greatcampsagamore.org; Sagamore Rd, Raquette Lake; tours adult/child $16/8; ☉Jun 22 – Oct 13) is one of the most well-known 'great camps', in part because the Vanderbilt family vacationed here for a half century. You can tour the property and in the summertime (and other limited times during the rest of the year) even spend a weekend (per person two nights $300) in this rustically elaborate retreat originally built in 1895.

Eating & Sleeping

Lake George ❶

✖ Prospect Mountain Diner — Diner $

(☎518-668-3147; Canada St; mains $4-12; ⊙7am-9pm) Rustic locals and wealthy second-homers all rub elbows here over inexpensive waffles, jumbo burgers and homemade pies. It's as old-school as it gets with polished chrome, spinning counter stools and checkered tile floors.

🛏 Surfside on the Lake — Motel $

(☎800-342-9795; www.surfsideonthelake. com; 400 Canada St; r from $60; ❋🛜♿) Towards the northern end of downtown Lake George's row of doo-wop era motels, Surfside's competitive edge is its renovated beachfront access and pool deck.

Essex

🛏 Essex Inn — Inn $$$

(☎518-963-4400; www.essexinnessex.com; 2297 Main St; r from $225; ❋🛜) Originally built in 1810 when this village was a port stop for boats hauling goods north, the soft-yellow boarding house with a wide veranda has all the rustic charm you'd expect from a 200-year-old landmark. However, a 2010 renovation means plush contemporary features have been added to the uniquely and tastefully designed nine rooms and two suites (down the block). The owner/chef serves up finely prepared meals in the cozy dining room.

Lake Placid ❺

✖ Big Mountain Deli & Creperie — Deli $

(2475 Main St; sandwiches $8; ⊙8am-4pm) Stop by this small family-run place to fuel up in the morning or pack a picnic lunch. Choose from filling and healthy oatmeal and veggie breakfast burritos or one of 46 sandwiches named after the Adirondack's 46 high peaks.

🛏 ADK Loj & Wilderness Campground — Cabin, Camping $

(☎518-523-3441; www.adk.org; 1001 Adirondack Loj Rd; tent site for two people winter/summer $20/40) South of Lake Placid town, Adirondack Loj, run by the Adirondack Mountain Club (ADK), is a rustic retreat surrounded by mountains on the shore of peaceful Heart Lake. Wilderness campsites, lean-tos and cabins suited for big groups are also available. Some of the best high-peak hikes in the region begin from here.

🛏 Golden Arrow Lakeside Resort — Resort $$

(☎800-582-5540; www.golden-arrow.com; 2559 Main St; r from $130; 🅿❋🛜♿🐾) Conveniently located on Main St a block from the Olympic Center and the only accommodation directly on the shore of downtown Lake Placid's Mirror Lake. When the lake is frozen, there are dogsled rides on offer; at other times hit the small beach or a gondola for a tour. A variety of room types cater to families and couples alike.

Saranac Lake

🛏 The Porcupine — B&B $$

(☎518-891-5160; www.theporcupine.com; 350 Park Ave; r incl breakfast $172-400; ❋🛜) Housed in a classic Adirondacks-style lodge run with loving care, the Porcupine feels like a cozy writerly retreat with book-lined shelves and antique furnishings. A hike up to nearby Moody Pond and Baker Mountain affords excellent views of the area.

Letchworth State Park *Lush forests surround magnificent waterfalls*

Niagara Falls & Around

6

There's more to this region than the famous Niagara Falls. Think Buffalo architecture, a remote park with a spectacular gorge, a town designed by artisans and history galore.

TRIP HIGHLIGHTS

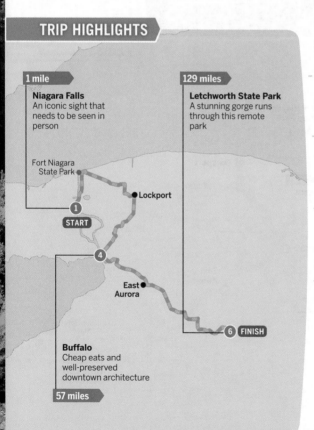

1 mile

Niagara Falls
An iconic sight that needs to be seen in person

Fort Niagara State Park

● Lockport

① START

④

129 miles

Letchworth State Park
A stunning gorge runs through this remote park

East ● Aurora

⑥ FINISH

Buffalo
Cheap eats and well-preserved downtown architecture

57 miles

3–4 DAYS
129 MILES / 207KM

GREAT FOR...

BEST TIME TO GO

May to early June and September to October to avoid crowds.

ESSENTIAL PHOTO

Bridal Veil Falls from Maid of the Mist.

BEST FOR OUTDOORS

Floating on a raft down the Genesee River.

6 Niagara Falls & Around

The history of western New York has been determined by the power of water: whether via the Erie Canal that once tethered the Great Lakes and Atlantic seaboard or the massive hydroelectric plants on the Niagara River, or even the long line of daredevils like Nik Wallenda who tightrope walked over Niagara Falls. And while industrial boom and bust cycles have come and gone, the canals, rivers, lakes and falls have never lost their sheen.

TRIP HIGHLIGHT

❶ Niagara Falls

These famous falls are in two separate towns: Niagara Falls, New York (USA) and Niagara Falls, Ontario (Canada). The towns face each other across the Niagara River, spanned by the Rainbow Bridge. Famous landscape architect Frederick Law Olmstead helped rescue and preserve the New York side, which by the 1870s was dominated by industry and gaudy signs. Today, the rather derelict

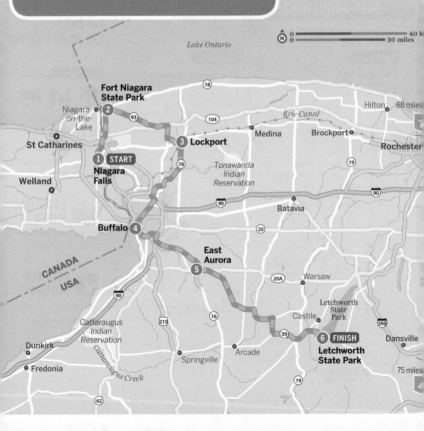

blocks are dominated by the purple, glass-covered Seneca Niagara Casino & Hotel.

Three waterfalls make up Niagara Falls. You can see views of the **American Falls** and part of the **Bridal Veil Falls**, which drop 180ft, from the **Prospect Point Observation Tower** (☑716-278-1796; admission $1, free from 5pm; ☻9:30am-7pm). Cross the small bridge to **Goat Island** for close-up viewpoints, including Terrapin Point, which has a fine view of **Horseshoe Falls** and pedestrian bridges to the Three Sisters Islands in the upper rapids. From the north corner of Goat Island, an elevator descends to the **Cave of the Winds** (☑716-278-1730; adult/child $11/8), where slippery

LINK YOUR TRIP

7 St Lawrence Seaway

Take I-90 E to Rochester and then to NY-104 to begin a trip along lake shores and to the Thousand Islands.

4 Finger Lakes Loop

From Letchworth, take NY-436 E and other rural back roads to Keuka Lake for a trip to wineries and beautiful falls.

walkways go within 25ft of the cataracts (raincoats provided), the closest viewpoint to the Canadian falls.

The **Maid of the Mist** (☑716-284-8897; www.maidofthemist.com; 151 Buffalo Ave; adult/child $15.50/9; ☻9am-7pm summer, times do vary so check website in advance) boat trip around the bottom of the falls has been a major attraction since 1846 and is highly recommended. Boats leave from the base of the Prospect Park Observation Tower on the US side and from the bottom of Clifton Hill on the Canadian side.

About 2 miles north of Niagara Falls, NY, is **Whirlpool State Park**, sitting just above a sharp bend in the Niagara River – a bend that creates a giant whirlpool easily visible from your vantage point. Steps take you 300ft to the gorge below and mind you don't tumble into the vortex.

 p91

The Drive » It's only a 15-mile drive north on the Robert Moses Parkway to the mouth of the Niagara River, not far from Lake Ontario, which you can see in the distance.

② Fort Niagara State Park

This park, occupying the once very strategic point where the Niagara River flows into Lake Ontario, is home to **Old**

Fort Niagara (☑716-745-7611; www.oldfortniagara.org; adult/child $12/8; ☻9am-5pm daily). The French originally built a garrison here in 1726 which was later used by the British and Americans in Revolutionary War battles. More recently, it was used for officers' housing during WWI. It has been stunningly restored and has engaging displays of Native American artifacts, small weapons, furniture and clothing as well as breathtaking views from its windblown ramparts. Surrounding the fort are well-maintained swimming pools and hiking trails.

The Drive » Take NY-93 east/Lockport Rd for around 14 flat, uneventful miles before turning right onto Stone Rd and then Mill St which runs down to the Erie Canal.

③ Lockport

Northeast of Niagara Falls is the town of Lockport, the western terminus of the Erie Canal, which was once the transportation lifeline connecting the Great Lakes and the Atlantic Ocean. Governor De Witt Clinton broke ground in 1817 on this public-works project of unprecedented scale; it was completed eight years later at a cost of $7 million (equivalent to around $4 billion today). The **Erie Canal Discovery Center** (☑716-439-0431;

24 Church St; adult/child $6/4; ⊙9am-5pm daily May-Oct, 10am-3pm Thu-Sat Nov-Apr) has an excellent museum explaining the canal's complex history and offers boat tours on the canal during the summer months (the official state canal museum is in Syracuse). To appreciate another angle on the infrastructure that went into making things hum in the mid-1800s, visit the offices of the **Lockport Cave & Underground Boat Tour** (☏716-438-0174; www.lockport.com; 5 Gooding St; adult/child $12/7; ⊙May 4-Oct 14, hours vary); the boat trip takes you through a water-filled tunnel blasted by engineers to help power industry and guides provide loads of historical info as you glide along the eerily motionless 1600ft channel.

NOPPAWAT "TOM" CHAROENSINPHON/GETTY IMAGES ©

The Drive » It's a straightforward drive on NY-78 south to I-990 south. The quickest way to downtown Buffalo from here is to get on I-290 west which skirts the northern 'burb of Tonawanda for about 6 miles. Then connect with I-290 south and take this another 7.5 miles until exit 8 for NY-266 north which brings you within a few blocks of the waterfront and center of town.

- - - - - - - - - - - -

TRIP HIGHLIGHT

❹ Buffalo

This often maligned working-class city does have long, cold winters and its fair share of abandoned industrial buildings, but Buffalo also has a vibrant community of college students and 30-somethings living well in cheap real estate and gorging on this city's unique and tasty cuisine. And most locals are united in their passion for their professional sports teams – the Bills for football, the Sabres for hockey and the Bisons, a AAA affiliate for baseball – which they live and die with every season.

Settled by the French in 1758 – its name is believed to derive from *beau fleuve* (beautiful river) – the city's illustrious past as a former trading post and later a booming manufacturing center and terminus of the Erie Canal means there's a certain nostalgia and hopefulness to the continual roll out and delay of ambitious revitalization plans.

The **Theodore Roosevelt Inaugural National Historic Site**

Niagara Falls A nighttime view from Prospect Point

(☏716-884-0095; www.nps. gov/thri; 641 Delaware Ave; adult/child $10/5; ⊙tours hourly 9:30am-3:30pm Mon-Fri, from 12:30pm Sat & Sun) has partly guided tours of the Ansley-Wilcox house where Teddy's emergency swearing in occurred following the assassination of William McKinley in 1901. There are interactive exhibits for the attention deficient.

North of downtown, sprawling Delaware Park was designed by Frederick Law Olmsted. Its jewel is the **Albright-**

Knox Art Gallery (☏716-882-8700; www.albrightknox. org; 1285 Elmwood Ave; adult/ child $12/5; ⊙10am-5pm, closed Mon; car 198 West to Elmwood Ave S/Art Gallery), a sizable museum including works by some of the best French Impressionists and American masters.

Frank Lloyd Wright fans should take a guided tour of the **Darwin Martin House** (☏716-856-3858; www. darwinmartinhouse.org; 125 Jewett Pkwy; basic tour $15; in-depth tour incl Barton

House $30; ⊙guided tours by reservation only, closed Tue), a 1904 Prairie-style home, and the neighboring Barton House.

 p91

The Drive » Leave the city on I-90 south and then connect to NY-400 south which cuts through Buffalo's outlying suburbs.

----

⑤ East Aurora

Not exactly a household name today, Elbert Hubbard is considered the 'grandfather of

NIAGARA FALLS, CANADA

When people say they are visiting the falls they usually mean the Canadian side which is blessed with superior views. Canada's Horseshoe Falls are wider and especially photogenic from Queen Victoria Park; at night they're illuminated with a colored light show. However, the city itself, especially the Clifton Hill and Lundy's Lane areas, which have grown up around the falls, is the equivalent of a kitschy beach boardwalk with arcades, a Ripley's Believe It or Not Museum, indoor water parks, T-shirt and souvenir shops and fast-food and chain restaurants. Whereas **Niagara on the Lake**, 15km to the north, is a small town full of elegant B&Bs and a famous summertime theater festival.

Crossing the Rainbow Bridge to Canada and returning costs US$3.25/0.50 per car/pedestrian. There are customs and immigration stations at each end – US citizens are required to have their passport or an enhanced driver's license.

Canadian citizens entering the US need one of the following: a passport, a NEXUS card, a Free and Secure Trade (FAST) card or an enhanced driver's licence/ enhanced identification card. Driving a rental car from the US over the border should not be a problem but check with your rental company before you depart.

modern marketing' and, at least as importantly, the founder of the Roycroft community in East Aurora. Unfulfilled by his financial success with the Larkin Soap Co in Buffalo, Hubbard took up the pen and became a writer, mostly of the motivational self-help genre. Inspired by William Morris, founder of the England Arts & Crafts movement, Hubbard returned to western New York and established his Roycroft campus here. From 1895 to 1938 it survived as a mostly self-sustaining community of talented artisans and craftspeople; they produced furniture, glass, books and metalwork. The **Roycroft Campus Corporation** (☎716-655-0261; www.

roycroftcampuscorporation. com; 31 S Grove St; tour $10; ☺tours Wed, Sat & Sun Jun-Oct) runs walking tours of the 14 original buildings and guides provide juicy tidbits and context to Hubbard's fascinating life story as a utopian reformer and entrepreneur.

🛏 p91

The Drive >> NY-78 south to NY-39 east takes you through rural countryside on this 41-mile drive; be sure you've filled up on gas before heading out this way. The Portageville entrance, in the southern part of the park, is on Denton Corners Rd.

- - - - - - - - - - - - -

TRIP HIGHLIGHT

❻ Letchworth State Park

Only 55 miles southeast of Buffalo is the little-

visited **Letchworth State Park** (☎585-493-3600; nysparks.com; Castile; car $8; ☺8am-9pm) encompassing 14,500 acres including the Genesee River and three magnificent waterfalls (no swimming allowed in the river), the surrounding gorge and lush forests. There's almost two dozen hiking trails, plus rafting from the end of April to October. Driving the 17 miles through the park from the Mt Morris entrance (open year-round) in the far north to Portageville without stopping should take only 30 minutes, and it's a very pretty drive. Camping sites are also available in the park.

🛏 p91

Sleeping & Eating

Niagara Falls ❶

✘ Buzzy's — Pizza $

(☎716-283-5333; 7617 Niagara Falls Blvd; mains $6-15; ⊙11am-11pm Sun-Thu, to midnight Fri & Sat) New York-style pizza, spicy buffalo wings, calzones, subs and hoagies for hungry crowds who like to drink beer and watch sports.

🛏 Giacomo — Boutique Hotel $$

(☎716-299-0200; www.thegiacomo.com; 220 First St; r from $150; [P] [✻] [📶]) The equal of any Canadian-side lodging in terms of stylish comfort, the Giacomo occupies a renovated 1929 art-deco office tower. While the majority of floors are taken up by high-end condos, the three dozen spacious rooms are luxuriously appointed and the 19th-floor lounge offers spectacular falls views.

Buffalo ❹

✘ Anchor Bar — American $$

(☎716-886-8920; 1047 Main St; 10/20 wings $13/20; ⊙10am-11pm Mon-Thu, 10am-1am Fri & Sat) For the famous deep-fried chicken wings covered in a spicy sauce, head to the landmark restaurant which claims credit for inventing the 'delicacy.' Motorcycles and other random paraphernalia line the walls and there's live music Thursday through Saturday nights.

✘ Ulrich's Tavern — German $$

(☎716-855-8409; 674 Ellicott St; mains $15; ⊙11am-3pm Mon-Wed, 11am-10pm Thu & Fri, 3-9pm Sat) One of Buffalo's oldest taverns, with warped floors and dark-wood walls. Try the gut-busting German fish fry, which comes with red cabbage, sauerkraut, potatoes and vegetables. Homemade potato pancakes ($7), liverwurst and red onions on rye ($11) are also recommended.

🛏 Hotel @ the Lafayette — Boutique Hotel $$

(☎716-853-1505; www.thehotellafayette.com; 391 Washington St; r $169, ste from $200; [P] [✻] [📶]) This grand seven-story French Renaissance building was designed by pioneering architect Louise Bethune in the early 1900s; it's been restored and stands impressively intact. The contemporary furnishings in the rooms and suites can't compete with the art-deco lobby and marble hallway; there's a steakhouse and bakery on the premises.

East Aurora ❺

🛏 Roycroft Inn — Inn $$

(☎716-652-5552; www.roycroftinn.com; 40 South Grove St; r/ste $165/$195-350; [✻] [📶]) Entering the salon of this inn, completed in 1905 to accommodate artisans and craftspeople making the pilgrimage to the Roycroft campus, is like stepping into a museum. Murals by Fournier adorn the walls, and Morris chairs and handcrafted lamps adorn the space – this is no ordinary hotel, but rather a cozy, rustic and living shrine to the Arts & Crafts movement.

Letchworth State Park ❻

🛏 Glen Iris Inn — Inn $$

(☎585-493-2622; www.glenirisinn.com; Letchworth State Park, Castile; r/ste $100/$180; [✻]) Next to the viewpoint for the Middle Falls near the Portageville entrance (closed winter) at the southern end of the park is this renovated Greek Revival home originally built in 1829. Wood-floored standard rooms are small but there's plenty of public space in the second-floor library lounge with falls views and front porch; a somewhat formal restaurant (mains $10) is on the ground floor. Open from late April to late October.

Salmon River
A fly fisherman's dream

St Lawrence Seaway

7

Twisting coastal roads along Lake Ontario to the fast-moving St Lawrence River take you through little fishing hamlets and picturesque harbors with dreamy islands just offshore.

TRIP HIGHLIGHTS

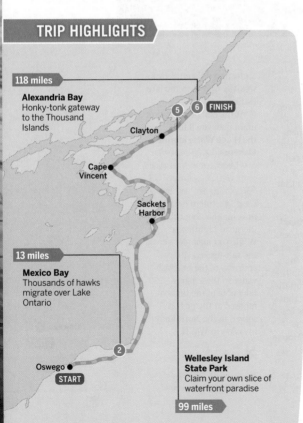

118 miles

Alexandria Bay
Honky-tonk gateway to the Thousand Islands

Clayton

Cape Vincent

Sackets Harbor

13 miles

Mexico Bay
Thousands of hawks migrate over Lake Ontario

Oswego
START

Wellesley Island State Park
Claim your own slice of waterfront paradise

99 miles

**2–3 DAYS
118 MILES / 189KM**

GREAT FOR...

BEST TIME TO GO
Get in or out on the water from May to September.

 ESSENTIAL PHOTO
Boldt Castle's full profile.

 BEST FOR FAMILIES
Drive-in movie theater near A-Bay.

CAVAN IMAGES, LLC/GETTY IMAGES ©

93

7 St Lawrence Seaway

Virtually unknown to downstate New Yorkers, mostly because of its relative inaccessibility, this region of more than 1800 islands – from tiny outcroppings with space for a towel to larger islands with roads and towns – is a scenic wonderland separating the US from Canada. Once a playground for the very rich, who built turn-of-the-century dream homes, today it's a watery world for boating, camping, swimming and even shipwreck scuba diving.

1 Oswego

The port town of Oswego is home to an old lighthouse that's open to the public and is just waiting to be explored – it involves a walk along a lengthy breakwater that juts well into the sea. An easier approach to **Oswego West Pierhead Lighthouse** (🕐1-5pm Sep-Jun, 10am-5pm Jul & Aug; adult/child $7/3) is to take in its delicate silhouette in the distance as you stroll the historic waterfront that's backed by gorgeous resort homes, including the **Richardson-Bates House Museum** (📞315-343-1342; www.rbhousemuseum.org; 135 E Third St; adult/child $5/2; 🕐1-5pm Thu-Sat Apr-Dec; 👪),

an Italian villa built by a wealthy family in the late 1800s.

At the end of the town's main pier, you'll find the **H Lee White Marine Museum** (📞315-342-0480; www.hleewhitemarinemuseum. com; 1 W 1st St; adult/child $7/3; 🕐1-5pm Sep-Jun, 10am-5pm Jul & Aug; 👪), full of detailed information about the Pierhead Lighthouse. While you meander across the salt-flecked stones – courtesy of the brackish water in these parts – take note of the tugboat moored at the pier; it served in the Normandy invasion in WWII.

🍴 p99

The Drive » This little-trafficked 16 mile stretch of

NY-104 heads east through flat countryside.

- - - - - - - - - -

TRIP HIGHLIGHT

② Mexico Bay

You'll pass the **Derby Hill Bird Observatory** (www.onandagaaudobon.com; 36 Grand View Ave; ⊙daily; 🚹) in the woodsy and rural area north of Oswego, a state park that also contains the famous **Salmon River** – the location fly-fishermen dream of when planning their perfect vacation. A walk around these challenging shores will bring you in close contact with northern New York's fiercely rampant nature – soaring trees and rough marsh grasses and big birds with sharp talons abound. In fact, Derby Hill, one of the premier hawk watching sites in the eastern US, sees an average of 40,000

🔗 LINK YOUR TRIP

4 **Finger Lakes Loop**
From Oswego head west on NY-104 and then south on NY-38 for Seneca Falls to begin exploring a region of lakeside wineries.

6 **Niagara & Around**
Follow the coastal road from Oswego and then I-90 west for a trip to the iconic falls and western New York.

of these birds of prey every spring, who use the thermals around the edge of the lake while migrating further north. April is the best month to see them but summers mean bald eagles, butterflies and local breeding birds.

Beach lovers shouldn't miss a pit stop at **Sandy Pond**, still on your northward route. This barrier beach has walkovers set up so pedestrians can enjoy the salty sand without disturbing fragile dunes and adjacent wetlands. There's plenty of wildlife to see, including frogs and turtles, especially if you arrive during the busy sunset hours when the night crawlers start to stir.

The Drive ≫ Rte 3, also known as 'The Seaway Trail,' continues north with a handful of ponds and estuaries on your left between the road and the lake. On this 35-mile trip you'll pass the access road for Southwick beach, a pretty stretch of sand with good swimming. Turn left on County Rd 75 about 1.5 miles before Sackets Harbor.

- - - - - - - - - - -

❸ Sackets Harbor

An old fishing village perched on a big lakeside bluff, Sackets Harbor was also the site of two important battles in the War of 1812. Swing by the grounds of the **Sackets Harbor Battlefield** (☎315-646-3634; www. sacketsharborbattlefield.org; W Main St; adult/child $3/ free; ☺10am-5pm Wed-Sat,

from 1pm Sun; 🚶); when the battle reenactments are on – performed by history-loving locals who enjoy wearing uniforms – you can practically smell the cannon smoke as old shooters are wheeled around to take aim at the retreating Red Coats. You can also learn more about the coastal trail you're now driving on with a stop at the **Seaway Trail Discovery Center** (☎315-646-1000; www. seawaytrail.com/discoverycenter; 401 West Main St; adult/child $4/2; ☺10am-5pm Wed-Sun Jul & Aug, Fri-Sun May-Jun & Sep–mid-Oct), comprising nine rooms full of interactive displays and features about life on the St Lawrence River and the shores of Lakes Erie and Ontario.

✗ 🛏 p99

The Drive ≫ Turn left onto NY-12E from NY-180 for a longer, more scenic route. You'll pass through the village of Chaumont before coming to the tiny Cape Vincent (p99). Follow signs to the white-stucco and red-roofed Tibbetts Point Lighthouse, now a lakeside hostel. Views are of the headwaters of the St Lawrence and Wolfe Island, Canada. It's another 15 miles to Clayton.

- - - - - - - - - - -

❹ Clayton

Next up is Clayton and the **Antique Boat Museum** (☎315-686-4104; www.abm.org; 750 Mary St; adult/child $13/free; ☺9am-5pm mid-May–mid-Oct; 🚶), which lets you actually sail (or sometimes row) the boats while you learn about them.

If you get a taste for boating, contact **T.I. Adventures** (☎315-686-2500; www.tiadventures.com; 1011 State St) to paddle the old-fashioned way – in a canoe or a kayak. Clayton native Jan Brabant leads tours along the historic coastline and into off-the-beaten-path wildlife reserves, but he saves his toughest trip – The Grinder – for those willing to muscle their way a mile and a half into the river to Grindstone Island.

Back on land, **Thousand Islands Museum** (☎315-686-5794; www.timuseum.org; 312 James St; admission $4; ☺10am-4pm May-Oct) has warehoused all kinds of

Alexandria Bay Boldt Castle on Heart Island

photography and writing about island culture dating from the 1800s. The museum also has a rotating exhibit of local artists, plus examples of the fine carving for which the region is famous.

Another big draw is the **Handweaving Museum and Arts Center** (☑315-686-4123; www.hm-ac.org; 314 John St; ☺9am-4:30pm Mon-Fri;). If you don't consider weaving an art, you'll know better by the time you leave Clayton.

✕ p99

The Drive » It's 7 miles on Rte 12 to the exit for I-81 north. Just over the bridge take the first exit

for County Rd 191; this crosses back under I-81 before turning north to the park.

- - - - - - - - - -

TRIP HIGHLIGHT

5 Wellesley Island State Park

Take the afternoon to visit **Wellesley Island State Park** (☑315-482-9825; http://nysparks.state.ny.us/parks; 44927 Cross Island Rd; ☺daily), a 2600-acre floating village that's connected to the mainland by the Thousand Islands International Bridge. Its abundant wildlife, plus marina, ponds and **Minna Anthony Common Nature Center** (☑315-482-2479;

44927 Cross Island Rd; ☺10am-4:30pm mid-Oct–mid-Jun, 8:30am-4:30pm rest of yr) – which has exhibits on the islands' animal life – will further pull you into the mysterious allure of these sparsely inhabited islands.

On the other side of Wellesley, at the end of the Thousand Islands International Bridge, is the fantastic **Skydeck** (☑613-659-2335; www.1000islandsskydeck.com; Hill Island, Lansowne, Ontario; adult/child $10/6; ☺9am-6pm mid-Apr–Oct), a 395ft observation tower that belongs to Canada – but you can enjoy it if you have valid ID on you (a passport is best). The elevator ride to the top gives excellent views of the sprawling Thousand Islands.

 p99

The Drive » It's simple – retrace your route back over the bridge to the mainland and exit onto Rte 12 north. If go-karts are your thing, stop at Alex Bay 500 Go-Karts, one of the state's longest tracks and only 1.5 miles from the exit. Alex Bay itself is another 3.5 miles down the road.

TRIP HIGHLIGHT

⑥ Alexandria Bay

Further east, Alexandria Bay (A-Bay or Alex Bay), an early-20th-century resort town, is still the center of tourism on the American side. While it's run down and tacky, there's enough to keep you occupied: go-karts, mini-golf and a **drive-in movie theater** (www.

baydrivein.com) are only minutes away.

It's also the departure point for ferries to Heart Island and **Boldt Castle** (📞315-482-9724; www.boldtcastle.com; adult/child $8/5.50; ⊙10am-6:30pm mid-May–mid-Oct), built by George C Boldt, the former proprietor of Manhattan's famed Waldorf-Astoria Hotel. Boldt began building this replica of a 120-room Rhineland, Germany, castle in 1900 for his dying wife Louise, who passed away well before it was finished. Boldt subsequently abandoned the project and it became the provenance of the island's woodland creatures. But since the late 1970s, millions have gone into its restoration, and now the structures are as magnificent as originally intended.

Another not-to-be-missed island experience

is a trip to neighboring **Singer Castle** (📞315-324-3275; www.singercastle.com; boat & admission adult/child $34/17; ⊙10am-4pm guided tours), perched on Dark Island. Built by the president of the Singer sewing machine company, this 20th-century delight was modeled on a Scottish castle, giving it long, spooky hallways and dimly lit passages.

Uncle Sam's Boat Tours (📞315-482-2611; www.usboattours.com; 45 James St; 2-nation tour adult/child $20/10) has several departures daily for its two-nation cruise (visiting the US and Canadian sides of the river), which allows you to stop at Boldt Castle and ride back on one of its half-hourly ferries for free.

✕ �📖 p99

💬 LOCAL KNOWLEDGE:
FREDERIC REMINGTON ART MUSEUM

Fewer people travel along the river north of A-Bay but it's worth a detour to the **Frederic Remington Art Museum** (📞315-393-2425; www.fredericremington.org; 303 Washington St; adult/child $9/free; ⊙11am-5pm Wed-Sat, from 1pm Sun) in Ogdensburg. Remington (1861–1909), an artist who romanticized the American West in paintings and sculpture, was born nearby in Canton and his family moved to Ogdensburg when he was 11. He led something of a peripatetic existence as a correspondent and illustrator for high-profile magazines of his day like *Collier's* and *Harper's Weekly*. The museum not only contains some of his sculptures and paintings but loads of personal ephemera like cigars he smoked and scrapbooks. A visit here goes well with one to the Rockwell Museum of Western Art (p71) in Corning.

From A-Bay, Rte 12 turns into Rte 37 just past Morristown, following the coastline. There are fewer islands in the river the further northeast you drive, but you can pull over at several turn-offs as well as two state parks – King Point and Jaques Cartier – to take in the views.

Eating & Sleeping

Oswego ①

✖ Rudy's Lakeside Drive-Thru   Seafood $

(☎315-343-2671; www.rudyshot.com; 78 County Rte 89; mains $8; ⏱10am-9pm, to 11pm Fri & Sat May 1-Sep 22, call for other times; 🚹) Join the locals lining up for the fresh fish and fries at this local institution that's straight out of the 1950s.

Sackets Harbor ③

✖ Tin Pan Galley   American $$

(☎315-646-3812; www.tinpangalley.com; 110 W Main St; mains $12-28; ⏱8am-9pm; 🚹) Pretty, wrought-iron tables and chairs in a blooming garden give this outdoor cafe a New Orleans feel.

🛏 Candlelight B&B   B&B $$

(☎315-646-1518; www.imcnet.net/candlelight; 501 Washington St; r $85-125; ✳🛜🚹) Big beds, love seats and armoires give this redbrick Georgian B&B a charming vibe. Views are of the battlefields.

Cape Vincent

🛏 Tibbetts Point Lighthouse Hostel   Hostel $

(☎315-654-3450; www.hihostels.com; 33439 Co Rt 6; dm $25; ⏱Jul 1-Sept 15) This 1854 whitewashed lighthouse marks the entrance to the St Lawrence River in dramatic, picturesque fashion. There are two-, five- and six-bed basic dorm rooms and a self-catering kitchen.

Clayton ④

✖ Lyric Coffee House   Cafe/American $$

(☎315-686-4700; 246 James St; mains $7-24; ⏱8am-8pm; 🛜) Surprisingly modern for this town, Lyric serves specialty coffee drinks, gelato, pastries and specials such as lasagna for lunch and a full 'fine dining' menu for dinner including gnocchi, roasted chicken and braised pork; there's live music some Fridays and Saturdays.

Wellesley Island State Park ⑤

🛏 Hart House Inn   B&B $$

(☎315-482-5683; www.harthouseinn.com; 21979 Club Rd, Wellesley Island; r/ste $95-255/$325; ✳🛜🚹) Expansive and lovely, Hart House is part homespun charm and part five-star resort, perfect for romantic getaways. Pedal your way down shady lanes and along the sandy coastline on the inn's free bikes, or just wander among the flower- and gazebo-filled gardens of this romantic B&B.

🛏 Wellesley Island State Park   Camping $

(☎518-482-2722; www.nysparks.com; campsites from $15) Camping on Wellesley Island is probably the best accommodations option even for the raccoon-averse. Many sites are almost directly on the riverfront and some have their own 'private' beaches. The island is only accessible by crossing a toll portion ($2.50) of the Thousand Islands Bridge.

Alexandria Bay ⑥

✖ Dockside Pub   American $$

(☎315-482-9849; 17 Market St; mains $7-18; ⏱11am-midnight Mon-Thu & Sun, to 2am Fri & Sat; 🚹) Unpretentious pub fare – burgers, fries, shepherd's pie – served dockside, overlooking the St Lawrence River.

🛏 Bonnie Castle   Resort $$

(☎800-955-4511; www.bonniecastle.com; 31 Holland St; r $100-250; ✳🛜🚹) Despite the name, this is actually a ritzy resort on the mainland. Its waterside bar, called Rum Runners, pulls in sunburned workers and tourists eager to unwind after a long day of island-hopping.

🛏 Capt Thomson's Resort   Hotel $$

(☎315-482-9961; www.captthomsons.com; 45 James St; r $130-200; 🅿✳🛜) This motel-style place on the waterfront is probably the best midrange choice in town.

STRETCH YOUR LEGS
NEW YORK CITY

Start/Finish: New Museum of Contemporary Art

Distance: 2.6 miles

Duration: 3 hours

A stroll through these downtown neighborhoods, home to successive waves of immigrants and lively ethnic communities, is a microcosm of how the city blends the old and the new.

Take this walk on Trips

New Museum of Contemporary Art

Housed in an architecturally ambitious building, the **New Museum of Contemporary Art** (☎212-219-1222; www.newmuseum.org; 235 Bowery btwn Prince & Rivington Sts; adult/child $14/free, 7-9pm Thu free; ☺11am-6pm Wed & Fri-Sun, to 9pm Thu) towers over this formerly gritty, but now rapidly gentrifying strip of the Lower East Side. The museum's cache of work will dazzle and confuse as much as the building's stacked-box facade; check out the rooftop viewing platform for a unique perspective on the landscape.

The Walk ≫ Head south on the relatively wide Bowery for a block until Spring St. Make a right and in three fashionable blocks you'll reach Mulberry St.

Mulberry Street

Although it feels more like a theme park than an authentic Italian strip, Mulberry St is still the heart of Little Italy. It's home to such landmarks as **Umberto's Clam House** (☎212-431-7545; www.umbertosclamhouse.com; 132 Mulberry St), where mobster Joey Gallo was shot to death in the '70s, and the old-time **Mulberry Street Bar** (☎212-226-9345; 176½ Mulberry St btwn Broome & Grand Sts), one of Frank Sinatra's favorite haunts. Waiters hawk their restaurant's menus as you pass, laying on the Italian shtick as heavily as they lay red sauce on their pastas.

The Walk ≫ In warm weather the restaurants that line Mulberry St set out tables on the sidewalk, making for a very tight fit. Cross over the wide, traffic-clogged Canal St (you'll explore it later) and continue south to Columbus Park.

Columbus Park

This is where outdoor mah-jongg and domino games take place at bridge tables while tai chi practitioners move through lyrical poses under shady trees. Judo-sparring folks and relaxing families are also common sights in this active communal space originally created in the 1890s.

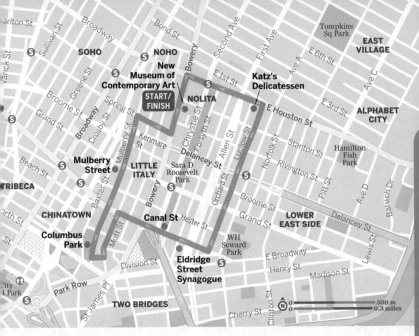

The Walk » Near the southern end of the park is a small alley that leads to Mott St. Follow Mott St back through Chinatown and make a right on Canal St – explore these blocks at your leisure.

Canal Street

This is Chinatown's main artery, where you'll dodge oncoming human traffic as you scurry into back alleys to scout for treasures from the Far East. You'll pass seafood stalls hawking slippery fish; herb shops displaying a witch's cauldron's worth of roots and potions; restaurants with whole roasted ducks hanging in the windows; and street vendors selling every iteration of knock-off designer goods.

The Walk » Walk east on Canal St and navigate the tricky intersection where the Manhattan Bridge on- and off-ramps converge. Continue for another two blocks before making a right on Eldridge St.

Eldridge Street Synagogue

Built in 1887 with Moorish and Romanesque ornamental work, this synagogue was flourishing at the turn of the 20th century but closed in the 1950s because of dwindling

membership. A 20-year restoration project was completed in 2007 and it now holds Friday evening and Saturday morning services; tours of the building are available. Perhaps the most breathtaking aspect of the interior is the massive circular stained-glass window above the ark (where torahs are kept).

The Walk » Take Orchard or Ludlow Sts, both lined with trendy cafes and shops, north to Katz's.

Katz's Delicatessen

One of the few remnants of the classic, old-world Jewish Lower East Side dining scene, this is the restaurant where Meg Ryan faked her famous orgasm in the 1989 flick *When Harry Met Sally*. If you love classic deli grub like massive pastrami, corned beef, brisket and tongue sandwiches, it might have the same effect on you. Hold on to the ticket you're handed when you walk in and pay cash only.

The Walk » Head west on East Houston St until you reach the Bowery; a left will take you back to the New Museum.

New Jersey & Pennsylvania Trips

AN UNDER-THE-RADAR REGION OF TREMENDOUS DIVERSITY. Where else could you visit an Amish family's farm, read the Declaration of Independence and ride a boardwalk roller coaster in a single day? These two states have dozens of parks where you can float down the Delaware, camp in out-of-the-way forests, sunbathe on a pristine beach or brush up on your pre-colonial American history.

Explore Philadelphia's burgeoning culinary scene after a long day learning about the nation's origins. Nearby in Jersey are the overlooked Pine Barrens and the riverside getaways of New Hope and Lambertville. The further west you go in Pennsylvania, the more rural it becomes until you reach Pittsburgh's bustling ethnic areas and top museums.

Longbeach Island Barnegat Lighthouse (Trip 8)
DAVID SUCSY/GETTY IMAGES ©

New Jersey & Pennsylvania Trips

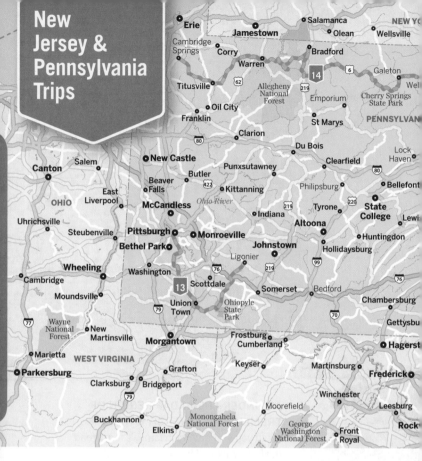

Through the Wilds Along Route 6
14 4 Days

This scenic highway runs past mountains, deep gorges and historic small towns. (p167)

DON'T MISS

The Music Man

Vaudeville-style performances at an ice-cream theater encapsulate the Jersey Shore culture. Stop by for a taste on Trip **8**

Princeton University Art Museum

The American gallery has masterworks of historic events that occurred nearby. Visit the museum on Trip **9**

Apple Pie Hill Fire Watch Tower

Climb to the top for 360-degree views of pinelands all the way to the horizon on Trip **11**

Gettysburg Cyclorama

Immerse yourself in the battle of Pickett's Charge by viewing this 377ft-long painting at the Gettysburg Museum on Trip **12**

Pennsylvania Macaroni

Between Thanksgiving and Christmas, this Pittsburgh market gives away homemade wine. Celebrate on Trip **13**

The Jersey Shore

8

Jersey girls in bikinis, tatted-up guidos, mile-long boardwalks, neon-lit Ferris wheels, steamed crabs, sweaty beers and 127 miles of Atlantic Ocean coast. Pack the car and hit the shore.

TRIP HIGHLIGHTS

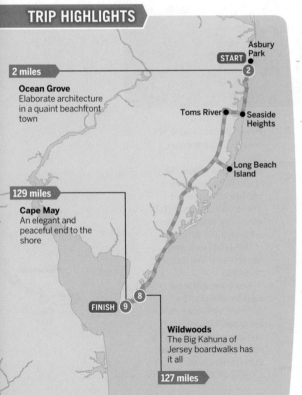

START
2
Asbury Park

2 miles

Ocean Grove
Elaborate architecture in a quaint beachfront town

Toms River ● ● Seaside Heights

● Long Beach Island

129 miles

Cape May
An elegant and peaceful end to the shore

FINISH 9 **8**

Wildwoods
The Big Kahuna of Jersey boardwalks has it all

127 miles

3–7 DAYS
120 MILES / 193KM

GREAT FOR ...

BEST TIME TO GO
Midweek in June – crowds are smaller and rooms cheaper than in the high season.

 ESSENTIAL PHOTO
Wildwood boardwalk roller coaster.

✔ **BEST TWO DAYS**
Polar opposites, Wildwood and Cape May: both classics.

Classic Trip

8 The Jersey Shore

The New Jersey coastline is studded with resort towns from classy to tacky that fulfill the Platonic ideal of how a long summer day should be spent. Super-sized raucous boardwalks – where singles more than mingle – are a short drive from old-fashioned inter-generational family retreats. When the temperature rises, the entire state tips eastward and rushes to the beach to create memories that they'll view later with nostalgia or perhaps some regret.

❶ Asbury Park

Let's start with the town that Bruce Springsteen, the most famous of a group of musicians who developed the Asbury Sound in the 1970s, immortalized in song. Several of these musicians – such as Steve Van Zandt, Garry Tallent, Danny Federici and Clarence Clemmons – formed Springsteen's supporting E Street Band. The main venues to check out are the still-grungy, seen-it-all club the **Stone Pony** (☏732-502-0600; 913 Ocean Ave) and **Wonder Bar** (1213 Ocean Ave); the latter is across the street from the majestic red-brick Paramount Theatre/Convention Hall where big acts perform (although the future of this landmark was uncertain at the time of research).

Led by wealthy gay men from NYC who snapped up blocks of forgotten Victorian homes and storefronts to refurbish, the **downtown** area (probably the hippest on the shore)

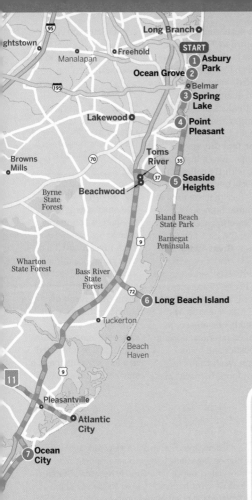

includes several blocks of Cookman and Bangs Aves, lined with charming shops, bars, cafes, restaurants and a restored art-house cinema.

The **boardwalk** itself is short and unspectacular by Jersey standards: at one end is the gorgeous but empty shell of a 1920s-era carousel and casino building, the Paramount Theatre is near the other end and there's an attractive, well-cared-for stretch of sand in front. Asbury Park's amusements tend to be more for adults than children: its clubs and bars rock late into the night, it has decent surf, and it has the shore's liveliest gay scene.

LINK YOUR TRIP

11 Brandywine Valley to Atlantic City

Atlantic City, the eastern shore's casino capital, and the forested Pine Barrens are easily accessible from the drive between Long Beach Island and Ocean City.

19 Delmarva

Hop on the Cape May–Lewes ferry across the Delaware Bay to this peninsula trip for a wonderful mix of more beach getaways.

Classic Trip

 p116

The Drive » There's no beachfront road to Ocean Grove – the two towns are separated by narrow Wesley Lake. Take the generically commercial Main St/Rte 71 and turn left on Ocean Grove's own Main Ave. However, it might be worthwhile to first head north on Rte 71 for a few miles to take a gander at the impressively grand homes in the community of Deal.

TRIP HIGHLIGHT

② Ocean Grove

Next to Asbury Park is Ocean Grove, one of the cutest Victorian seaside towns anywhere, with a boardwalk boasting not a single business to disturb the peace and quiet. Known as 'God's Square Mile at the Jersey Shore,' Ocean Grove is perfectly coifed, sober, conservative and quaint. Founded by Methodists in the 19th century, the place retains what's left of a post–Civil War **Tent City** revival camp – now a historic site with 114 cottage-like canvas tents clustered together that are used for summer homes.

Towering over the tents, the 1894 mustard-yellow **Great Auditorium** (☏732-775-0035, tickets 800-965-9324; www.oceangrove. org; Pilgrim Pathway; recitals free, concerts $13; ⏰recitals 7:30pm Wed, 10am or noon Sat; 🚶) shouldn't be missed: its vaulted interior, amazing acoustics and historic organ recall Utah's Mormon Tabernacle. Make sure to catch a recital or concert or one of the open-air services held in a boardwalk pavilion.

✕ 🛏 p116

The Drive » Follow Rte 71 south through a string of relatively sleepy towns (Bradley Beach, Belmar) for just over 5 miles to reach Spring Lake.

❸ Spring Lake

The quiet streets of this prosperous community, once known as the 'Irish Riviera,' are lined with grand oceanfront Victorian houses set in meticulously manicured lawns. As a result of Hurricane Sandy, the gorgeous beach was extremely narrow at high tide. If you're interested in a low-key quiet base, a stay here is about as far

HURRICANE SANDY

In late October 2012 Hurricane Sandy devastated much of the New York and New Jersey coastline, destroying homes, breaching barrier islands, ripping away boardwalks and washing away entire waterfront communities. In New York, Staten Island, the Rockaways and Red Hook were the hardest hit, while the Jersey Shore from Sandy Hook to Atlantic City suffered the brunt of the hurricane's impact. The dimensions and profiles of many beaches were diminished and it remains to be seen whether rebuilding efforts will add dunes and other storm surge impediments where none existed before.

More than six months later, there are still significant pockets of desolation: piles of debris rise higher than sand dunes; entire sides of houses are ripped away, others teeter precariously at gravity-defying angles. While a new boardwalk was being built in Seaside Heights for the 2013 summer season, the *Star Jet* roller coaster, in perhaps the most dramatically symbolic posture of displacement, still remained perched in the ocean like a remnant of an antedeluvian civilization. This book was researched just prior to the start of the 2013 summer season when state officials and locals alike were promising to be ready to welcome sun-worshipping throngs with open arms.

from the typical shore boardwalk experience as you can get.

Only 5 miles inland from Spring Lake is the quirky **Historic Village at Allaire** (☎732-919-3500; www.allairevillage.org; adult/child $3/2; ☺noon-4pm Wed-Sun late May-early Sep, noon-4pm Sat & Sun Nov-May), the remains of what was a thriving 19th-century village called Howell Works. You can still visit various 'shops' in this living history museum, all run by folks in period costume.

🛏 p116

The Drive » For a slow but pleasant drive, take Ocean Ave south – at Wreck Pond you turn inland before heading south again. At Crescent Park in the town of Sea Girt (the boardwalk has a couple casual restaurants), Washington Ave connects back to Union Ave/Rte 71 which leads into Rte 35 and over the Manasquan Inlet. The first exit for Broadway takes you past several marina-side restaurants.

4 Point Pleasant

Point Pleasant is the first of five quintessential bumper-car-and-Skee-Ball boardwalks. On a July weekend, Point Pleasant's long beach is jam-packed: squint, cover up all that nearly naked flesh in striped unitards, and it could be the 1920s, with umbrellas shading every inch of sand and the surf clogged with bodies and bobbing heads.

Families with young kids love Point Pleasant,

TOP TIP: PLAN AHEAD

We love the shore but let's be honest, in summer months, the traffic's a nightmare, parking's impossible and the beaches are overflowing. Pack the car – the night before. Leave at dawn, or soon thereafter. If at all possible, come midweek. If you want to stay, make reservations. And if you want something besides a run-down, sun-bleached, musty, three-blocks-from-the-water, sand-crusted flea box to stay in, make reservations six months to a year in advance.

as the boardwalk is big but not overwhelming, and the squeaky-clean amusement rides, fun house and small aquarium – all run by **Jenkinson's** (☎732-295-4334, aquarium 732-899-1659; www.jenkinsons.com; 300 Ocean Ave; aquarium adult/child $10/6; ☺rides noon-11pm, aquarium 10am-10pm, hours vary off-season; 👶) – are geared to the height and delight of the 10-and-under set. That's not to say Point Pleasant is only for little ones. **Martell's Tiki Bar** (☎732-892-0131; www.tikibar.com; Boardwalk; mains $5-30; ☺11am-11pm, to 12:30am Fri & Sat), a place margarita pitchers go to die, makes sure of that: look for the neon-orange palm trees and listen for the live bands.

The Drive » Head south on Rte 35 past several residential communities laid out on a long barrier island only a block or two wide in parts – Seaside Heights is where it's at its widest on this 11-mile trip.

5 Seaside Heights

Coming from the north, Seaside Heights has the first of the truly overwhelming boardwalks: a sky ride and two rollicking amusement piers with double corridors of arcade games and adult-size, adrenaline-pumping rides, roller coasters, and various iterations of the vomit-inducing 10-story drop. During the day, it's as family friendly as Point Pleasant, but once darkness falls Seaside Heights becomes a scene of such hedonistic mating rituals that an evangelical church has felt the need for a permanent booth on the pier. Packs of young men – caps askew, tatts gleaming – check out packs of young women in micro-dresses as everyone rotates among the string of loud bars with live bands playing Eagles tunes. It's pure Jersey.

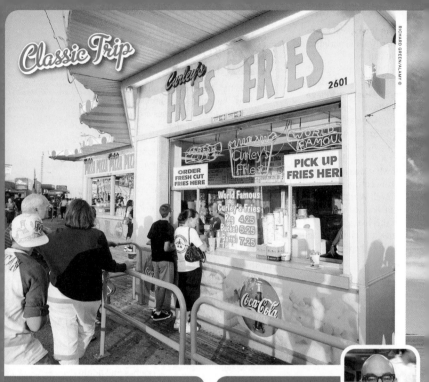

RICHARD GREEN/ALAMY ©

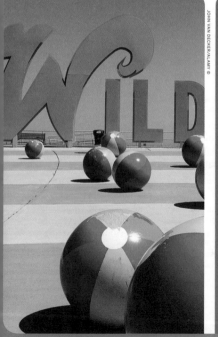

JOHN VAN DECKER/ALAMY ©

LOCAL KNOWLEDGE
DAVE POWITZ
OWNER, SKIPPER
DIPPER ICE CREAM

The Barnegat Lighthouse is beautiful from nearly every angle, but I think it looks best from the water. Don't have access to a boat? A great view is from the beach in the neighborhood of High Bar Harbor. Drive to the end of Sunset Blvd, and look across Barnegat Bay to enjoy the best view on the island.

Top: Snack time at the beach
Left: Wildwoods boardwalk sign
Right: Barnegat Lighthouse

Detour south on Rte 35 to the 10 mile–long **Island Beach State Park** (weekday/weekend $12/20 summer; 8am-8pm), a completely undeveloped barrier island backed by dunes and tall grasses separating the bay from the ocean.

✗ p116

The Drive » To reach the mainland, take Rte 37 from Seaside Heights; you cross a long bridge over Barnegat Bay before reaching the strip-mall filled sprawl of Tom's River. Hop on the Garden State Parkway south, then Rte 72 and the bridge over Manahawkin Bay.

----

⑥ Long Beach Island

Only a very narrow inlet separates this long sliver of an island, with its beautiful beaches and impressive summer homes, from the very southern tip of Island Beach State Park and northern shore towns. Within throwing distance of the park is the landmark **Barnegat Lighthouse** (☎609-494-2016; www.njparksandforests.org; off Long Beach Blvd; ⊘8am-4pm) which offers panoramic views at the top. Fishermen cast off from a jetty extending 2000ft along the Atlantic Ocean and a short nature trail begins just in front of a visitor center with small history and photography displays.

Classic Trip

Nearly every morning practically half the island is jogging, walking, blading or biking on Beach Ave, the 7.5 mile stretch of asphalt that stretches from Ship Bottom to Beach Haven (south of the bridge); it's a great time to exercise, enjoy the sun and people watch. Tucked down a residential street is **Hudson House** (13th St, Beach Haven), a nearly locals-only dive bar about as worn and comfortable as an old pair of flip-flops. Don't be intimidated by the fact that it looks like a crumbling biker bar – it is.

The Drive » The only way in and out of Long Beach Island is via the bridge between Ship Bottom and Beach Haven West. The Garden State Parkway heads south past the marshy pinelands area and Atlantic City (see p142). Take exit 30 for Somers Point; Laurel Dr turns into Mac Arthur Blvd/Rte 52 and then a long causeway crosses Great Egg Harbor Bay. All up, this is a 48-mile drive.

----

❼ Ocean City

An almost heavenly amalgam of Ocean Grove and Point Pleasant, Ocean City is a dry town with a roomy boardwalk packed with genuine family fun and facing an exceedingly pretty beach. There's a small water park, and Gillian's Wonderland has a heart-thumpingly tall Ferris wheel, a beautifully restored merry-go-round, kiddie rides galore – and no microphoned teens hawking carnie games. The mood is light and friendly (a lack of alcohol will do that).

Minigolf aficionados: dingdingdingding! You hit the jackpot. Pint-size duffers can play through on a three-masted schooner, around great white sharks and giant octopus, under reggae monkeys piloting a helicopter and even in black light. If you haven't yet, beat the heat with a delicious Kohr's soft-serve frozen custard, plain or dipped. While saltwater taffy is offered in many places, **Shriver's Taffy** (☎877-668-2339, 609-399-0100; www.shrivers.com; 9th & Boardwalk; ☺9am-midnight, shorter hours off-season; 👶) is, in our humble opinion, the best: watch machines stretch and wrap it, and then fill a bag with two dozen or more flavors.

🛏 p117

The Drive » If time isn't a factor, cruise down local streets and several small bridges over inlets and channels ($1.50 toll on two of the four in each direction; no E-Z Pass) through the beachfront communities of Strathmere, Sea Isle City, Avalon and Stone Harbor); this is roughly a 26-mile drive. Otherwise, head back to the Garden State Parkway and get off at one of two exits for the Wildwoods on a 30-mile drive.

TRIP HIGHLIGHT

❽ Wildwoods

A party town popular with teens, 20-somethings and the young, primarily Eastern Europeans who staff the restaurants and shops, Wildwood is the main social focus here (North Wildwood and Wildwood Crest are

---

WE'RE HAVIN' A PARTY

Yes, in summer, every day is a party at the Jersey shore. But here are some events not to miss:

» Gay Pride Parade, Asbury Park, early June (www.gayasburypark.com)

» Polka Spree by the Sea, Wildwood, late June (www.northwild.com/events.asp)

» New Jersey Sandcastle Contest, Belmar, July (www.njsandcastle.com)

» New Jersey State Barbecue Championship, Wildwood, mid-July (www.njbbq.com)

» Ocean City Baby Parade, Ocean City, early August (www.ocnj.us)

to the north and south respectively). Access to all three beaches is free, and the width of the beach – more than 1000ft in parts, making it the widest in NJ – means there's never a lack of space. Several massive piers are host to water parks and amusement parks – easily the rival of any Six Flags Great Adventure – with roller coasters and rides best suited to aspiring astronauts anchoring the 2-mile-long Grand Daddy of Jersey Shore boardwalks. Glow-in-the-dark 3D mini-golf is a good example of the Wildwood boardwalk ethos – take it far, then one step further. Maybe the best ride of all, and one that doesn't induce nausea, is the tram running the length of the boardwalk from Wildwood Crest to North Wildwood. There's always a line for a table at Jersey Shore staple pizzeria **Mack & Manco's** on the boardwalk (it also has other shore boardwalk locations).

Wildwood Crest is an archaeological find, a kitschy slice of 1950s Americana – whitewashed motels with flashing neon signs, turquoise curtains and pink doors. Check out eye-catching motel signs like the **Lollipop** at 23rd and Atlantic Aves.

🛏 p117

Cape May Victorian architecture

The Drive » Take local roads: south on Pacific Ave to Ocean Dr, which passes over a toll bridge over an estuary area separating Jarvis Sound from Cape May Harbor. Then left on NJ-109 over the Cape May harbor itself. You can turn left anywhere from here, depending on whether you want to head to town or the beach.

- - - - - - - - - - -

TRIP HIGHLIGHT

9 Cape May

Founded in 1620, Cape May – the only place in the state where the sun both rises and sets over the water – is on the state's southern tip and is the country's oldest seashore resort. Its sweeping beaches get crowded in summer, but the stunning Victorian architecture is attractive year-round.

In addition to 600 gingerbread-style houses, the city boasts antique shops and places for dolphin-, whale- (May to December) and bird-watching, and is just outside the **Cape May Point State Park** (www.state.nj.us/dep/parksandforests; 707 E Lake Dr; 🕗8am-4pm) and its 157ft **Cape May Lighthouse** (adult/child $7/3) (there's 199 steps to the observation deck at the top); there's an excellent visitor center and museum with exhibits on wildlife in the area as well as trails to ponds, dunes and marshes. A mile-long loop of the nearby **Cape May Bird Observatory** (✆609-898-2473, 609-861-0700; www.birdcapemay.org; 701 East Lake Dr; 🕗9am-4:30pm) is a pleasant stroll through preserved wetlands. The wide sandy beach at the park (free) or the one in town is the main attraction in summer months. **Aqua Trails** (✆609-884-5600; www.aquatrails.com; from single/double $40/70) offers kayak tours of the coastal wetlands.

🍴🛏 p117

Classic Trip

Eating & Sleeping

Asbury Park ①

✖ Sunset Landing   Cafe $

(☏732-776-9732; 1215 Sunset Ave; mains $5-8; ⏱7am-2pm Tue-Sun; 🖶) On Deal Lake, about 10 blocks from the beach, Sunset Landing is like a Hawaiian surf shack transported to a suburban Asbury lakeside. Vintage longboards crowd the wooden rafters, cheesy omelets are super-fresh, and delicious specialty pancakes come with cranberries, cinnamon, coconut, macadamia nuts and other island flavors. Cash only.

Ocean Grove ②

✖ Moonstruck   Italian $$$

(☏732-988-0123; www.moonstrucknj.com; 517 Lake Ave; mains $16-30; ⏱5-10pm Wed-Thu & Sun, to 11pm Fri & Sat) There's nothing staid or proper about this bustling, popular restaurant housed in a striking Victorian building with tables on the wraparound porches. The menu is eclectic, though it leans towards Italian with a good selection of pastas; the meat and fish dishes have varied ethnic influences.

✖ Starving Artist   Cafe $

(☏732-988-1007; 47 Olin St; mains $3-9; ⏱8am-3pm Mon-Sat, to 2pm Sun, closed Wed; 🖶) The menu at this adorable eatery with a large outdoor patio highlights breakfast, the grill, and fried seafood; tasty ice cream is served at the adjacent shop.

🛏 Quaker Inn   Inn $$

(☏732-775-7525; www.quakerinn.com; 39 Main St; r $90-150; 🖶) The 135-year-old inn has 29 small, well-priced rooms, all with air-con and TV, and some with balconies. Open year-round; no breakfast.

Spring Lake ③

🛏 Grand Victorian at
Spring Lake   Inn $$

(☏732-449-5237; www.grandvictorian springlake.com; 1505 Ocean Ave; r with shared/ private bath with breakfast from $100/150; ❄🗢) A stay at this bright and airy Victorian directly across the street from the beach is about as far from the TV version of a shore break as you can get. Rooms are simple and tastefully done and a wraparound porch and excellent attached restaurant add to the general air of oceanfront elegance.

Seaside Heights ⑤

✖ Music Man   Ice Cream $

(☏732-854-2779; www.njmusicman.com; 2305 Grand Central Ave (Rte 35), Lavallette; mains $3-8; ⏱takeout 6am-midnight, shows 6pm-midnight; 🖶) Stop in Lavallette for an ice cream at this true crowd-pleaser where every evening is 'dessert theater,' with servers belting out Broadway show tunes tableside. Go on, order a sundae; you'll smile all the way home.

✖ Shut Up and Eat!   Breakfast $

(☏732-349-4544; 213 Rte 37 East) About 6 miles west of Seaside Heights, tucked away in the Kmart shopping plaza in Tom's River, this sarcastically named place could be the silliest breakfast joint ever: there are waitresses in pajamas (wear yours for a 13% discount), snappy repartee, mismatched furniture and a cornucopia of kitsch. The food's even better: try stuffed French toast with real maple syrup, plus top-quality omelets, pancakes and more.

Ocean City ⑦

🛏 Flanders Hotel   Hotel $$$

(☎609-399-1000; www.flandershotel.com; 719
E 11th St; r $260-440; 🏊) Shake off those sandy
motel blues at Ocean City's Flanders Hotel:
every room is a modern, immaculate, 650-sq-ft
(or larger) suite with full kitchen, and the blue-
and-yellow decor evokes a pleasantly low-key
seaside feel.

Wildwoods ⑧

🛏 Heart of Wildwood   Hotel $$

(☎609-522-4090; www.heartofwildwood.com;
Ocean & Spencer Aves, Wildwood; r $125-245;
🏊) If you're here for waterslides and roller
coasters, book a room at Heart of Wildwood,
facing the amusement piers. It's not fancy, but
gets high marks for cleanliness (the tile floors
help), and from the heated rooftop pool you can
watch the big wheel go round and round.

🛏 Starlux   Hotel $$

(☎609-522-7412; www.thestarlux.com; Rio
Grande & Atlantic Aves, Wildwood; r $130-310; 🏊)
The sea-green-and-white Starlux has the soaring
profile, the lava lamps, the boomerang-decorated
bedspreads and the sailboat-shaped mirrors, plus
it's clean as a whistle. Even more authentically
retro are its two chrome-sided Airstream trailers.

🛏 Summer Nites B&B   B&B $$

(☎609-846-1955; www.summernites.com;
2110 Atlantic Ave, Wildwood; r $145-275) North

of the noise and lights, in an unassuming white
house, is the coolest vintage experience of all:
real jukeboxes play 45s; the breakfast room is a
perfectly re-created diner and the eight themed
rooms are dominated by wall-size murals and
framed, signed memorabilia.

Cape May ⑨

🍴 Lobster House   Seafood $$

(906 Schellengers Landing Rd, Fisherman's
Wharf; mains $12-27; ⏱11:30am-3pm &
4:30-10pm Apr-Dec, to 9pm other times) Talk
about locally sourced ... You know the fish is
fresh at this classic surf and turf because the
restaurant's own boats haul the day's catch in.
There are no reservations which means very
long waits are a possibility; in that case try to
grab a seat at the dockside raw seafood bar.

🍴 Uncle Bill's Pancake House   American $

(Beach Ave at Perry St; mains $7; ⏱6:30am-
2pm) The size (and decor) of a high-school
cafeteria from the 1950s, Uncle Bill's has been
drawing in crowds for its flapjacks for 50 years.

🛏 Congress Hall   Hotel $$

(☎609-884-8421; www.congresshall.com; 251
Beach Ave; r $100-465) The classic and regal-
looking Congress Hall has a range of beautiful
quarters to suit various budgets, plus a long,
oceanfront porch lined with rocking chairs. An
ideal location, onsite restaurant and downstairs
bar called the Boiler Room (with live music some
nights) make this hard to beat.

Easton A historic city with a bohemian vibe

Bucks County & Around

9

A drive along the lower Delaware River leads past lovely scenery and to atmospheric and history-filled towns, from finely coiffed Princeton to more gritty Bethlehem and historic Philadelphia.

TRIP HIGHLIGHTS

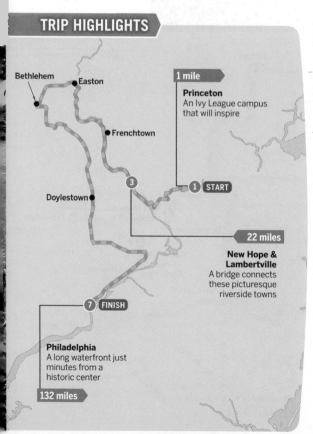

Bethlehem • **Easton**

1 mile

Princeton
An Ivy League campus that will inspire

• **Frenchtown**

 3

Doylestown •

1 START

22 miles

New Hope & Lambertville
A bridge connects these picturesque riverside towns

 7 FINISH

Philadelphia
A long waterfront just minutes from a historic center

132 miles

3–4 DAYS
132 MILES / 212KM

GREAT FOR ...

BEST TIME TO GO
Spring and fall for lush green and gold foliage.

ESSENTIAL PHOTO
Erie blast furnaces of Bethlehem Steel.

BEST FOR FAMILIES
Coloring with Crayolas in Easton.

9 Bucks County & Around

Since the turn of the 20th century painters have found inspiration in the soothing beauty of the region's tree-lined riverbanks and canals. And despite the fact that Revolutionary War struggles took place amid its picturesque setting, the flowing Delaware has a way of softening not only the afternoon light but one's mood as well. It's no surprise artists and city dwellers seeking to commune with nature continue to flock here.

TRIP HIGHLIGHT

❶ Princeton

It was here, on January 3, 1777, that George Washington and his untrained, ill-equipped troops won their first victory against British Regulars, then the world's most powerful army. Today's town is home to **Princeton University**, the country's fourth oldest and a bastion of the Ivy League. Its impressive campus with wrought iron gates, Gothic spires and manicured quads

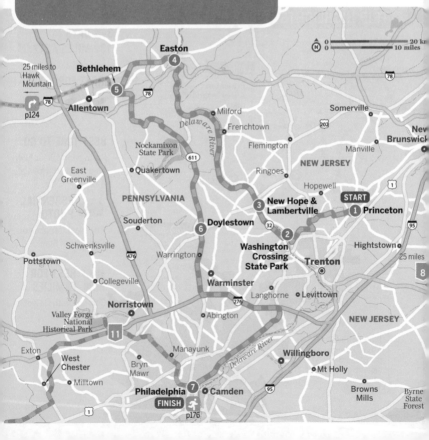

personify the ideals of a classic liberal arts education. Running along the campus' edge is Nassau St, the town's principle commercial thoroughfare where Albert Einstein once window-shopped – he lived in Princeton from 1933 until his death in 1955.

The **Princeton University Art Museum** (☎609-258-3788; www.princetonartmuseum.org; McCormack Hall, Princeton University Campus; ⏱10am-5pm, to 10pm Thu) is akin to a mini-Metropolitan Museum of Art in terms of its variety and quality of works, which range from ancient Greek pottery to pieces by Andy Warhol. Afterwards, stop by the nearby **Morven Museum & Garden** (☎609-924-8144; www.morven.org; 55 Stockton St; adult/child

 LINK YOUR TRIP

11 Brandywine Valley to Atlantic City

Start on I-95 south from Philly to access the rural byways and gardens of the Brandywine Valley.

8 The Jersey Shore

It's a straight shot down the Atlantic City Expwy to Atlantic City, from where all of the shore is within reach.

$6/free; ⏱11am-3pm Wed-Fri, noon-4pm Sat & Sun) for fine displays of decorative arts and fully furnished period rooms; other galleries change their exhibitions periodically. The gardens and house itself, a perfectly coiffed colonial revival mansion originally built by Richard Stockton, a prominent lawyer in the mid-18th century and signer of the Declaration of Independence, are worth a visit in and of themselves.

 p126

The Drive » Surrounding Princeton, to the west especially, gorgeous homes line the streets – surely only the most tenured professors could afford to live here. Take local roads – Rosedale Rd, right on Carter, left on Elm Ridge and then left on Pennington Rocky Hill Rd. Take one more left on Rte 31/Pennington Rd and finally a right on Washington Crossing Pennington Rd.

- - - - - - - - - - - - - -

② Washington Crossing State Park

Ten days before the battle at Princeton on Christmas night 1776, George Washington led his army across the ice-packed Delaware River from the Pennsylvania side to the New Jersey side in a raging snowstorm. He took the risk knowing that if he didn't win something before winter closed in, his army might come entirely come spring. **Washington Crossing State Park** (☎609-737-

0623; www.state.nj.us/dep/parksandforests; Washington Crossing Pennington Rd, Titusville; per vehicle $7 Memorial Day–Labor Day; no charge rest of year; ⏱9am-4pm) offers an overstuffed exhibit in the visitor center, historic buildings and nice trails through pretty woods. Though good for a picnic, the park isn't very evocative. A copy of the painting *Washington Crossing the Delaware* is on the Pennsylvania side (Washington Crossing Historic Park); the original is in the Metropolitan Museum of Art in NYC. According to historians, the artist, Emanuel Leutze, got almost none of the details right: the boats, the light, the river, Washington himself – all wrong. Rather, the scene is a caricature that captures not the moment itself but how everyone felt about it afterward.

Just 4 miles south on the Jersey side of the river is the **New Jersey State Police Museum** (☎609-882-2000; www.njspmuseum.org; 1020 River Rd, Ewing Township; ⏱10am-4pm Mon-Fri). Where else can you gawk at confiscated sawed-off shotguns, Colt .45s, or the electric chair that killed Bruno Hauptmann? Yes, the guy who kidnapped Lindbergh's baby – or did he? A fantastic exhibit guides you through the trial. Then test your detective skills on a fictional crime-scene.

The Drive » The 13-mile drive north is prettier on the PA side so cross the extremely narrow bridge and turn right on River Rd. You'll pass Washington Crossing Historic Park and, further along, the Delaware Canal State Park. Across the street from the latter is the entrance to Bowman's Hill Wildflower Preserve. The meadows and ponds are worth a stroll.

TRIP HIGHLIGHT

❸ New Hope & Lambertville

These two towns built along the banks of the wide Delaware River separating New Jersey and Pennsylvania are connected by a pedestrian-friendly bridge. The intersection of Bridge and Main Sts is the center of New Hope's action, mostly small craft, vintage and antique shops as well as a number of restaurants with outdoor patios – great spots for drinks when the weather permits. On Main St, you'll find Coryell's Ferry, which offers pleasant paddle wheel cruises (11am May to September; adult/child $10/5) with colonial history narrated by Bob Gerenser, New Hope's star George Washington re-enactor. Buy your tickets at Gerenser's Exotic Ice Cream on Main Street.

Smaller and quainter Lambertville has antique shops, art galleries and a few cozy coffee shops and restaurants. The restored 19th-century train station near the foot of the bridge now houses the town's signature restaurant. About a mile south of town on Rte 29 is the **Golden Nugget Antique Market** (☎609-397-0811; www.gnmarket.com; 1850 River Rd; ◷6am-4pm) where over 250 dealers congregate, along with food vendors every Wednesday, Saturday and Sunday year round. Seven miles north is **Bull's Island Recreation Area**, a lovely place to stroll along the canal; a pedestrian bridge crosses the Delaware to the tiny, historic hamlet of Lumberville, PA, which has a general store where you can pick up deli food.

✗ ⊨ p126

The Drive » Settle in for a picturesque 34-mile stretch; River Rd on the PA side is an especially scenic drive, nestled between the river and forested hills and picturesque homes along the way. It's worth crossing the bridges and pausing at the blink-and-you'll-miss-it villages of Frenchtown and Milford on the Jersey side before continuing onwards. Cross the Delaware once more to enter Easton.

❹ Easton

The historic city of Easton, home to Lafayette College, is in the Lehigh Valley, just over the New Jersey border and on the banks of the Delaware River. While there's a few charming cobblestone blocks and bohemian elements, there's also an undeniable air of decay around the fringes of this otherwise picturesque town. Families with kids should head to the **Crayola Factory** (☎610-515-8000; www.crayolaexperience.com; 30 Centre Sq; admission $16; ◷10am-6pm May-Sep, times vary Oct-Apr; ♿) – it's decidedly not a factory, rather more an interactive 'museum' where you can watch crayons and markers get made, plus enjoy hands-on exhibits where you're *supposed* to write on the walls.

No longer awkwardly sharing space with the Crayola Factory, the **National Canal Museum** (☎610-923-3548; www.canals.org; 2750 Hugh Moore Park Rd; adult/child $11.75/9; ◷noon-5pm Wed-Sun) is now housed in a plain two-story brick building that's, appropriately enough, along the canal. With fascinating exhibits on the integral role canals played in fostering the nation's economy, it's less dry than you might imagine. You can also hop aboard the *Josiah White II*, a rebuilt 19th-century boat, or learn about the life of a lock tender from a costumed interpreter.

✗ ⊨ p126

The Drive » It's only 4 miles on the Lehigh Valley Thruway to the exit at PA-191 south/Nazareth Bethlehem Pike. It turns into Linden St and takes you straight into downtown Bethlehem.

Princeton Nassau Hall, Princeton University

⑤ Bethlehem

From its initial founding by a small religious community to a heavy industry center to its current incarnation as a gambling destination, the city of Bethlehem on the Lehigh River retains a charming historic quality. On Christmas Eve 1741, the leader of a group of Moravian settlers from Saxony in Germany christened the town 'Bethlehem' and ever since its Christmas celebrations have drawn visitors from afar. Fourteen acres of the original community in which men, women and children lived in separate housing have been granted a national historic landmark status and you can tour several buildings including the **Moravian Museum of Bethlehem** (☎610-882-0450; www.historicbethlehem.org; adult/child $12/6; ⊙11am-4pm Fri-Sun), housed in the oldest still-standing structure in town.

The 10-acre campus of **SteelStacks** (☎610-332-1300; www.steelstacks.org; 101 Founders Way), an arts and culture organization, is located directly underneath the towering, prehistoric-looking blast furnaces of the former Bethlehem Steel factory, left neglected and decaying for years. This formerly forlorn site has been revitalized and now includes **ArtsQuest Center** (☎610-332-1300; www.artsquest.org; Banana Factory, 25 W 3rd St), a state-of-the-art performance space with a cinema, restaurant and more, the Levitt Pavilion, which hosts free outdoor concerts, and walking tours (adult/child $15.50/9.50) explaining the history and architecture of this industrial giant.

Even if you don't intend on throwing down

DETOUR: HAWK MOUNTAIN

Start: ⑤ Bethlehem

When the East Coast gratefully turns the page on August's heat and humidity, it's time to head for the mountains. Cooler temperatures make hiking more pleasant and as the leaves turn, nature paints the mid-Atlantic's deciduous forests every shade of red and yellow. With so many mountains to choose from, why pick Hawk Mountain? Because raptors start their annual migration south, and during September, October and November some 18,000 hawks, eagles, osprey, kestrels and vultures pass this particular windy updraft along the Kittatinny Ridge. From Hawk Mountain's North Lookout, you can see more than 17 species fly by, some at eye-level. On a good day, observers count a thousand birds, though broad-winged hawks, the rare raptor that flies in a group, have been known to arrive 7000 at a time. At other times of the year, the soft carpeted hills of the Appalachians are just as beautiful, and those for whom Hawk Mountain's relatively short trails are not enough can pick up the Appalachian Trail from here. The **Hawk Mountain Visitor Center** (☎601-756-6961; www.hawkmountain.org; 1700 Hawk Mtn Rd, Kempton, PA; trail admission adult/child $6/3; ⊙9am-5pm) has loaner optics and trail guides.

To get to Hawk Mountain, leave Bethlehem on PA-378 north to connect to US 22 west – after 10.5 miles this merges with I-78 west for another 16 miles. Take exit 35 at Lenhartsville and head north on Rte 143 for another 4 miles. Turn left onto Hawk Mountain Rd (there's a blue Hawk Mountain sign here); it's another 7 miles to the parking lot at the top of the mountain.

any cash, the massive casino built on the site of the former factory (it takes its design cues from its utilitarian past) is worth a drive-by.

🛏 p127

The Drive » It's only 30 miles south through the heart of Bucks County to Doylestown. You'll pass by Nockamixon State Park, a large lake with a few miles of hiking trails, shortly before Rte 412 turns into Rte 611.

- - - - - - - - - - -

⑥ Doylestown

In 1898–99, painters Edward Redfield and William Langson Lathrop moved to New Hope and co-founded an artists' colony that changed American painting. Redfield, in particular, became famous for painting outside (*en plein air*) in winter storms so bad he had to tie his easel to a tree. He worked fast, not even sketching first, creating moody, muted landscapes in a day. For the whole story on the New Hope School of painters and other top flight American artists, head to Doylestown's **Michener Art Museum** (📞215-340-9800; www.michenermuseum.org; 138 S Pine St; adult/child $15/7.50; ⏰10am-4:30pm Tue-Fri, to 5pm Sat, noon-5pm Sun). Housed in an impressive looking stone building, a refurbished prison from the 1880s, the museum is named after the popular

Pulitzer Prize–winning author James A Michener (*Tales of the South Pacific* is probably his most well known work) who supported the museum. A small permanent exhibition includes Michener's writing desk and other objects from his Bucks County home, including a collection of this inveterate traveler's personal road maps to cities and countries around the world.

The Drive » Continue south on Rte 611 to I-276 east; a shortcut to I-95 south, which takes you to Penn's Landing, is to exit onto US 1 toward Philadelphia and then take PA-63 east. Otherwise, keep going on I-276 east until you can take another exit for I-95 south.

- - - - - - - - - - -

TRIP HIGHLIGHT

⑦ Philadelphia

Penn's Landing – Philadelphia's waterfront area along the Delaware River between Market and Lombard Sts, where William Penn landed on a barge in 1682 – was a very active port area from the early 18th-century into the 20th. Today most of the excitement is about boarding booze cruises, or simply strolling along the water's edge. The 1.8-mile Benjamin Franklin Bridge, the world's largest suspension bridge when completed in 1926, spans the Delaware River and dominates the view. Check out the

Independence Seaport Museum (📞215-413-8655; www.phillyseaport.org; 211 S Columbus Blvd; adult/child $13.50/10; ⏰10am-5pm, to 7pm Thu-Sat summer; 🚻; 🚇No 21, 25, 76) which highlights Philadelphia's role as an immigration hub; its shipyard closed in 1995 after 200 years.

Old City – the area bounded by Walnut, Vine, Front and 6th Sts – picks up where Independence National Historical Park (p138) leaves off. And, along with Society Hill, Old City was early Philadelphia. The 1970s saw revitalization, with many warehouses converted into apartments, galleries and small businesses. Today it's a quaint place for a stroll, especially along tiny, cobblestoned **Elfreth's Alley** – its 32-well-preserved brick row houses make up what's believed to be the oldest continuously occupied street in the USA. Stop into **Elfreth's Alley Museum** (📞215-574-0560; www.elfrethsalley.org; No 126; adult/child $5/2; ⏰10am-5pm Wed-Sat, from noon Sun) which was built in 1755 by blacksmith and alley namesake Jeremiah Elfreth; it's been restored and furnished to its 1790 appearance.

For another look at Philadelphia, see p138 or follow the walking tour on p176.

🍴 🛏 p127

Sleeping & Eating

Princeton ①

✕ Mediterra Restaurant
& Taverna   Mediterranean $$

(📞609-252-9680; 29 Hulfish St; mains $15-30;
🕑11:30am-10pm, to 11pm Fri & Sat) Centrally
located in Palmer Square, Mediterra is the sort
of upscale, contemporary place designed for a
college town, for visiting parents, flush students
and locals craving menus that highlight locally
sourced and organic ingredients. It's worth
leaning towards the fish and small plates like
bruschetta.

✕ Olives   Bakery/Deli $

(22 Witherspoon St; sandwiches $7; 🕑7am-
8pm) Visit Olives for reasonably priced,
healthy Mediterranean-style food with a Greek
emphasis – it's like Whole Foods' deli section
only with better selection and quality. There's
very limited counter space so aim for take-out,
especially at lunch time when it's crowded.

⚏ Nassau Inn   Inn $$

(📞609-921-7500; www.nassauinn.com; 10
Palmer Sq; r incl breakfast from $169; 🏵🛜🏊)
A Princeton favorite, evoking 18th-century
elegance with 21st-century comforts.
Downstairs is the Yankee Doodle Tap Room
where professors, students and out-of-towners
gather for local brews and hearty meals.

New Hope ③

✕ Marsha Brown
Creole Kitchen and Lounge   Southern $$

(📞215-862-7044; 15 S Main St; mains $15-30;
🕑11:30am-10pm Mon-Thu, to 11pm Fri & Sat,
to 9pm Sun) For a divine meal in a renovated
former church, this unique New Hope creation is
inspired by the Louisiana cooking and Southern
roots of its owner. Catfish, steaks and lobster
are served in the gorgeous light-filled dining
room.

⚏ Black Bass Hotel   Inn $$$

(📞215-297-9260; www.blackbasshotel.com;
3774 River Rd, Lumberville; r wkdays/wkends

from $195/225; 🏵🛜) Originally a small tavern
popular with Tory loyalists – that's right, 1740s
Tories – this elegant and comfortable inn is
steeped in history. Extensively renovated in
2009 after falling on hard times, the antique
furnishings, memorabilia and artwork were
restored and mixed with contemporary
amenities. Only 6 miles north of New Hope,
most of the rooms have views of the Delaware
Canal and River which runs behind the property.

⚏ Porches on the Towpath   B&B $$

(📞215-862-3277; www.porchesnewhope.
com; 20 Fisher's Alley; r from wkdays/wkends
$115/155) Romantic and quirky, this cozy
Victoriana with porches and canal views doesn't
take itself too seriously (just like the inn's
affable owner). It's a relatively secluded spot
off the main drag with six uniquely designed
rooms in the main house and another six in an
atmospheric 19th-century carriage house.

Lambertville ②

✕ DeAnna's   Mediterranean $$

(📞609-397-8957; 54 N Franklin St; mains
$18-25; 🕑5-9:30pm Tue-Thu, to 10pm Fri & Sat)
This long-running owner/chef driven place with
an eclectic menu and romantic vibe serves up
homemade pasta and simple but delicious meat
and fish dishes. Reservations recommended.

Easton ④

✕ Sette Luna   Italian $$

(219 Ferry St; mains $15; 🕑11:30am-9:30pm,
to 10:30pm Fri & Sat) A small gem a few blocks
from the center of town, this sophisticated
Tuscan trattoria has a large selection of pastas
and thin-crusted pizzas as well as skilfully
prepared fish and meat dishes. The dining room
can get loud when groups are in; the best seats
are at one of the few sidewalk tables.

⚏ Lafayette Inn   Inn $$

(📞610-253-4500; www.lafayetteinn.com; 525
W Monroe St; r incl breakfast from $125, ste from
$225; 🅿🏵🛜) This 18-room Georgian-style

mansion with antiques and big breakfasts has warm and cozy rooms and suites, some with fireplaces and one with a full kitchen. It's perched at the top of College Hill, a block from the campus of Lafayette College and with several restaurants in easy walking distance.

Bethlehem ⑤

🛏 Hotel Bethlehem   Hotel $$

(☎800-607-2384; www.hotelbethlehem.com; 437 Main St; r from $149; ❄🛜) Centrally located and embodying a more regal and grand moment in the town's history, this is the place to stay in Bethlehem. While the room decor is hardly fashionable or stylish, the bedding is plush and rooms come with every modern amenity. There's an elegant restaurant as well as a bar with live jazz.

Philadelphia ⑦

✗ Cuba Libre   Caribbean $$

(☎215-627-0666; www.cubalibrerestaurant. com; 10 S 2nd St; dinner $15-24; ⏰11:30am-11pm Mon-Fri, from 10:30am Sat & Sun) Colonial America couldn't feel further away at this festive, multistoried Cuban eatery and rum bar. The creative, inspired menu includes Cuban sandwiches, guava-spiced BBQ, and savory black beans and salads tossed with smoked fish.

✗ Farmicia   Organic $$

(☎215-627-6274; 15 S 3rd St; mains $10-29; ⏰11:30am-3pm & 5:30-10pm Tue-Fri, 8:30am-3pm & 5:30-11pm Sat & Sun) Dedicated to simply crafted, local and organic foods, the meals at this BYOB spot – including an organic Angus burger with caramelized onions, and Alaskan salmon with roasted beets and lentils – are creative and soul satisfying. Vegetarians are well cared for, with a variety of tofu, pasta and veggie-and-grain plates to choose from. Weekend brunch rocks, too.

🛏 Rittenhouse 1715   Hotel $$$

(☎215-546-6500; www.rittenhouse1715.com; 1715 Rittenhouse Sq; r $249-305, ste $309-699; ❄🛜) Just steps from Rittenhouse Sq, this is an elegant, top-notch choice. Housed in a 1911 mansion and infused with old-world sophistication, it's brimming with modern amenities – iPod docking stations, plasma TVs and rain showerheads. The friendly and efficient staff is also worth noting.

🛏 Society Hill Hotel   Hotel $$

(☎215-925-1919; sochill301@aol.com; 301 Chestnut St; ⏰check in at 3pm) Philly's smallest hotel has a European atmosphere and friendly staff, and is right near Independence Park. Its very small but quaint rooms feature brass beds and private baths, and the first floor of the place is a congenial bar and restaurant.

Bushkill Falls An undeniably beautiful series of eight falls

Down the Delaware

10

Visit small riverside towns along the Delaware as you traverse the region between the Catskills proper and the Pocono Mountains.

TRIP HIGHLIGHTS

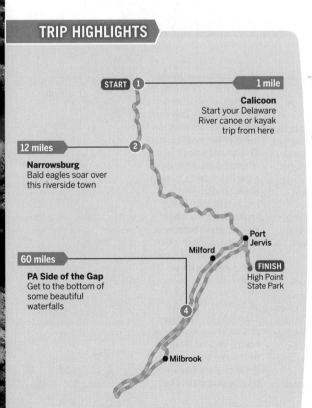

START ① — **1 mile**

Calicoon
Start your Delaware River canoe or kayak trip from here

12 miles ②

Narrowsburg
Bald eagles soar over this riverside town

60 miles

PA Side of the Gap
Get to the bottom of some beautiful waterfalls

Port Jervis

Milford

FINISH
High Point State Park

④

Milbrook

3–4 DAYS
125 MILES / 201KM

GREAT FOR...

BEST TIME TO GO
Mid-April through October for boating.

 ESSENTIAL PHOTO
River and Mt Minsi from Mt Tammany.

 BEST FOR OUTDOORS
Paddle your way down the Delaware.

10 Down the Delaware

Flowing along the New York and Pennsylvania border and then through New Jersey, the Delaware River is a particularly scenic state boundary. Snaking past riverside towns where locals coexist with downstaters discovering the pleasures of rural living, it makes its most dramatic appearance at an S-shaped curve in a gap in the mountains. Whatever side you're on, beautiful waterfalls – some hidden deep in the forest – can be found down little-known back-country roads.

TRIP HIGHLIGHT

① Calicoon

Calicoon was settled in the 1760s when lumbering was all the rage; the railroad, which still runs through this postage-stamp-sized town, linked the Great Lakes to the eastern seaboard a century later. Today Calicoon is a mix of year-round residents and second-homers, rural rhythms and independently minded retirees, artists and farmers. Built in the 1940s, the Calicoon movie theater has daily 7:30pm showings (plus another screening at 2pm on weekends), generally Hollywood blockbusters, in its single-screen cavernous Quonset-hut style theater. Throw in a sophisticated wine shop, several antiques stores and restaurants, including the newly redesigned Peppino's Pizzeria and Cafe Devine, where you can while away a few hours, and a farmer's market on Sundays (🕙11am to 3pm) in the summer and you might start window-shopping at the local real-estate office.

Rent a canoe or kayak from **Lander's River Trips** (📞800-252-3925; www.landersrivertrips.com; per day Mon-Fri/Sat & Sun $39/45) in the Shell gas station at the foot of the bridge for a relaxing float down the Delaware. Between Calicoon and Narrowsburg, the river

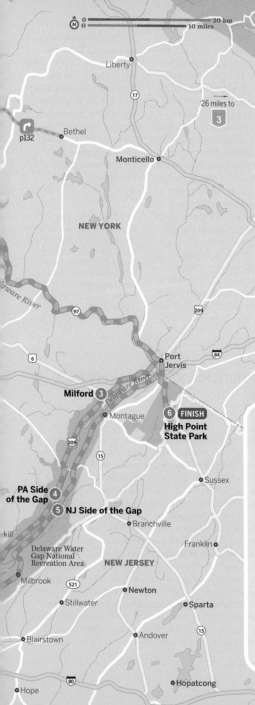

is wide and slow (with a few bends and islets of tall grass) and flotillas of family and friends on hot days – hop in, grab your boat's funnel and cool off.

✕ p135

The Drive » The quick way is Rte 97 south. A scenic alternative is River Rd on the Pennsylvania side of the Delaware – after crossing the bridge in Calicoon, turn left onto a rough dirt road. Just 5.5 miles later at an intersection with the bridge to Cochecton (cuh-SHEK-ton), make a right and then a quick left back onto the paved portion of River Rd.

TRIP HIGHLIGHT

② Narrowsburg

Another small, essentially one-street town, Narrowsburg overlooks the deepest (113ft) and widest spot on the Delaware. There's an

LINK YOUR TRIP

③ Tranquil Catskills

Calicoon is already in the southern tier of the Catskills; head north to access the heart of this mountains region.

⑨ Bucks County & Around

From Stroudsburg at the southern end of the Gap, take Rte 33 to historic Bethlehem and a trip with other perspectives on the Delaware.

overlook with excellent views on Main St where you can spot bald eagles soaring overhead. The National Park Service office has animal skulls and skins on display – fox, raccoon, otter, beaver – that kids can touch and try to identify.

Two NYC fashion-world transplants own the **River Gallery** (www.rivergalleryny.com; 8 Main St; ☺11am-5pm Mon-Thu, to later Fri-Sun), a high-end boutique filled with an eclectic mix of oil paintings, handcrafted glassware and other whimsically designed home accessory items.

Just up the road from town, past Peck's grocery store, is **Fort Delaware**

Museum (☎845-252-6660; 15 Rte 97; adult/child $7/4; ☺10am-5pm Sat-Mon summer months), a reconstructed log fort (not a military outpost) from the 1750s when English settlers and Lenape (Native Americans) coexisted in what was then wilderness territory. Interpreters in period dress demonstrate skills like candle-making, quilting, weaving and food preparation and will explain how the A, B, Cs were taught in the late 18th century.

If you've canoed or kayaked down from Calicoon you can take out at the Lander's office just under the single-lane bridge from Milanville.

The slightly more adventurous can carry on through **Skinners Falls**, where there's a little white water, and end at Narrowsburg (tubing the falls is $12). When the water's low, the rocks around Skinners Falls create small pools and eddies – a great place for sunbathing and swimming.

 p135

The Drive » Heading south on Rte 97, you'll initially head inland before hugging the river all the way to the city of Port Jervis. Stop in the Zane Grey Museum – famous novelist of the American West – in Lackawaxen on the Pennsylvania side if you have time. Milford is 7 miles to the southwest from here.

DETOUR:
WHERE WOODSTOCK REALLY HAPPENED: BETHEL

Start: ❶ Calicoon

About 13 miles southeast of Calicoon on Rte 17B is Bethel, the site of the former pig farm that for three rainy summer days in 1969 hosted Woodstock, a concert that came to symbolize the dreams and aspirations of an entire generation. These days, it's a bucolic rolling field of green. The **Bethel Woods Center for the Arts** (☎866-781-2922; www.bethelwoodscenter.org; 200 Hurd Rd), a state-of-the-art performance and recital center, is designed to be perfectly in harmony with the terrain. As you walk the stone pathways, you can get a bird's-eye view of the gorgeous Pavilion Stage, which has about 50,000 seats set into a sloping lawn, and the outdoor Terrace Stage, which is like a Greek amphitheater set down in a mossy field. Big acts like Joan Baez, Blake Shelton, John Mayer and Yo-Yo Ma perform in the summer.

The jewel of the complex is the **Museum at Bethel Woods** (☎866-781-2922; adult/child $15/6; ☺10am-7pm daily late May-early Sep, 10am-5pm Thu-Sun early Sep–late Dec) at the center's entrance, a groovy look back at the tumultuous, spontaneous concert that's come to define the Summer of Love. The captivating multimedia displays use a combination of stock footage, documentaries, retrospectives, letters, books and – above all else – music to capture the '60s all-embracing spirit. A 21-minute film runs every half hour. You can pick up undeniably non-freelove, commercialized souvenirs like tie-dies and key chains emblazoned with a Woodstock logo in the gift shop.

❸ Milford

Gifford Pinchot, the first director of the US Forest Service and two-term governor of Pennsylvania, has left his mark on this small town at the northern end of the Delaware Water Gap. Pinchot, who took the position in 1905 with the support of his friend President Roosevelt and was fired five years later by President Taft, oversaw spectacular growth in the number and size of federally managed forests and is widely considered a pioneer of American conservation. From May to the end of October you can take a guided tour of **Grey Towers** (📞570-296-9630; www.greytowers. org; Old Owego Turnpike; tours adult/child $8/free; ⏰grounds dawn-dusk), the gorgeous French chateau-style home built by Gifford's parents in the 1880s; otherwise, much of the 1600-acre property is open for wandering year-round.

The gray, slate and stone of Grey Towers can be seen in other buildings on Main St in Milford, but there's also been something of a resurgence in recent years with a new library and the refurbishing of the old movie theater. The latter hosts the **Black Bear Film Festival** every October, featuring

PA Side of the Gap Bushkill Falls

independent films with a local focus.

🍴 🛏 p135

The Drive » It's a simple drive south on Rte 209 to the entrance of the Delaware Water Gap National Recreation Area on the Pennsylvania side.

TRIP HIGHLIGHT

❹ PA Side of the Gap

River Rd, the 30-mile stretch of good paved road on the Pennsylvania side of the **Delaware Water Gap National Recreation Area** (📞570-828-2253; www.npa.gov/dewa) includes several worthwhile stops. **Raymondskill Falls** is a stunningly beautiful multilevel cascade and the highest in Pennsylvania;

a steep mile-long trail descends to the creek at the bottom. If you want a nearby shortcut over to the Jersey side, the Dingman's Ferry bridge ($1 toll) is your chance. Otherwise, the Swiss chalet-style Dingman's Falls Visitor Center is the place to begin a 0.25 mile boardwalk trail to the base of the eponymous falls.

The **Pocono Environmental Education Center** (📞570-828-2319; www.peec.org; 538 Emery Rd, Dingman's Ferry; ♿) offers workshops on fly fishing, nature photography, birding and other related outdoor skills; five self-guided hiking trails begin from here as well.

Further south, the privately owned and very

133

developed **Bushkill Falls** (☎570-588-6682; Rte 209, Bushkill; adult/child $12.50/7; 9am, closing times vary, closed Dec-Mar) encompasses a miniature golf course, ice-cream parlor, gift shop and paddleboat rentals so it's far from a wilderness experience. Nevertheless, the series of eight falls surrounded by lush forest is undeniably beautiful.

Finally, the hamlet of Shawnee, towards the southern end of the park, has a general store with sandwiches and burgers, and a large resort with a golf course along the river. Nearby **Adventure Sports** (☎570-223-0505, 800-487-2628; www.adventuresport.com; Rte 209; per day canoe/kayak $40/44; ⊙9am-6pm Mon-Fri, from 8am Sat & Sun May-Oct) is one of a half-dozen companies that rent canoes and kayaks for trips down the river.

🛏 p135

The Drive ≫ To reach Old Mine Rd/Rte 606 on the Jersey side, get on I-80 east and take the exit to your right signposted as Kittatinny Point Visitor Center (closed indefinitely), through an underpass, past a pullout for the Appalachian Trail and back onto I-80 west. Then take exit 1, again on your right, towards Milbrook/ Flatbrookville. Just before the river veer right onto River Rd.

- - - - - - - - - - - - - -

⑤ NJ Side of the Gap

Old Mine Rd, one of the oldest continually operating commercial roads in the US, meanders along the eastern side of the Delaware. A few miles inland, a 25-mile stretch of the Appalachian Trail runs along the Kittatinny Ridge. Day hikers can climb to the top of the 1547ft Mt Tammany in **Worthington State Forest** (☎908-841-9575; www.njparksandforests.org) for great views (the 1.8-mile Blue Dot trail is the easiest route, though it's still strenuous) or walk to the serene-looking glacial Sunfish Pond. Hawks, bald eagles and ravens soar over the hemlock forest.

The recreated site of **Milbrook Village**, composed of about two dozen buildings, some original, others moved or built here since the 1970s, is meant to evoke a late 19th-century farming community. From a peak of 75 inhabitants in 1875, by 1950 only a blacksmith remained. On Saturdays and other select days in summer, as well as the first weekend in October during the Milbrook Days Festival, costumed interpreters perform period skills. Otherwise, it's a picturesque ghost town.

A steep wooden stairway takes you to the top of the spectacular **Buttermilk Falls** but it's equally impressive from the bottom. It's accessed down a dirt road after turning right after the cemetery in Walpack Center.

The Drive ≫ Head towards Port Jervis, then take Rte 23 to High Point State Park.

- - - - - - - - - - - - - -

⑥ High Point State Park

A 220ft monument marks the highest point in the park and New Jersey at 1803ft. Here and at several other viewpoints in the aptly named **High Point State Park** (☎973-875-4800; www.njparksandforests.org; 1480 Rte 23, Sussex; ⊙8am-8pm Apr-Oct, to 4:30pm other months), there are wonderful panoramas of the surrounding lakes, hills and farmland – the Poconos to the west, the Catskills to the north and the Wallkill River Valley to the southeast. Trails snake off into the forests and there's a small beach with a lake to cool off in during the summer. If you only have time for one walk, try the 2.3-mile Dryden Kuser National Area interpretive trail through a white cedar bog with a variety of birdlife. In winter months, contact the information center for snowshoe 'tracking' programs where you learn how to search for the snowy footprints of weasels, bobcats and coyotes.

Sleeping & Eating

Calicoon ❶

✖ Matthew's on
Main Street American $$

(19 Main St; mains $10-24; ⏱11am-9pm, to 11pm Sat & Sun) The husband-and-wife team who own Matthew's serve up juicy burgers, sandwiches and salads at lunchtime, and more expensive, elaborate seafood and meat dishes at dinnertime; locals cozy up to the bar from the afternoon on.

Narrowsburg ❷

✖ The Heron Modern American $$

(☎845-252-3333; 40 Main St; mains $10-30; ⏱ 10am-3pm Sun, Mon & Thu, 5-9pm Thu, 10am-2pm & 6-10pm Fri & Sat, bar 5-9pm Wed) For those seeking a little bit of Brooklyn on the Delaware, the Heron has reclaimed wood picnic tables, tin ceilings and refined menu touting locavore credentials. The oysters and fried chicken are especially recommended. The best tables are on the back deck overlooking the river. Opening hours can be irregular so call in advance.

Milford ❸

✖ Dairy Bar Ice Cream $

(307 W Hartford St; ⏱noon-9pm summer) Stop by for great homemade ice-cream, gelato, sorbet and smoothies, a perfect way to cap off a day on the river.

✖ The Fork at
Twin Lakes Modern American $$$

(☎570-296-8094; 814 Twin Lakes Rd, Shohola; mains $23-33; ⏱6-10pm Thu-Sat, to 9pm Sun)

In Shohola, 8 miles northwest of Milford, this husband-and-wife-run restaurant rivals any NYC foodie destination. Even though you could easily fill up on the excellent sourdough bread and small plates like smoked fishcakes with quinoa cucumber salad, save some room for the beautifully plated fish and meat mains.

🛏 Hotel Fauchere Boutique Hotel $$$

(☎570-409-1212; www.hotelfauchere.com; 401 Broad St; r incl breakfast from $200; ✳🛜) This immaculately restored mid-19th century inn offers luxurious amenities and sophisticated decor – landscape paintings, wood floors and banister – and a great restaurant/bar in the basement called Bar Louis. There's also the Delmonico Room, a more formal restaurant with a menu of locally sourced and hearty fare.

PA Side of the Gap ❹

🛏 Deer Head Inn Inn $$

(☎570-424-2000; www.deerheadinn.com; 5 Main St, Delaware Water Gap; r from $90; ✳🛜) This four-story Victorian with wraparound porch is only a few miles from the Gap itself and just around the corner from the highway. Furnishings in the eight comfortable rooms don't always match but it's worth a stay, especially for the top-flight live jazz music Thursdays through Sundays.

🛏 Delaware Water
Gap Camping Camping $

(www.nps.gov/dewa; tent site from $15) River camping – that is, traveling by canoe or kayak with an overnight stay on an island – is a special experience. Whether via boat or hiking – there's loads of campsites – come prepared with all your food and cooking supplies and remember to bear-proof everything at night.

Longwood Gardens *A display of blooming good design*

Brandywine Valley to Atlantic City

11

Travel down back roads, from refined gardens and mansions to forested wilderness in the heart of Jersey, and end your trip at the boardwalk gambling capital of Atlantic City.

TRIP HIGHLIGHTS

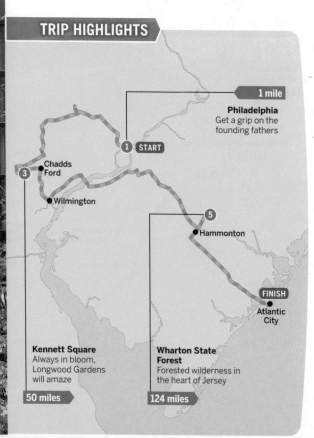

1 mile

Philadelphia
Get a grip on the founding fathers

1 **START**

Chadds Ford

3

Wilmington

5

Hammonton

FINISH

Atlantic City

Kennett Square
Always in bloom, Longwood Gardens will amaze

50 miles

Wharton State Forest
Forested wilderness in the heart of Jersey

124 miles

4 DAYS
165 MILES / 265KM

GREAT FOR ...

BEST TIME TO GO
May through October for camping in the Pines.

ESSENTIAL PHOTO
Fountain show at Longwood Gardens, Kennett Square.

BEST FOR ART LOVERS
Tour the Wyeth studios – both father and son.

137

11 Brandywine Valley to Atlantic City

From the beginnings of American democracy to the height of American aristocracy, from pine forests as far as the eye can see to endless rows of slot machines, this trip covers the gamut. Only a short drive from isolated wilderness, as far from stereotypical Jersey as you get, is Atlantic City – perhaps its epitome. Bone up on the founding fathers' principles to grasp these dizzying shifts in culture and landscape.

TRIP HIGHLIGHT

❶ Philadelphia

Independence National Historic Park (☎215-965-2305; www.nps.gov/inde; 3rd & Chestnut Sts; ☺ visitor center & most sites 9am-5pm), along with Old City, has been dubbed 'America's most historic square mile.' Once the backbone of the United States government, it has become the backbone of Philadelphia's tourist trade. Stroll around and you'll see storied buildings in

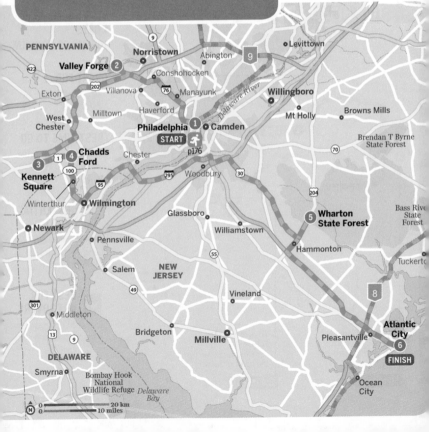

which the seeds for the Revolutionary War were planted and the US government came into bloom. You'll also find beautiful, shaded urban lawns dotted with plenty of squirrels, pigeons, and costumed actors.

Independence Hall (📞215-597-8974; Chestnut St, btwn 5th & 6th Sts) is the 'birthplace of American government,' where delegates from the 13 colonies met to approve the Declaration of Independence on July 4, 1776. An excellent example of Georgian architecture, it sports understated lines that reveal Philadelphia's Quaker heritage.

The **Liberty Bell** is Philadelphia's top tourist attraction. Made in London and tolled at the first public reading

LINK YOUR TRIP

8 The Jersey Shore

From AC, you have your pick of shore beaches. Head north or south on the Garden State Parkway or Route 9.

9 Bucks County & Around

You're already in Philly, this trip's last stop, so just put it in reverse to explore this scenic stretch of the Delaware.

of the Declaration of Independence, the bell became famous when abolitionists adopted it as a symbol of freedom. The highly recommended **National Constitution Center** (📞215-409-6700; www.constitutioncenter.org; 525 Arch St; adult/child $14.50/8; ⏰9:30am-5pm Mon-Fri, to 6pm Sat, noon-5pm Sun; 🚇) makes the United States Constitution interesting for a general audience through theater-in-the-round reenactments. There are exhibits including interactive voting booths and Signer's Hall, which contains lifelike bronze statues of the signers in action.

 p143

The Drive » Access I-76 west just over the Schuylkill River which you follow for around 12½ miles until the exit for 202 north toward King of Prussia. Then quickly take a right onto US 422 west; the exit for Valley Forge is a few miles further on.

2 Valley Forge

After being defeated at the Battle of Brandywine Creek and the British occupation of Philadelphia in 1777, General Washington and 12,000 continental troops withdrew to Valley Forge. Today, Valley Forge symbolizes Washington's endurance and leadership. The **Valley Forge National Historic Park** (📞610-

783-1099; www.nps.gov/vafo; cnr N Gulph Rd & Rte 23, park grounds; ⏰6am-10pm, welcome center & Washington's Headquarters 9am-5pm) contains 5½ sq miles of scenic beauty and open space 20 miles northwest of downtown Philadelphia – it's a remembrance of where 2000 of George Washington's 12,000 troops perished from freezing temperatures, hunger and disease, while many others returned home. Its wide fields are dotted with soldier's huts and light-blue cannons and despite the occasional statue of a horse-mounted general, the park has an egalitarian focus.

The Drive » US 202 south/US 322 east passes along the eastern edge of the town of West Chester – the quaint downtown is only a few blocks long and has several good restaurants and cafes (p143). A couple miles further south make a right on W Street Rd/PA-926 west.

TRIP HIGHLIGHT

3 Kennett Square

The small town of Kennett Square, which was founded in 1705, boasts several art galleries, bistros and cafes but is generally known for two things: it is the 'mushroom capital' of the United States (60% of the nation's mushrooms come from the area) and the spectacular **Longwood Gardens** (☎610-388-1000; www.longwoodgardens.org; 1001 Longwood Rd, Kennett Square; adult/child $18/8; ⊙from 9am, check website for closing times), only 3 miles to the east. Pierre du Pont, the great-grandson of the DuPont chemical company founder, began designing the property in 1906 with the grand gardens of Europe in mind – especially French and Italian ones. Virtually every inch of the 1,050 acres has been carefully sculpted into a display of horticultural and floricultural magnificence. Whatever your mood, it can't help but be buoyed by the colors of the tulips which seem too vivid to be real and the overwhelming variety of species testifying to nature's creativity. With one of the world's largest greenhouses and 11,000 kinds of plants, something is always in bloom. There's also a Children's Garden with a maze, fireworks, fountains, outdoor concerts in summer and lights at Christmas.

The Drive » In summer months traffic can be backed up heading east on Rte 1. Midway between the gardens and the Brandywine River Museum is **Chaddsford Winery** (⊙noon-6pm Tue-Sun) – grab a glass of vino and an Adirondack chair for a pleasant afternoon break.

- - - - - - - -

❹ Chadds Ford

A showcase of American artwork, the **Brandywine River Museum** (☎610-388-2700; www. brandywinemuseum.org; cnr Hwy 1 & Rte 100; adult/child $12/free; ⊙9:30am-4:30pm), at Chadds Ford, includes the work of the Brandywine School – Howard Pyle, Maxfield Parrish and of course three generations of

---

BRANCH OUT IN THE PINE BARRENS

Despite the name, the Pine Barrens are anything but. Here are some sights in the area:

» The 27,000 acre **Bass River State Forest** (www.state.nj.us), New Jersey's first state park, typifies the strange character of the Pine Barrens where it's quite easy to feel as if you're in isolated wilderness, forgetting there's a major highway within throwing distance. **Lake Absegami** (weekdays/weekends vehicle fee summer $5/10), near the park offices, is packed with swimmers in summer months, but you can take the half-mile interpretive trail on a boardwalk that passes over a section of eerie and mysterious looking white cedar bog.

» For a short detour when traveling on Rte 539 between Bass River and Brendan T Byrne State Forest, turn onto the ominously named **Bombing Range Rd** – a sign reads '177th FW/DETI Warren Grove Air to Ground Range'. A half-mile on this dirt road provides unobstructed views of the surrounding pygmy forest (mostly dwarf Pitch Pine trees all the way to the horizon). Oh, and you can't go any further – there's a large gate and fence marking the site where Air National Guard units practice bombing and strafing runs nearby.

» New Jersey is one of the largest producers of cultivated blueberries in the US and the world. **Whitesbog**, in Brendan T Byrne State Forest – where blueberries were first cultivated – is really nothing more than a ghost town out of blueberry season, but is worth visiting during the annual June festival (www.whitesbog.org).

» Camping in the Pine Barrens, the most recommended way to experience the true wilderness of the parks, can be 'buggy'. In summer, prepare for mosquitoes, strawberry flies, greenheads and other quaintly named biting pests, all of which diminish in spring and fall.

Wharton State Forest View from Apple Pie Hill fire tower

Wyeths (N.C., Andrew and Jamie). N.C.'s illustrations for popular books like *The Last of the Mohicans* and *Treasure Island* are displayed along with rough sketches and finished paintings. One of our favorite paintings by Andrew that's not among his iconic works is *Snow Hill*, a large canvas that despite the snowy, playful scene somehow manages to evoke menace and a haunted quality. Also check out the back story behind Jamie's *Portrait of a Pig* and the *trompe l'oeil* paintings in separate third-floor galleries. The handsome building is a converted mill with pinewood floors and walls of glass overlooking the slow-moving Brandywine River. **N.C.'s house and studio** are open to the public on guided tours, as are **Andrew's studio** and the **Kuerner Farm**, the noticeable setting for some of Andrew's most famous works. He roamed there every fall and winter for 70 years and found much of his inspiration. Tours of each site cost $8 in addition to museum admission, and can be booked at and leave from Brandywine River Museum.

✕ p143

The Drive ›› Only a mile further east on Rte 1 is Brandywine Battlefield State Park; Batsto, in the Wharton State Forest, is about 66 miles further. Take Rte 100 south past lovely rolling hills. Winterthur (see p242) is close by off Rte 52. Take I-95 north to the Commodore Barry Bridge over the Delaware, then I-295 north towards Camden and exit at US 30 east. It's more

141

rural approaching Hammonton where Rte 206 and Rte 542 lead into the forest.

- - - - - - - - - -

TRIP HIGHLIGHT

⑤ Wharton State Forest

Your introduction to this region, variously referred to as 'the Pines', 'the Pinelands' the 'Pine Barrens' and 'the Pine Belt' (locals are 'Pineys'), is the 12,000 acre Wharton State Forest.

To understand the region's early history, begin at the well-preserved village of **Batsto**. Founded in 1766, Batsto forged 'bog iron' for the Revolutionary War and remained an important ironworks until the 1850s; a self-guided cell phone audio tour provides a dry primer on the uses of the various structures. The **visitor center** (9am-4:30pm, $5 vehicle fee in summer), also the primary one for Wharton State Forest, has an interesting collection of exhibits dedicated to the economic, cultural and natural history of the Pinelands. Several 1- to 4-mile loop trails start here and pass through scrub oak and pine, swamp maple and Atlantic white cedar, a typical mix found in the forests' woodlands.

The most well-known trail is the epic 50-mile **Batona Trail** that cuts through several state parks and forests; look for endangered pitcher plants, which get nutrients they can't get from the soil from hapless insects. Stop and climb the **Apple Pie Hill fire tower** – the Batona Trail passes by it – for magnificent 360-degree views of hundreds of square miles of forests. The climb to the top is completely exposed and the steps and railing feel less than sturdy, so it's not for the acrophobic.

✕ 🛏 p143

The Drive ≫ From Batsto, it's the AC Expressway all the way for 28 miles.

- - - - - - - - - -

⑥ Atlantic City

It's not exactly Vegas, but for many a trip to AC conjures *Hangover*-like scenes of debauchery. And inside the casinos that never see the light of day, it's easy to forget there's a sandy beach just outside and boarded-up shop windows a few blocks in the other direction. The AC known throughout the late 19th and early 20th century for its grand boardwalk and oceanside amusement pier, and the glamorously corrupt one of the HBO series *Boardwalk Empire* (set in 1920s Prohibition-era AC), have been thoroughly overturned. Gray-haired retirees and vacationing families are at least as common as bachelors and bachelorettes.

It's worth nothing that AC's famous boardwalk, 8 miles long and still the lifeline of the city, was the first in the world. Built in 1870 by local business owners who wanted to cut down on sand being tracked into hotel lobbies, it was named in honor of Alexander Boardman, who came up with the idea – Boardman's Walk later became 'Boardwalk'.

The **Steel Pier** (📞866-386-6659; www.steelpier. com; cnr Boardwalk & Virginia Ave; 🕙1pm-midnight Mon-Fri, noon-1am Sat & Sun), directly in front of the Taj Mahal casino, was the site of the famous high-diving horses that plunged into the Atlantic before crowds of spectators from the 1920s to the '70s. Today it's a collection of amusement rides, games of chance, candy stands and a Go-Kart track.

If it's open, drop in on the informative **Atlantic City Historical Museum** (📞609-347-5839; www. acmuseum.org; Garden Pier; 🕙10am-5pm daily). It was closed for repairs at the time of writing due to damage from Hurricane Sandy. The museum is run by a quirky old-timer and provides a suitably quirky look at AC's past.

✕ 🛏 p143

Sleeping & Eating

Philadelphia ①

✖ Morimoto   Japanese $$$
(☎215-413-9070; 723 Chestnut St; mains $25; ⊘11:30am-10pm Mon-Fri, to midnight Fri & Sat) High concept and heavily stylized, from the dining room that looks like a futuristic aquarium to a menu of globe-spanning influence and eclectic combinations, a meal at this *Iron Chef* regular's restaurant is a theatrical experience.

🛏 Morris House Hotel   Boutique Hotel $$
(☎215-922-2446; www.morrishousehotel.com; 225 S 8th St; r incl breakfast from $179; ❄🛜) If Benjamin Franklin were a hotelier he would have designed a place like this. The upscale Federal-era building has the friendly charm and intimacy of an elegant B&B and the professionalism and good taste of a designer-run 21st-century establishment.

🛏 Penn's View Hotel   Boutique Hotel $$
(☎215-922-7600; www.pennsviewhotel.com; cnr Front & Market Sts; r from $149-329; ❄🛜) Housed in three early 19th–century buildings overlooking the Delaware waterfront, Penn's View is ideal for exploring the Old City district. It's quaint and full of character but not overly nostalgic. An authentic Italian trattoria and charming wine bar are part of the hotel.

West Chester

🛏 Hotel Warner   Hotel $$
(☎610-692-6920; www.hotelwarner.com; 120 N High St; r incl breakfast from $118; ❄@🛜🏊) The Art Deco facade and entryway of this 'downtown' West Chester hotel was fashioned out of a 1930s movie theater, lending it a dash of old-time elegance when it opened in 2012. It's modern and fairly generic inside, but it offers plush king-sized beds and large bathrooms.

Chadds Ford ④

✖ Mushrooms   Cafe $
(878 Baltimore Pike (Rte 1); sandwich $7; ⊘7am-3pm Tue-Fri, 8am-4pm Sat & Sun) This bright little cafe serves good coffee, omelets, salads, quiche, sandwiches and, of course, mushrooms – in a soup, dip, stuffed with sausage and by the pound. When you're full of 'shrooms, wander around the attached overstuffed antiques store.

Wharton State Forest ⑤

✖ Penza's   Cafe $
(☎609-567-3412; 51 Myrtle St, Hammonton; mains 5-$10; ⊘8am-5pm) Housed in an old red barn between Hammonton and Atsion, having a meal here feels like you're eating in your grandmother's den. The breakfast omelets are especially recommended, as are the homemade fruit pies laid out in a mouthwatering display.

🛏 Atsion Family Campground   Camping $
(☎609-268-0444; www.state.nj.us; 31 Batsto Rd; tent sites $20; ⊘Apr 31-Oct 1) Try to reserve a lakeside spot (there's a two night minimum policy during summer) at this campground in the Wharton State Forest. You can swim and fish and there's an interpretive trail that's an excellent introduction to the flora and fauna of the area.

Atlantic City ⑥

✖ Angelo's Fairmount Tavern   Italian $
(2300 Fairmount Ave; mains $7; ⊘11:30am-3pm & 5-10pm) The outdoor patio at this beloved family-owned Italian restaurant is a nice spot to take in the sunset and have a pint and a burger.

✖ White House Subs   Sandwiches $
(2301 Arctic Ave; sandwiches $6-15; ⊘10am-8pm Mon-Thu, to 9pm Fri-Sun; 🚻) An icon of old AC with an impressive range of photos on its wall of fame. Its gigantic oily subs and cheesesteaks could feed a family of four. There's another White House Subs located inside the Trump Taj Mahal.

🛏 Chelsea   Boutique Hotel $
(☎800-548-3030; www.thechelsea-ac.com; 111 S Chelsea Ave; r from $80; 🅿❄@🛜🏊) A non-casino place that's trendy with art-deco-style furnishings. Rooms in the attached annex are less expensive. Also houses a retro diner, steakhouse and cabana club.

Lancaster *Lush farmland produces gastronomic delights*

Pennsylvania Dutch Country

12

This fairly compact trip takes you to rural Amish communities where farmers markets and roadside stalls offer homemade goods, and traditions and history are preserved in everyday life.

TRIP HIGHLIGHTS

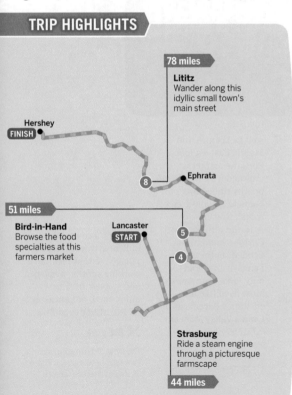

78 miles

Lititz
Wander along this idyllic small town's main street

Hershey
FINISH

Ephrata

51 miles

Bird-in-Hand
Browse the food specialties at this farmers market

Lancaster
START

8

5

4

Strasburg
Ride a steam engine through a picturesque farmscape

44 miles

3–4 DAYS
102 MILES / 164KM

GREAT FOR...

BEST TIME TO GO
Less crowded in early Spring or September.

 ESSENTIAL PHOTO
A windmill or grain silo with a horse-drawn plow in the foreground.

 BEST FOR FOODIES
Almost everything can be jarred at the Intercourse Canning Co.

12 Pennsylvania Dutch Country

The Amish really do drive buggies and plow their fields by hand. In Dutch Country, the pace is slower, and it's no costumed reenactment. For the most evocative Dutch Country experience, go driving along the winding, narrow lanes between the thruways — past rolling green fields of alfalfa, asparagus and corn, past pungent working barnyards and manicured lawns, waving to Amish families in buggies and straw-hatted teens on scooters.

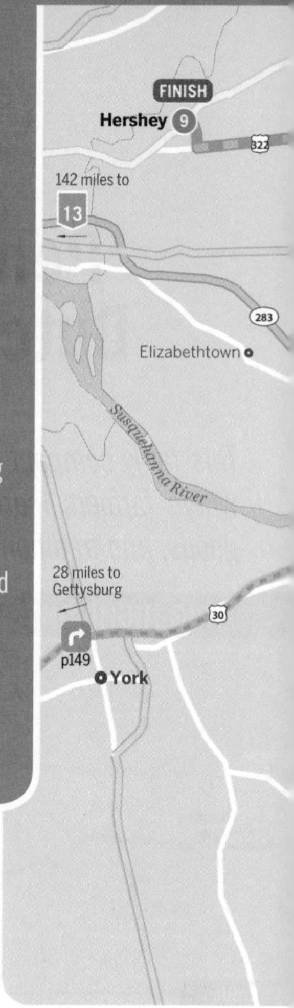

FINISH
Hershey 9
322

142 miles to
13

283
Elizabethtown

Susquehanna River

28 miles to
Gettysburg
30

p149
York

1 Lancaster

A good place to start is Lancaster's (LANK-uh-stir) walkable, red-brick historic district, just off Penn Sq. The Romanesque Revival style **Central Market** (www.centralmarketlancaster. com; 23 N Market St; ⊙6am-4pm Tue & Fri, to 2pm Sat), has regional gastronomic delicacies – fresh horseradish, whoopie pies, soft pretzels, sub sandwiches stuffed with cured meats and dripping with oil – as well as Spanish and Middle Eastern food. Plus, the market is crowded with handicraft booths staffed by bonneted, plain-dressed Amish women.

In the 18th century, German immigrants flooded southeastern Pennsylvania, and only some were Amish. Most lived like the costumed docents at the **Landis Valley Museum** (717-569-0401; www. landisvalleymuseum.org; 2451 Kissel Hill Rd; adult/child $12/8; ⊙9am-5pm, from noon Sun), a re-creation of Pennsylvania German village life that includes a working smithy, weavers and stables. It's a few miles north of Lancaster off Rte 272/Oregon Pike.

✕ ⊨ p154

The Drive » From downtown Lancaster head south on Prince St, which turns into Rte 222

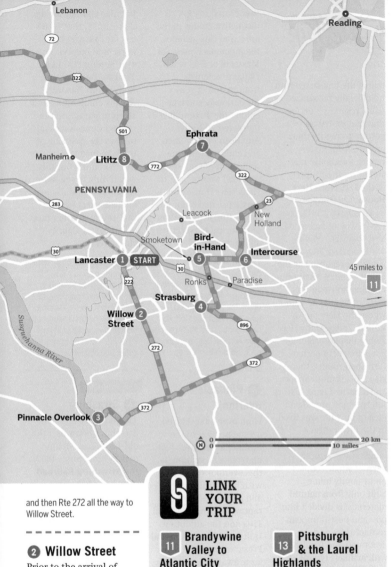

and then Rte 272 all the way to Willow Street.

- - - - - - - - - - - - - - - -

② Willow Street

Prior to the arrival of European émigrés, Coney, Lenape, Mohawk, Seneca and other Native Americans lived in the area. However, Pennsylvania remains

§ LINK YOUR TRIP

11 Brandywine Valley to Atlantic City

Take US 30 east to West Chester to explore gardens and rural byways before heading to the Jersey Shore.

13 Pittsburgh & the Laurel Highlands

US 30 west winds through southern PA before beginning a trip with architectural highlights and urban fun.

one of the few states with no officially recognized tribal reserves – or, for that matter, tribes. In a gesture to rectify their erasure from history, a replica longhouse now stands on the property of the **1719 Hans Herr House** (☎717-464-4438; www.hansherr.org; 1849 Hans Herr Dr; combined guided tour adult/child $15/7; ☺9am-4pm Mon-Sat Apr 1-Nov 30), generally regarded as the oldest original Mennonite meeting house in the western hemisphere and where the Herr family settled. Today, Hans Herr House displays colonial-era artifacts in period-furnished rooms; there's also a blacksmith shop and a barn. 'Living history interpreters' provide an idea of how life was lived in the 18th century.

The interior of the longhouse, a typical narrow, single room, multi-family home built only from natural materials, is divided into pre- and post-European contact sides and decorated and furnished with artifacts typical of each era. The primary mission is to teach visitors about the history of Native American life in Lancaster County from around 1570 to 1770 when for all intents and purposes

they ceased to exist as distinctive groups in the area. And this includes the infamous Conestoga Massacre of 1763 when vigilante colonists from Paxton (given the curiously anodyne epithet the 'Paxton Boys') murdered 20 Native American men, women and children from the settlement of Conestoga. A guided tour of both the Hans Herr House and the longhouse makes for an interesting juxtaposition of historical perspectives and culture.

The Drive >> The simplest route is Rte 272 south to Rte 372 west. However, if you have time head west on Long Ln or W Penn Grant Road, then right on River Rd, a pretty but hard-to-follow backcountry road. You'll pass by Tucquan Glen Nature Preserve – park and hike to the river.

- - - - - - - - - - - - - - -

③ Pinnacle Overlook

High over Lake Aldred, a wide portion of the Susquehanna River just up from a large dam, is this overlook (☺8am-9pm) with beautiful views and eagles and other raptors soaring overhead. This and the adjoining Holtwood Environmental Preserve are parts of a large swath of riverfront property maintained by the Pennsylvania Power & Light Co (PPL). But electrical plant infrastructure and truck traffic is largely kept at bay, making this a

popular spot for locals, non-Amish, that is (it's too far to travel by horse and buggy). The 4-mile-long Fire Line Trail to the adjoining Kelly's Run Natural Area is challenging and steep in parts and the rugged Conestoga Trail follows the east side of the lake for 15 miles. It's worth coming out this way if only to see more rough-hewn landscape and the rural byways that reveal another facet of Lancaster County's character.

The Drive >> You could retrace your route back to Willow Street and then head to Strasburg, but to make a scenic loop, take Rte 372 east, passing agrarian scenes, to the small hamlet of Georgetown. Make a left onto Rte 896 – vistas open up on either side of the road.

- - - - - - - - - - - - - - -

TRIP HIGHLIGHT

④ Strasburg

The main attraction in Strasburg is trains – the old-fashioned, steam-driven kind. Since 1832, the **Strasburg Railroad** (☎717-687-7522; www.strasburgrailroad.com; Rte 741; coach class adult/child $14/8; ☺multiple trips daily, times vary by season; ♿) has run the same route (and speed) to Paradise and back that it does today, and wooden train cars are gorgeously restored with stained glass, shiny brass lamps and plush burgundy seats. Several classes of seats are offered including the private President's Car; there's also a wine and cheese option.

The **Railroad Museum of Pennsylvania** (☏717-687-8628; www.rrmuseumpa.org; Rte 741; adult/child $10/8; ☺9am-5pm Mon-Sat, noon-5pm Sun, closed Sun Nov-Mar; 🚻) has 100 gigantic mechanical marvels to climb around and admire, but even more delightful is the HO-scale **National Toy Train Museum** (☏717-687-8976; www.nttmuseum.org; 300 Paradise Lane; adult/child $6/3; ☺10am-5pm May-Oct, call for hours off-season; 🚻). The push-button interactive dioramas are so up-to-date and clever (such as a 'drive-in movie' that's a live video of kids working the trains), and the walls are packed with so many gleaming railcars, that you can't help but feel a bit of that childlike Christmas-morning wonder. Stop at the Red Caboose Motel next to the museum – you can climb the silo in back for wonderful views ($0.50) and kids can enjoy a small petting zoo.

🛏 p155

The Drive » Continue north on S Ronks Rd past farmland scenery in Ronks (p155), cross busy Rte 30 and carry on for 2 miles to Bird-in-Hand. Hungry? Smoketown's Good 'N Plenty Restaurant (p154) is a mile west of Bird-in-Hand on Rte 340 at the intersection with Rte 896.

--- --- --- --- --- --- --- ---

TRIP HIGHLIGHT

⑤ Bird-in-Hand

The primary reason to make your way to this

DETOUR: GETTYSBURG

Start: ❶ Lancaster

Take US 30 west (also called Lincoln Hwy) for 55 miles into downtown Gettysburg. This tranquil, compact and memorial-laden town saw one of the Civil War's most decisive and bloody battles for three days in July, 1863. It's also where, four months later, Lincoln delivered his Gettysburg Address consecrating, eulogizing and declaring the mission unfinished. At only 200-plus words, it's one of the most defining and effective rhetorical examples in US history. Much of the ground where Robert E Lee's Army of Northern Virginia and Major General Joseph Hooker's Union Army of the Potomac fought can be explored – either in your own car with a map and guide, on an audio CD tour, a bus tour or a two-hour guided ranger tour ($65 per vehicle). The latter is most recommended but if you're short on time it's still worth driving the narrow lanes past fields with dozens of monuments marking significant sites and moments on the battle.

Don't miss the massive new **Gettysburg National Military Park Museum & Visitor Center** (☏717-334-1124; www.gettysburgfoundation.org; 1195 Baltimore Pike; adult/child $12.50/8.50; ☺8am-5pm Nov-Mar, to 6pm Apr-Oct) several miles south of town, which houses a fairly incredible museum filled with artifacts and displays exploring every nuance of the battle; a film explaining Gettysburg's context and why it's considered a turning point in the war; and Paul Philippoteaux's 377-foot cyclorama painting of Pickett's Charge. The aforementioned bus tours and ranger-led tours are booked here. While overwhelming, in the very least, it's a foundation for understanding the Civil War's primacy and lingering impact in the nation's evolution.

The annual Civil War Heritage Days festival, held from the last weekend of June to the first weekend of July, features living history encampments, battle re-enactments, a lecture series and book fair that draws war reenactment aficionados from near and wide. You can find re-enactments throughout the year as well.

WHY THIS IS A CLASSIC TRIP
MICHAEL GROSBERG, AUTHOR

One of the best things about eating Pennsylvania Dutch food – it's certainly not its nutritional content – is how it's eaten: communally, at long tables where you actually have to sit next to and converse with strangers. You won't be strained for conversation, as the massive offerings give you plenty to chat about – the food keeps coming until you can't take another bite.

Top: A horse-drawn buggy drives towards a farm
Left: An Amish girl makes handicrafts at the Bird-in-Hand Farmers Market
Right: Cranberry harvest

KELLY-MOONEY PHOTOGRAPHY/CORBIS ©

delightfully named Amish town is the **Bird-in-Hand Farmers Market** (☎717-393-9674; 2710 Old Philadelphia Pike; ⏰8:30am-5:30pm Wed-Sat Jul-Oct, call for other times of year), which is pretty much a one-stop shop of Dutch Country highlights. There's fudge, quilts and crafts, and you can buy scrapple (pork scraps mixed with cornmeal and wheat flour, shaped into a loaf and fried), homemade jam and shoofly pie (molasses pie sprinkled with a crumbly mix of brown sugar, flour and butter). Two lunch counters sell cheap sandwiches, homemade pretzels and healthy juices and smoothies. It's worth bringing a cooler to stock up for the drive home.

The Drive » It's less than 4 miles east on Old Philadelphia Pike/Rte 340 but traffic can back up, in part because it's a popular route for tourist horse and buggy rides.

- - - - - - - - - - - - - -

❻ Intercourse

Named for the crossroads, not the act, Intercourse is a little more amenable to walking than Bird-in-Hand. The **horse-drawn buggy rides** (☎717-391-9500; www.aaabuggyrides.com; 3529 Old Philadelphia Pike; adult/child $12/6; ⏰9am-7pm Mon-Sat, hours vary; 👶) on offer can also be fun. How much fun depends largely on your driver: some Amish are strict, some liberal, and Mennonites are different again. All drivers strive to present Amish culture to

the 'English' (the Amish term for non-Amish, whether English or not), but some are more openly personal than others.

Kitchen Kettle Village, essentially an open-air mall for tourists with stores selling smoked meats, jams, pretzels and tchotchkes, feels like a Disneyfied version of the Bird-in-Hand Farmers Market. It offers the commercialized 'PA Dutch Country experience' which means your perception of it will depend on your attitude toward a parking lot jammed with tour buses.

The **Quilt Museum at the Old Country Store** (www.ocsquiltmuseum.com; 3510 Old Philadelphia Pike; ⊘9am-5pm, closed Sun)

displays museum-quality artisan quilts and the **Intercourse Canning Company** (13 Center St; ⊘9:30am-5pm Mon-Sat) shows that almost anything can be pickled and put in a mason jar.

✗ p155

The Drive » Head north on Rte 722 and make your first right onto Centerville Rd, a country lane that takes you to Rte 23. Turn right here and it's a few miles to Blue Ball – which has a restaurant and country store or two – and then left on the busier Rte 322 all the way to Ephrata.

⑦ Ephrata

One of the country's earliest religious communities was founded in 1732 by Conrad Beissel, an émigré escaping religious persecution in his native Germany. Beissel, like others throughout human history dissatisfied with worldly

ways and distractions (difficult to imagine what these were in his pre-pre-pre digital age), sought a mystical, personal relationship with God. At its peak there were close to 300 members including two celibate orders of brothers and sisters, known collectively as 'the Solitary,' who patterned their dress after Roman Catholic monks (the last of these passed away in 1813), as well as married 'households' who were less all-in, if you will.

Today, the collection of austere, almost medieval-style buildings of the **Ephrata Cloister** (☏717-733-6600; www.ephratacloister.org; 632 W Main St; adult/child $10/6; ⊘9am-5pm Mon-Sat, from noon Sun) have been preserved and are open to visitors; guided tours are offered or take an audio cell phone tour on your own. There's a small museum and a short film in the visitor

---

THE AMISH

The Amish (ah-mish), Mennonite and Brethren religious communities are collectively known as the 'Plain People.' All are Anabaptist sects (only those who choose the faith are baptized) who were persecuted in their native Switzerland, and from the early 1700s settled in tolerant Pennsylvania. Speaking German dialects, they became known as 'Dutch' (from 'Deutsch'). Most Pennsylvania Dutch live on farms and their beliefs vary from sect to sect. Many do not use electricity, and most opt for horse-drawn buggies – a delightful sight in the area. The strictest believers, the Old Order Amish who make up nearly 90% of Lancaster County's Amish, wear dark, plain clothing (no zippers, only buttons, snaps and safety pins) and live a simple, Bible-centered life – but have, ironically, become a major tourist attraction, thus bringing busloads of gawkers and the requisite strip malls, chain restaurants and hotels that lend this entire area an oxymoronic quality. Because there is so much commercial development – fast-food restaurants, mini-malls, big-box chain stores, tract housing – continually encroaching on multigenerational family farms, it takes some doing to appreciate the unique nature of the area.

center that tells the story of Ephrata's founding and demise – if the narrator's tone and rather somber *mise-en-scène* are any indication, not to mention the extremely spartan sleeping quarters, it was a demanding existence. No doubt Beissel would disapprove of today's Ephrata, whose commercial Main Street is anchored by a Walmart.

If you're around on a Friday, be sure to check out the **Green Dragon Farmers Market** (www.greendragonmarket.com; 955 N State St; 9am-9pm Fri).

The Drive » This is a simple 8.5 mile drive; for the most part, Rte 772/Rothsville Rd between Ephrata and Lititz is an ordinary commercial strip.

TRIP HIGHLIGHT

8 Lititz

Like other towns in Pennsylvania Dutch Country, Lititz was founded by a religious community from Europe, in this case Moravians who settled here in the 1740s. But unlike Ephrata, Lititz was more outward looking and integrated with the world beyond its historic center. Many of its original handsome stone and wood buildings still line its streets. Take a stroll down E Main from the **Sturgis Pretzel House** (717-626-4354; www.juliussturgis.com; 219 E Main St; admission $3; 9am-5pm Mon-Sat;), the first pretzel

✓ **TOP TIP: FARM STAY**

If you like your vacations to be working ones, check out **A Farm Stay** (www.afarmstay.com; r from $60-180) which represents several dozen farm stays that range from stereotypical B&Bs to Amish farms. Most include breakfast, private bathrooms and some activity like milking cows or gathering eggs or simply petting a goat.

factory in the country – you can try rolling and twisting the dough. Across the street is the Moravian Church (c 1787); then head to the intersection with S Broad. Rather than feeling sealed in amber, the small shops, which do seem to relish their small-town quality, are the type that sophisticated urbanites cherish. There's an unusual effortlessness to this vibe, from the Bulls Head Public House, an English-style pub with an expertly curated beer menu, to Greco's Italian Ices, a little ground-floor hole-in-the-wall where local teens and families head on weekend nights for delicious homemade ice cream.

✕ ⊨ p155

The Drive » It's an easy 27 miles on Rte 501 to US 322. Both pass through a combination of farmland and suburban areas.

9 Hershey

Hershey is home to a collection of attractions that detail, hype and, of course, hawk the many trappings of Milton

Hershey's chocolate empire. The pièce de résistance is **Hersheypark** (800-437-7439; www.hersheypark.com; 100 W Hersheypark Dr; adult/child $52/31; 10am-10pm Jun-Aug, 9am-6pm or 8pm Sep-May), an amusement park with more than 60 thrill rides, a zoo and a water park plus various performances and frequent fireworks displays. Don a hairnet and apron, punch in a few choices on a computer screen and voilà, watch your very own chocolate bar roll down a conveyor belt at the Create Your Own Candy Bar ($15) attraction. This forms part of Hershey's Chocolate World, a mock factory and massive candy store with over-stimulating features like singing characters and free chocolate galore. For a more informative visit, try the **Hershey Story**, The Museum on Chocolate Avenue, which explores the life and fascinating legacy of Mr Hershey through interactive history exhibits; try molding your own candy in the hands-on Chocolate Lab.

Eating & Sleeping

Lancaster ❶

✖ Bube's
Brewery Continental, Brewery $$

(www.bubesbrewery.com; 102 North Market St, Mt Joy) This well-preserved 19th-century German brewery-cum-restaurant complex is in Mt Joy, 15 miles northwest of Lancaster off Rte 283. It contains several atmospheric bars and four separate dining rooms (one underground), hosts costumed 'feasts' and, naturally, brews its own beer.

✖ Lancaster
Brewing Co American, Brewery $$

(302 N Plum St; mains $9-22; ⊙11:30am-10pm) Just around the corner from the Cork Factory hotel, the bar here draws young neighborhood regulars and the menu is a big step-up from standard pub fare – rack of wild boar and cranberry sausage is an example. But you can't beat specials like 35¢-wing night.

✖ Ma(i)son French/Italian $$$

(☎717-293-5060; www.maisonlancaster.com; 230 N Prince St; mains $25 ; ⊙5-11pm Wed-Sat) Every worthy current trend of the slowfood, farm-to-table culinary movement is embodied in this sophisticated, though of course rustically furnished, Lancaster restaurant. It's run by a husband-and-wife team who like to keep things local; they value the bounty from the area's farms and live above the restaurant. Expect the menu to change with the seasons – it may include meticulously prepared mains such as Madeira-braised veal and wild nettle sausage pasta. BYOB and reservations recommended.

⌂ Cork Factory Boutique Hotel $$

(☎717-735-2075; www.corkfactoryhotel.com; 480 New Holland Ave; r incl breakfast from $125; ❄🛜) An abandoned-brick behemoth now

houses a stylishly up-to-date hotel only a few miles northeast of the Lancaster city center. Sunday brunch at the hotel's restaurant is a fusion of seasonal new American and down-home comfort cooking.

⌂ Lancaster Arts Hotel Hotel $$

(☎866-720-2787; www.lancasterartshotel.com; 300 Harrisburg Ave; r from $180; P❄🛜) For a refreshingly hip and urban experience, make a beeline to the snazzy **Lancaster Arts Hotel**, housed in an old brick tobacco warehouse and featuring a groovy boutique-hotel ambience.

⌂ Landis Farm Guest House $$

(☎717-898-7028; www.landisfarm.com; 2048 Gochlan Rd, Manheim; d incl breakfast $125; 🛜) A slightly upscale and modern (complete with cable TV and wifi) homestay farm experience can be had **here**, a 200-year-old stone home with pinewood floors.

Smoketown

✖ Good 'N Plenty
Restaurant American $$

(Intersection Rte 896 & Rte 340; mains $11; ⊙11:30am-8pm Mon-Sat, closed Jan; 🚻) Sure, you'll be dining with busloads of tourists and your cardiologist might not approve, but hunkering down at one of the picnic tables here for a family-style meal ($21) is a lot of fun. Besides the main dining room, which is the size of a football field, there are a couple of other mini-areas where you can order from an à la carte menu.

⌂ Fulton Steamboat Inn Hotel $$

(☎717-299-9999; 1 Hartman Bridge Rd; r from $100; ❄🛜🏊) A nautically themed hotel in landlocked Amish country seems like a gimmick even if the inventor of the steamboat was born nearby. The slight kitsch works, however – shiny brass old-timey light fixtures and painterly wallpaper, the hotel's interior is rather elegant and rooms are spacious and comfy. It's located at a crossroads convenient for trips to farm country or Lancaster.

Ronks

✕ Miller's Smorgasbord   Buffet $

(2811 Lincoln Hwy; mains from $8; ⏲11:30am-8pm Mon-Fri, 7:30am-8pm Sat & Sun; 🚗) To smorgasbord ($23) or not to smorgasbord – there's no question. Otherwise, the alternative menu of diner-style dishes is fairly ordinary. The anchor of a touristy complex of shops, this pavilion-size restaurant draws crowds for the buffet featuring Amish-style entrees and desserts.

🛏 Red Caboose Motel & Restaurant   Motel $$

(📞888-687-5005; www.redcaboosemotel.com; 312 Paradise Lane; r from $120; ❄🛜) There's nothing very hobo-esque about a night's sleep in one of these 25-ton cabooses – TVs and mini-fridges included – though the basic furnishings aren't the draw. Spaces are narrow – the width of a train car – but the setting, on a rural lane surrounded by picturesque countryside, is beautiful.

Intercourse ❻

✕ Stoltzfus Farm Restaurant   Diner $$

(📞768 -8156; www.stoltzfusmeats.com; 3718 E Newport Rd; ⏲11:30am-8pm Mon-Sat Apr-Oct,

Fri-Sat only in Nov) An all-you-can-eat, family-style Dutch restaurant with chow-chow (a sweet pickled relish made from a combination of vegetables), pepper cabbage, fried chicken, homemade sausage, shoofly pie and more. It's just country cooking, plain and plentiful, but served by waitresses so preternaturally friendly you wonder for your own hardened soul.

Lititz ❽

✕ Tomato Pie Cafe   Sandwiches $

(23 N Broad St; mains $6; ⏲7am-9pm Mon-Sat; 🛜) Housed in a charming yellow and green home just around the corner from Main St, this cafe gets crowded, especially at lunchtime on weekends. Besides the signature tomato pie, the menu has salads and sandwiches like a peanut butter, Nutella and banana panini, excellent breakfasts and baristas who take their coffee seriously.

🛏 General Sutter Inn   Inn $

(📞717-626-2115; www.generalsutterinn.com; 14 East Main St; r from $70; ❄🛜) The bones of this atmospheric and charming inn anchoring one end of Lititz's Main St date to 1764. Ten wood-floored and cheerful rooms are tastefully furnished with antiques. A new top-floor annex called the Rock Lititz Penthouse has six decidedly modern suites with a playful rock n' roll theme. Attached is the extremely popular craft beer-centric Bull's Head Pub.

Fallingwater A Frank Lloyd Wright masterpiece that blends with its natural setting

Pittsburgh & the Laurel Highlands

13

Visit architectural masterpieces and enjoy whitewater fun around the historically rich highlands region south of Pittsburgh – and check out this culturally vibrant city, too.

TRIP HIGHLIGHTS

104 miles

5 FINISH

Pittsburgh
Sports can't overshadow a vibrant cultural scene

START ● Ligonier

Donegal ●

29 miles

2

Fallingwater
Tour a Frank Lloyd Wright masterpiece

Union
● Town

3

Ohiopyle State Park
Raft the rapids through this park's moutains

38 miles

3–4 DAYS
104 MILES / 167KM

GREAT FOR ...

BEST TIME TO GO

April to November for snow-free outdoor activities.

ESSENTIAL PHOTO

Fallingwater from the waterfall side.

BEST FOR ARCHITECTURE

Tour two Frank Lloyd Wright homes and sleep in another in a single day.

157

13 Pittsburgh & the Laurel Highlands

Most people forget that the British, French and their Native American allies once struggled for control of this southwestern corner of Pennsylvania. The fate of empires hung in the balance in the 1750s when it was primarily a rugged wilderness. The forested landscape remains, of course less wild, but a scenic backdrop nevertheless. And Pittsburgh, its skyscrapers nestled in a compact downtown, provides a civilizing influence.

❶ Ligonier

Compared to the Revolutionary War and the Civil War, the French & Indian War, oft referred to as the 'first world war' and known as the Seven Years War in Europe, is less indelibly stamped as a turning point in America's national narrative. The excellent **Fort Ligonier** (☎724-238-9701; www.fortligonier.org; 200 South Market St; adult/child $10/6; ☉10am-4:30pm Mon-Sat, noon-4:30pm Sun mid-Apr–mid-Nov), both a museum and a reconstructed fort

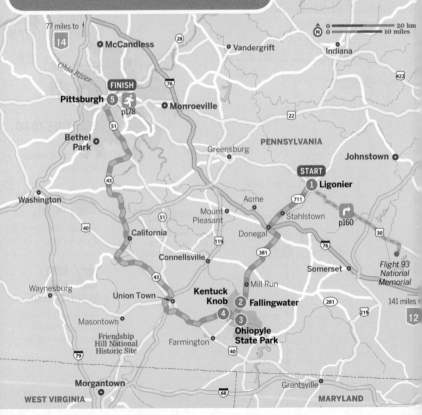

with enthusiastic and knowledgeable historical interpreters, helps correct this oversight, providing an overview of this war over territory and its significance, both in America and elsewhere.

In the fall of 1758 when nearly 5400 soldiers manned the fort it was the second most populated place in Pennsylvania outside of Philadelphia. It takes a leap of imagination today to picture this otherwise ordinary spot, at a relatively busy intersection surrounded by small homes, as a valuable frontier outpost in a clash of empires.

Brigadier General John Forbes meant for Ligonier to be the final link in a chain of fortifications

LINK YOUR TRIP

14 Through the Wilds Along Rte 6

From Pittsburgh take I-79 north to explore small towns and the forested northern tier.

12 Pennsylvania Dutch Country

Follow the PA Turnpike (I-76) south and east or the Lincoln Hwy/Rte30 for a slower, more scenic route to a compact patchwork of Amish farms.

built across Pennsylvania and the staging post for an attack on the French at Fort Duquesne (today the site of Point State Park in Pittsburgh). Artifacts include one of the few intact British red coat uniforms and George Washington's saddle pistols, once owned by General Andrew Jackson. Battle reenactments are held twice a year.

✕ p165

The Drive ›› It's a pretty 12½ miles on Rte 711 south to Donegal and the unsightly PA Turnpike. The overpass will take you to Rte 31 east where you quickly come to the Fire Cafe and Old General Store, two good places to stop for a bite to eat. Take Rte 381 south the rest of the way.

- - - - - - - - - - - -

TRIP HIGHLIGHT

② Fallingwater

A Frank Lloyd Wright masterpiece and a national historic landmark, **Fallingwater** (🖉724-329-8501; www.fallingwater.org; 1491 Mill Run Rd; adult/child $23/17; ⊙hours vary, closed Jan & Feb) looks like an architectural fantasy. Completed in 1938 (when Pittsburgh was called the 'Smoky City') as a weekend retreat for the Kaufmanns, owners of the Pittsburgh department store, the project was extremely over budget at a total of $155,000 though Wright's commission was only $8000 (to give you a sense of building costs at that time, master masons working on the home earned around $0.85

an hour). Built to bring the outside and inside together in harmony, it blends seamlessly with its natural setting, echoing its surroundings through terraces, ledges, cantilevering, circles and semi-circles. One of the most inventive features, which operates as a natural air conditioner, is the open stairway leading directly down to Bear Run stream. Photos can't do it justice – nor can they transmit the sounds of Fallingwater – and you'll likely need a return visit or two to really appreciate Wright's ingenuity and aesthetic vision.

To see inside you must take one of the hourly guided tours (these began in 1964); during busy times tours leave nearly every six minutes, and reservations several months in advance are highly recommended. The earlier in the morning the better, otherwise it can feel crowded; however, unlike tours of other similar sights, there are no velvet ropes. A two-hour tour with photography permitted is offered ($55; times vary depending on day and month). The 2000 acres of attractive forested grounds open at 8:30am and the charming cafe serves seasonally inspired salads and sandwiches made from locally sourced ingredients. Pick up Neil Levine's *The Architecture of Frank*

Lloyd Wright either in the gift shop or before a visit for an excellent overview of Wright's career.

The Drive » It's a simple and quick hop to Ohiopyle only 4 miles away south on Rte 381.

❸ Ohiopyle State Park

During the off-season no more than 70 people call Ohiopyle, a postage-stamp-sized riverside and falls-side hamlet, home. But from the end of May to the beginning of September, this gateway to the 20,000-acre state park of the same name swells with visitors. Most come looking to run the rapids on the Youghiogheny River (locals simply say 'the Yough,' pronounced 'yawk') with one of four well-equipped operators in town including the highly recommended **Laurel Highlands River Tours** (☎800-472-3846; www.laurelhighlands.com). Families and beginners run the middle Yough, while the lower Yough has class III and IV whitewater. But for those who find rafting too tame, kayak clinics and rock climbing are offered. Or take a walk on the nearby Ferncliff Peninsula or the Backman trail which starts in town and heads up to an overlook. There's a swimming beach at a dam on the Yough 12 miles to the south and an extensive network of cross-country skiing trails for the snowbound winter months.

The farmers market, coffee shop, ice cream parlor, restaurants, bar, and a handful of guesthouses are even busier in the summer now that the Great Allegheny Passage, a bike path running from Washington, DC, to Pittsburgh has finally reached Ohiopyle. The viewing spot in front of the falls in town was a construction site at the time of our visit – a new park office and modern visitor center is scheduled to open here in 2014. So far wifi service has generally failed to reach the town or park, allowing you to appreciate the joys of being disconnected for a time.

🛏 p165

The Drive » It's only another 3 miles to Kentuck Knob – cross the bridge at the southern end of Main St and turn right to take the steep and winding Chalk Hill/Ohiopyle Rd to the top. One more left on Kentuck Rd and you're there.

❹ Kentuck Knob

Less well known than Fallingwater, **Kentuck Knob** (☎724-329-1901; www.kentuckknob.com; 723 Kentuck Rd; adult/child $20/14; ⏱hours vary, closed Jan 2–Mar 2), another Frank Lloyd Wright home, is built into the side of a rolling hill with stunning panoramic views. It was completed in 1956 for $82,000 for the Hagan family, friends of the Kaufmans

DETOUR: FLIGHT 93

Start: ❶ Ligonier

If you're driving between the Laurel Highlands and Gettysburg or PA Dutch country further east, you might want to pay your respects to the 40 passengers and crew who struggled to retake control of their plane from hijackers on September 11, 2001. The **Flight 93 National Memorial** (☎814-893-6322; www.nps.gov/flni; Shanksville), about 28 miles southeast of Ligonier on Rte 30/Lincoln Hwy, marks the crash site in a field in rural Somerset Country, only 18 minutes of flying time from the hijacker's intended target, Washington, DC. It's a solemn site with the names of the dead carved on a marble wall aligned in the direction of the flight path leading to a fence, beyond which is their final resting place. Future plans call for extensive landscaping and tree planting on what is now a fairly barren hill.

WHEN HISTORY TURNED IN THE HIGHLANDS

George Washington surrendered once: on July 3, 1754 at **Fort Necessity** (www.nps.gov/fone; 1 Washington Pkwy, Rte 40, Farmington; ⊙9am-5pm daily) when he was a 22-year-old colonel. The first of the French & Indian War battles pitted the undermanned British against the French and their Native American allies. Burned to the ground, the small and rudimentary fort was reconstructed in the 1930s. An excellent visitors center run by the NPS explains the significance of the battle and the war, as does the museum at Fort Ligonier (p158).

A year later and only 2 miles northwest of the fort, Washington officiated at the burial of Major General Edward Braddock, the commander in chief of all British forces in North America and the man responsible for blasting through the forests leading to the major French outpost at Fort Duquesne (now Point State Park in Pittsburgh). Much of Braddock's Road eventually became part of the **National Road**, the first federally financed highway and the busiest in America in the early 1800s. A 90-mile corridor of today's Rte 40 follows the general route of the National Road, which originally led from Maryland to Illinois and was the primary thoroughfare for Americans making their way to the western frontier. Alas, new technology brought change and when the first locomotive-powered train reached the Ohio Valley in 1853, the road's demise began in earnest.

In a curious historical coda, Thomas Edison, Henry Ford and Harvey Firestone – friends and business partners – hopped in their Ford motorcars in 1921 to explore the area along **Rte 40** (primarily western Maryland, but they did make it to the Summit Inn in Uniontown, PA). They spent two weeks every summer from 1915 to 1925 exploring the country, preferring dirt roads like Rte 40 to their paved counterparts. Historians point to their trips as the first to famously link camping, cars and the outdoors and perhaps popularize the idea of the road trip.

and owners of an ice cream manufacturing company, who lived here full time for 28 years. It was purchased by Peter Palumbo (aka Lord Palumbo) in 1986 for $600,000 and opened to the public a decade later – Wright himself never saw the house in its finished state. In general, it's a cozier, family friendly, more modest application of Wright's genius than at Fallingwater.

Of a comparably small scale and a fairly plain exterior typical of Wright's Usonia-style (which stands for United States of North America), the obsessively designed interior – note the hexagonal design and honeycomb skylights – and creative attention applied to the most trivial detail is singularly Wright. Every nook and cranny of the 22,000 sq ft home balances form and function, especially Wright's signature built-ins, like the room-length couch and cabinets. While incredibly impressive and inspiring, a visit might lead to a little dispiriting self-reflection upon comparison to one's own living situation: matching towels to a shower curtain no longer seems like much of an achievement.

House tours last about an hour and you can return to the visitor center, with a small shop and cafe, via a wooded path and a sculpture garden with works by Andy Goldsworthy, Ray Smith and others.

The Drive » US 40 east, part of the historic National Road, passes by Farmington (p165), Fort Necessity National Battlefield and Christian W. Klay Winery, the highest mountaintop vineyard east of the Rockies. Carry on down the mountain and around the city of Uniontown to PA-43 north before merging

Pittsburgh

with PA-51 north to Pittsburgh to complete this 71-mile leg.

- - - - - - - - - - -

⑤ Pittsburgh

Scottish-born immigrant Andrew Carnegie made his fortune here by modernizing steel production, and his legacy is still synonymous with the city and its many cultural and educational institutions. However, the city's industrial buildings are now more likely to house residential lofts and film production studios and the city's abundant greenery, museums and sports teams have long since supplanted the image of billowing smokestacks.

Pittsburghers are proudly over-the-top obsessive fans of their hometown sports teams – the Steelers (football), Penguins (hockey) and Pirates (baseball). If you want to fit in, pony up (around $100) for a classic Franco Harris or Mario Lemieux jersey or the current Pirate all-star Andrew McCutchen. Keep in mind that the 6th St/Roberto Clemente bridge is closed to vehicular traffic when the Steelers and Pirates are in town.

For a taste of the city's ethnic texture, head to the **Strip District** just east of downtown stretching from 14th to 30th St between the Allegheny River and Liberty Ave. Stroll along Penn Ave from 17th to 23rd; it's the city's bustling heart, where one-of-a-kind food markets like **Stamoolis Brothers**, **Pennsylvania Macaroni** and **Wholey** have been selling goods in bulk as well as retail with a heaping of pride and character for the past hundred years.

Between 10am and 3pm is the best time to visit; during the holiday season (when parking is close to impossible), it's especially celebratory and intoxicating, literally, as homemade wine is typically offered for free.

The historic **funicular railroads** (one way adult/child $2.50/1.25; ⊙5:30am-12:40am Mon-Sat, from 7am Sun), circa 1877, that run up and down Mt Washington's steep slopes afford great city views, especially at night. At the start of the Monongahela Incline is Station Square, a group of beautiful, renovated railway buildings that now comprise what is essentially a big ol' mall with restaurants and bars.

For a look around downtown and to check out Pittsburgh's North Shore, follow the walking tour on p178.

✗ ⊨ p165

WRIGHT-EOUS ACCOMMODATION

There's a frisson of excitement when you're sleeping in a house designed by a world famous architect, in this case Frank Lloyd Wright. Part of Polymath Park, a wooded property with three other homes designed by Wright apprentices, **Duncan House** (☑877-833-7829; www.polymathpark.com; 187 Evergreen Ln, Acme; $400 up to three people, $50 per person additional, up to six; ✻⊚) was taken apart piece by piece from its original site in Illinois, transported in four trailers 600 miles to Johnstown, PA and put back together before finally finding its way here and opening to the public in 2007. Don't expect Wright pyrotechnics – the house is a modest Usonia-style design built for just $7000 in 1957. None of the furniture or interior pieces were designed by Wright but are rather standard mid-century modern furnishings.

If you plan to stay at Duncan House while you're on this road trip, you can access it during the drive from Ligonier to Fallingwater. After heading south from Ligonier for 8.5 miles, make a right onto PA-130 heading west for 3 miles. Then make a left onto Ridge Rd which turns into Evergreen Rd a little less than 2 miles later. A half-mile further along you come to Treetops Restaurant where you can check-in.

Sleeping & Eating

Ligonier ➊

✘ Ligonier Tavern — American $$

(137 West Main St; mains $10-20; ⏱11:30am-9pm, to 10pm Fri & Sat, to 8pm Sun) This warm and friendly restaurant, the finest in town, is housed in a thoroughly renovated Victorian home just off the central square. There's a variety of salads and sandwiches at lunch as well as interesting appetizers like lobster wontons, while the dinner menu includes crab cakes, shepherd's pie and cranberry walnut chicken. There's a second-floor outdoor patio and live music some weekend nights. It's a short walk to Fort Ligonier.

Ohiopyle State Park ➌

🛏 Laurel Guesthouse — Guesthouse $$

(☏724-329-8531; www.laurelhighlands.com/lodging; Grant St, Ohiopyle; s/d $80/90; ❄) This small place has three bedrooms, two shared bathrooms and a kitchen and living room furnished like a comfortable suburban-style home. It's especially good for groups, although this and two other similar setups (with the same pricing and contact info), the Ferncliff and MacKenzie guesthouses, get filled in advance during summer months.

Farmington

🛏 Nemacolin Woodlands Resort & Spa — Resort $$$

(☏724-329-8555; www.nemacolin.com; 1001 Lafayette Dr; r from $200; ❄@❄✈🐾🎱) Occupying 2000 acres 8 miles south of Ohiopyle with a grand French chateau–style hotel as the centerpiece, Nemacolin offers a variety of accommodations and restaurants catering to every taste. Rooms in the chateau are large and have high ceilings and chandeliers. Take off-roading lessons, get a gander at the $50 million private art collection, go dog sledding in the winter, tour the 'wildlife habitat' and of course end the day with a massage in Nemacolin's first-class multi-floored spa facilities. Kids are especially well looked after.

Pittsburgh ➎

✘ Primanti Bros — Fast Food $

(☏412-263-2142; www.primantibros.com; 18th St, close to the intersection with Smallman St; sandwiches $6; ⏱24hr) A Pittsburgh institution on the Strip, this always-packed place specializes in greasy and delicious hot sandwiches – from knockwurst and cheese to the 'Pitts-burger cheesesteak.' Other outlets are in Oakland, Market Square in downtown and the South Side.

✘ The Original Oyster House — Seafood $

(20 Market Sq; sandwich $6; ⏱10am-10pm Mon-Sat) Operating in one form or another since 1870 and still drawing crowds of devotees for its deep-fried-fish sandwiches (Pittsburgh wouldn't do it any other way), it's fair to call this restaurant-tavern a Pittsburgh classic. A mix of locals of all stripes form a line out the door at lunchtime but it's a strictly lowdown, pretension-free place with paper plates and plastic cutlery.

🛏 Inn on the Mexican War Streets — Boutique Hotel $$

(☏412-231-6544; www.innonthemexican warstreets.com; 604 W North Ave; r incl breakfast $139-199; P❄❄) This historic mansion on the North Side is near several museums. Expect hearty homemade breakfasts, charming hosts, stunning antique furnishings and an elegant porch, plus a martini lounge and the four-star restaurant Acanthus.

🛏 Omni William Penn Hotel — Hotel $$$

(☏412-281-7100; www.omnihotels.com; 530 William Penn Place; r from $200; P❄❄) Though originally built by Henry Clay Frick nearly 100 years ago, his European inspiration is alive and well in this elegant and stately downtown behemoth. High tea is served in the grand lobby which is (surprisingly) otherwise a welcoming meeting place for non-guests who tend to grab coffees from, yes, the attached Starbucks. Above-average service, contemporary room furnishings, a spa, several dining options and a newly reopened basement speakeasy bar round out the offerings.

Pine Creek Gorge *Get back to nature at the PA Grand Canyon*

Through the Wilds Along Route 6

14

Travel through a region where the oil industry was born, past an endless canopy of flowering hardwood trees, with detours for canyon hikes and gorge views.

TRIP HIGHLIGHTS

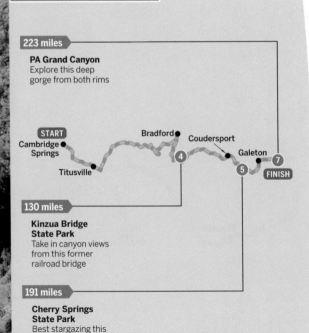

223 miles

PA Grand Canyon
Explore this deep gorge from both rims

START
Cambridge Springs

Titusville

Bradford

Coudersport

Galeton

FINISH

130 miles

Kinzua Bridge State Park
Take in canyon views from this former railroad bridge

191 miles

Cherry Springs State Park
Best stargazing this side of the Mississippi

4 DAYS
223 MILES / 359 KM

GREAT FOR...

BEST TIME TO GO
Fall foliage season is mid-September to October.

ESSENTIAL PHOTO
Gorge views from Leonard Harrison State Park, PA Grand Canyon.

BEST FOR HIKING
Thousands of miles of trails and parks galore.

14 Through the Wilds Along Route 6

Interspersed throughout this rural region are regal buildings and grand mansions, remnants of a time when lumber, coal and oil brought great wealth and the world's attention to this corner of Pennsylvania. Several museums tell the boom and bust industrial story. But natural resources of another kind remain – known as 'the Wilds', roads and hundreds of miles of trails snake through vast national forests and state parks.

1 Cambridge Springs

The **Riverside Inn & Dinner Theatre** (☎814-398-4645; www. theriversideinn.com; One Fountain Ave; r from $100; ❋☎) is a rambling throwback to another era, when Cambridge Springs was a resort town booming with visitors seeking the medicinal properties of its mineral springs. Several restorations, the most recent in 2010, have rehabilitated some

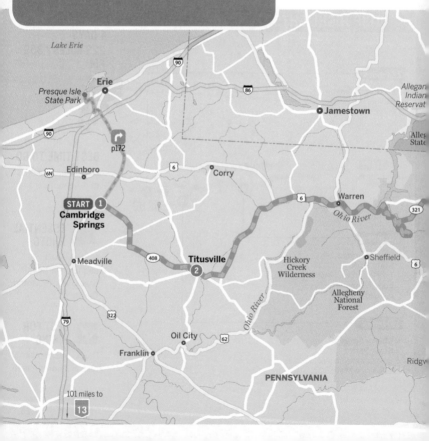

of this grand survivor's Victorian charm and elegance, however not much has been updated: floorboards are still warped and many of the decorations are tchotchkes typical of a roadside garage sale. And sure, the mattress may sag a little and lighting can be dim but hey, you're here for the atmosphere.

It's definitely worth timing a visit for the third weekend in April for the inn's **Bluegrass Music Festival,** when dozens of talented

musicians gather in ad hoc groupings in every nook and cranny. There are also more organized performances in the downstairs theater. If you can pluck a banjo

or a fiddle feel free to sit in.

The Drive » Most of the 27 miles to Titusville are on the fairly flat and rural PA-408 east past farms and patches of forest.

LINK YOUR TRIP

 Finger Lakes Loop

It's less than an hour north on Rte 15 from Wellsboro to Corning, NY, the southern end of a tour to beautiful lakeside wineries.

13 Pittsburgh & the Laurel Highlands

From Cambridge Springs, it's less than two hours south on I-279 to Pittsburgh and the highlands.

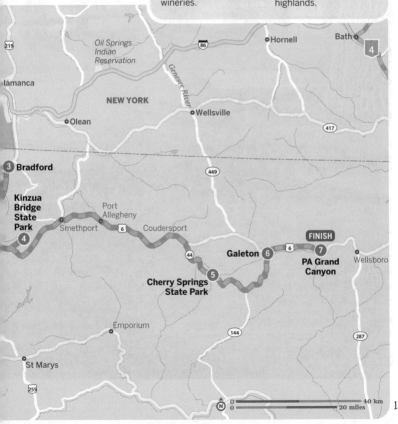

DETOUR:
PRESQUE ISLE STATE PARK

Start: ❶ Cambridge Springs

Jutting out from the city of Erie into the lake of the same name, Presque Isle State Park shoots north and then curves back upon itself like Cape Cod in Massachusetts. A slow crawl on the 13-mile loop road that circumnavigates the sandy peninsula takes you past windswept swimming beaches and walking and biking trails that lead past ponds and wooded areas. In warm weather, the picnic areas get crowded and cyclists, runners and rollerbladers compete for space. The modern and comprehensive **Tom Ridge Environmental Center** (📞814-833-7424; www.trecpi.org; 301 Peninsula Dr; ⊗10am-6pm), on the mainland side just before the park entrance and across the street from an amusement park, pretty much covers everything you'd want to know about the park, with interactive exhibits for kids. Things pretty much shut down from November to January when snow squalls and cold air blanket the region.

To visit, head north on US 19 from Cambridge Springs for 27 miles to Erie and the park.

❷ Titusville

Before there was oil, coal and timber – with a boost from railroads – fueled Pennsylvania's economy. But even before Edwin Drake's Eureka moment in August 1859 (after many failed attempts) when he invented a new method of drilling for oil without collapsing the hole, oil had been seeping from the ground reportedly for centuries. After that first year, wells were producing 4500 barrels. Only three years later the total was three million. And 10 years later kerosene was the nation's fuel. When Edison electrified part of lower Manhattan in 1882, kerosene's relevance was threatened, but along

came the automobile and once again gas was king.

To get a sense of this chapter in Pennsylvania's history, head to the **Drake Well Museum** (📞814-827-2797; www.drakewell.org; 202 Museum Ln; adult/child $10/5; ⊗9am-5pm, from noon Sun) which has a replica of Drake's engine house, working antique machinery, a large gallery of exhibits and even an olfactory challenge asking you to smell oil from around the world. Learn about the local boom towns that drew more migrants than California's Gold Rush and how Drake never capitalized on his invention and died virtually broke.

The Drive ⟫ After leaving Titusville on Rte 27 heading

east, take the junction to the left onto Enterprise-Titusville Rd for about 3.5 miles before hooking up again with Rte 27 heading north. Connect with Rte 6 east and then to Rte 59 closer to the Allegheny Reservoir. If you have time, turn right on Forest Rd/Rte 262 just before the reservoir and follow it to the southern end of Kinzua Creek before connecting with Rte 321 N to take you back to Rte 59. Views from this high plateau are worth the detour while you're on this 72-mile drive. Then it's Rte 770 to Rte 219 which turns into a four-lane highway.

❸ Bradford

Evidence of Bradford's glory days when oil barons called the town home can still be seen in a handful of impressive buildings on Main Street. Otherwise, downtown feels neglected and vacant, highlighting the disparity between the present and the past, when this small corner of northwestern Pennsylvania was an economic powerhouse. The **Penn Brad Oil Museum** (☏814-362-1955; www.pennbradoilmuseum. org; 901 South Ave; adult/child $5/free; ⊙10am-4pm Tue-Sat), like the Drake Well Museum in Titusville, tells the story of the world's first billion-dollar oil field and includes a 'model home' of an oil field worker and an 80ft tall working rig typical of the boom time in the late-1800s. Perhaps unsurprisingly, the museum comes off as something of an oil industry booster, even a promoter of today's controversial method of fracking, which has unlocked the region's vast natural gas deposits in the Marcellus Shale – at what cost is the question. If you were to continue driving on Rte 6 all the way east to the Poconos, you'd notice the enormous infrastructure supplying fracking's boom – trucks, equipment suppliers, etc – is the most striking new feature of the landscape.

🛏 p175

The Drive 》 Rte 219 south takes you all the way back to Rte 6 at Lantz Corners where you head east to Mt Jewett on this 28-mile drive.

TRIP HIGHLIGHT

❹ Kinzua Bridge State Park

The Kinzua railroad viaduct, once the highest and one of the longest railroad suspension bridges in the world, was built in 1882 to transport coal across the valley to customers to the north. In 2003, as it was undergoing repairs to reinforce its deteriorating structure, a tornado swept through the valley destroying a portion of the bridge. After finally being decommissioned, it was reopened as a 'skywalk' in 2011 and it and the surrounding 329 acres became the **Kinzua Bridge State Park** (☏814-965-2646; www. visitanf.com; 1712 Lindholm Rd). The remaining six towers now carry people instead of trains 600ft out where it dead-ends in an overlook – a small section here has a glass floor so you can see directly to the valley floor 225 ft below.

The Drive 》 Head through Smethport towards Port Allegheny on this 59-mile drive. After Port Allegheny, Rte 6 follows the Allegheny River, but further east it narrows into a stream. Several miles after Coudersport (p175) – that garish gold-colored behemoth on Main St is the former headquarters of cable giant Adelphia Communications Co – make a right onto PA-44 south.

TRIP HIGHLIGHT

❺ Cherry Springs State Park

Ponder the immensity of the universe at this dark sky park, considered one of the best places for stargazing east of the Mississippi. **Cherry Springs** (☏814-435-5010; www. visitpaparks.com; PA 44, Potter Cty) is one of only five parks in the country (the others are in Big Bend, Texas; Death Valley, California; Natural Bridges, Utah; and Clayton Lake, New Mexico), to have received the highest rating or certification by the organization in charge of these sorts of things – the International Dark Sky Association (www. darksky.org).

Essentially two large open fields, one a former runway, at an elevation of 2300 ft, Cherry Springs is blessed to be surrounded by the hills of the 262,000-acre Susquehannock State Forest that tend to block any artificial light. The area also has an extremely low population density. Beginning about an hour after sunset on Friday and Saturday nights from Memorial Day to Labor Day (Saturdays only from mid-April to end of May and September to the end of October), the park hosts free laser-guided and telescope-assisted tours of the constellations. Crowds of several hundred people are common on clear nights in July and August when the Milky Way is almost directly overhead.

🛏 p175

The Drive » Take PA-44 south to PA-144 north to Galeton. Both roads twist and turn down the mountain until 144 levels out near Rte 6.

⑥ Galeton

Looking out from any vista in the area, it's difficult to imagine that Galeton was once almost completely denuded of tress, logged until hardly any were left standing. Until the early 1800s only the Seneca and other Native Americans encountered these dense woods, but at the turn of the last century, the lumber industry arrived, scraping the land bare but also bringing prosperity and employment. The men who worked in the camps were called 'wood hicks'. Springtime melt meant water was plentiful to float log rafts, white pine and hemlock primarily, to lumber mills along the Susquehana River.

The **Pennsylvania Lumber Museum** (📞814-435-2652; www.lumbermuseum.org; 5660 US Rte 6 West; ⏰9am-5pm Wed-Sun, call for winter hrs) includes a re-created lumber camp typical of the late 1800s, two large locomotives housed

in a saw mill and a modernized new visitor center due to open in 2014 with exhibits on the history of our relationship with forests. Logging companies are still active in the northern tier but are subject to regulations to keep deforestation at bay. Wildlife such as deer, beaver, elk and river otters were slowly reintroduced throughout the 1900s. Consider a visit during the annual **Bark Peeler's Convention** (July 6–7), an Olympics for lumberjacks with events like grease pole fighting, sawing, burling (running on a log in a pond) and the more tongue-in-cheek tobacco spitting and frog jumping. Coming immediately after Galeton's large 4th of July celebration, accommodation is extremely tight.

The Drive » Head east on Rte 6 and hang a right onto Forest/Colton Rd just before the Ansonia cemetery; a sign for Colton Point State Park marks the turn. It's another 5 miles up a narrow and winding paved road until you reach the overlook.

TRIP HIGHLIGHT

⑦ PA Grand Canyon

Two state parks on either side of the 47-mile-long Pine Creek Gorge make up what's commonly referred to as the 'PA Grand Canyon'. Access

to the west rim of the canyon is from **Colton Point State Park** which has a several view points, camping grounds and trails into the forest of maple, oak, poplar, aspen and beech trees. The more visited and developed **Leonard Harrison State Park** (📞570-724-3061; www.visitPAparks.com) on the east rim has possibly better, fuller views of the 800ft canyon (it's 1450 ft at its deepest) and Tioga State Forest beyond. It's a trade-off, however, since it has a paved plaza with steps down to an observation area and there's a gift shop next to the park office.

The way out here is via a turnoff on Rte 6 not far past the one for the Colton Point side. Eventually, you take Rte 660 west past some suburban style homes and pretty farmland. Both parks have a trail called the **Turkey Path** that descends to the canyon floor – it's a tough 3-mile round-trip on the Colton Point Side but you can catch your breath with a stop at a 70-ft waterfall.

If you want to explore the east rim of the canyon one day and the west rim the next, consider staying overnight in nearby Wellsboro (p175) – it's just 10 miles east from the canyon on Rte 660.

Eating & Sleeping

Bradford ❸

🛏 Lodge at Glendorn   Lodge $$$

(☎800-843-8568; www.glendorn.com; 1000 Glendorn Dr; r from $450) It's no surprise that this 1200-acre estate is easily the most luxurious accommodation in the region; after all, it was built as the family retreat for the scions of Clayton Glenville Dorn who made a fortune during the late 18th century oil boom. There's a 'big house' and a dozen cabins done up in log cabin, rustic panache with more than 50 fireplaces throughout the property. Outdoor activities like snowmobiling, skeet shooting and fishing are offered.

Coudersport

🍴 Fezz's Diner   Diner $

(Mill Creek Plaza, Rte 6; mains $6; ⏰6am-3pm Mon-Wed, to 9pm Thu-Sat, 8am-3pm Sun) This proudly retro diner doesn't seem to have changed much since it was shipped lock, stock and barrel from Bethlehem, PA in the mid-1950s. Expect good burgers, large portions and at times, old-school – ie delayed and less than solicitous – service.

Cherry Springs State Park ❺

🛏 Cherry Springs State Park Campsite   Camping $

(☎in Galeton 814-435-5010; PA Rte 44, Cherry Springs State Park; tent sites $15; ⏰Apr 15–Nov

15) There's no reason to call it quits when there's constellations and stars still overhead. Pitch a tent on this primitive site – no electricity, no showers, vault toilets, no pets and no reservations. It's a small area nestled between the two stargazing fields. The campsite at nearby Lyman Run State Park has hot showers and flush toilets.

Galeton ❻

🛏 Susquehannock Lodge   Inn $

(☎814-435-2163; www.susquehannock-lodge.com; 5039 Rte 6, Ulysses; r with breakfast $75; ❄🢄) A homey and comfortable place halfway between Coudersport and Galeton and 20 miles from Cherry Springs State Park. The owners, a couple who relocated from Philadelphia decades ago, are happy to help sort out activities in the area.

Wellsboro

🛏 Penn Wells Hotel & Lodge   Hotel $$

(☎800-545-2446; www.pennwells.com; 62 Main St; r incl breakfast from $100; ❄🢄🢅) This large, historic hotel circa 1869 conveniently located in 'downtown' Wellsboro has a variety of rooms, some dated. A new, modern annex is just down the block; it's more bland although it does have a small swimming pool and gym.

STRETCH YOUR LEGS
PHILADELPHIA

Start/Finish: Rittenhouse Square

Distance: 2.8 miles

Duration: 2.5 hours

Historic Philadelphia, so well-known, lives side by side with contemporary skyscrapers and fashionable squares. This walk takes in the old and the new, which often means regal-looking spaces and structures from centuries past revitalized for a vibrant modern city.

Take this walk on Trips

Rittenhouse Square

This elegant square, with its wading pool and fine statues, marks the heart of the prosperous Center City neighborhood. Several excellent restaurants with sidewalk seating in warm weather line the east side of the square – a great spot for people watching.

The Walk » It's only 10 steps or so from the southeast corner of the square to the next stop.

Philadelphia Art Alliance

Housed in a Gilded Age mansion, one of the few buildings on the square to escape the skyscraper age, is the **Philadelphia Art Alliance** (☏216-646-4302; www.philartalliance.org; 261 S 18th St; adult/child $5/3; ⏰11am-5pm Tue-Fri, from noon Sat & Sun). Its exhibits of modern crafts are always interesting.

The Walk » Walk back through the square and exit on the west side onto Locust St. Turn left on 21st before making a left on Delancey Pl.

Rosenbach Museum & Library

This three-story brick townhouse is an unassuming repository of treasures and a bibliophiles dream. The collection includes 30,000 rare books, drawings by William Blake, James Joyce's original manuscript for *Ulysses* and a re-creation of the modernist poet Marianne Moore's Greenwich Village apartment.

The Walk » Head east on Delancey Pl for three blocks, then left on 17th St and then right on Spruce. The modern Kimmel Center for the Performing Arts is on the right side of the intersection at Broad St.

Avenue of the Arts

Tours of **Kimmel Center for the Performing Arts** (☏215-790-5800; www.kimmelcenter.org; cnr Broad & Spruce Sts), Philadelphia's most active center for fine music, are available at 1pm Tuesday through Saturday. When walking north on Broad St (aka 'the Avenue of the Arts'), look up. The facades of these early incarnations of skyscrapers have signature flourishes like terracotta roofs and elaborate filigree work

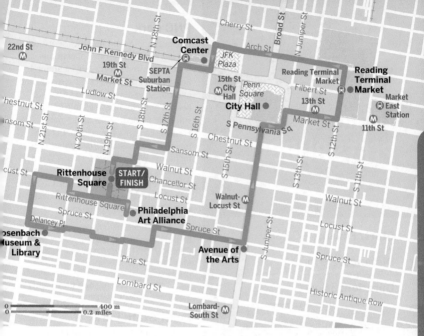

highlighted even more when they're illuminated at night.

The Walk » City Hall is dead center down Broad St; it's visible the entire way. Entering from the south portal, look for the keystone sculpture of Moses.

City Hall

The majestic 548-ft tall **City Hall** sits in the center of the original orderly city between the Delaware and Schuykill Rivers. Standing at the intersection of Market and Broad Sts, the avenues shoot out in plumb-straight lines. It was the world's tallest occupied building until 1909 and the tallest in Philly until 1987. Check out the 250 sculptures including a 37-ft tall, 27-ton statue of William Penn on the top.

The Walk » Walk through the east-side portal; look for the Benjamin Franklin keystone. Tower and building tours leave from here. The two-block stretch of Market St isn't the prettiest; turn left at 12th.

Reading Terminal Market

Housed in the railroad terminal since 1892 and renovated in the 1990s, the

Reading Terminal Market (☎215-922-2317; www.readingterminalmarket.org; 51 N 12th St; ⏰8am-5:30pm Mon-Sat, 9am-4pm Sun) is a bustling cornucopia of cuisines, crowded with tourists and locals at lunchtime. The market has everything: cheesesteaks, Amish crafts, regional specialties, ethnic eats, top-quality butchers, produce, cheese, flowers, bakeries and more.

The Walk » Head west on Arch until you reach JFK Plaza and Robert Indiana's *LOVE* sculpture. Good food trucks congregate here at lunchtime.

Comcast Center

An entrance to this skyscraper, the tallest in the city, leads into a massive all-glass atrium. On the back wall is the world's largest high-definition screen. It's always on, displaying curious, sometimes *trompe l'oeil* images.

The Walk » Walking south on 17th you'll pass a Lichtenstein sculpture and several hotels. Go right on Sansom for a block of nice little boutiques and then left on 18th or 19th to return to Rittenhouse Square.

STRETCH
YOUR LEGS
PITTSBURGH

Start/Finish: PNC Park

Distance: 2.9 miles

Duration: 3 hours

To those aware only of the city's well-known industrial past, this walk – which includes riverfront parkways, world-renowned arts institutions and a gleaming place of pilgrimage for its rabid sports fans – will come as a revelation.

Take this walk on Trip

13

PNC Park

Pittsburgh lives and breathes sports and the city's beloved Pirates play in this widely admired fan-friendly stadium. It has spectacular views of the city's skyline and the Allegheny River that runs just behind outfield; only a couple of home run have made it as far as the river. Four of the park's five entrances have massive bronze statues of Pirates legends including Willie Stargell, Honus Wagner, Bill Mazeroski and Roberto Clemente. You can enter the gates near the Clemente and Mazeroski statues without a ticket to walk along the river promenade.

The Walk » Cross the Allegheny River on the pedestrian-friendly, bright-yellow Roberto Clemente/6th St Bridge (no cars are allowed when the Pirates or Steelers are in town). Take the stairway on your right down to the riverfront trail; follow westward then take a stairway up to 'woodlands' section of the park.

Point State Park

At the tip of the city's downtown triangle and spot of its founding is a newly renovated waterfront park which has spectacular unobstructed views of the Ohio, Allegheny and Monongahela rivers (the Ohio River flows from here into the Gulf of Mexico) and south and north shore neighborhoods. The sole remaining part of Fort Pitt, the oldest in the city, and a museum have excellent exhibits displaying 18th-century artifacts. The lovely landscaped pathways and lawns are popular with strollers, cyclists, loungers and runners.

The Walk » Exit the park at the Blvd of the Allies. Turn left at Stanwix St where you'll see the distinctive lattice pattern of the United Steelworkers Union headquarters and then right on Forbes Ave.

Market Square

In the late 18th century there were a few market stalls and a courthouse here. Now downtown's cobblestone central plaza includes a mix of generic fast-food restaurants as well as a few genuine Pittsburgh institutions. Grab

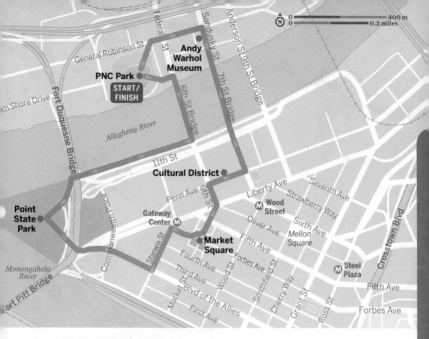

a sandwich from Primanti Bros or the Original Oyster House. Towering over the southern end of the square is the oddly imposing Philip Johnson designed PPG Place skyscraper, a marriage between gothic medievalism and all-glass postmodernism.

The Walk » Exit onto Market St at the northern side of the plaza and walk two blocks to Liberty Ave; make a left onto 6th St to begin exploring the Cultural District.

Cultural District

This once-seedy neighborhood has been revitalized and its 19th-century loft buildings have been converted into contemporary art galleries, shops, restaurants and performance spaces. The ornately designed Heinz Hall, once the site of an abandoned movie theater, now houses the Pittsburgh Symphony Orchestra. Take a break at Agnes R Katz Plaza at the corner of Penn and Seventh St; the granite benches and fountain here were designed by the renowned artist Louise Bourgeois.

The Walk » Cross back over the Allegheny to the North Shore on the Andy Warhol/7th St Bridge; the two other 'three sisters' bridges, identical suspension bridges built in the late 1920s, are on either side.

Andy Warhol Museum

The seven floors of the **Andy Warhol Museum** (📞412-237-8300; www.warhol.org; 117 Sandusky St; adult/child $20/10; ⏰10am-5pm Tue-Thu, Sat & Sun, to 10pm Fri) celebrate Pittsburgh's coolest native son, who became famous for his pop art, avant-garde movies, celebrity connections and Velvet Underground spectaculars. The collection includes his first works on canvas, such as his Campbell's soup can series, his award-winning commercial art, Brillo boxes, *Interview* covers and Elvis portraits. The museum's theater hosts frequent film screenings and quirky performers. Friday night cocktails at the museum are popular with Pittsburgh's gay community.

The Walk » It's only two blocks west on General Robinson St back to PNC Park.

Washington DC, Maryland & Delaware Trips

AMERICA IS CONDENSED INTO HER CAPITAL AND THE REGION THAT SURROUNDS IT. Maryland's unofficial motto is 'America in Miniature,' and since Delaware is basically an extension of Maryland, you could say the 42nd- and 49th-largest states in the union encapsulate said Republic.

Culturally, Delaware balances the gritty northeast edge of Philly with a certain laid-back charm. Maryland's tougher to pin down. Green mountains in the panhandle to aristocratic horse country in the center, Chesapeake Bay running throughout, a north–south intermarriage of cultures and the cross-pollination of immigrant groups create a state that mixes small towns and wealthy estates with sharp cliffs and soft, tide-kissed wetlands.

Washington, DC Thomas Jefferson Memorial (Trip 15)
ALTRENDO TRAVEL/GETTY IMAGES ©

Washington DC, Maryland & Delaware Trips

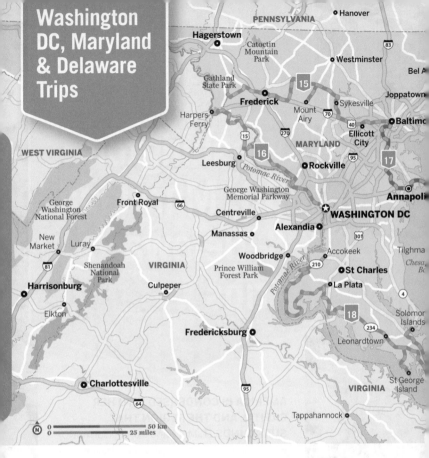

Maryland's National Historic Road 2 days
Drive from Baltimore's docks to the tiny villages of the Catoctin Mountains. (p185)

Along the C&O Canal 2 days
Ferries, bike paths and mountain valleys all line this old canal path. (p195)

Classic Trip
Maritime Maryland 4 days
Get into seaside towns, miles of marsh and sweaty Chesapeake crab shacks. (p203)

Southern Maryland Triangle 2 days
Historical trails, preserved colonial towns and pine-studded beaches converge south of DC. (p217)

Delmarva 3 days
Miles of beach and boardwalks abut barrier islands and summer resort towns. (p227)

Eastern Shore Odyssey 3 days
Fishing villages and farm towns await on this isolated wetland peninsula. (p237)

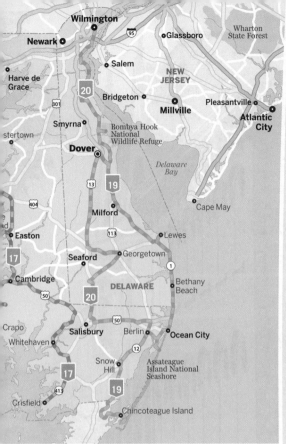

✓ DON'T MISS

Urban Exploration

Cities like Baltimore and Frederick are steeped in history, good eats and hot nightlife. See them on Trip 15

River Runs

The Potomac River snakes by Maryland, West Virginia and Virginia, framed by mountains and cultural hotspots. Follow the river path on Trip 16

Isolated Adventures

Southern Maryland lays off the beaten path, and there are miles of lonely back roads to stomp down. Get romantically lost on Trip 18

Get Tanned

There are beach resorts a-plenty and even more quiet parks and nature reserves near the Atlantic. Swim ashore or sun away on Trip 19

Eat Crabs

Enjoy Maryland's favorite pastime of tucking into crabs, beer and corn. Get spicy with these crustaceans on Trip 17

Baltimore Inner Harbour

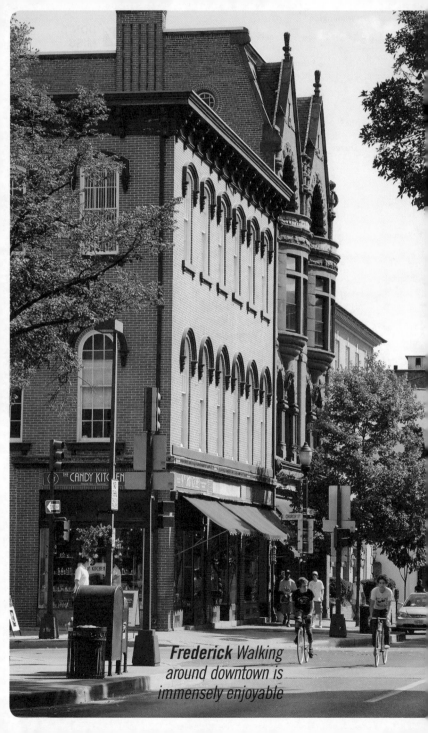

Frederick *Walking around downtown is immensely enjoyable*

Maryland's National Historic Road

15

From Baltimore's salty docks to the forested foothills around old Frederick, delve into the past of one of the most diverse states in the country.

26 miles

Sykesville
Old rail town on a bucolic hill

Gathland
State Park

FINISH

7

New Market

Mount Airy

3

2

Baltimore

START

Frederick
Picture-perfect town center framed by lively arts district

73 miles

Patapsco Valley
Green nature hikes by a rushing river

13 miles

2 DAYS
92 MILES / 150KM

GREAT FOR...

BEST TIME TO GO
April to June to soak up late spring's sunniness and warmth.

ESSENTIAL PHOTO
The historic buildings lining New Market, MD.

BEST FOR OUTDOORS
Hiking along the bottom of Patapsco Valley.

185

WILLIAM S. KUTA/ALAMY ©

15

Maryland's National Historic Road

For such a small state, Maryland has a staggering array of landscapes and citizens, and this trip engages both of these elements of the Old Line State. Move from Chesapeake Bay and Baltimore, a port that mixes bohemians with blue-collar workers, through the picturesque small towns of the Maryland hill country, into the stately cities that mark the lower slopes of the looming Catoctin Mountains.

❶ Baltimore

Maryland's largest city is one of the most important ports in the country, a center for the arts and culture and an entrepôt of immigrants from Greece, El Salvador, East Africa, the Caribbean and elsewhere. These streams combine into an idiosyncratic culture that, in many ways, encapsulates Maryland's depth of history and prominent diversity – not just of race, but creed and socioeconomic status.

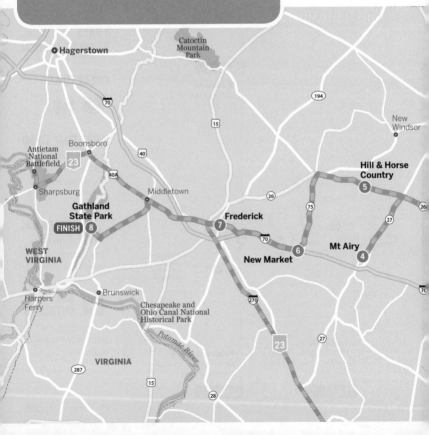

Baltimore was a notable hold-out against the British military during the War of 1812, even after Washington DC fell. The morning after an intense shelling, staring 'through the rockets' red glare,' local lawyer Francis Scott Key saw that 'our flag was still there' and wrote *The Star-Spangled Banner*. The history of that battle and the national anthem are explored at **Fort McHenry** (☏410-962-4290; 2400 E Fort Ave; adult/child $7/free; ☺8am-5pm), located in South Baltimore.

Have a wander through nearby **Federal Hill Park** (300 Key Hwy), a 70-acre hill that rises above the city, and admire the view out over the harbor.

✕ 🛏 p193

The Drive » Get on US 40 (Baltimore National Pike – and the basis of the National Historic Road this trip is named for) westbound in Baltimore. The easiest place to access it is at Charles and Franklin St. Franklin becomes US 40/the Pike as you head west out of downtown Baltimore, into the woods that mark the edges of the Patapsco Valley. The whole drive takes about 30 minutes in traffic.

TRIP HIGHLIGHT

② Patapsco Valley

The Patapsco river and river valley are the defining geographic features of the region, running through Central Maryland to Chesapeake Bay. To explore the area, head to **Patapsco Valley State Park** (☏410-461-5005; 8020 Baltimore National Pike, Ellicott City; ☺9am-sunset), an enormous protected area – one of the oldest in the state – that runs for 32 miles along a whopping 170 miles of trails. The main visitor center provides insight into the settled history of the area, from Native Americans to the present, and is housed in a 19th-century stone cottage that looks as though it were plucked from a CS Lewis bedtime story.

LINK YOUR TRIP

17 Maritime Maryland

Head south then east from Baltimore into Maryland's rural bayside villages.

23 The Civil War Tour

In Gathland State Park, head 10 miles west to Antietam to begin exploring America's seminal internal conflict.

The Drive ›› Get back on the Pike/US 40 westbound until you see signs to merge onto I-70W, which is the main connecting road between Baltimore and Central and Western Maryland. Get on 70, then take exit 80 to get onto MD-32 (Sykesville Rd). Follow for about 5 miles into Sykesville proper.

TRIP HIGHLIGHT

③ Sykesville

Like many of the towns in the Central Maryland hill country between Baltimore and Frederick, Sykesville has a **historic center** that looks and feels picture perfect. **Main Street**, between Springfield Ave and Sandosky Rd, is filled with structures built between the 1850s and 1930s, and almost looks like an advertisement for small-town America.

The old Baltimore & Ohio (B&O) train station, now **Baldwin's** restaurant (7618 Main St), was built in 1883 in the Queen Anne style. The station was the brainchild of E Francis Baldwin, a Baltimore architect who designed many B&O stations, giving that rail line a satisfying aesthetic uniformity along its extent.

Fun fact: Sykesville was founded on land James Sykes bought from George Patterson. Patterson was the son of Elizabeth Patterson and Jerome Bonaparte, brother of Napoleon. The French emperor insisted his brother marry royalty and never let his sister-in-law (the daughter of a merchant) in to France; her family estate (which formed the original parcel of land that the town grew from) is the grounds of Sykesville proper.

✕ p193

The Drive ›› Although this trip is largely based on US 40 – the actual National Historic Road – detour up to Liberty Rd (MD-26) and take that west 8 miles to Ridge Rd (MD-27). Take Ridge Rd/27 south for 5.5 miles to reach Mt Airy.

---

④ Mt Airy

Mt Airy is the next major (we use that term with a grain of salt) town along the B&O railroad and US 40/the National Historic Road. Like Sykesville, it's a handsome town, with a stately center that benefited from the commerce the railway brought westward from Baltimore. When the railway was replaced by the highway, Mt Airy, unlike other towns, still retained much of its prosperity thanks to the proximity of jobs in cities like DC and Baltimore.

Today the town centers on a **historic district** of 19th- and early 20th-century buildings, many of which can be found around Main Street. The posher historical homes near 'downtown' Mt Airy

ATLANTIDE PHOTOTRAVEL/CORBIS ©

DETOUR:
CALVERT CLIFFS

Start: ❶ Baltimore

In Southern Maryland, 75 miles south of Baltimore via US 301 and MD-4, skinny Calvert County scratches at Chesapeake Bay and the Patuxent River. This is a gentle landscape ('user-friendly' as a local ranger puts it) of low-lying forests, estuarine marshes and placid waters, but there is one rugged feature: the Calvert Cliffs. These burnt umber pillars stretch along the coast for some 24 miles, and form the seminal landscape feature of **Calvert Cliffs State Park** (📞301-743-7613; 9500 H. G. Trueman Road, Lusby; ☺sunrise to sunset; 🅿️🚻🐾), where they front the water and a pebbly, honey-sand beach scattered with driftwood and drying beds of kelp.

Back in the day (10–20 million years ago), this area sat submerged under a warm sea. Eventually, that sea receded and left the fossilized remains of thousands of prehistoric creatures embedded in the cliffs. Fast forward to the 21st century, and one of the favorite activities of Southern Maryland families is coming to this park, strolling across the sand and plucking out fossils and sharks' teeth from the pebbly debris at the base of the cliffs. Over 600 species of fossils have been identified at the park. In addition, a full 1079 acres and 13 miles of the park are set aside for trails and hiking and biking.

While this spot is pet- and family-friendly, fair warning: it's a 1.8 mile walk from the parking lot to the open beach and the cliffs, so this may not be the best spot to go fossil hunting with very small children unless they can handle the walk. Also: don't climb the cliffs as erosion makes this an unstable and unsafe prospect.

were built in the Second Empire, Queen Anne and Colonial Revival styles, while most 'regular' homes are two-story, center gable 'I-houses,' once one of the most common housing styles in rural America in the 19th century, now largely displaced in this region by modern split-levels.

The Drive ›› Take Ridge Rd/ MD-27 back to Liberty Rd/MD-26. Turn left and proceed along for 10 miles to reach Elk Run.

❺ Hill & Horse Country

Much of Frederick, Carroll, Baltimore and Hartford counties consist of trimmed, rolling grassy hills intersected by copses of pine and broadleaf woods and tangled hedgerows; it's the sort of landscape that could put you in mind of the bocage country of northern France or rural England. A mix of working farmers and wealthy city folks live out here, and horse breeding and raising is a big industry.

It can be pretty enchanting just driving around and getting lost on some of the local back roads, but if you want a solid destination, it's tough to go wrong

with **Elk Run Vineyards** (📞410-775-2513; www.elkrun. com; 15113 Liberty Road, Mt Airy; tastings from $5, tours free; ☺10am-5pm Tue-Sat, 1-5pm Sun), almost exactly halfway between Mt Airy and New Market. Free tours are offered at 1pm and 3pm, and tastings can be arranged without reservations for at least two people.

The Drive Continue west on Liberty Rd/ MD-26 for 6 miles, then turn left (southbound) onto MD-75/Green Valley Rd. After about 7 miles, take a right onto Old New Market Road to reach New Market's Main Street.

6 New Market

Pretty New Market is the smallest and best preserved of the historical towns that lies between Baltimore and Frederick. **Main Street**, full of antique shops, is lined with Federal and Greek Revival houses. More than 90% of the structures are of brick or frame construction, as opposed to modern vinyl, sheet rock and/ or dry wall; the National Register of Historical places deems central New Market 'in appearance, the quintessence of the c[irca] 1800 small town in western central Maryland.'

The Drive » Frederick is about 7 miles west of New Market via I-70. Take exit 56 for MD-144 to reach the city center.

TRIP HIGHLIGHT

7 Frederick

Frederick boasts a historically preserved center, but unlike the previously listed small towns, this is a mid-sized city, an important commuter base for thousands of federal government employees and a biotechnology hub in its own right.

Central Frederick is, well, perfect. For a city of its size (around 65,000), what more could you want? A historic, pedestrian-friendly center of redbrick rowhouses with a large, diverse array of restaurants usually found in a larger town; an engaged, cultured arts community anchored by the excellent events calender at the **Weinberg Center for the Arts** (☎301-600-2828; www.weinbergcenter. org; 20 West Patrick St); and meandering Carroll Creek running through the center of

DETOUR: WASHINGTON DC

Start: 1 Baltimore

A natural complement to your historical tour is the nation's capital, just 40 miles south of Baltimore on the BWI Parkway. The **National Mall**, part of which is covered in our Stretch Your Legs tour (p246), is the site of some of the nation's most iconic protests, from Martin Luther King's March on Washington to recent rallies for the legalization of gay marriage.

The east end of the Mall is filled with the (free!) museums of the **Smithsonian Institution**. All are worth your time. We could easily get lost amid the silk screens, Japanese prints and sculpture of the often-bypassed **Sackler & Freer Gallery** (1050 Independence Ave SW).

On the other side of the Mall is a cluster of memorials and monuments. The most famous is the back of the penny: the **Lincoln Memorial** (⊙24hr). The view over the reflecting pool to the Washington Monument is as spectacular as you've imagined. The **Roosevelt Memorial** (www.nps.gov/fdrm; W Basin Dr SW; ⊙24hr) is notable for its layout, which explores the entire term of America's longest-serving president.

On the north flank of the Lincoln Memorial (left if you're facing the pool) is the immensely powerful **Vietnam Veterans Memorial** (Constitution Gardens; ⊙24hr), a black granite 'V' cut into the soil inscribed with names of the American war dead of that conflict. Search for the nearby but rarely visited **Constitution Gardens** (⊙24hr), featuring a tranquil, landscaped pond and artificial island inscribed with the names of the signers of the Constitution.

SOME MORE OF BALTIMORE'S BEST

Everyone knows DC is chock a block replete with museums, but the capital's scruffier, funkier neighbor to the northeast gives Washington a run for her money in the museum department.

Out by the Baltimore waterfront is a strange building, seemingly half enormous warehouse, half explosion of intense artsy angles, multicolored windmills and rainbow-reflecting murals, like someone had bent the illustrations of a Dr. Seuss book through a funky mirror. This is quite possibly the coolest art museum in the country: the **American Visionary Art Museum** (☎410-244-1900; www.avam. org; 800 Key Hwy; adult/child $16/10; ☺10am-6pm Tue-Sun). It's a showcase for self-taught (or 'outsider' art), which is to say, art made by people who aren't formally trained artists. It's a celebration of unbridled creativity utterly free of arts-scene pretension. Some of the work comes from asylums, others are created by self-inspired visionaries, but it's all rather captivating and well worth a long afternoon.

The Baltimore & Ohio railway was (arguably) the first passenger train in America, and the **B&O Railroad Museum** (☎410-752-2490; www.borail.org; 901 W Pratt St; adult/child $16/10; ☺10am-4pm Mon-Sat, 11am-4pm Sun; ⚐) is a loving testament to both that line and American railroading in general. Train spotters will be in heaven among more than 150 different locomotives. Train rides cost an extra $3; call for the schedule.

If you're traveling with a family, or if you just love science and science education, come by the **Maryland Science Center** (☎410-685-5225; www.mdsci.org; 601 Light St; adult/child $17/14, IMAX film only $8; ☺10am-5pm Mon-Fri, 10am-6pm Sat, 11am-5pm Sun; summer hours 10am-6pm Sun-Thu, to 8pm Fri & Sat). This awesome center features a three-story atrium, tons of interactive exhibits on dinosaurs, outer space and the human body, and the requisite IMAX theater.

it all. Walking around downtown is immensely enjoyable.

Said creek is crossed by a lovely bit of community art: the mural on **Frederick Bridge**, at S. Carroll St between E. Patrick & E. All Saints. The trompe l'oeil-style art essentially transforms a drab concrete span into an old, ivy-covered stone bridge from Tuscany.

✗ ⌂ p193

The Drive » Head west on old National Pike (US 40A) and then, after about 6.5 miles, get on MD-17 southbound/ Burkittsville Rd. Turn right on Gapland Rd after 6 miles and follow it for 1.5 miles to Gathland.

- - - - - - - - - - - - - -

❽ Gathland State Park

This tiny **park** (☎301-791-4767; ☺8am-sunset) **FREE** is a fascinating tribute to a profession

that doesn't lend itself to many memorials: war correspondents. Civil War correspondent and man of letters George Alfred Townsend fell in love with these mountains and built an impressive arch decorated with classical Greek mythological features and quotes that emphasize the needed qualities of a good war correspondent.

Sleeping & Eating

Baltimore ❶

✖ Chaps   American
(☎410-483-2379; 5801 Pulaski Hwy; mains under $10; ⏰10:30am-10pm, to midnight Fri & Sat) This is the go-to stop for pit beef, Baltimore's take on barbeque – thinly sliced top round grilled over charcoal. Park and follow your nose to smoky mouth-watering goodness, and get that beef like a local: shaved onto a kaiser roll with a raw onion slice on top, smothered in tiger sauce (a creamy blend of horseradish and mayonnaise).

✖ Dukem   Ethiopian $$
(☎410-385-0318; 1100 Maryland Ave; mains $13-22; ⏰11am-10:30pm) Dukem is a standout among Baltimore's many Ethiopian places. Delicious mains, including spicy chicken, lamb and vegetarian dishes, all sopped up with spongy flatbread.

✖ PaperMoon Diner   Diner $$
(227 W 29th St; mains $7-16; ⏰7am-midnight Sun-Thu, to 2am Fri & Sat) Like a kaleidoscopic dream, this brightly colored, quintessential Baltimore diner is decorated with thousands of old toys, creepy mannequins and other quirky knickknacks. The real draw here is the anytime breakfast – fluffy French toast, crispy bacon and bagels with lox.

✖ Vaccaro's Pastry   Italian $
(222 Albemarle St; desserts $7; ⏰9am-10pm Sun-Thu, to midnight Fri & Sat) Vacarro's serves some of the best desserts and coffee in town. The cannoli are legendary, and the gelato and tiramisu are also quite good.

🛏 Peabody Court   Hotel $$
(☎410-727-7101; www.peabodycourthotel.com; 612 Cathedral St; r from $120; P❄🛜) Smack dab in the middle of Mt Vernon, this upscale larger hotel with a boutique feel has large, handsomely appointed guest rooms with all-marble bathrooms and top-notch service. Often has great-rate deals online.

Sykesville ❸

✖ E.W. Beck's   Pub $
(☎410-795-1001; 7565 Main Street; mains $9-15; ⏰11:30am-10pm, bar to 1am) In the middle of Sykesville's historic district, Beck's feels like a traditional pub, with wooden furnishings, soused regulars and serviceable pub grub mains.

Frederick ❼

✖ Brewer's Alley   Gastropub $$
(☎301-631-0089; 124 N Market St; burgers $9-13, mains $18-29; ⏰11:30am-11:30pm Mon & Tue, to midnight Wed & Thu, to 12:30am Fri & Sat, noon-11:30pm Sun; 🛜) This bouncy brewpub is one of our favorite places in Frederick, for several reasons. First, the beer: homemade, plenty of variety, delicious. Second, the burgers: enormous, half-pound monstrosities of staggeringly yummy proportions. Third, the rest of the menu: excellent Chesapeake seafood and Frederick county farm produce and meats. Finally: the beer. Again. The beer.

✖ Cacique   Latin $$
(☎301-695-2756; 26 N. Market Street; $11-29; ⏰11:30am-10pm Sun-Thu, to 1:30pm Fri & Sat) This interesting spot mixes up a menu of Spanish (as in Spain) favorites like paella and tapas with Latin American gut busters like enchiladas ceviche. That said, the focus and the expertise seems bent more towards the Iberian side of the menu; the shrimp sauteed in garlic and olive oil is wonderful.

🛏 Hollerstown Hill B&B   B&B $$
(☎301-228-3630; www.hollerstownhill.com; 4 Clarke Pl; r $135-145; P❄🛜) The elegant, friendly Hollerstown has four pattern-heavy rooms, two resident terriers and an elegant billiards room. It's right in the middle of the historic downtown area of Frederick, so you're within easy walking distance of all the goodness.

Seneca Creek State Park *Miles of hiking and biking trails await*

Along the C&O Canal

16

Lush forests, river valleys, a thin towpath trail, hiking, biking, living history, and an anachronistic car ferry: welcome to the C&O Canal, y'all.

85 miles

Harpers Ferry
Unwind in this city perched on a forested gorge

FINISH 7 • Brunswick

5

3

START
Georgetown

White's Ferry
Cross the Potomac on a river ferry from the past

40 miles

Great Falls National Park
Relax on a slow boat up the old C&O Canal

15 miles

2 DAYS
185 MILES / 297KM

GREAT FOR...

BEST TIME TO GO
May to Jun, Oct to Nov; pleasant spring weather, gorgeous autumnal mountain foliage.

 ESSENTIAL PHOTO
Panorama shot of Harpers Ferry.

BEST FOR FAMILIES
Pottering around Harpers Ferry.

195

16 Along the C&O Canal

In its day, the Chesapeake and Ohio Canal was both an engineering marvel and a commercial disaster. Today, it's one of the nicest national parks in the mid-Atlantic. Drive along the the former canal path from Washington DC to West Virginia, now a popular hiking and biking trail (because this was a canal towpath, it's almost completely flat), and experience the lush scenery of the Potomac watershed.

❶ Georgetown

Georgetown is Washington, DC's toniest neighborhood, but it's not all hyper-modern lounges and boutiques. On Thomas Jefferson St, enthusiastic college students dress in scratchy 19th-century costumes, while the adventurous set out on one of the country's great rights-of-way.

This is the beginning of the C&O Canal and **Chesapeake & Ohio Canal National Historical Park** (www.

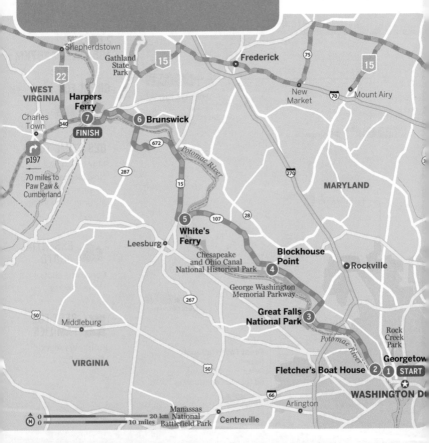

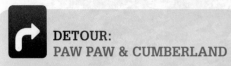

DETOUR:
PAW PAW & CUMBERLAND

Start: ⑦ Harpers Ferry

Northwest of Harpers Ferry, the canal continues into West Virginia and Western MD. Paw Paw Tunnel, in Paw Paw, WV, runs directly into the mountains and out of them again; the edifice speaks to both the will of the canal's builders and the somewhat quixotic nature of their enterprise, as all of this (literal) moving of mountains did nothing to save their investment. Oh well – still makes a nice walk.

Once you hit Cumberland, this is, as the Doors would say, the end – of the C&O Canal. Cumberland, MD, is Mile 184.5, the trail's terminus, marked by the C&O's **Cumberland Visitor Center** (☎301-722-8226; www.nps.gov/choh; 13 Canal Pl; ☻9am-5pm Mon-Fri; P), itself an excellent museum on all things related to the canal. Go have a beer, and consider delving into one of our many Appalachian trips.

To get to Paw Paw, take US 340W to VA-7W to hit Winchester. Then take VA-127N to WV-29N and follow signs to Paw Paw. From Paw Paw, take MD-51N to reach Cumberland (two hours from Harpers Ferry).

nps.gov/choh; ☻daylight hours;). The pathway runs from here, on Washington, DC's southwestern shores, 184.5 miles up the Potomac River to Cumberland, MD, over 74 elevation-changing locks.

In Georgetown, the canal runs along a verdant, willow-shaded tunnel of trees. There's a convincing reconstruction of the first leg of the canal path, staffed by the aforementioned costumed interpreters working out of the **Georgetown Visitor Center** (☎202-653-5190; 1057 Thomas Jefferson Rd, Georgetown; ☻9:30am-4:30pm Jun-Aug).

✗ p201

The Drive ≫ The drive from Georgetown to Fletcher's Boat House is short but sweet. Head directly west on M St (and be ready to deal with traffic). After 0.5 miles M St becomes Canal Rd, which parallels the towpath. Follow Canal Rd for 1.7 miles; Fletcher will be on your left.

LINK YOUR TRIP

22 Across the Appalachian Trail

Head west from Harpers Ferry into the Appalachian wilderness.

15 Maryland's National Historic Road

From Brunswick, head northeast into the historical downtown of Frederick.

② Fletcher's Boat House

The first stop for almost all travelers leaving the towpath from Georgetown is **Fletcher's Boat House** (☎202-244-0461; www.fletcherscove.com; 4940 Canal Rd NW; watercraft per hr/day from $11/25; ☻7am-7pm Mar-Nov), a good spot for a picnic or, if you're looking to boat around, organizing gear rental. Be careful as you go; while the Potomac is beautiful, the currents can be dodgy, despite the calm appearance of the water.

The Drive ≫ Continue northwest along Canal Rd, which becomes the Clara Barton Pkwy when you cross the Maryland border (after 1 mile). Continue along the Clara Barton Pkwy for about 7 miles, then turn left onto MacArthur Blvd. Follow for 3.5 miles into Great Falls National Park.

SKIP BROWN/GETTY IMAGES ©

TRIP HIGHLIGHT

❸ Great Falls National Park

While you've been driving, the towpath has been twisting and turning for 15 miles to the **Great Falls Tavern Visitor Center** (☎301-767-3714; 11710 MacArthur Blvd, Potomac, MD; ☻9am-4:30pm Wed-Sun, boat rides 11am & 3pm Wed-Fri, 11am, 1:30pm & 3pm Sat & Sun). From here you can book a canal boat ride, a favorite activity among kids. The one-hour trips are a leisurely introduction to the rhythms of the waterway, and are well worth the $8/5 price tag for adults/children. The 4.7-mile **Billy Goat Trail**, which begins near the visitor center, takes you on an enjoyable scramble over rugged, river-smoothed boulders.

✕ p201

The Drive » Head back on MacArthur Blvd for 1.2 miles, then turn left onto Falls Rd. Follow it for about 2 miles, then turn left onto River Rd and follow it for 6 miles through some of the poshest suburbs of Montgomery County.

- - - - - - - - - -

❹ Blockhouse Point

A little further up the river, Montgomery County has carved the pretty little **Blockhouse Point Conservation Park** (☎301-670-8080; 14750 River Road, Darnestown; ☻sunrise-sunset; Ⓟ) out of this corner of the Potomac River Valley. From Blockhouse Point, you'll see views of the Potomac Valley and ruins of Civil War bunkers. Nearby **Seneca Creek State Park** (☎301-924-2127; 11950 Clopper Road Gaithersburg; ☻8am-sunset Mar-Oct, from 10am Nov-Feb; Ⓟ🖼) is a much larger affair, consisting of the woods that hug Seneca Creek, which winds a twisty course to the Potomac.

Miles of hiking and biking trails and boating opportunities await in Seneca Creek, though if you're a horror film buff, you may already be familiar with these woods – this is where 1999's *Blair Witch Project* was filmed.

The Drive » Stay westbound on River Rd for 3 miles, then turn right to get onto Partnership Rd. Take Partnership for about 4 miles through meadows and

Great Falls National Park Canal barge on the C&O Canal

farmland, then turn left onto Maryland 107/Fisher Ave. After about 5 miles, this will become White's Ferry Rd; follow it to the ferry.

- - - - - - - - - - -

TRIP HIGHLIGHT

5 White's Ferry

White's Ferry (☎301-349-5200; 24801 Whites Ferry Rd, Dickerson, MD; car/bicycle/pedestrian $5/2/1; ⊙5am-11pm) is the last functioning river service between Maryland and Virginia. The ferry runs continuously from 5am to 11pm, and during rush hour it's pretty packed. The process is easy: line your car up at the ferry office and wait to board the good ship *Jubal A Early*. Once you drive on or board the boat, the surliest ferry operator ever will snatch your fare (cash only) and then you quickly chug across the Potomac to Leesburg, VA.

The Drive » If you want a pretty detour, head northwest of White's Ferry to the small town of Boyd (p201), nestled in green foothills. Otherwise, take the ferry to Leesburg, then take VA-15 north for 8 miles. Then turn left onto State Route 672/Lovettsville and follow it for 6 miles. Turn right onto VA-287 N/N Berlin Pike and follow it for 2.5 miles to Brunswick.

199

6 Brunswick

The C&O Canal's little **Brunswick Visitor Center** (☎301-834-7100; 40 West Potomac Street, Brunswick; rail museum adult/child $7/4; ⏰10am-2pm Fri, to 4pm Sat, 1-4pm Sun) doubles as the Brunswick Rail Museum. As quiet as this town is, it was once home to the largest rail yard (7 miles long) owned by a single company in the world. Those days are long past, but the museum will appeal to trainspotters, and you have to have a heart of stone not to be charmed by the 1700-sq-ft model railroad that depicts the old Baltimore & Ohio Railway.

The Drive ›› Go west on Knoxville Rd until it becomes MD-180; follow this road and merge onto US 340 and follow it for 5 miles to Harpers Ferry.

TRIP HIGHLIGHT

7 Harpers Ferry

In its day, Harpers Ferry was the gateway to the American West. This geographic significance turned the town into a center of industry, transportation, and commerce. Today you'd hardly know the Ferry was once one of the most important towns in the country, but it does make for a bucolic, calculatedly cute day trip.

If you'd like to pause here for a break from the towpath you'll want to first get a pass from the **Harpers Ferry National Historic Park Visitor Center** (☎304-535-6029; www.nps.gov/hafe; 171 Shoreline Dr; per person/vehicle $5/10; ⏰8am-5pm), which opens the town's small public museums, located within walking distance of each other, for your perusal. All of these little gems are worth their own small stop; one deals with the area's importance to the development of modern firearms and African American history.

✖ 🛏 p201

THE C&O: YESTERDAY AND TODAY

In case you were wondering: no one uses the C&O Canal today for its original purpose of moving goods. Originally plotted as a transportation line between the Eastern seaboard and the industrial heartland west of the Appalachian Mountains, the 'Grand Old Ditch' was completed in 1850, but by the time it opened, it was as advanced as a Walkman in a store full of iPhones. The Baltimore and Ohio Railway was already trucking cargo west of the Alleghenies; in a stroke of alphabetical justice, the B&O had supplanted the C&O.

A series of floods, coupled with the canal's own lack of profitability, led to the death of the C&O in 1924, and for some 30 years plans for the land were thrown back and forth: should the canal towpath become a parkway or a park? US Supreme Court Justice William O Douglas firmly believed the latter. The longest-serving justice in history was an environmentalist who argued rivers could be party to litigation, was the lone dissenter on over half of his 300 dissenting opinions, wrote the most speeches and books as a justice, and had the most marriages (four) and divorces (three – his last marriage, to a 23-year-old law student, lasted till his death) on the bench. As part of his commitment to making the C&O a park, he hiked the full length of the path with 58 companions (only nine made it to the end). Public opinion was swayed, and the C&O was saved.

Eating & Sleeping

Georgetown ❶

✕ J Paul's — Gastropub $$

(📞202-333-3450; 3218 M St NW; mains $13-29; ⊙from 11:30am Mon-Fri, from 10:30am Sat & Sun) Politicians, lobbyists, students and other locals belly up at J Paul's to knock beers back and enjoy great burgers, steaks, ribs and seared salmon. Join the clientele at the long mahogany shotgun bar, especially during happy hour (4–7pm Monday to Thursday) when deals on oysters and other items off the restaurant menu prevail.

✕ Pizzeria Paradiso — Italian $$

(📞202-337-1245; 3282 M St NW; mains from $11; ⊙11:30am-11pm Mon-Thu, to midnight Fri & Sat, noon-10pm Sun) This casual restaurant serves wood-oven Neapolitan-style pizzas with scrumptious toppings to crowds of patrons with rave results. The pizza crust is perfect – light, crisp and a little flaky.

Great Falls ❸

✕ Old Angler's Inn — American $$$

(📞301-365-2425; 10801 MacArthur Blvd, Potomac; mains $26-40; ⊙11:30am-2:30pm Tue-Sun, 5:30-9:30pm Mon-Thu, to 10pm Fri & Sat, to 9pm Sun; 🅿) While it sounds like a salty-seadog hangout, the Old Angler's Inn is actually one of the poshest restaurants in Potomac, MD, and makes for a nice detour from C&O's outdoor activities. Inside the warm, rustic-chic dining room, French Laundry-inspired fare mixed with Chesapeake flavor comes to the table. It's 2 miles from the Great Falls Tavern Visitor Center.

Boyd

⊨ Pleasant Springs Farm B&B — B&B $$

(📞301-972-3452; www.pleasantspringsfarm. com; 16112 Barnesville Road, Boyd; r $195) The grounds of this farm-turned-bed-and-breakfast encapsulate the beauty of rural Maryland. Situated in rolling green hill country, it manages to come off as appealingly rough around the edges. The owners are local historians and experts on all things Montgomery County, and the breakfasts are wonderful. Located 15 miles northeast of White's Ferry.

Harpers Ferry ❼

✕ Anvil — American $$

(📞304-535-2582; 1270 Washington St; lunch mains $8-12, dinner mains $15-24; ⊙11am-9pm Wed-Sun) High-end mountain cuisine of the fresh field-and-stream variety is done up in any number of mouthwatering ways here. If crab, country ham and a rurally pleasant dining setting doesn't get you to the door, what will?

⊨ Jackson Rose — B&B $$

(📞304-535-1528; www.thejacksonrose.com; 1167 W Washington St; r weekday/weekend $135/150; ❋ 🛜) This marvelous brick 18th-century residence with stately gardens has three attractive guestrooms, including a room where Stonewall Jackson briefly lodged during the Civil War. It's a 600m walk downhill to the historic district. No children under 12 allowed.

⊨ Town Inn — B&B $$

(📞877-489-2447, 304-702-1872; www. thetownsinn.com; 175 & 179 High St; r $70-140; ❋) This lovely B&B consists of two pre–Civil War residences (Heritage and Mountain house) smack dab in the heart of historic Harpers Ferry. Small, cozy and a bit contemporary, it's well-positioned for exploring town on foot.

Baltimore Discover marine life at
the National Aquarium.

Classic Trip

Maritime Maryland

17

Crack steamed crabs, poke around the marshlands, sit in the salt breeze and soak up the estuarine identity of Maryland's maritime cultural spaces.

TRIP HIGHLIGHTS

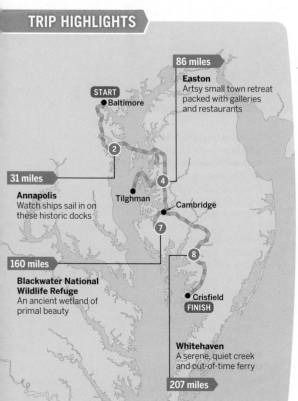

86 miles

Easton
Artsy small town retreat packed with galleries and restaurants

START
● Baltimore

②

31 miles

Annapolis
Watch ships sail in on these historic docks

Tilghman

④

● Cambridge

⑦

160 miles

Blackwater National Wildlife Refuge
An ancient wetland of primal beauty

⑧

● Crisfield
FINISH

Whitehaven
A serene, quiet creek and out-of-time ferry

207 miles

**4 DAYS
320 MILES / 515KM**

GREAT FOR...

BEST TIME TO GO
May to September, when it's warm, sunny and sultry.

 ESSENTIAL PHOTO

The marshes at Blackwater Wildlife Refuge.

 BEST FOR FOODIES

Enjoy stupefyingly huge meals at Red Roost.

Classic Trip

17 Maritime Maryland

Inside the marshy silent spaces of a preserve like Wye Island or Blackwater Wildlife Refuge, you'll realize: this state is utterly tied to the water. You'll know it when you roll past a dozen little towns on the Eastern Shore, each with a small and public pier still used by commercial watermen and local pleasure boaters. This, trippers, is Chesapeake Bay, Maryland's defining geographic and cultural keystone.

1 Baltimore

Start in Baltimore, which calls itself the 'Crab Cake' to New York's Big Apple. B'more has always been built around its docks, and is a port city through and through its watery veins. Indeed, the state's most prominent urban renewal project was the **Inner Harbor** overhaul, which turned a rough dock into a waterfront playground for families. The most prominent landmark, and the best way to learn about the state's aquatic

fauna (and aquatic wildlife anywhere) is the excellent **National Aquarium** (☏410-576-3800; www.aqua.org; 501 E Pratt St, Piers 3-4; adult/child $35/22; ☺9am-5pm Mon-Thu, to 8pm Fri, 8:30am-8pm Sat, 8:30am-6pm Sun). Standing seven stories high and capped by a pyramid, it houses 16,500 specimens of 660 species, a rooftop rainforest, a central ray pool and a multistory shark tank.

Ship-lovers should consider a visit to the **Baltimore Maritime Museum** (☏410-396-3453; www.historicships.org; 301 E

Pratt St, Piers 3 & 5; admission adult 1/2/4 ships $11/14/18, child $5/6/7; ⏱10am-4:30pm), which offers ship tours aboard a Coast Guard Cutter, lightship and submarine. The highlight of the Inner Harbor is the separately operated **USS Constellation**, one of the last sail-powered warships built by the US Navy. A joint ticket gets you on board all four ships and the Seven Foot Knoll Lighthouse on Pier 5.

Afterward, stroll around historic **Fells Point**, a cobblestone district of typical Baltimore rowhouses clustered by the water. Fells is now largely filled with bars and is a fun nightlife area.

✕ ⌂ p214

The Drive » Get on the Baltimore beltway (I-695)

🔗 LINK YOUR TRIP

15 Maryland's National Historic Road

From Baltimore, you can head west into the Maryland hill country and picturesque Frederick.

20 Eastern Shore Odyssey

Drive to Laurel, DE, to begin exploring the back roads and small towns of the Eastern Shore.

and head south on I-97 for 18 miles. Keep left at the fork, and follow signs for 50 E/301 to Annapolis/the Bay Bridge. There's convenient parking at a garage on the corner of Colonial Avenue and West Street.

TRIP HIGHLIGHT

2 Annapolis

The state's capital is a city of yachts and pleasure boats as opposed to commercial fisheries. The **city docks** off Randall and Dock street are where you can see the ships quite literally come in.

Nearby is the country's oldest state capitol in continuous legislative use, the stately 1772 **State House** (📞410-974-3400; 91 State Circle; 🕘9am-5pm Mon-Fri, 10am-4pm Sat & Sun, tours 11am & 3pm), which also served as national capital from 1733 to 1734. The Maryland Senate is in action here from January to April. The upside-down giant acorn atop the dome stands for wisdom.

Probably the surest sign of Annapolis' ties to the water is the **Naval Academy**, the officer candidate school of the US Navy. The **Armel-Leftwich Visitor Center** (📞410-293-8687; www.usnabsd.com; Gate 1, City Dock entrance; tours adult/child $9.50/7.50; 🕘9am-5pm) is the place to book tours and immerse yourself in all things Navy. Come for the formation weekdays at 12:05pm sharp, when the 4000 midshipmen and midshipwomen conduct a 20-minute military marching display in the yard. Photo ID is required for entry.

🍴 p214

The Drive » Get on US 50/US 301 and head east over the Chesapeake Bay Bridge (commonly known as the Bay Bridge), which extends 4.3 miles (7km) over Chesapeake Bay. Once you hit land – Kent Island (p214) – travel 12.5 miles eastbound on US 50/US 301, then turn right onto Carmichael Road. Go about 5 miles on Carmichael and cross the Wye Island Bridge.

3 Wye Island

Our introduction to the Shore is a wild one – specifically the **Wye Island Natural Resource Management Area** (Wye Island NRMA; 📞410-827-7577; 632 Wye Island Road, Queenstown; 🕘sunrise to sunset).

This small, marshy island encapsulates much of the soft-focus beauty of the Eastern Shore. It's all miles of gently waving sawgrass and marsh prairie, intercut with slow blackwater and red inlets leeching tannins from the thick vegetation. Six miles of easy, flat trails run through the NRMA, weaving under hardwood copses and over rafts

LOCAL KNOWLEDGE:
MARYLAND CRAB FESTS

Maryland goes gaga for blue crabs – they even appear on state driver's licenses. Here, the most hallowed of state social halls is the crab house, where crabs are steamed in water, beer and Old Bay seasoning to produce sweet, juicy white flesh cut by cayenne, onion and salt. Crab houses also offer these favorites: crab cakes (crabmeat mixed with breadcrumbs and secret spice combinations, then fried); crab balls (as above, but smaller); soft crabs (crabs that have molted their shells and are fried, looking like giant breaded spiders – they're delicious); red crab or cream of crab soup; and fish stuffed with crab imperial (crab sautéed in butter, mayonnaise and mustard, occasionally topped with cheese). Join the locals in a crab fest – eating together in messy camaraderie can't be beat.

THE EAST COAST COWBOYS

After you drive over the Bay Bridge, the first community you cross into on the Eastern Shore is Kent Island. This is where, in 1631, English trader William Claiborne set up a rival settlement to the Catholic colonists of St Mary's City in Southern Maryland (see p223). Where those Catholics sought religious freedom from the Church of England, Claiborne sought the American dream: profit, in this case from the beaver-fur trade.

In later days Kent became a major seafood-processing center. A dozen packing houses processed the catches of hundreds of watermen. Also known as the 'East Coast cowboys,' watermen usually operate as individuals, piloting their own boats and catching crabs, oysters and fish. Today the industry still exists, but it is fading – independent commercial fisheries yield small profits and have expensive overheads. The cost of a boat can equal a home loan, and the maintenance needed to provide upkeep is prohibitive.

The state enforces environmental regulations on catch size, and the bounty of the Bay is declining thanks largely to run-off pollution. In the meantime, many watermen prefer to send their children to college, away from the uncertain income and backbreaking manual labor of independent commercial fishing.

Still, the waterman is an iconic symbol of the Eastern Shore, an embodiment of the area's independent spirit and ties to the land (and water). On Kent Island, drive under the Kent Narrows Bridge (the way is signed from US 50) to see the **Waterman's Monument**. The sculpture depicts two stylized watermen in a skiff laden with their daily catch, and is a small slice of tradition in an area now given over to outlet malls and tourism.

WASHINGTON DC, MARYLAND & DELAWARE TRIPS **17** MARITIME MARYLAND

of wetland flora. The interlacing tide pools and waterways look like a web, especially in the morning sun. Keep an eye out for bald eagles, osprey, white-tailed deer and red foxes.

The Drive » Drive back on Carmichael to US 50 and turn right. Take US 50 eastbound (though really, you're going south) for 14 miles and exit onto MD-322 southbound. Follow signs for central Easton.

- - - - - - - - - -

TRIP HIGHLIGHT

④ Easton

Easton, founded in 1710, is both a quintessential Shore town and anything but. The historic center,

seemingly lifted from the pages of a children's book, is wedding cake cute; locals are friendly; the antique shops and galleries are well stocked. That's because this isn't what Shore people would call a 'working water town,' which is to say, a town that relies on Bay seafood to live.

Rather, Easton relies on the Bay for tourism purposes. It has retained the traditional *appearance* of a working water town by being a weekend retreat for folks from DC, Baltimore and further afield.

The main thing to do here is potter around and

feel at peace. The area between Washington St, Dover St, Goldsborough St and East Ave is a good place to start. **First Saturday gallery walks** (☎410-820-8822; ⏰5-9pm) are also a lovely way of engaging with old Easton.

There's a superlative number of good restaurants around for a town of 16,000; be sure to try at least one.

✕ 🛏 p214

The Drive » Get on MD-33 in Easton and take it westbound for 10 miles to reach St Michaels. Tilghman Island is 14 miles further west of St Michaels via 33.

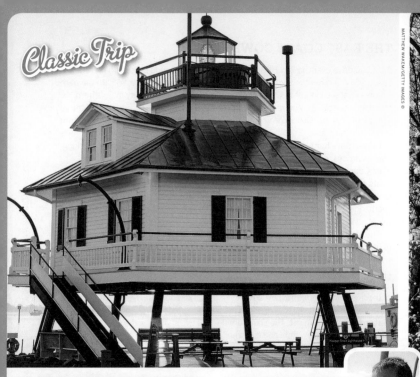

Classic Trip

WHY THIS IS A CLASSIC TRIP
ADAM KARLIN, AUTHOR

Maryland is essentially a giant coastline, intersected by miles of estuary, wetland, rivers and oceans. By exploring the seashore (and bay shore, and marsh shore) one can get an (excuse the pun) under-the-surface glimpse of a state where a body of water is rarely more than a quick drive away. You'll also be exposed to small town charm and fantastic seafood – bonus!

Top: Hooper Strait Lighthouse, Chesapeake Bay Maritime Museum
Left: Crabs are a regional specialty
Right: Washington St, Easton

PHILIP SCALIA/ALAMY ©

⑤ St Michaels & Tilghman Island

Tiny St Michaels has evolved into a tourism-oriented town, but for centuries this village was known for building some of the best boats in the country. Later, this became a waterman community, and many watermen still set out from the local docks.

If you want to learn about these watermen, their community and the local environment, head to the lighthouse and the **Chesapeake Bay Maritime Museum** (☎410-745-2916; www.cbmm.org; 213 N Talbot St; adult/child $13/6; ☻9am-6pm summer; 🚶), which delves into the deep ties between Shore folk and America's largest estuary.

When those Shore folk work the water, they are often joined by the **Rebecca T Ruark** (☎410-829-3976; www.skipjack.org; 2hr cruises adult/child $30/15), one of the last surviving skipjacks on the Bay. Skipjacks are sail-powered oyster dredgers; there's a real art to the way they work the breeze and the Bay floor simultaneously, and it makes for fascinating viewing.

The Ruark sails out of Tilghman Island, an even smaller, quieter town than St Michaels, where many come to arrange fishing and hunting

expeditions; if this interests you, check out Harrison's Chesapeake House (p215).

 p215

The Drive >> Take MD-33 back to US 50E and go south for 15 miles to reach Cambridge.

6 Cambridge

First settled in 1684, Cambridge is one of the oldest towns in the country. Situated on the Choptank River, it has historically been a farming town.

Cambridge's city center has lots of historic buildings fashioned in Federal Style; it may not be quite as picture perfect as Easton, but the town's populace is less transplant-heavy and more authentically of the Shore, and it's diverse to boot (almost 50-50 split between white and African American).

Have a wander around the local galleries at the **Dorchester Center for the Arts** (321 High Street) and check out the **farmers market** at **Long Wharf Park** (High St & Water St), which runs on Thursdays from 3pm to 6pm from mid-May to October.

The Drive >> Take Race St to MD-16W/Church Creek Rd and follow it for 5 miles to MD-335. Follow Route 335 for about 4 miles and turn east on Key Wallace Drive. The visitor center is about 1 mile from the intersection on the right.

TRIP HIGHLIGHT

7 Blackwater National Wildlife Refuge

The Atlantic Flyway is the main route birds take between northern and southern migratory trips, and in an effort to give our fine-feathered friends a bit of a rest stop, the **Blackwater National Wildlife Refuge** (☎410-228-2677; www.fws.gov/blackwater; 2145 Key Wallace Dr; per vehicle $3; ☉ sunrise-sunset) was established.

The Blackwater is technically in the state of Maryland, yet by all appearances it could have fallen from the cutting room floor of *Jurassic Park*. This enormous expanse of marsh and pine forest contains a third of Maryland's wetland habitat. Thousands upon thousands of birds call the refuge home, or at least stop there during their long migratory routes. Driving or cycling around the paved 4-mile **wildlife drive** is perhaps the seminal wildlife experience on the Eastern Shore. A few small walking trails and an observation tour can be accessed via the drive.

Harriet Tubman, 'the Moses of her people' who led thousands of black slaves to freedom, was born on nearby Greenbrier Rd. At the time of writing, work had begun (set to be finished by 2015) on a **national monument** (www.nps.gov/hatu; 2145 Key Wallace Dr) dedicated to Tubman and the Underground Railroad, the pipeline that sent escaped slaves north.

The Drive >> Get back on MD-16 and take it 11 miles north to US 50. Get on 50 east and drive 23 miles, then turn right on Rockawalkin Rd and connect to MD-340 southbound (Nanticoke Rd). Take this for 3 miles,

BEST. SEASONING. EVER.

You see it everywhere down here: Old Bay seasoning, the deep red, pleasantly hot and unmistakably estuarine spice of Maryland. It's made from celery salt, mustard, black and red pepper and other secret ingredients, and Marylanders put it on corn, french fries, potato chips and, of course, crabs. A large container of the stuff is the perfect Maryland souvenir, but beware of wiping your face after partaking of the spice: Old Bay in the eyes is incredibly painful.

DETOUR:
SALISBURY

Start: ❽ Whitehaven

About 30 minutes east of Whitehaven (take Whitehaven Road to MD-349 and head east for 7 miles) is Salisbury, the main commercial and population hub of the Eastern Shore.

If you're around in the fall, drop by for the **Maryland Autumn Wine Festival** (www.autumnwinefestival.org), held around the third weekend of October. You can get an enjoyable sousing courtesy of more than 20 state vineyards and wineries, many of which are located on the Eastern Shore.

Our favorite spot in town is the **Ward Museum of Wildfowl Art** (☏410-742-4988; www.wardmuseum.org; adult/child $7/3; ☺10am-5pm Mon-Sat, noon-5pm Sun). It's a museum based on...well, duck decoys. Let's put it another way – a museum built around a little-known but fascinating art form that was largely perfected by two brothers who rarely left the small town of Crisfield, MD. The Eastern Shore's flat marshes and tidal pools have always attracted a plethora of waterfowl, along with dedicated fowl hunters. In the early 20th century, Stephen and L.T. Ward spent a lifetime carving and painting waterfowl decoys that are wonderful in their realism and attention to detail. The Ward Museum exhibits the works of the Brothers Ward, as well as decoy art gathered from around the world.

On the campus of Salisbury University, the **Nabb Research Center** (☏410-543-6312; http://nabbhistory.salisbury.edu; 1101 Camden Avenue; ☺10am-4pm Tue-Fri, to 8pm Mon) contains what is likely the world's most comprehensive archive of artifacts related to the Delmarva Peninsula (Delaware and the Maryland and Virginia Eastern Shore). If you have family ties to the area, staff can do a professional genealogical search on your behalf for $30; otherwise, small rotating exhibits on local history are the main attraction.

then turn left on MD-352W/ Whitehaven Rd and follow for 8 miles to Whitehaven.

TRIP HIGHLIGHT

❽ Whitehaven

Nestled in a heart-melting river-and-stream-scape, Whitehaven is a quintessential small Shore town where it feels like the 17th century was yesterday. It boasts one of the finest family restaurants and crab shacks in the state: the low-slung, laughter-packed Red Roost (p215).

When you have devoured your fill of food, enjoy the surrounding countryside and consider taking a short ride in your car across the Wicomico River on the **Whitehaven Ferry** (☏410-543-2765), which dates back to 1685 and is the oldest publicly operated ferry in the country (ie it's free!).

The ferry runs from 7am to 5:30pm if there's traffic (there often isn't, so you may need to call the above number); it only takes five minutes to cross the river. The ferry doesn't run if the river is frozen or the wind is over 35 knots, in which case you will need to go all the way back to Salisbury to cross the river.

✕ 🛏 p215

The Drive ❯❯ Take the ferry across the river and follow Whitehaven Rd to MD-362; take this road for 5 miles to US 13. Take 13 south for 5.5 miles until it becomes 413; follow this for 14 miles to reach Crisfield.

TREVOR CLARK/GETTY IMAGES ©

Classic Trip

⑨ Crisfield

Crisfield is a true working water town, where the livelihood of residents is tied to harvesting Chesapeake Bay. Catch the local watermen at their favorite hangout, having 4am coffee at **Gordon's Confectionary** (831 W Main St) before shipping off to check and set traps. Or just drop in to Gordon's for some scrapple (a local specialty – it's pig...bits) before sunset. There will usually be a waterman hanging around willing to bend your ear with a story.

For a more formal education on watermen, head to the **J Millard Tawes Historical Museum** (☎410-968-2501; www. crisfieldheritagefoundation. org/museum; 3 Ninth St; adult/ child $3/1; ⊙10am-4pm Mon-Sat), which gives an insight into the ecology of the Bay and the life of working watermen. Local docents also lead walking tours of Crisfield. End your trip on the Crisfield docks, by the old crab-shelling and packing plants, and let the salt breeze move you while you're in a most maritime spot, in the most maritime of states.

Blackwater National Wildlife Refuge

Eating & Sleeping

Baltimore ❶

🍴 LP Steamers   Seafood $$

(☏410-576-9294; 1100 E Fort Ave; mains $8-28; ⊕lunch & dinner) The best sit-down crab joint in Baltimore is LP Steamers, which is a quick drive from Fort McHenry, the historic structure that defended Baltimore during the War of 1812. The 'LP' stands for Locust Point, one of Charm City's blue-collar southside 'hoods; lots of residents here have been employed on the Baltimore docks or are related to people working on the waterfront.

🛏 Admiral Fell Inn   Hotel $$$

(☏522 7377, 800 292 4667; www.harbormagic. com/admiral-fell-inn; 888 S Broadway; r from $200; 🛜) This old Fells Point sailors' hotel has been converted into a lovely inn with Federal-style furniture and four-poster beds. It's got the best of both of Baltimore's worlds, with historic and nautical details abounding on the one hand, and plenty of modern amenities on the other.

Annapolis ❷

🍴 Cantler's   Seafood $$$

(☏410-962-5379; 400 E Saratoga St; mains from $20; ⊕7am-2pm Mon-Fri) The by-consensus best crab house in Annapolis is a little ways outside of the city. But like many crab houses, Cantler's can be approached by road (Forest Beach Rd) or boat (a waterfront location is crab-eating industry standard). The soft crabs are particularly well-respected, probably due to large on-site peeling sheds, where crabs are allowed to molt.

Kent Narrows

🍴 Harris Crab House   Seafood $$

(☏410-827-9500; 425 Kent Narrow Way; mains $11-30; ⊕lunch & dinner) Off Rte 50 in the Kent Narrows, just after crossing the Bay Bridge, Harris Crab House is highly regarded for its food and enormous wooden waterfront deck, even if it's a bit of a tourist trap.

Easton ❹

🍴 Mason's   American $$$

(☏410-822-3204; 22 S. Harrison Street; mains $25-34; ⊕11:30am-2:30pm Mon-Sat, 5:30-9:30pm Tue-Sat) Food lovers are happy to trek the extra mile (well, many miles) to reach Mason's and its New American goodness. As great as this place is, it's not stuffy; portions are big, as is the restaurant itself, so there's a pleasant buzz accompanying your pan-seared scallops and poached lobster with leek and goat cheese ravioli.

🍴 Out of the Fire   Fusion $$$

(☏410-770-4777; 22 Goldsborough St; mains $15-38; ⊕11:30am-2:30pm Tue-Sat, 5-9pm Tue-Thu, to 10pm Fri & Sat; 🍴) For all that Out of the Fire put forward a playful attitude, this spot is serious about several things, most prominently sourcing sustainable ingredients and turning said ingredients into delicious food that bridges the globe, but is often influenced by Chesapeake Bay. The crispy polenta with gorgonzola sauce and mushroom ragout – oh yes. Yes. Yes!

Scossa
Italian $$$

(☎410-822-2202; 8 N Washington St; mains
$15-28; ⏰11:30am-3pm Thu-Sun, 4-9pm Mon-
Thu, to 10pm Fri & Sat, to 8pm Sun) The Eastern
Shore is not the first place we go to for great
Northern Italian cuisine, but then along comes
Scossa. Maybe we should change our priorities.
The food is authentic, rustic, delicious and
served in a dining room with the right amount of
chic; a crispy sweetbread risotto is daring and
delightful in turn.

Bishop's House
Bed & Breakfast
B&B $$

(☎410-820-7290, 800-223-7290; www.
bishopshouse.com; 214 Goldsborough Street;
$185-195; P) As B&Bs go, the Bishop's House
is pretty luxurious. No bog-standard scratchy
sheets here; there's 1000-thread count softness
and a decor scheme that nicely balances some
modern touches along with the historical bric-a-
brac you expect of towns like Easton. Located in
a Victorian mansion built in 1880.

Tidewater Inn
Hotel $$$

(☎410-822-1300; www.tidewaterinn.com;
101 East Dover Street; r from $180; P🛜) The
Tidewater is an excellent all-around hotel.
Located in a handsome brick building in
downtown Easton, you'll have easy walking
access to some of the town's seminal sights,
and the chance to sleep in rooms with modern
touches but a stately, Victorian elegance.

St Michaels ❺

Crab Claw
Seafood $$

(☎410-745-2900; 304 Burns St; mains $15-30;
⏰11am-10pm) Next door to the maritime
museum, the Crab Claw serves up tasty
Maryland blue crabs and has splendid views
over the harbor. It's a quintessential crab shack,
but there's a good variety of seafood and some
landlubber fare as well (read burgers).

Harrison's
Chesapeake House
Seafood $$

(☎410-886-2121; 21551 Chesapeake House Drive,
Tilghman Island; $15-30; ⏰9am-10pm; 🚗) The
venerable Harrison has had a bit of an overhaul,
going from old-school crab shack decked out
in maritime paraphernalia to...a slightly newer-
school crab shack with maritime paraphernalia.
And that's fine! Let the Harrison be the salty-dog
seafood spot generations of seafood lovers know
and love, because sometimes you want fried
seafood, and this place does fried seafood *right*.

Parsonage Inn
B&B $$

(☎410-745-8383; www.parsonage-inn.com; 210
N Talbot St; r incl breakfast $150-210; P❄)
Laura Ashley's most lurid fantasies probably
resemble the rooms in the red-brick Parsonage
Inn, which is run by a pair of lovely, awfully
hospitable innkeepers. Ask them about organizing
outdoor expeditions into the nearby countryside,
especially if you're into fishing.

Whitehaven ❽

Red Roost
American $$

(☎410-546-5443; 2670 Clara Rd; mains $15-40;
⏰dinner) The original legend: tell someone from
the Eastern Shore you cracked crabs here and
your street (well, Bay) cred rises immediately.
It's all-you-can-eat taken to postmodern levels
of silliness: fried chicken, steamed corn, hush
puppies and buckets and buckets of crabs. Don't
forget about the frequent corny performances of
live piano music.

Whitehaven Hotel
B&B $$

(☎410-873-2000; http://whitehaven.tripod.
com; 2685 Whitehaven Rd; r $110-150; P) Run
by some lovely Baltimore ladies, the Whitehaven
has excellent rooms and views and is nestled in a
registered historic mansion perched on a small,
picturesque corner of the Eastern Shore.

Maryland
*A Catholic colony full
of natural beauty*

Southern Maryland Triangle

18

Between the nation's capital, the Potomac River and Chesapeake Bay is a micro-region filled with natural beauty, great food and a unique cultural heritage.

TRIP HIGHLIGHTS

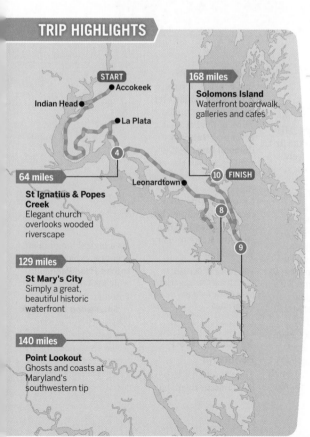

START ● Accokeek

Indian Head ●

● La Plata

4

168 miles

Solomons Island
Waterfront boardwalk, galleries and cafes

Leonardtown ●

10 **FINISH**

64 miles

St Ignatius & Popes Creek
Elegant church overlooks wooded riverscape

8

9

129 miles

St Mary's City
Simply a great, beautiful historic waterfront

140 miles

Point Lookout
Ghosts and coasts at Maryland's southwestern tip

**2 DAYS
170 MILES / 273KM**

GREAT FOR...

BEST TIME TO GO
April to June, when it's warm but not sultry.

 ESSENTIAL PHOTO

The river flowing past Historic St Mary's City.

 BEST FOR FOODIES

Steamed hard crabs at Courtney's.

18 Southern Maryland Triangle

The little-known slice of the Old Line State known as Southern Maryland is a patchwork of marsh, fields and forests, the state's oldest European settlements and stunning riverscape vistas – all an hour or so from Washington DC. On this trip you'll shift from down home crab shacks to upscale wine bars, all while probing back roads that are often quite removed from the tourist radar.

1 Accokeek

About 23 miles south of Washington DC via the Indian Head Hwy (MD-210), Accokeek is the first community that feels more Southern Maryland than DC suburb.

This quilt of farms, fields and forests was (and to a degree, remains) a popular retreat for scientists and intellectuals who wanted to live in a rural community within DC's orbit. The aesthetic they were attracted to is exemplified by **Piscataway Park** (☎301-763-4600; www.nps.gov/pisc; 3400 Bryan Point Rd; ☺sunrise to sunset), a small satellite of the National Park System (NPS) that consists of nature trails, boardwalks over freshwater wetlands, views of the Potomac River and **National Colonial Farm** (☺10am-4pm, Tue-Sun, mid-Mar–mid-Dec, 10am-4pm weekends-only other months), a living history museum that recreates a middle-class Maryland family farm circa the Revolutionary War period.

The Drive » Get back on MD-210 and head south for 8 miles to reach the entrance to Indian Head.

2 Indian Head Peninsula

There's not a lot to see in little Indian Head, but it's a logical jumping off point for exploring the Indian Head Peninsula, which is hugged by the Potomac River.

Smallwood State Park (☎301-743-7613; www.dnr.state.md.us/publiclands/southern/smallwood.asp; 2750 Sweden Point Road, Marbury; $5; ☺5am-sunset Apr-Oct, 7am-sunset Nov-Mar) sits

between said Potomac and Mattawoman creek. There's a few very easy nature trails that run through local hardwood forests, and the **Retreat House**, a restored tidewater plantation and tobacco barn; these historic properties are open on Sunday from 1pm to 5pm.

LINK YOUR TRIP

17 Maritime Maryland

Take MD 2-4 to Annapolis, then cross the Bay Bridge to explore Maryland's watery edges.

15 Maryland's National Historic Road

Head north to Frederick along I-270 to see the small, historical towns of Central Maryland.

About 12 miles down Rte 224 is **Purse State Park** (☏301-743-7613; www.dnr.state.md.us/publiclands/southern/purse.asp; Rte 224; ☼sunrise-sunset), a wooded area that fronts the Potomac; you've got nice views clear to Virginia and the Marine Corps base at Quantico.

The Drive » You can drive around the entire peninsula on MD-224. When you're ready to move on, hop on MD-425N and take it to MD-6; take 6 eastbound for 11 miles through bucolic countryside to reach La Plata.

- - - - - - - - - - - - -

❸ La Plata

Named for a river in Argentina, La Plata is the seat of Charles County. It's a prosperous little country town, but for all that, it's subject to the sprawl that creeps south from DC.

The **Port Tobacco Players** (☏301-932-6819; www.ptplayers.com; 508 Charles Street) is a local theater company that puts on Broadway and off-Broadway standards, plus a few lesser-known pieces. Catch a show – not for the production values, but for the chance to peek into a hyper-local arts scene.

✖ p225

The Drive » Get back on MD-6 and backtrack west for around 2 miles. Turn left at Chapel Point Rd and follow it for 4 miles. When you see an amazing view of the Potomac

next to a charming church, you're in business.

- - - - - - - - - - - - -

TRIP HIGHLIGHT

❹ St Ignatius & Popes Creek

On a gentle slope overlooking the Potomac River is **St Ignatius Church** (www.chapelpoint.org/; 8855 Chapel Point Rd, Port Tobacco), which hosts the oldest continuously active Catholic parish in the country. The church itself has a lovely exterior profile. If you visit, you can content yourself with wandering the cemetery, which offers great sightlines out to the water. The forested bottomlands visible from Ignatius' backslope constitute 600 acres of state-owned land; you're welcome to stomp around, but there are no trails.

If you continue on Chapel Point Rd you'll hit US 301; take this for 1.5 miles, then turn right onto **Pope's Creek Rd**. This 2-mile country lane is quite pretty, and was also the escape route John Wilkes Boothe took to Virginia after assassinating Abraham Lincoln.

The Drive Turn around on Pope's Creek Rd and head back to US 301. Turn left (north) onto 301, then almost immediately turn right onto MD-234, Budds Creek Rd. After barely a mile you'll pass Allen Fresh Run, a

magnificent marshscape – pull over and take a picture. It's about 7 miles to the speedway.

- - - - - - - - - - - - -

❺ Budds Creek

Before you properly explore St Mary's County, the first county in the state and one of the oldest counties in the country, consider this: you have been driving (hopefully) responsibly for perhaps thousands of miles on our trips. Maybe it's time to see some people drive like maniacs. Enter **Budds Creek** (☏301-475-2000; www.buddscreek.com; 27963 Budds Creek Rd, Mechanicsville), one of the premier motocross racetracks on the Eastern seaboard. It's always a blast here – a blast of hot exhaust and speed across your face, but a blast nonetheless.

The Drive » Continue on MD-234 for 12 miles (you'll pass through a traffic circle). 234 hits MD-5; turn right here and continue through Leonardtown for about 2 miles. Turn right on Washington St and look for the Bank of America building; this small square is 'downtown' Leonardtown.

- - - - - - - - - - - - -

❻ Leonardtown

The seat of St Mary's county has worked hard to maintain its small-town atmosphere. The central square (Fenwick & Washington Sts) is the closest thing this

Point Lookout State Park Fishing is a popular pastime

community has to a town green. Maryland is a border state between the North and South, a legacy evident in the square's onsite **WWI memorial**, divided into 'white and 'colored' sections.

Look for a rock in front of the nearby **circuit courthouse** (Courthouse Dr & Washington); legend has it that Moll Dwyer, a local 'witch', froze to death while kneeling on said rock and cursed the town with her dying breath. Her faint knee imprints are supposedly still visible in the stone. Nearby **Fenwick St Used Books & Music** (☏301-475-2859; www.fenwickbooks.com; 41655 Fenwick Street;

⊙11am-5pm) is a good spot for learning about local history and current events. On the first Friday of each month, music fills the town square and businesses throw their doors open.

🍴 🛏 p225

The Drive » Continue south on MD-5 for 7.5 miles. Turn right onto Piney Point Rd (MD-249) and follow that route for 10 miles, which includes crossing a small bridge at the end, to get to St George's Island.

- - - - - - - - - - - - - -

❼ St George's Island

This beautiful little island shifts between woods of skeletal loblolly pines and acres of waving marsh grass and cattails. The pines

were once so prevalent the British utilized the island as a base during the War of 1812; the trees were used to repair their ships during raids up the Potomac and Chesapeake. It takes maybe 20 minutes to drive around the island; while here, you'll pass by the **Paul Hall Center**, one of the largest merchant marine training academies in the country.

The Drive » Head back up Piney Point Rd. Turn right onto MD-5 and follow it south for 8 miles. When you enter the campus of St Mary's College, you'll see the 'Freedom of Conscience' statue (a man emerging from a rock wall); take a slight right onto Trinity Church Rd and follow to the Historic St Mary's City parking lot.

TOBACCO BARNS OF THE TIDEWATER

The Bridges of Madison County just *sounds* like a great novel, right? How about 'The Tobacco Barns of Southern Maryland?' No?

Well, those barns are in a similar vein to those flashy covered bridges: a piece of hyper-regional American architectural heritage. Tobacco was once the cash crop of Southern Maryland. It was the crop that made the original Maryland colony economically viable, and the area's stubborn loyalty to tobacco, coupled with Southern Maryland's geographic position under the I-95 corridor, was largely what kept the region rural for so many centuries. But declining profits, and a 2001 state-sponsored buyout of tobacco farms, largely ended the industry in the past decade.

Tobacco was stored in frame-built barns with gabled roofs and adjustable ventilation slats. The frames provided space for 'sticks' (poles) that were hung with tobacco leaf, which was cured and air-dried through a combination of the elements and charcoal or (later) propane fires.

Preservation Maryland (www.preservationmaryland.org) and similar organizations have made tobacco barn preservation a cause celebre, and as such, hundreds of rickety tobacco barns dot the Southern Maryland triangle. They have a creaky, spidery aesthethic, like they were drawn by children's book illustrator Stephen Gammell, and they're as integral to the local landscape as the water and the woods.

ST MARY'S FIRSTS

Massachusetts and Virginia are usually in a tight race to prove whoever has the most 'historical' state (whatever that means), but Maryland gives them a run for their money, especially when it comes to historic firsts. All of the following are specific to St Mary's City:

» Maryland was the first Catholic colony in British North America. The first Catholic mass in the British colonies was held here.

» The Maryland Toleration Act (1649), also known as the Act Concerning Religion, created the first legal limitations on hate speech in the world, and was the second law requiring religious tolerance in British North American colonies.

» Mathias de Sousa, who served in the colony's 1642 assembly of freemen, *may* have been the first man of African descent to participate in a legislative assembly in British America. Contemporary accounts describe him as a mulatto, which at the time referred to people of mixed African descent.

» Margaret Brent was the first woman in British North America to appear before a court of the Common Law. She was also appointed executor of the estate of Governor Leonard Calvert upon his death (1647), and publicly demanded a vote within the colonial assembly.

» In 1685 William Nuthead owned the first printer in Maryland. Upon his death, his wife, Dinah, inherited the business and became the first woman licensed as a printer in America.

- - - - - - - - - - - -

TRIP HIGHLIGHT

❽ St Mary's City

The Potomac and its tributary, St Mary's River, along with Chesapeake Bay, cuts a lush triangle of land out of the southern edge of Southern Maryland. This is where, in 1634, on high green bluffs overlooking the water, Catholic settlers began the state of Maryland.

The settlement has been recreated into **Historic St Mary's City** (HSMC; ☎240-895-4990, 800-762-1634; www. stmaryscity.org; 18751 Hogaboom Lane; adult/child $10/6; ☉10am-4pm; P🚻),

a living history museum romantically positioned among the surrounding forests, fields and farmlands. Given its distance from anything resembling a crowd, HSMC feels more of the colonial era than similar places like Williamsburg.

A recreation of the Maryland *Dove*, the supply ship that accompanied the original British colonists, sits docked on the St Mary's River. Next door **Trinity Church** and **St Mary's College of Maryland** are both lovely – they're easy to walk around and get satisfyingly lazy in.

The Drive » Getting to Point Lookout is straightforward: roll

south for 10 miles on MD-5, and there you are.

- - - - - - - - - - - -

TRIP HIGHLIGHT

❾ Point Lookout

The western shore of Maryland – that is, the western peninsula created by Chesapeake Bay – terminates here, in a preserved space of lagoons, pine woods and marshes managed by **Point Lookout State Park** (☎301-872-5688; www.dnr.state. md.us/publiclands/southern/ pointlookout.asp; 11175 Point Lookout Road, Scotland; summer/off-season $7/5; ☉6am-sunset; P🚻). There's a playground for kids and a sandy beach that's OK for swimming, but watch out for jellyfish in summer;

they're not deadly, but their stings hurt.

During the Civil War, the Union Army imprisoned thousands of Confederate POWs here, overseen by black soldiers. Swampy conditions and harsh treatment by guards led to the death of some 4000 Confederates. A controversial shrine to their memory has been built, and legends persist of Confederate ghosts haunting local swamps at night.

 p225

The Drive » Take MD-5 north for 6 miles and bear right onto MD-235 when it splits. (For a little detour, turn left just after MD-5 splits instead; you'll get to Ridge, an unincorporated community with popular seafood restaurants, p225) Take MD-235 north through the town of Lexington Park; after 16.5 miles, turn right onto MD-4. Follow for 4 miles over the dramatic Thomas Johnson Bridge and immediately bear right as the bridge terminates to reach Solomons Island.

- - - - - - - - - - - -

TRIP HIGHLIGHT

🔟 Solomons Island

Solomons is a seaside (but not a beachy) town of antique shops, cafes, diners and one of the most famous bars in the state: the **Tiki Bar** (📞410-326-4075; 85 Charles St; ⊘noon-2am). We're not entirely sure *why* the bar is so famous; it's got a sandy beach, some Easter Island heads and Tiki torches (and *very* strong drinks), and that's about it. Nonetheless people come from as far away as DC and Baltimore to drink here on weekends, and the bar's grand opening for the summer season literally attracts thousands of tourists to Solomons Island.

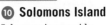 p225

THE AMISH OF ST MARY'S

St Mary's County has always had a rural feel to it, but horse and buggy carriages? Straw hats? One-room schoolhouses? In the 21st century? Yes, thanks to a sizable presence of Amish settlers, who have been in the county since 1940.

The Amish are a Christian sect that embraces simplicity, humility, manual labor and the countryside; conversely, they are reluctant to adopt modern technology, although they do not, as stereotypes would have it, reject it wholesale. Men usually wear their beards long and women wear head coverings, and internally, Amish communities speak a dialect of German known as Pennsylvania German.

The local Amish live in northern St Mary's County, near the town of Mechanicsville. Their farms are sprinkled along Rte 236 South and Rte 247, and their homes can be found on quiet country lanes like Parsons Mill Rd, Friendship School Rd and the perhaps ironically dubbed Busy Corner Rd. You'll know you're in Amish country when you see horse-drawn buggies clop-clop by on the roadside, or when you see German surnames like Kurtz, Hertzler and Zimmerman on mailboxes.

It is important to remember the Amish aren't frozen in amber. Farmers sometimes carry cell phones for emergencies. And local markets now often feature bilingual signage, a testament to the growing Latino population of the area, particularly within the agricultural sector.

If you'd like to interact with the Mechanicsville Amish, the easiest way is at the **North St Mary's County Farmers Market** (📞301-475-3200; 37600 New Market Turner Road, Charlotte Hall; ⊘7am-sunset Mon-Sat), where local Amish farming families sell produce and crafts. To really see the Pennsylvania Dutch in their element, check out the **produce auction** held during spring and summer harvest seasons on Monday, Wednesday and Friday at 40454 Bishop Road, in the town of Loveville.

Sleeping & Eating

La Plata

✗ Casey Jones — American $$

(☎301-392-5116; 417 East Charles St, La Plata; mains $14-29; ⏱11:30am-11pm Tue & Wed, to 2am Thu-Sat, 3:30pm-11pm Mon; 🅿) There are lots of restaurants in America that try to come off as high-end gastropubs, and they should all be more like Casey Jones. There's an excellent beer selection and a New American cuisine menu, featuring dishes from wild grilled salmon to zested-up meatloaf.

Leonardtown ⑥

✗ Cafe des Artistes — French $$

(☎301-997-0500; 41655 Fenwick St, Leonardtown; mains $13-26; ⏱11am-2pm Tue-Fri, 5-9pm Tue-Sat, 11am-8pm Sun; 🅿) We love this restaurant for its unapologetic embrace of old-school French food – boeuf bourguignon, croque monsieur, rack of lamb and an excellent steak frites. The interior has a jazzy bistro atmosphere; it's dark enough to be intimate, but buzzing enough to feel relaxed as opposed to stuffy.

🛏 The Victorian Candle — B&B $$

(☎301-373-8800; www.victorian-candle.com; 25065 Peregrine Way, Hollywood; $105-160) This enormous, dollhouse-like bed & breakfast is frilly in the extreme, with dainty rooms and friendly service. Rooms are good value for money, and rates drop during the week.

Ridge

✗ Courtney's — Seafood $$

(☎301-872-4403; 48290 Wynne Rd, Ridge; mains $10-23; ⏱8am-9pm; 🅿) This fish shack, which isn't that far in exterior decor from a bomb shelter (it doesn't get significantly better inside), is run by Tom Courtney, local fisherman and all-round surly character. So what's to love? Fish, crabs and oysters. Tom catches them, his wife cooks them, and everything is fresh and tasty.

🛏 Woodlawn — B&B $$

(☎301-872-0555; www.woodlawn-farm.com; 16040 Woodlawn Ln, Ridge; r $170-260; 🅿🛜) Seven well-kept suites, all individually decked out with rustic charm (think boxwood gardens, fireplaces and vanity chests) and modern amenities (such as glassed-in showers and Jacuzzis with views of the water) characterize the lodging at this farm, which has been converted into an excellent rural resort in the cornfields of southern St Mary's county.

Solomons Island ⑩

✗ CD Cafe — American $$

(☎410-326-3877; 14350 Solomons Island Rd, Solomons; mains $11-26; ⏱11:30am-9:30pm Mon-Sat, to 9pm Sun; 🍴) Intensely fresh seafood and produce characterize the menu at this sunny spot, where natural light, friendly service, crisp salads and tasty pastas are the order of the day. The fresh flounder sandwich is a seafood-lover's delight, while the shepherd's pie is hearty and filling on a chilly day.

🛏 Back Creek Inn — B&B $$

(☎410-326-2022; www.backcreekinnbnb.com; 210 Alexander Lane, Solomons; r $120-170, cottage $225; 🅿🛜) This rather lovely B&B is positioned over the eponymous back bay. Pretty rooms are named after herbs (for example: thyme and rosemary. Maybe the owners are Simon & Garfunkel fans?) and manage to be twee without being frilly.

Rehoboth Beach
Boardwalk fun in the sun

Delmarva | 19

Discover countless beaches, boardwalks and miles of wild coastline on this trip, which takes in some of the Mid-Atlantic's best seaside resorts.

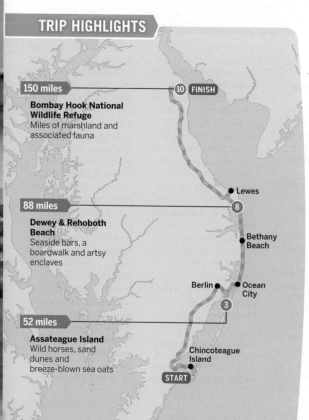

150 miles — 10 FINISH

Bombay Hook National Wildlife Refuge
Miles of marshland and associated fauna

● Lewes

8

88 miles

Dewey & Rehoboth Beach
Seaside bars, a boardwalk and artsy enclaves

Bethany Beach

Berlin ● ● Ocean City

3

52 miles

Assateague Island
Wild horses, sand dunes and breeze-blown sea oats

Chincoteague Island

START

3 DAYS
150 MILES / 241KM

GREAT FOR...

BEST TIME TO GO
Visit from June to September to get the most out of summer.

ESSENTIAL PHOTO
Wild horses pounding the beach at Assateague Island National Seashore.

BEST FOR FAMILIES
The charms and nostalgia of Bethany Beach.

227

19 Delmarva

Yes: there is sun, surf and sand here. But also: wild horses, salt marshes, estuarine deltas and stretches of surprisingly isolated oceanfront scenery, considering we're mere miles from the most densely populated urban corridor in the country. Find neon lights and a greasy batch of boardwalk fries, or a patch of sea oats and a view of the ocean – either option exists in abundance on the Delmarva Peninsula, named for its constituent three states: Delaware, Maryland and Virginia.

❶ Chincoteague Island

Way, way out at the edge of anywhere – a uniform three hours and 20 minutes from Washington DC, Baltimore, Philadelphia *and* Richmond – we begin this trip at the isolated end of the road.

That said, Chincoteague (Shink-oh-teeg) hardly feels lonely. Rather, this is a cheerful resort island, populated by fishermen and folks seeking an escape in the coastal salt marshes of an Atlantic barrier island.

The best activity around is exploring said unique environment, and we recommend boarding a boat with **Captain Dan** (☏757-894-0103; www.captaindanstours.com; tours adult/child $40/35). His personable Around the Island Tours take around 2 to 2.5 hours and are excellent value. You can also rent your own boat or arrange fishing charters at **Captain Bob's Marina** (☏757-336-6654; www.captbobsmarina.net; 2477 Main Street; boat rental from $75/99 half/full-day; ⏱6am-6pm).

The big event in these parts is the Chincoteague Pony Swim (p232).

The Drive » In the town of Chincoteague, follow Maddox Blvd south to the traffic circle at the Chamber of Commerce. Take the exit into Beach Access

❷ Chincoteague National Wildlife Refuge

Part of the appeal of exploring the Delmarva Peninsula is encountering an incredibly rich environment and ecosystem, one where several biomes are packed into exceptionally small physical spaces. The **Chincoteague National Wildlife Refuge** (www.fws.gov/northeast/chinco; 8231 Beach Road, Chincoteague Island; daily/weekly pass $8/15 ; ⏱5am-10pm Mon-Sat May-Sep, 6am-6pm Nov-Feb, 6am-8pm Mar, Apr & Oct; P ♿) epitomizes this. Within these 14,000 acres you'll encounter breeze-kissed beaches with no crowds, dunes, maritime forest and freshwater and saltwater marshes; keep an eye out for snapping turtles, Virginia opossums, river otters, great blue herons and of course, a herd of Chincoteague ponies. Six trails web across the wetlands and woodlands, ranging from a quarter mile to 3.25 miles in length; none offer any serious elevation gain. The jewel of the reserve is the **Herbert H Bateman Educational and Administrative Center** (⏱9am-4pm spring, fall & winter, to 5pm

in summer), a marvel of green architecture that, set against the marshes, seems to resemble a futuristic, solar-powered duck blind.

The Drive » Head back into town, then west on Chincoteague Rd til it hits State Route 679/Fleming Rd, then turn right. Rte 679 will cross into Maryland and become MD-12. Follow it north for 11 miles, then turn onto US 113. Take 113 north for 16 miles, then right (east) onto MD-376. Drive 4 miles, then turn right (south) onto MD-611; follow it for 4 miles to Assateague Island.

- - - - - - - - - - - - - - - - - -

TRIP HIGHLIGHT

③ Assateague Island

While there are two entrances to **Assateague Island National Seashore** (☎410-641-1441; www.nps. gov/asis; Rte 611; admission/ vehicles/campsites per week $3/15/20; ☉visitors

LINK YOUR TRIP

20 **Eastern Shore Odyssey**

Head west from Ocean City to reach Berlin, MD and the small towns of the interior Eastern Shore.

27 **Bracketing the Bay**

From Chincoteague, head down the Virginia Eastern Shore and cross into the tidewater historic triangle.

center 9am-5pm), we are directing you to the one in Maryland, 8 miles south of Ocean City.

Assateague is another barrier island, a low, sandy sweep of land peppered with the feral horses this region is so famous for. Kayaking, canoeing and particularly cycling are all popular on the island. There are some 37 miles of beach here, all considerably quieter than nearby Ocean City.

Plus: you can **camp** ([📞]877-444-6777; www. recreation.gov; Assateague National Seashore; campsites from $20; [P]) on the Maryland side of the island. The facilities are basic but decently comfortable. We recommend just bringing your tent and waking up to the wind – who can object to a morning with an Atlantic sunrise and wild horses cantering by the waves?

The Drive Get back on Rte 611 and take it north to reach the southern outskirts of Ocean City. After a little over 8 miles you'll hit Ocean Gateway Rd; turn right here and it's 1.5 miles to the OC.

PHOTO BY SCOTT DUNN/GETTY IMAGES ©

- - - - - - - - - - - - -

④ Ocean City

Ocean City – the 'OC', as some call it – is like the Platonic ideal of an Atlantic seaside resort. You see it from afar as you cross Assawoman Bay, a name that's

provoked giggles for generations of Maryland schoolkids: a skyline of silver condos, neon, all-you-can-eat buffets and, of course, the boardwalk.

Ah, the **boardwalk** (www.ocboards.com): built in 1902, it extends from Ocean City Inlet at the southern end of the island to 27th St, a distance of some 2.3 miles. Along the way there's a sandy beach on one side and endless tacky T-shirt shops and

purveyors of grease on the other. The most visible landmark is **Ocean Gallery** ([📞]410-289-5300; www.oceangallery. com; Boardwalk & 2nd St; [🕐]10am-4pm, to 7pm Fri & Sat), an enormous art gallery stuffed with prints of varying quality (mostly bad, but there are a few gems) with an exterior papered in vibrant folk art.

If you really want to engage in tacky seaside fun to the fullest extent

Rehoboth Beach

possible, hit up **Trimpers Rides** (☎410-289-8617; www.trimpersrides.com; S. First St and The Boardwalk; ☺ Mon-Fri 3pm-midnight, Sat & Sun noon-midnight), one of the oldest of old-school amusement parks. Have some fries with vinegar, play the games and enjoy watching the teenage staff dance the ballet of summer hormonal overload.

✗ ⊫ p235

The Drive >> Allow about 30 minutes, depending on traffic, for this trip. Drive north on the Coastal Hwy – also known as Philadelphia Ave and MD-258 – until you hit the Delaware border, where the road becomes DE-1. Fenwick Island State Park is almost immediately across the border.

⑤ Fenwick Island State Park

Cross into Delaware and Ocean City's neon gives way to peaceful groves and miles – three, to be exact – of quiet beach and wooded trails. Welcome to **Fenwick Island State Park** (☎302-227-2800; www.destateparks.com/park/fenwick-island; Rte 1; $8; ☺sunrise-sunset).

Within the park you'll find **Coastal Kayak** (☎302-539-7999; www.coastalkayak.com; DE-1; tours from $50, kayak/SUP/sailing rentals from $45/55/85 per day; ☺9am-6pm Jun-Oct, by appt other times), a well-regarded outdoor

231

SALTWATER COWBOYS

Roughly 300 horses, more commonly referred to as 'ponies' by locals, roam Assateague Island, itself split by a fence between **Assateague Island National Seashore** (in Maryland) and **Chincoteague National Wildlife Refuge** (in Virginia). While they're often described as wild, the horses are in fact feral; their ancestors were domesticated, but for generations they have lived a wild existence.

The small (average 13.2 hands high) animals are officially classified as 'Assateague horses,' and they're a sight, galloping across the dunes and surf like something out of a fantasy novel. The horses come in solid and pinto colors, and were made famous by Marguerite Henry's children's book *Misty of Chincoteague* (later adapted for the big screen as *Misty*). Legend has it the herd is descended from the equine survivors of wrecked Spanish galleons, but a more plausible theory is they were released by colonists looking to avoid stock taxes.

Rangers give the Assateague ponies contraceptives to prevent overpopulation, but they are otherwise left alone. The Chincoteague ponies, on the other hand, are owned by the Chincoteague Volunteer Fire Company. Every year, in midsummer, thousands of spectators gather for the **Chincoteague Pony Swim** (www.chincoteague.com/pony_swim_guide). During this event, 'Saltwater Cowboys' herd the wild horses on the Virginia side of the island and swim them across Assateague Bay to Chincoteague Island. The horses make landfall at **Memorial Park** (7427 Memorial Park Dr, Chincoteague Island) and are paraded to local carnival grounds for a next-day auction (at the time of writing, the average price of a horse was about $1440). Some horses are sent back to the wild to replenish the herd.

If you're in Delmarva during July, we highly recommend checking out the swim and attendant fair, which we'd go as far as to say is the biggest regional holiday in the area.

adventure outfit that can take you on paddling tours of the nearby wetlands and sea islands, and arrange rentals of kayaks, stand-up paddleboards (SUP) and sailing craft (small Hobies).

The Drive » Bethany Beach is 5 miles north of Fenwick Island State Park on DE-1. Along the way you'll pass a few private beach communities; be warned that there are children at play and speed limits in these parts are enforced pretty mercilessly.

----

6 Bethany Beach

If you're coming from the south, Bethany Beach is the first of the three Delaware resort towns – Bethany, Dewey and Rehoboth. You'll know you've reached Bethany when you see **Chief Little Owl**, a 24ft stylized totem pole meant to represent the indigenous Nanticoke Indians, sculpted by Hungarian artist Peter Wolf Toth.

Bethany is the most family-friendly beach in the area. It also boasts something like a real town center, which neither of the other two beaches can claim. In the early 20th century, the only way here was via an exhausting series of travel exchanges: by train to Baltimore, then a boat across the Chesapeake, a train to Rehoboth Beach and finally a small boat to Bethany.

A **trolley** (25 cents) runs throughout town from 9:30am to 10pm during the summer. Kids and the science-inclined will enjoy the exhibits and nature trail at the **Bethany Beach Nature Center** (☎302-537-7680; 807 Garfield Pkwy; ◷10am-3pm Thu-Sat, to 2pm Sun). A **bandstand** in the middle of town features live performances on weekends.

✕ 🛏 p235

The Drive » Pretty straightforward: head north on DE-1 for about 8 miles, and you're at Delaware Seashore State Park.

- - - - - - - - - -

❼ Delaware Seashore State Park

In between Bethany and Dewey Beach, you'll find six miles of dramatically wind-whipped dunes, sea oats and crashing Atlantic waves. When skies are gray and the sea is rough, **Delaware Seashore State Park** (📞302-227-2800; www.destateparks.com/park/delaware-seashore; 39415 Inlet Rd; $4; ⏰8am-sunset) looks remarkably rugged considering the generally placid nature of Delmarva's, well, nature.

There are several miles of hiking trails, and during the summer rangers lead daily cultural and wilderness activities. Mainly, we like this spot because it offers, in our opinion, some of the prettiest stretches of beach in the region.

🛏 p235

The Drive » Dewey Beach is 4 miles north of here via DE-1; Rehoboth is 2.5 miles north of Dewey Beach.

- - - - - - - - - -

TRIP HIGHLIGHT

❽ Dewey & Rehoboth Beaches

Dewey is the wild child of the Delaware beach towns. This is the spot for spring breakers and teenagers and 20-somethings from further north looking to party.

Rehoboth isn't quite as hedonistic, but that's a relative distinction. People still come here to let loose, but the crowd is more slanted toward older professionals from DC, Baltimore and Philadelphia. Rehoboth has also been a popular artist colony and, by extension, LGBT destination for decades; as such, a small but vibrant gallery scene is manifest.

The main public **beach** for both communities is in Rehoboth, and the intermixing of frat boys

DETOUR: FURNACE TOWN

Start: ❶ Chincoteague

As you drive to Assateague from Chincoteague, you'll have the option, at the MD-12/US 113 split, of detouring northwest on MD-12. Follow this road for 4 miles and you'll enter a woolly patch of pine woods and soggy bottomlands.

For years, children who grew up in the far eastern reaches of the Eastern Shore whispered about a ghost town by these bogs, an abandoned settlement known as 'Furnace Town' named for an old smelting furnace. The ghost of an old African American man, the town's last inhabitant, supposedly stalked the site.

Good story, right? Well, it's true, except for the ghost bit (as far as we know). And whereas in the past this was a cautionary tale about the wild woods, today **Furnace Town** (📞410-632-2032; www.furnacetown.com; Old Furnace Rd; adult/child $6/3; ⏰10am-5pm Mon-Sat Apr-Oct, from noon Sun; 🅿🚻) is a living history museum in the same vein as Colonial Williamsburg (p316). Seven artisans, including a blacksmith, a weaver and a printer, bring the town to life. The reenactors are pretty scrupulous about doing everything the way it was done back in the day, and they're quite willing to teach, especially if you've got children along. If you need to combine a historical trip with the trappings of a nature walk, Furnace Town is a perfect detour.

in Eagles caps and older gay couples coming from their bohemian summer houses is a sight in and of itself.

If you're partying in Dewey and need to get back to Rehoboth, or vice versa, don't stress. During the summer the two towns are connected by the **Jolly Trolley** (one way/round-trip $3/5; ⊙8am-2am summer), which runs late into the night for you party people.

 p235

The Drive » Take DE-1 north out of Rehoboth for 3.5 miles, then turn right onto Rd 268 (you'll see signs for Lewes). You'll drive a little over a mile on 268 to reach Lewes.

⑨ Lewes

It's fair to say Lewes once had one of the prettiest names (or at least pretty name meanings) in the state. For the brief period of time that this was a Dutch colony (about 300 years ago), it was known as Zwaanedael (Valley of the Swans). Then the Dutch, after a clumsy overture of friendship to the local Leni Lenape tribe, were massacred by the Native Americans. The Dutch were eventually replaced by British colonists and now we all eat cheddar instead of gouda.

This history and other stories of this small, gingerbread-pretty town is explained at the **Zwaanendael Museum** (102 Kings Hwy; ⊙10am-4:30pm Tue-Sat, 1:30-4:30pm Sun). If you want some beach time away from the crowds of Rehoboth's boardwalk, head to adjacent **Cape Henlopen State Park** (☏302-645-8983; www.destateparks.com/park/cape-henlopen; 15099 Cape Henlopen Dr; $4; ⊙8am-sunset). And if you want to leave Delaware altogether, the **Cape May-Lewes Ferry** (☏800-643-3779; www.capemaylewesferry.com; 43 Cape Henlopen Dr; per motorcycle/car $36/44, plus per adult/child passenger $10/5) runs services across Delaware Bay to New Jersey.

 p235

The Drive » Take DE-1 north for about 30 miles, then take the exit for DE-9N. Follow it for 13 miles, past miles of marsh and sedge, then turn right at Whitehall Neck Rd and follow it into the refuge.

TRIP HIGHLIGHT

⑩ Bombay Hook National Wildlife Refuge

You're not the only person making a trip to **Bombay Hook National Wildlife Refuge** (☏302-653-9345; www.fws.gov/refuge/Bombay_Hook; 2591 Whitehall Neck Road, Smyrna; ⊙sunrise-sunset). Hundreds of thousands of waterfowl use this protected wetland as a stopping point along their migration routes.

A 12-mile wildlife driving trail through 16,251 acres of sweet-smelling saltwater marsh, cordgrass and tidal mud flats is the highlight of this stop, which manages to encapsulate all of the soft beauty of the Delmarva Peninsula in one perfectly preserved ecosystem.

There are also five walking trails, two of which are handicapped accessible, as well as observation towers overlooking the entire affair. Across the water you may see the lights and factories of New Jersey, an industrial yin to this area's wilderness yang.

✓ TOP TIP:
OFF-SEASON INFO

Note that we cover seasonal summer towns on this trip that are busy from Memorial Day (last weekend in May) to Labor Day (first Monday in September). Hotel rates plunge in the winter, but many tours, activities and museums are closed then as well.

Sleeping & Eating

Ocean City

✘ Liquid Assets Modern American $$

(☎410-524-7037; 94th St & Coastal Hwy; mains
$10-28; ⏱11:30am-11pm, to midnight Fri & Sat)
Like a diamond in the rough, this bistro gem
and wine shop complex is hidden in a strip mall
in north OC. The menu is a refreshing mix of
innovative seafood, grilled meats and regional
classics (Carolina pork BBQ, 'ahi tuna burger).

🛏 Inn on the Ocean B&B $$$

(☎410-289-8894; www.innontheocean.com;
1001 Atlantic Ave, at the Boardwalk; r $275-395
incl breakfast) This six-roomed B&B is an elegant
escape from the usual OC big box lodging.

Bethany Beach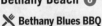

✘ Bethany Blues BBQ American $$

(☎302-537-1500; www.bethanyblues.com; 6 N
Pennsylvania Ave; mains $14-24; ⏱4:30-9pm, to
10pm Fri & Sat) For a nice change of pace from
the usual seafood fare, this spot has falling-
off-the-bone ribs and pulled-pork sandwiches.
There's also a general boozy vibe, constituting
one of the few nightlife-y options in Bethany.

🛏 Westward Pines Motel $$

(☎302-752-4962; www.westwardpinesmotel.
com/; 33309 Kent Ave; r low/high season
$150/200; 📶♿) This little low-slung motel,
located down a wooded lane, doesn't look like
much, but it's great value for money, especially
considering its relative proximity to the beach.
Rooms are simple, clean and comfy.

Delaware Seashore State Park ⑦

🛏 Cottages at Indian
River Marina Cottages $$$

(☎302-227-3071; www.destateparks.com/
camping/cottages/rates.asp; Inlet 838,

Rehoboth Beach; weekly peak/shoulder/off-
season $1800/1350/835, 2 days off-season
$280 ; 🅿❄) These cottages are some of our
favorite local vacation rentals, with patios and
unadulterated views across the pristine beach
to the ocean. Each cottage has two bedrooms
and a loft, and while they must be rented out by
the week during the summer, they're available in
two-day increments in the off-season.

Rehoboth Beach ⑧

✘ Dogfish Head Microbrewery $$

(www.dogfish.com; 320 Rehoboth Ave; mains
$9-25; ⏱noon-late) When a place mixes its own
brewery with some of the best live music on the
Eastern Shore, you know you've got a winning
combination.

🛏 Hotel Rehoboth Boutique Hotel $$$

(☎302-227-4300; www.hotelrehoboth.com; 247
Rehoboth Ave; r $230-320; 🅿❄@📶♿) This
boutique hotel has gained a reputation for great
service and luxurious amenities, including a free
shuttle to the beach.

Lewes ⑨

✘ Wharf Seafood $$$

(☎302-645-7846; 7 Anglers Rd; mains $15-29;
⏱7am-1am; 🅿♿) The Wharf is a family-
friendly waterfront spot that's a good option if
you're into sitting above dock pilings, watching
seagulls and chowing on fried clams, seared
scallops and fisherman's stew.

🛏 Hotel Rodney Hotel $$

(☎302-645-6466; www.hotelrodneydelaware.
com; 142 2nd St; r $160-260; 🅿❄📶♿) This
charming boutique hotel features exquisite
bedding and antique furniture, but it also has
some modern touches: iPod clock radios,
flat-screen televisions and duochromatic
color schemes that contrast with dark-stained
wooden floors and clean white linen.

Wilmington 'Crying Giant' by
Tom Otterness is part of a
vibrant arts scene

Eastern Shore Odyssey

20

Plunge into a landscape of quilted patches of cornfields and chicken farms, red-brick small towns and miles of rippling marshland in rural Maryland and backwater Delaware.

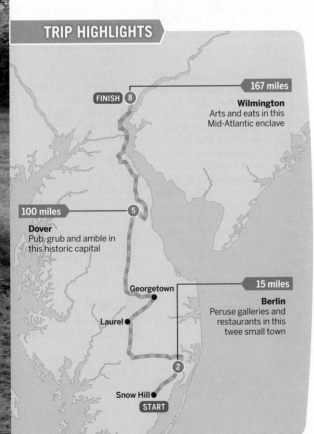

TRIP HIGHLIGHTS

167 miles

FINISH 8

Wilmington
Arts and eats in this Mid-Atlantic enclave

100 miles — 5

Dover
Pub, grub and amble in this historic capital

15 miles

Berlin
Peruse galleries and restaurants in this twee small town

Georgetown

Laurel

2

Snow Hill
START

3 DAYS
165 MILES / 265.5KM

GREAT FOR...

BEST TIME TO GO

April to September for sunny weather and blue skies.

 ESSENTIAL PHOTO

Grab a shot of downtown Berlin's twee city center in the early evening.

 BEST FOR OUTDOORS

Kayaking at Trap Pond State Park.

20 Eastern Shore Odyssey

The Eastern Shore of Maryland and the state of Delaware are made up of bucolic farming villages and postcard-perfect small towns, but there's an urban edge further north, including Wilmington, one of the Eastern seaboard's undiscovered major cities. Cross this green slice of America that sits in the shadow of the Eastern seaboard's concrete superhighways but still feels romantically removed from them.

1 Snow Hill

Attractive Snow Hill, a village of a little over 2000 people, sits on the banks of the Pocomoke River. It's a postcard-perfect slice of Americana, with its antique shops, cafes and brick buildings, all arrayed in loose grid around a town hall and a church.

Located in a little house that itself resembles a set piece from a historical movie, the **Julia A Purnell Museum** (☑410-632-0515; 208 W Market St; adult/child $2/50¢; ☺10am-4pm Tue-Sat, from 1pm Sun Apr-Oct) is a veritable attic of all things Snow Hill. The attraction isn't so much the exhibits as the town's obvious pride in them.

About 3.5 miles outside of town, **Pocomoke River State Park** (☑410-632-2566; 3461 Worcester Highway; ☺sunrise to sunset; 🚻🎣), part of the 15,000-acre Pocomoke State Forest, is an exquisite state park, especially for kids. There are trails, paddling opportunities, wetlands, woods, a nature center and a pool ($6 for day use).

Show Hill is almost equidistant (two hours and 45 minutes) from Washington DC and Baltimore.

✖️ ⨠ p244

The Drive ⟫ Drive north on US 113, through a patchwork of cornfields, woodsy groves and flower banks, for 20 miles until you see signs for Berlin.

TRIP HIGHLIGHT

2 Berlin

There's a red-brick stateliness to Berlin's town center that is quite compelling to travelers, and we're not the first people to notice. The films *Runaway Bride* and *Tuck Everlasting* both used Berlin as their stand-in for a quintessential American small town.

So, what is there to do? Potter about, browse the ubiquitous antique shops, or hit the local **farmers market** on Friday (200 Main St, ☺10am to 3pm). Or check out a show at the local **Globe Theater** (☑410-641-0784; www.globetheater.com; 12 Broad St; lunch mains $6-12, dinner $11-25; ☺11am-10pm; 🛜), a dinner theater-cum-bar with excellent nosh and a packed performance schedule that's always good for a date night.

✖️ ⨠ p244

The Drive ⟫ Take US 50 westbound from Berlin for about 20 miles til you hit the outskirts of Salisbury, MD. Merge onto the ramp towards US 13 north and follow that for about 8 miles, then turn left onto Bi State Rd. Follow Bi State for 8 miles until you hit Laurel.

3 Laurel

Laurel, the first town you'll come to in Delaware, is...well, it's *nice*. There's not a lot to do besides walk around and soak up the vibe. We like vibe.

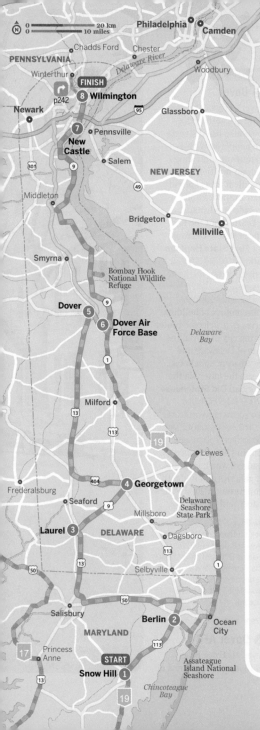

If you want to balance small-town tranquility with intense, nerve-shattering adrenalin (why not?), get in touch with **Skydive Delmarva** (📞888-875-3540; www.skydivedelmarva.com; 32524 Aero Drive; tandem/freefall jumps weekdays from $215/315, weekends from $225/325). The jumps take in some killer views: the Atlantic to your east, the Chesapeake, DC and the Appalachians to the west and the entirety of Delmarva all around.

Six miles east of Laurel, **Trap Pond State Park** (📞302-875-5153; www.destateparks.com/park/trap-pond; 33587 Baldcypress Lane, Laurel; ⏱8am-sunset; 🅿🚻🎠) is the site of the northernmost bald cypress habitat – a flooded forest that looks like it lurched out of the Louisiana bayou – in the USA.

✖ p244

LINK YOUR TRIP

19 **Delmarva**
From Georgetown, head east to Rehoboth Beach along Rte 9 to get some sun, sand and surf.

17 **Maritime Maryland**
In Snow Hill, go west to Crisfield via US 113 and US 13 for culinary culture and cracking crabs.

The Drive >> Take Rte 9 northeast from Laurel for about 10.5 miles, cutting through farmland, fields, forests, no-name unincorporated areas and the fantastically named Hardscrabble Road to reach Georgetown.

4 Georgetown

The most attractive buildings in the seat of Sussex County are arranged around Georgetown Circle, an atypical round town green (in these parts, town centers are usually square) anchored by a handsome **courthouse** on its northeast side.

Georgetown's economy is largely linked to a nearby chicken-processing plant. The facility is staffed by many workers from Central America, giving this small town a surprisingly large Latin enclave.

Five miles northwest is the **Redden State Forest**, the largest state forest (9500 acres) in Delaware. You can access some 44 miles of trails, primarily from E Redden Rd, which leads past the **Redden State Forest & Education Center** (☏302-698-4500; gail.ingram-smith@state.de.us; 18074 Redden Forest Drive; ☺ 8am-4:30pm by appointment).

✖ p244

The Drive >> You could get to your next destination via DE-1, but it's not the most attractive road. Instead, head west on DE-404 for 11 miles, then turn right (north) on US 13 and

follow it for 30 miles until you reach Dover.

TRIP HIGHLIGHT

5 Dover

Dover's city center is quite attractive; the rowhouse-lined streets are peppered with restaurants and shops and, on prettier lanes, broadleaf trees spread their branches and provide good shade.

Learn about the first official state – Delaware – at **First State Heritage Park** (☏302-744-5055; 121 Martin Luther King Blvd North; ☺8am-4:30pm Mon-Fri, from 9am Sat, 1:30-4:30pm Sun). This complex of buildings serves as a welcome center for the city of Dover, the state of Delaware and the adjacent statehouse. Access the latter via the Georgian **Old Statehouse** (☏302-744-5055; http://history.delaware.gov/museums; 25 The Green; ☺9am-4:30pm Mon-Sat, from 1:30pm Sun), built in 1791 and since restored, which contains art galleries and in-depth exhibits on the First State's history and politics.

The Drive >> It's a quick 7-mile drive southeast on DE-1 to Dover AFB. Take exit 91 for Delaware 9 toward Little Creek/Kitts Hummock, and keep an eye out for signs leading to the Air Mobility Command Museum.

6 Dover AFB

Dover Air Force Base (AFB) is a visible symbol of

PAT & CHUCK BLACKLEY/ALAMY ©

New Castle William Penn statue

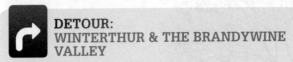

DETOUR:
WINTERTHUR & THE BRANDYWINE VALLEY

Start: ⑧ Wilmington

Head out of Wilmington on the Kennett Pike and then turn north onto Montchanin Rd. Head north for about 6 miles and you're in the intersection of some of the wealthiest suburbs of Wilmington, West Chester, PA, and Philadelphia, a green and lush region also known as the Brandywine Valley.

The grandest of the grand homes that pepper the valley is **Winterthur** (📞302-888-4600; www.winterthur.org; 5105 Kennett Pike (Route 52); adult/child $18/5; ⊙10am-5pm Tue-Sun) (Winter-tour), the palatial mansion of the du Pont family, whose wealth built much of Delaware. Today, the residence and its magnificent gardens are open to the public. Curators maintain the home as both a testament to Henry Francis du Pont's love of early-American architectural styles and American decorative arts and antiques.

Friendly docents lead tours around the grounds, pointing out design and architectural oddities and generally sharing an infectious enthusiasm.

The nearby gardens include flower beds that bloom in alternating seasons, which means the grounds are always swathed in some floral fireworks display. Kids will love the Enchanted Forest, built to resemble a children's book come to life.

Just minutes away is **Brandywine Creek State Park** (📞302-577-3534; www.destateparks.com/park/brandywine-creek; 41 Adams Dam Road, Wilmington; $3; ⊙8am-sunset). This green space would be impressive anywhere, but is doubly so considering how close it is to prodigious urban development. Nature trails and shallow streams wend through the park; contact **Wilderness Canoe Trips** (📞302-654-2227; www.wildernesscanoetrips.com; 2111 Concord Pike; kayak/canoe trip from $46/56, per tube $18) for information on paddling or tubing down the dark-green Brandywine creek.

American military muscle and a poignant reminder of the cost of war. This is the location of the Department of Defense's largest mortuary, and traditionally the first stop on native soil for the remains of American service members killed overseas.

The base is the site of the **Air Mobility Command Museum** (📞302-677-5938; www.amcmuseum.org; cnr Hwys 9 & 1 (1301 Heritage Rd); ⊙9am-4pm Tue-Sun) **FREE**. If you're into aviation, you'll enjoy it; the nearby airfield is filled with restored vintage cargo and freight

planes, including C-130s, a Vietnam War-era C-7 and WWII era 'Flying Boxcar.'

Two miles from the base is the **John Dickinson Plantation** (📞302-739-3277; http://history.delaware.gov/museums; 340 Kitts Hummock Road, Dover; ⊙10am-3:30pm; Ⓟ), the restored 18th-century home of the founding father of the same name, also known as the Penman of the Revolution for his eloquent written arguments for independence.

🍴 🛏 p244

The Drive » The longest drive on this trip is also the simplest and prettiest. Follow DE-9 north for 50 miles, passing several protected wetlands along the way, all the way to New Castle.

- - - - - - - - - - - -

❼ New Castle

Like a colonial playset frozen in amber, downtown New Castle is all grey cobbles and beige stonework, with wrought iron details throughout. In fact, the entire four- by five-block area has been designated a National Historic Landmark. The local **Old**

Court House (📞302-323-4453; 211 Delaware Street; 🕐10am-3:30pm Wed-Sat, 1:30-4:30pm Sun) dates back to the 17th century and is now operated as a museum by the state.

The New Castle Historical Society owns and operates **Amstel House** (📞302-322-2794; www.newcastlehistory.org; 2 East Fourth Street; adult/child $5/2; 🕐10am-4pm Wed-Sat, from noon Sun) and **Dutch House** (32 East Third Street; 🕐10am-4pm Wed-Sat, from noon Sun), which are usually visited as part of a joint tour ($9/3 admission for adult/child to both properties). Amstel House is a surviving remnant of 1730s colonial opulence; Dutch House is a example of a smaller working residence.

 p245

The Drive » Follow DE-9 northeast for 7 miles into downtown Wilmington.

- - - - - - - - - - - - -

TRIP HIGHLIGHT

⑧ Wilmington

Delaware's biggest city is full of muscular art-deco architecture and a vibrant arts scene, plus a diverse populace that blends Baltimore charm with Philly saltiness.

The **Delaware Art Museum** (📞302-571-9590; www.delart.org; 800 S Madison St; adult/child $12/6, Sun free; 🕐10am-4pm Wed-Sat, from noon Sun) anchors the local creative community, and exhibits the work of the local Brandywine School, including Edward Hopper, John Sloan and three generations of Wyeths. The **Wilmington Riverfront** (www.riverfront wilm.com) is made up

of several blocks of redeveloped waterfront shops, restaurants and cafes; the most striking building is the **Delaware Center for the Contemporary Arts** (📞302-656-6466; www. thedcca.org; 200 S Madison St; 🕐10am-5pm Tue & Thu-Sat, from noon Wed & Sun) **FREE**, which consistently displays innovative exhibitions.

In the art-deco Woolworth's building, the **Delaware History Museum** (📞302-656-0637; www.hsd.org/dhm; 200 S Madison St; adult/child $6/4; 🕐11am-4pm Wed-Fri, 10am-4pm Sat) proves the First State's past includes loads more than being head of the line to sign the Constitution.

 p245

THE POTATO HOUSE RULES

The most hyper-regional architectural oddity we encountered on our road trips – besides Southern Maryland's tobacco barns (see Tobacco Barns of the Tidewater, p222) – are the potato houses of Sussex County, Delaware. These tall and narrow two-story wooden-frame structures were storage facilities for sweet potatoes (yams), once a cash crop of this region. Potato houses can be spotted throughout southern Delaware, often on lonely back roads.

The skinny potato houses held crops from October to February; their proportions allowed them to be heated easily, but also facilitated air circulation. High windows provided a ventilation counterpoint to the heat – sweet potatoes require a uniform, constant temperature of 50ºF (10ºC).

Eleven potato houses are concentrated near Laurel. They can be a bit tough to find, though, and most reside on private property. Contact the **Laurel Historical Society** (📞302-875-1344; www.laureldehistoricalsociety.org; 502 E 4th Street; 🕐 1-4pm Sun Jun-Oct or by appointment) for directions. If you're driving around, the rather appropriately dubbed **Chipman Potato House** is at the intersection of Chipmans Pond and Christ Church Rds (GPS: 38.561004,-75.537342), 2.5 miles east of Laurel.

Sleeping & Eating

Snow Hill ❶

✕ Palette — American $$

(☎410-632-0055; 104 W Market St; mains $14-22; ⊗11am-3pm Tue-Wed, to 9pm Thu-Sat, 10am-2pm Sun; 🖋) An ever-shifting innovative menu always keeps us guessing when it comes to the Palette, yet we're never disappointed with whatever this excellent standby comes up with, from gourmet grilled cheese to roasted quail or lamb and pea risotto.

🛏 River House Inn — B&B $$

(☎410-632-2722; www.riverhouseinn.com; 201 E Market St; r $160-190, cottage $250-300; P ✳ 🛜 🐾) The Victorian River House Inn overlooks a breathtakingly pretty bend of the Pocomoke River. The grounds are spacious and beautiful; on a sunny day, or even blanketed under the snow, this spot could remind one of an English manor house, but the service and friendliness are pure Eastern Shore laid back (we mean that in a good way).

Berlin ❷

✕ Drummer's Cafe — American $$

(2 N Main St; lunch mains $9-14, dinner $17-34; ⊗11am-3pm & 5-10pm Mon-Sat, 10am-3pm Sun) The dining room of the Atlantic Hotel is as grand as the hotel itself, all big windows, natural sunshine and – come evening – flickering candlelight. The food references the best of the Chesapeake; filet mignon gets even more decadent with a crab cake, and the fish tacos are fresh, citrus-y and superb.

✕ Southside Deli — Deli $

(☎410-208-3343; 11021 Nicholas Ln #7; mains under $10; ⊗9am-9pm) The Southside encapsulates the odd regional culinary predilections of the area – a deli in a small, seemingly Southern town that serves one of the best Italian subs this side of New York. Actually, any sandwich here is grand; finish them off with cannolis imported from Vaccaro's, one of Baltimore's most famous Italian bakeries.

🛏 Atlantic Hotel — Hotel $$

(☎410-641-3589; www.atlantichotel.com; 2 N Main St; r $115-245; P ✳) This handsome, Gilded-era lodger gives guests the time-warp experience but with modern amenities. It's centrally located within walking distance to most of the best things that Berlin's historic downtown has to offer. The 18 rooms are individually appointed, but they all blend Victorian posh with Southern rustic charm.

Laurel ❸

✕ Laurel Pizzeria — Italian $

(☎302-877-0660; 411 N Central Ave; pizzas $6-17; ⊗11am-10pm Mon-Sat, to 9pm Sun) Nothing anchors a small town like Laurel like an excellent pizza place, so kudos to the Laurel Pizzeria. The price is right too; at $6 for a small cheese pizza, this is one budget slice of pie.

Georgetown ❹

✕ Restaurante Mi Laurita — Latin $

(☎302-856-3393; 10 N Race St; mains under $10; ⊗9am-10pm; P) Georgetown has a big Latin American population, and this is where they eat. Dishes are as cheap, delicious and fresh as the best street food south of the border – that's a compliment. Give 'em credit for serving *tacos de tripa* (intestine tacos) – sounds funny to a conservative palate, but delicious to anyone who tries them.

Dover ❺

✕ Flavors of India — Indian $$

(☎302-677-0121; 348 N Dupont Hwy; $11-16; ⊗11am-10pm; P 🖋 🐾) To say this place is an unexpected delight would be the grossest understatement. First: it's in a Super 8 Motel off the highway. Second: *it's great*. The standards – vindaloos and kormas and tikka masalas – are all wonderful, as are some new dishes. Goat Palakwala? Goat curry with a spinach base. Amazing. By far the best vegetarian option in the area.

✗ Golden Fleece — Pub $

(☎302-674-1776; 132 W Loockerman St; mains under $10; ⏲4pm-midnight, til late on weekends, from noon Sun) The best bar in Dover also serves up pizza, cheesesteaks and burgers. It has the atmosphere of an old English pub, and an outdoor patio for summer nights.

🛏 State Street Inn — B&B $$

(☎302-734-2294; www.statestreetinn.com; 228 N State St; r $125-135) Although it's a bit over the top in its cuteness and flowery-patterned wallpapers and sheets, the State Street remains a solid accommodation choice, with friendly, knowledgeable service and an unbeatable central location.

New Castle ❼

✗ Dog House — American $

(☎302-328-5380; 1200 Dupont Hwy; mains under $10; ⏲10:30am-midnight) Don't be fooled by the name; while this unassuming counter top does hot dogs and does them exceedingly well (the chili dogs are a treat), they also whip out mean subs and cheesesteaks that could pass muster in Philly.

✗ Jessop's Tavern — American $$

(☎302-322-6111; 114 Delaware St; mains $12-24; ⏲11:30am-10pm, to midnight Fri & Sat) There are big, mouthwatering colonial dishes like roast duck and honey-drop biscuits at this colonial-style tavern. Half the fun is watching the bored teenage staff chafe in their colonial-era garb. The bar has a good beer selection.

🛏 Terry House B&B — B&B $

(☎302-322-2505; www.terryhouse.com; 130 Delaware St; r $90-110; 🅿🛜) The owner of the five-room Terry House B&B will play the piano for you while you enjoy a full breakfast. That's a treat for sure, but we're more impressed by the historical grounds and supremely cozy rooms; there's nothing like stepping from a historical village into historical accommodation.

Wilmington ❽

✗ Leo & Jimmy's Deli — Deli $

(☎302-656-7151; 728 Market St; mains $4-10; ⏲5:30am-4pm Mon-Fri) This deli is a Wilmington standby, well loved for its excellent sandwiches and service – friendly with just the right touch of endearing surliness.

🛏 Hotel du Pont — Hotel $$$

(☎302-594-3100; www.hoteldupont.com; cnr Market & 11th Sts; r $230-480; 🅿❄🛜) The premier hotel in the state, the du Pont is luxurious and classy enough to satisfy its namesake (ie one of America's most successful industrialist families). The spot exudes an art-deco majesty that Jay Gatsby would have been proud of, but the goodness goes beyond the impressive lobby to well-appointed rooms and proximity to a handsome shopping arcade.

STRETCH YOUR LEGS
WASHINGTON, DC

Start/Finish: Library of Congress

Distance: 3 miles

Duration: 3 hours

Washington, DC, is more than monuments, museums and memorials, but it is still partly defined by these structures. All along the National Mall, you'll find symbols of the American dream, the physical representation of the nation's highest ideals and aspirations.

Take this walk on Trips

Library of Congress

To prove America was just as cultured as the Old World, second US president John Adams established the Library of Congress, now the largest library in the world. The motivation behind the library is simple: 'universality,' the concept that all knowledge is useful. Stunning in scope and design, the building's baroque interior and flourishes are set off by a Main Reading Room that looks like an ant colony constantly harvesting 29 million books.

The Walk >> Head across the street to the underground Capitol Visitor Center.

Capitol Visitor Center

The US Capitol – that would be the big domed building that dominates the eastern end of the National Mall – is the seat of the legislative branch of government, otherwise known as Congress. The underground **Capitol Visitor Center** (www.visitthecapitol.gov; 1st St NE & E Capitol St; ⊘8:30am-4:30pm Mon-Sat) is an introduction to the history and architecture of this iconic structure. Use the center's website to book tours of the Capitol itself.

The Walk >> Walk along the edge of the Capitol towards the Washington Monument (the big obelisk in the middle of the Mall). At the traffic circle, walk onto Maryland Ave; the Botanic Garden will be on your right.

United States Botanic Garden

Resembling London's Crystal Palace, the **United States Botanic Garden** (www.usbg.gov; 100 Maryland Ave SW; ⊘10am-5pm; 👬) provides a beautiful setting for displays of exotic and local plants. Check out titan arum, also known as *Amorphophallus titanum* ('giant misshapen penis'). If you're lucky, the plant's 'corpse flower' will be on display. This Sumatran native only blooms every three to five years; when it does, it smells like rotten meat. Mmm!

The Walk >> Continue on Maryland Ave for a little over 500ft; the National Museum of the American

Indian is on your right-hand side. The curving exterior, fashioned from amber kasota limestone, blobs like an amoeba.

National Museum of the American Indian

The **National Museum of the American Indian** (www.americanindian.si.edu; cnr 4th St & Independence Ave SW; ◷10am-5:30pm; 👶) uses native communities' voices and their own interpretive exhibits to tell respective tribal sagas. The ground-floor **Mitsitam Native Foods Cafe** (www.mitsitamcafe.com; mains $8-18; ◷11am-5pm) is the best dining option on the Mall.

The Walk » Walk west across the Mall, following Jefferson Ave. After about 2000ft you'll reach the doughnut-shaped Hirshhorn Museum.

Hirshhorn Museum and Sculpture Garden

The **Hirshhorn Museum** (www.hirshhorn.si.edu; cnr 7th St & Independence Ave SW; ◷10am-5:30pm, sculpture garden 7:30am-dusk; 👶) houses the Smithsonian's modern art collection. Just across Jefferson

Dr, the sunken **Sculpture Garden** feels, on the right day, like a bouncy jaunt through a Lewis Carroll-style Wonderland. Young lovers, lost tourists and serene locals wander by sculptures such as Rodin's *The Burghers of Calais*.

The Walk » Walk up 7th Ave towards Pennsylvania Ave. Turn left on Pennsylvania Ave and you're at the National Archives.

National Archives

It's hard not to feel a little in awe of the big documents in the **National Archives** (www.archives.gov; 700 Constitution Ave NW; ◷10am-7pm mid-Mar–early Sep, to 5:30pm early Sep–mid-Mar). The Declaration of Independence, the Constitution and the Bill of Rights, plus one of four copies of the Magna Carta: viewed together, it becomes clear just how radical the American experiment was for its time.

The Walk » Getting back to the Library of Congress is easy – just head down Pennsylvania Ave towards the Capitol Building, skirt the Capitol and there you are. But feel free to explore the National Mall while you're down here.

STRETCH YOUR LEGS
BALTIMORE

Start/Finish: Washington Monument

Distance: 1.6 miles

Duration: 3 hours

The Mt Vernon neighborhood of Baltimore is an incredibly handsome collection of brownstone townhouses, Federal architecture and slate-grey stateliness. Experience its considerable charms on this walk, which takes in classic museums, old libraries and great eats.

Take this walk on Trips

Washington Monument

For the best views of Baltimore, climb the 228 steps of this 178ft-tall Doric column, better known as Baltimore's **Washington Monument** (699 Washington Pl; suggested donation $5; ⊙10am-5pm Wed-Sun). The ground floor contains a museum about Washington's life. The surrounding circle of cobblestones and green lawns is known as Mt Vernon Place, and is one of the most attractive photo opportunities in Baltimore.

The Walk » Walters Art Museum is only 500ft away. Walk downhill on Charles St, then turn right on Centre St to reach the entrance.

Walters Art Museum

Do not pass up the **Walters** (☎410-547-9000; www.thewalters.org; 600 N Charles St; ⊙10am-5pm Wed-Sun, to 9pm Thu), a fantastic art museum whose collection spans over 55 centuries, from ancient to contemporary, with excellent displays of Asian treasures, rare and ornate manuscripts and books, and a comprehensive French paintings collection. It is, essentially, a repository of every kind of cool stuff, and we could lose a week wandering its galleries. And by the way – it's free.

The Walk » Continue west on Centre St and turn left on Cathedral St. The Pratt Library is on your right after 500ft.

Enoch Pratt Free Library

The **Enoch Pratt Free Library** (400 Cathedral St; ⊙10am-8pm Mon-Wed, to 5pm Thu-Sat, 1-5pm Sun; 🛜) was established in 1882 when philanthropist Enoch Pratt gave the city a $1 million endowment towards the remarkably progressive idea of establishing a library that 'shall be for all, rich and poor without distinction of race or color.' The grand central reading room is marvelous, all natural light and baroque-esque design flourishes.

The Walk » The Basilica of the Assumption is just around the corner. Walk down Cathedral St, then turn left on Mulberry to get there.

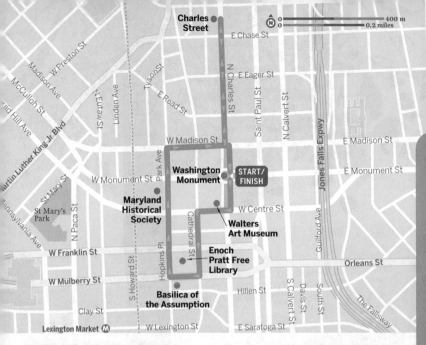

Basilica of the Assumption

Also known as America's First Cathedral, the **Basilica of the National Shrine of the Assumption of the Blessed Virgin Mary** (☎410-727-3565; www.baltimorebasilica.org; 409 Cathedral St; ⏰7am-4pm Mon-Fri, to 5:30pm Sat, to 4:30pm Sun), commonly known as the Basilica of the Assumption, is one of the city's most prominent landmarks. The structure, with its prominent dome and twin spires, is considered the masterpiece of architect Benjamin Henry Latrobe.

The Walk » Head west on Mulberry St for 500ft, then turn right on Park Ave. Walk this way for 1000ft and turn left on Monument St; the Historical Society will be 200ft ahead on your left.

Maryland Historical Society

With more than 5.4 million artifacts, the **Maryland Historical Society** (www.mdhs.org; 201 W Monument St; adult/child $9/6; ⏰10am-5pm Wed-Sat, noon-5pm Sun) is one of the largest collections of Americana in the world, including Francis Scott Key's original manuscript of the *Star-Spangled Banner*. Fascinating permanent exhibits trace Maryland's colonial, Civil War and 19th-century history.

The Walk » Head back the way you came and turn left on Park Ave. Follow for 1000ft and turn right on Madison St. After 500ft turn left on Charles St and follow it uphill for 1500ft.

Charles Street

This residential neighborhood is one of the most pleasant parts of Baltimore. Charles St is the main thoroughfare through the area, meandering past row houses and sidewalk cafes. We recommend eating at **Brewer's Art** (☎410-547-6925; 1106 N Charles St; sandwiches $9-12, mains $19-26; ⏰4pm-2am Mon-Sat, 5pm-2am Sun), which is divided into two portions: a subterranean cave that mesmerizes the senses with an overwhelming selection of beers, and a great upstairs restaurant serving New American cuisine.

The Walk » The Washington Monument is back on Charles St down the hill, about 2000ft from Brewer's Art.

Virginia Trips

VIRGINIA IS DECEPTIVELY BIG, BY WHICH WE MEAN, JEEZ, VIRGINIA IS ENORMOUS. With a western mountain spine, beach-studded ocean coastline, miles of farmland, stately Southern cities, liberal Northeastern-esque suburbs and a political climate that consistently makes her a toss-up in national elections, it's hard to imagine a state with more diversity.

Actually, Virginia is both a state and technically a Commonwealth. The Old Dominion has both produced more presidents than any other state, and led the Confederacy that rebelled against the nation those presidents led.

Admire Jeffersonian architecture. Stew over politics outside DC. Wind along Skyline Drive, or hike in the Blue Ridge Mountains' shadow.

Blue Ridge Parkway Autumn vista (Trip 25)
DAVID SUCSY/GETTY IMAGES ©

Virginia Trips

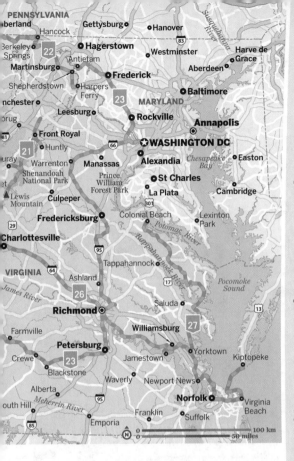

Hear Music

Southwestern Virginia is the soil that American country music and bluegrass are rooted in. Toe tap to fiddles on Trip 24

Beach Bumming

From Virginia Beach's golden sand to quiet corners of the Eastern Shore, there's plenty of watery diversions. Cruise the coast on Trip 27

Oddities Abound

Eccentrics have indulged their creative passions in the small towns and roadside attractions that line the Blue Ridge. Find fun on Trip 25

Peep Into the Past

Living history towns like Williamsburg abut the actual places where America was founded and achieved her independence. Get old-schooled on Trip 26

Trail Trekking

Many trails arc along Skyline Drive, plunging past forests, white waterfalls and lonely mountains. Get your boots on for Trip 21

25 Blue Ridge Parkway 3 Days
Travel through college towns, back-road hamlets and miles of woolly wilderness trails. (p299)

26 Peninsula to the Piedmont 3 days
Visit living history museums, go on sunny wine tours, and dip into university culture and presidential palaces. (p313)

27 Bracketing the Bay 2 days
Enjoy cheesy beach boardwalks and quiet tidewater inlets, with great food in between. (p323)

Luray Caverns *Beautiful limestone stalactites under the Shenandoah Valley*

Classic Trip

Skyline Drive

21

Skyline Drive is one of America's classic road trips. Befittingly, it comes studded like a leather belt with natural wonders and stunning scenery.

TRIP HIGHLIGHTS

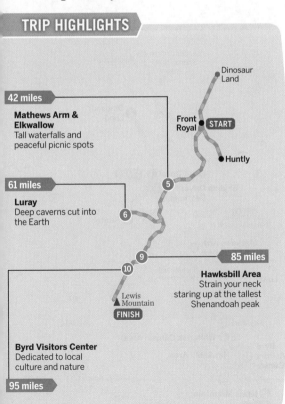

42 miles

Mathews Arm & Elkwallow
Tall waterfalls and peaceful picnic spots

61 miles

Luray
Deep caverns cut into the Earth

85 miles

Hawksbill Area
Strain your neck staring up at the tallest Shenandoah peak

Byrd Visitors Center
Dedicated to local culture and nature

95 miles

**3 DAYS
150 MILES / 240KM**

GREAT FOR...

BEST TIME TO GO

May to November for great weather, open facilities and top views.

 ESSENTIAL PHOTO

The fabulous 360-degree horizon at the top of Bearfence Rock Scramble.

 BEST FOR CULTURE

Byrd Visitors Center offers an illuminating peek into Appalachian folkways.

255

The centerpiece of the ribbon-thin Shenandoah National Park is the jaw-dropping beauty of Skyline Drive, which runs for just over 100 miles atop the Blue Ridge Mountains. Unlike the massive acreage of western parks like Yellowstone or Yosemite, Shenandoah is at times only a mile wide. That may seem to narrow the park's scope, yet it makes it a perfect space for traversing and road-tripping goodness.

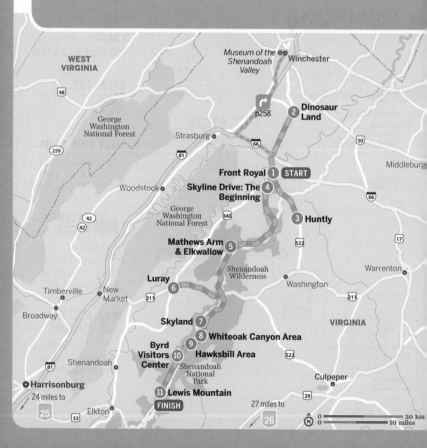

WEST VIRGINIA

48

George Washington National Forest

259

Strasburg

81

Woodstock

42

42

George Washington National Forest

Timberville

New Market

211

Broadway

81

Shenandoah

Harrisonburg

24 miles to

25

Elkton

33

Museum of the Shenandoah Valley

Winchester

p258

2 Dinosaur Land

66

50

Middleburg

Front Royal 1 START

Skyline Drive: The Beginning 4

66

3 Huntly

340

Mathews Arm & Elkwallow 5

523

17

Shenandoah Wilderness

Luray 6

211

Washington

Warrenton

211

Skyland 7

8 Whiteoak Canyon Area

9

Byrd Visitors Center 10

Hawksbill Area

VIRGINIA

523

Shenandoah National Park

11 Lewis Mountain

FINISH

Culpeper

27 miles to

26

29

0   20 km
0   10 miles
N

1 Front Royal

Straddling the northern entrance to the park is the tiny city of Front Royal. Although it's not among Virginia's fanciest ports-of-call, this lush riverside town offers all the urban amenities one might need before a camping or hiking trip up in the mountains.

If you need to gather your bearings, an obvious place to start is the **Front Royal Visitor Center** (☎800-338-2576; 414 E Main St; ◷9am-5pm). Friendly staff are on hand to overwhelm you with information about what to do in the area.

For a summer night under the stars with endangered species, check out

LINK YOUR TRIP

26 Peninsula to the Piedmont

At the end of this trip, continue on to the park exit, then turn east to Charlottesville to explore the Piedmont's breweries and wineries.

25 Blue Ridge Parkway

You can also head from the park exit to Staunton, VA, about 20 minutes away, to start America's favorite drive.

TOP TIP: MILEPOSTS

Handy stone mileposts (MP) are still the best means of figuring out just where you are on Skyline Drive. They begin at MP 0 near Front Royal, and end at MP 105 at the park's southern entrance near Rockfish Gap.

the Smithsonian Conservation Biology Institute (p262).

🍴🛏 p264

The Drive » Dinosaur Land is 10 miles north of Front Royal, towards Winchester, via US 340 (Stonewall Jackson Highway).

2 Dinosaur Land

Before you head into the national park and its stunning natural beauty, visit **Dinosaur Land** (☎540-869-2222; www.dinosaurland.com; 3848 Stonewall Jackson Hwy, White Post; adult/child $6/5; ◷9:30am-5:30pm Mar-May, to 6:30pm in summer, to 5pm Sep-Dec; ⊞) for some fantastic man-made tackiness. This spectacularly low-brow shrine-to-concrete sculpture is not to be missed. Although it's an 'educational prehistoric forest,' with more than 50 life-size dinosaurs (and a King Kong for good measure), you'd probably learn more about the tenants by fast-forwarding through *Jurassic Park 3*. But that's not why you've stopped here, so grab

your camera and sidle up to the triceratops for memories that will last a millennium.

The Drive » Head back to Front Royal, then go south on US 522 (Remount Rd) for about 9 miles to reach Huntly.

3 Huntly

Huntly is a smallish town nestled in the green foothills of the Shenandoahs, lying just in the southern shadows of Front Royal. It's a good spot to refuel on some cosmopolitan culture and foodie deliciousness in the form of **Rappahannock Cellars** (☎540-635-9398; www.rappahannockcellars.com; 14437 Hume Road; $8 tasting; ◷11:30am-5pm, to 6pm Sat), one of the nicer wineries of north-central Virginia. Frankly, you get a lot of wine for your buck here, although the real draw is the vineyard-covered hills shadowing the horizon, like some slice of Northern Italian pastoral prettiness that got lost somewhere in the upcountry of the Old Dominion. Give the port

a whirl (well, maybe not if you're driving).

The Drive » Head back to Front Royal, as you'll enter Skyline Drive from there. From the beginning of Skyline Drive, it's 5.5 miles to Dickey Ridge.

- - - - - - - - - - -

④ Skyline Drive: The Beginning

Skyline Drive (☎540-999-3500; www.nps.gov/shen; north entrance at Front Royal; car $10; 🚶) is the scenic drive to end all scenic drives. The 75 overlooks, with views into the Shenandoah Valley and the Piedmont,

are all breathtaking. In spring and summer, endless variations on the color green are sure to enchant, just as the vibrant reds and yellows will amaze you in autumn. This might be your chance to finally hike a section of the Appalachian Trail, which crosses Skyline Drive at 32 places.

The logical first stop on an exploration of Skyline and Shenandoah National Park is the **Dickey Ridge Visitors Center** (☎540-635-3566; Skyline Dr, mile 4.6; ⏰9am-5pm Apr-Nov). It's not just an informative leaping-off point; it's a building with a fascinating history all of its own. This spot originally operated as a

'wild' dining hall in 1908 (back then, that simply meant it had a terrace for dancing). However, it closed during WWII and didn't reopen until 1958, when it became a visitor center. Now it's one of the park's two main information centers and contains a little bit of everything you'll need to get started on your trip along Skyline Drive.

The Drive » It's a twisty 19 more miles along Skyline Drive to Mathews Arm.

- - - - - - - - - -

TRIP HIGHLIGHT

⑤ Mathews Arm & Elkwallow

Mathews Arm is the first major section of Shenandoah National Park you encounter after leaving Dickey's Ridge. Before you get there, you can stop at a pullover at MP 19.4 and embark on a 4.8-mile loop hike to **Little Devils Stairs.** Getting through this narrow gorge is as tough as the name suggests; expect hand-over-hand climbing for some portions.

At Mathews Arm there's a campground as well as an amphitheater, and some nice breezes; early on in your drive, you're already at a 2750ft altitude.

From the amphitheater, it's a 6.5 mile moderately taxing hike to lovely **Overall Run Falls**, the tallest in the

---

DETOUR: MUSEUM OF THE SHENANDOAH VALLEY

Start: ① Front Royal

Of all the places where you can begin your journey into Shenandoah National Park, none seem to make quite as much sense as the **Museum of the Shenandoah Valley** (☎540-662-1473, 888-556-5799; www.shenandoahmuseum.org; 901 Amherst St; adult/student $10/8; ⏰10am-4pm Tue-Sun), an institution dedicated to its namesake. Located in the town of Winchester, some 25 miles north of Front Royal, the museum is an exhaustive repository of information on the valley, Appalachian culture and its associated folkways, some of the most unique in the USA. Exhibits are divided into four galleries, accompanied by the restored Glen Burnie historical home (closed until 2014) and six acres of gardens.

To get there, take I-66 west from Front Royal to I-81 and head north for 25 miles. In Winchester, follow signs to the museum, which is on the outskirts of town.

Shenandoah Valley Colorful Virginian town in the valley

national park (93 ft). There's plenty of rock ledges where you can enjoy the view and snap a picture, but be warned that the falls sometimes dry out in the summer.

Elkwallow Wayside, which includes a nice picnic area and lookout, is at MP 24, just past Mathews Arm.

The Drive » From Mathews Arm, proceed south along Skyline for about 10 miles, then take the US 211 ramp westbound for about 7 miles to reach Luray.

- - - - - - - - - - - -

TRIP HIGHLIGHT

6 Luray

Luray is a good spot to grab some grub and potentially rest your head if you're not into camping. It's also where you'll find the wonderful

Luray Caverns (☎540-7 43-6551; www.luraycaverns. com; Rte 211; adult/child $21/10; ⏰9am-7pm Jun-Aug, to 6pm Sep-Nov, Apr & May, to 4pm Mon-Fri Dec-Mar), one of the most extensive cavern systems on the East Coast.

Here you can take a one-hour, roughly 1-mile guided tour of these caves, opened to the public more than 100 years ago. The rock formations throughout are quite stunning, and Luray boasts what is surely a one-of-a-kind attraction – the Stalacpipe Organ – in the pit of its belly. This crazy contraption has been banging out melodies on the rock formations for decades. As the guide says, the caves are 400

million years old '*if* you believe in geological dating' (if the subtext is lost on you, understand this is a conservative part of the country where creationism is widely accepted, if hotly debated). No matter what you believe in, you'll be impressed by the fantastic underground expanses.

✖ ⭘ p265

The Drive » Take US 211 east for 10 miles to get back on Skyline Drive. Then proceed 10 miles south along Skyline to get to Skyland. Along the way you'll drive over the highest point of Skyline Drive (3680ft). At MP 40.5, just before reaching Skyland, you can enjoy amazing views from the parking overlook at Thorofare Mountain (3595ft).

Classic Trip

GREG DALE/GETTY IMAGES ©

PAT & CHUCK BLACKLEY/ALAMY ©

WHY THIS IS A CLASSIC TRIP
ADAM KARLIN, AUTHOR

Skyline Drive is one of America's original scenic drives. The Shenandoah Valley is a mind-bendingly beautiful combination of two seemingly at odds ecosystems: the rough, forested mountains of the Appalachians on one hand, and the manicured hills of the Virginia Piedmont on the other. We've included plenty of grand hikes and great food to accompany you on your way among the clouds.

Top: Bearfence Mountain
Left: Black bear cub
Right: Dinosaur Land, White Post

FRANCK FOTOS/ALAMY ©

❼ Skyland

Horse-fanciers will want to book a trail ride through Shenandoah at **Skyland Stables** (📞540-999-2210; guided group rides 1/2½hr $30/50; 🕘9am-5pm May-Oct). Rides last up to two-and-a-half hours and are a great way to see the wildlife and epic vistas. Pony rides are also available for the wee members of your party. This is a good spot to break up your trip if you're into hiking (and if you're on this trip, we're assuming you are).

You've got great access to local trailheads around here, and the sunsets are fabulous. The accommodations are a little rustic, but in a charming way (the Trout Cabin was built in 1911, and it feels like it, but we mean this in the most complimentary way possible.) The place positively oozes nostalgia, but if you're into amenities, you may find it a little dilapidated.

The Drive >> It's only 1.5 miles south on Skyline Drive to get to the Whiteoak parking area.

❽ Whiteoak Canyon Area

At MP 42.6, Whiteoak Canyon is another area of Skyline Drive that offers unmatched hiking and exploration opportunities. There are several parking areas that all provide

Classic Trip

different entry points to the various trails that snake through this ridge- and stream-scape.

Most hikers are attracted to Whiteoak Canyon for its **waterfalls** – there are six in total, with the tallest topping out at 86ft high. At the Whiteoak parking area, you can make the 4.6-mile round trip hike to these cascades,

but beware – it's both a steep climb up and back to your car. To reach the next set of waterfalls, you'll have to add 2.7 miles to the round trip and prepare yourself for a steep (1100ft) elevation shift.

The **Limberlost Trail** and parking area is just south of Whiteoak Canyon. This is a moderately difficult 1.3-mile trek into spruce upcountry thick with hawks, owls and other birds; the boggy ground is home to many salamanders.

The Drive » It's about 3 miles south of Whiteoak Canyon to the Hawksbill area via Skyline Drive.

TRIP HIGHLIGHT

9 Hawksbill Area

Once you reach MP 45.6, you've reached **Hawksbill**, the name of both this part of Skyline Drive and the tallest peak in Shenandoah National Park. Numerous trails in this area skirt the summits of the mountain.

Pull into the parking area at Hawksbill Gap (MP 45.6). You've got a

LOCAL KNOWLEDGE:
SMITHSONIAN CONSERVATION BIOLOGY INSTITUTE

If you're into wildlife, one of the coolest adventures you can embark upon on the Eastern seaboard is a Conservation Campout with the **Smithsonian Conservation Biology Institute** (SCBI; 202-633-2614, 540-635-6500; http://nationalzoo.si.edu/ActivitiesAndEvents/Activities/ConservationCampout; 1500 Remount Road, Front Royal; $125; Jun-Aug;) The Smithsonian Institution is a collection of museum and research centers dedicated to 'the increase and diffusion of knowledge;' the SCBI is the umbrella organization for the Smithsonian's conservation work and research.

Based in Front Royal, the SCBI is generally closed to the public. But during the summer months, via the Friends of the National Zoo (FONZ), SCBI hosts overnight trips during the weekends that put you face to face with its conservation efforts. You'll be allowed (under the supervision of SCBI staff) to explore an animal habitat area; some of the species based at the center include maned wolves, cheetahs, black-footed ferrets and clouded leopards. Following this, you'll camp under the stars in four-person tents and have a continental breakfast the next day, along with family-oriented activities throughout your stay.

This activity is aimed at families (a maximum of six people can register per campout), but some campouts are adults only. In addition, children must be aged six or older, and anyone under 18 must be accompanied by a paying adult. With all that said, the experience comes highly recommended; you're having a wildlife encounter with trained, very knowledgeable professionals. Registration for campouts begins in spring (check website for details); register fast, as this is a popular event.

– Adam Karlin

few hiking options to pick from. The **Lower Hawksbill Trail** is a steep 1.7-mile round trip that circles Hawksbill Mountain's lower slopes; that huff-inducing ascent yields a pretty great view over the park. Another great lookout lays at the end of the **Upper Hawksbill Trail**, a moderately difficult 2.1-mile trip. You can link up with the Appalachian Trail here via a spur called the Salamander Trail.

If you continue south for about 5 miles you'll reach **Fishers Gap Overlook**. The attraction here is the **Rose River Loop**, a 4-mile, moderately strenuous trail that is positively Edenic. Along the way you'll pass by waterfalls, under thick forest canopy and over swift-running streams.

The Drive » From Fishers Gap, head about a mile south to the Byrd Visitors Center, technically located at MP 51.

- - - - - - - -

TRIP HIGHLIGHT

⑩ Byrd Visitors Center

The **Byrd Visitors Center** (☎540-999-3283; Skyline Dr, MP 50; ◷9am-5pm Apr-Nov) is the central visitor center of Shenandoah National Park, marking (roughly) a halfway point between the two ends of Skyline Drive. It's devoted to explaining

the settlement and development of the Shenandoah Valley via a series of small but well-curated exhibitions; as such, it's a good place to stop and learn about the surrounding culture (and pick up backcountry camping permits). There's camping (p264) and ranger activities in the **Big Meadows** area, located across the road from the visitor center.

The **Story of the Forest** trail is an easy, paved, 1.8-mile loop that's quite pretty; the trailhead connects to the visitor center. You can also explore two nearby waterfalls. **Dark Hollow Falls**, which sounds (and looks) like something out of a Tolkien novel, is a 70ft high cascade located at the end of a quite steep 1.4-mile trail. **Lewis Falls**, accessed via Big Meadows, is on a moderately difficult 3.3-mile trail that intersects the Appalachian Trail; at one point you'll be scrabbling up a rocky slope.

The Drive » The Lewis Mountain area is about 5 miles south of the Byrd Visitors Center via Skyline Drive. Stop for good overlooks at Milam Gap and Naked Creek (both clearly signposted from the road).

- - - - - - - -

⑪ Lewis Mountain

Lewis Mountain is both the name of one of the major camping areas (p265) of Shenandoah National Park and a nearby 3570ft mountain. The trail to the mountain is only about a mile long with a small elevation gain, and leads to a nice overlook. But the best view here is at the **Bearfence Rock Scramble.** That name is no joke; this 1.2-mile hike gets steep and rocky, so don't attempt it during or after rainfall. The reward is one of the best panoramas of the Shenandoahs. After you leave, remember there are still about 50 miles of Skyline Drive between you and the park exit at Rockfish Gap.

Eating & Sleeping

Front Royal ❶

✕ Apartment 2G Fusion $$$

(☏540-636-9293; 206 S Royal Ave; 5 courses $50, tapas $6-14; ⊘from 6:30pm Sat & third Thurs) The best restaurant in Front Royal is only open once a week (well, twice if you count the third Thursday of the month, when it serves tapas). Owned and operated by a husband-and-wife team (two chefs from the acclaimed Inn at Little Washington), the Apartment's culinary philosophy is simple and wonderful: uncompromisingly fresh ingredients fashioned into ever-changing five-course fixed menus.

✕ Element Fusion $$

(☏540-636-9293; jsgourmet.com; 206 S Royal Ave; mains $12-22; ⊘11am-3pm & 5-10pm Tue-Sat; ✍) Element is the casual-but-gourmet-quality cousin of Apartment 2G, owned and operated by that restaurant's proprietors. It's a superior spot for sandwiches and soup, and the dinner mains, which revolve around a fusion of Asia and Appalachia (think quail with shitaake mushrooms), are excellent. Vegetarian options (including a righteous avocado sandwich and vegetables cooked in Caribbean jerk spices) are plentiful and delicious.

✕ Jalisco's Mexican $

(☏540-635-7348; 1303 N Royal Ave; mains $8-15; ⊘11am-10pm Mon-Thu, to 11pm Fri & Sat, to 9:30pm Sun) Jalisco's has pretty good Mexican food. It's definitely the sort of Mexican that derives flavor from refried beans and melted cheese, but that's not such a terrible thing (well, unless we're talking about your heart). The chili relleños go down a treat, as do the margaritas.

✕ Main Street Mill & Tavern Cafe $

(☏540-636-3123; 500 E Main St; mains $6-15; ⊘10:30am-9pm Sun-Thu, to 10pm Fri & Sat; ♿) This folksy restaurant is located in a spacious renovated 1880s feed mill. There are no big surprises when it comes to the cuisine, which is of the soup and sandwich and salad school of cookery, but it is filling and satisfying and does the job.

⌂ Killahevlin B&B B&B $$

(☏800-847-6132, 540-636-7335; www.vairish.com; 1401 N Royal Ave; r/ste $155-225/255-285) This Irish-style B&B is located in a lovely old building that's on the National Register of Historic Places. There's free beer on tap for guests, because clichés sell as well as quaintness, we suppose. Rooms are quite flowery and service is friendly.

⌂ Woodward House on Manor Grade B&B $$

(☏800-635-7011, 540-635-7010; www.acountryhome.com; 413 S Royal Ave/US 320; r $110-155, cottage $225; ℗🔊) This cluttered B&B has eight bright rooms complemented by owners who bring a lot of cheerful energy to the table. Serves as a lovely base for exploring the northern reaches of Shenandoah National Park.

Shenandoah National Park

The following three accommodation options are all operated by the same concessionaire. There are also four **campgrounds** (☏877-444-6777; www.recreation.gov; sites $15-25) in the park if you're so inclined.

⌂ Big Meadows Lodge Lodge $$

(☏540-999-2255; www.goshenandoah.com/Big-Meadows-Lodge.aspx; Skyline Dr, MP 51.2; r $130-210; ⊘late May-Oct; 🔊♿) This *Wonder Years*–reminiscent lodge and campsite is located in the heart of Skyline Drive at MP 51.2 (Byrd Visitors Center). The atmosphere here is very peaceful, as chipmunks and birds go flitting about the branches. You can stay in either the 1939 stone lodge or one of the rustic cabins that are the picture of 1950s vacation paradise. Wi-fi is available in the central buildings of the lodge campus.

🛏 Lewis Mountain Cabins   Cabins $

(📞877-247-9261; www.goshenandoah.com/
Lewis-Mountain-Cabins.aspx; Skyline Dr, MP
57.6; cabins $90-100, campsites $16; 🕘Apr-Oct;
P🐾) Lewis Mountain has several furnished
cabins complete with private bathrooms for a hot
shower. The complex also has a campground with
a store, a laundry and showers. This is the most
rustic accommodation option in the area short of
camping. Bear in mind many cabins are attached,
although we've never heard our neighbors here.

🛏 Skyland Resort   Resort $$

(📞877-247-9261; www.goshenandoah.com/
Skyland-Resort.aspx; Skyline Dr, MP 41.7; r from
$140, incl breakfast $150; 🕘Apr-Oct; P🐾)
Founded in 1888, this beautiful resort has
fantastic views over the countryside, which is
unsurprising as it occupies one of the highest
points within Shenandoah National Park
(the elevation of the hotel is around 3680ft).
You'll find simple, wood-finished rooms and a
full-service dining room, and you can arrange
horseback rides from here.

Luray ❻

🍴 Gathering Grounds
Patisserie & Cafe   Bakery $

(📞540-743-1121; 55 E Main St; baked goods
under $5, mains $5-7; 🕘7am-6pm Mon-Thu, to
7pm Fri, 8am-7pm Sat, 11am-3pm Sun; 🛜📶)
If you need a bit of caffeine or an internet
break, Gathering Grounds is the spot to stop
by in Luray. The coffee is served strong and
the pastries are all tasty, but what really sets
this place apart is the interior, a refreshingly
innovative, airy space that combines warm
artsy-hippie cafe chic with modern hip.

🍴 West Main Market   Deli $

(📞540-743-1125; 123 W Main St; mains
$5-7; 🕘10am-6pm Tue-Thu, to 7pm Fri & Sat;
P📶🐾) Exploring Skyline Drive lends itself
to picnic lunches, and there are few better
places to pick up said lunch then the salad and
sandwich counter at West Main. The grilled
turkey and avocado is wonderful, while the fresh
garden salad kept us rolling all the way down
Skyline Drive.

🛏 Yogi Bear's Jellystone
Park Campsite   Camping $

(📞800-420-6679; www.campluray.com; 2250
Hwy 211 East; campsites/cabins from $30/85;
🐾) Miniature-golf courses, waterslides and
paddleboats all await inside this fanciful
campus. Bargain-basement campsite and
cabin prices don't reflect the possibility you
might strike it rich while panning for gold at Old
Faceful Mining Company. For those interested
in passing by and peeking in, there are a few
oversized figures of Yogi and Boo Boo that are
ready-made photo ops.

Berkeley Springs
*Roman-style bathhouse
fed by mineral springs*

Across the Appalachian Trail

22

Who doesn't love a good nature hike? On this trip we shadow the back roads that run by the mountains, waterfalls and small towns of the Eastern seaboard's most rugged up-country.

TRIP HIGHLIGHTS

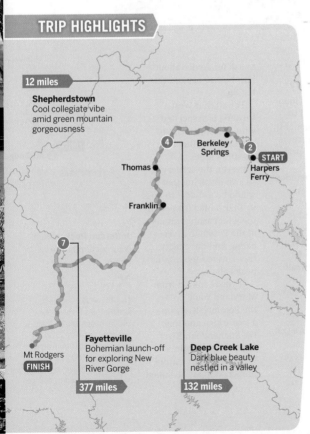

12 miles

Shepherdstown
Cool collegiate vibe amid green mountain gorgeousness

4 Berkeley Springs

Thomas ●

2 **START**
Harpers Ferry

Franklin ●

7

Mt Rodgers
FINISH

Fayetteville
Bohemian launch-off for exploring New River Gorge

377 miles

Deep Creek Lake
Dark blue beauty nestled in a valley

132 miles

5 DAYS
495 MILES /
796KM

GREAT FOR...

BEST TIME TO GO

From September to November; brisk fall air is good for hikes.

 ESSENTIAL PHOTO

The cascades at Muddy Falls, Deep Creek Lake.

BEST FOR CULTURE

Live music at The Purple Fiddle.

22 Across the Appalachian Trail

The Appalachian Trail runs 2175 miles from Maine to Georgia, across the original American frontier and some of the oldest mountains on the continent. This journey fleshes out the unique ecological-cultural sphere of the greater Appalachians, particularly in Maryland, West Virginia and Virginia. Get your hiking boots on and get ready for sun-dappled national forests, quaint tree-shaded towns and many a wild, unfettered mountain range.

OHIO

Parkersburg

77

Spen

79

◉ Charleston

Fayetteville 7

Guyandotte River

77

Princeton

Bluefield

Jefferson National Forest

Marion

81

Wyth

24 **FINISH**

8 Mt Rodgers

TENNESSEE

NORTH CAROLI

---

1 Harpers Ferry

While the Appalachian Trail isn't integral to this trip, we do honor it where we can. Harpers Ferry, a postcard-perfect little town nestled between the Shenandoah and Potomac Rivers, is home to some of the most beautiful scenery along said trail. Conveniently, this is also the headquarters for the **Appalachian Trail Conservancy** (304-535-6331; www.appalachiantrail. org; 799 Washington Trail, cnr Washington & Jackson Sts; 9am-5pm Mon-Fri Apr-Oct). The visitor center is located in the heart of town on Washington St and is a great place to ask for advice about how best to explore this region.

For all that West Virginia is associated with the Appalachian Trail, it's only home to a scant 4 miles of it. However, the scenery is so awe-inspiring that it would be a shame to miss it. Take a hike framed by the wild rushing rapids of the Potomac River below, and the craggy, tree-covered mountain peaks above.

If you're hiking from Maryland you'll cross the Potomac River on a footbridge and then the Shenandoah River to pass into Virginia. While in West Virginia proper, stop at the famed **Jefferson Rock**, which is an ideal place for a picnic.

 p275

The Drive » Head west from Harpers Ferry on US 340 for about 3 miles, then turn right onto WV-230N. It's about 9 miles from here to Shepherdstown. Parking downtown is heavily regulated because of the nearby college,

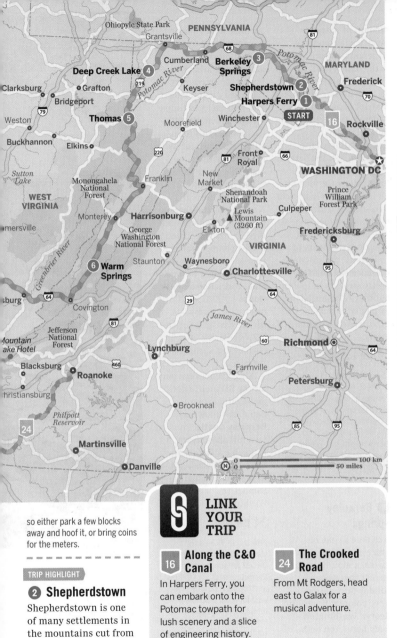

so either park a few blocks
away and hoof it, or bring coins
for the meters.

- - - - - - - - - - - - - - - -

TRIP HIGHLIGHT

② Shepherdstown

Shepherdstown is one
of many settlements in
the mountains cut from
a similar cloth – artsy
college towns that
balance a significant

**LINK
YOUR
TRIP**

**16 Along the C&O
Canal**

In Harpers Ferry, you
can embark onto the
Potomac towpath for
lush scenery and a slice
of engineering history.

**24 The Crooked
Road**

From Mt Rodgers, head
east to Galax for a
musical adventure.

amount of natural beauty with a quirky, bohemian culture. This is the oldest town in West Virginia, founded in 1762, and its **historic district** is packed with Federal-style brick buildings that are heartrendingly cute.

The bulk of the best preservation can be found along German St; all of the cutest historical twee-ness is within walking distance of here. The historic center is also close to Shepherd University; the student presence can be felt pretty strongly in town, but they're balanced out by plenty of pick-up-driving West Virginia locals.

 p275

The Drive >> Head west on WV-45 (the Martinsburg Pike) for around 8 miles. Then turn right onto US 11 N/WV-9 W (which quickly becomes just WV-9) and follow it to the northwest, through the mountains, for 24 miles. Follow the signs for Berkeley Springs.

- - - - - - - - - - - - -

③ Berkeley Springs

Welcome to one of America's original spa towns, a mountainside retreat that's been a holiday destination since colonial times (did George Washington sleep here? You bet). The draw has always been the warm mineral springs, long rumored to have healing properties; such rumors have attracted a mix of people, from country folk with pickup trucks and gun racks to hippie refugees from the '60s.

Although this town is still best known for its spas, one of the more enjoyable activities here is strolling around and soaking up the odd New-Age-crystal-therapy-meets-the-Hatfields-and-the-McCoys vibe. If you do need a pamper, immerse yourself in the relaxation that is Berkeley Springs State Park's **Roman Bath House** (☎304-258-2711; www. berkeleyspringssp.com/spa. html; 2 S Washington St; bath $22; ⏱10am-6pm) and its enchanting, spring-fed pools.

Also: keep an eye out for the Samuel Taylor Suit Cottage, more popularly known as **Berkeley Castle**. Perched on a hill above town, it looks like a European fortress and was built in 1885 for Colonel Samuel Taylor Suit of Washington, DC.

 p275

The Drive >> Head into Maryland by going north on US 522 for about 6 miles; take the exit towards US 40/I-68 westbound. Follow this road west for around 62 miles through Maryland's western mountain spine. Take MD-495 south for 3.5 miles, then turn right onto Glendale Rd and follow it to Deep Creek Lake.

HARRISON SHULL/GETTY IMAGES ©

- - - - - - - - - - - -

TRIP HIGHLIGHT

④ Deep Creek Lake

Deep in Western Maryland, plunked into a blue valley at the end

Fayetteville Bridge over New River Gorge

of a series of tree-ridged mountains, is Maryland's largest lake: Deep Creek. With some 69 miles of shoreline stretching through the hills, there's a lot of outdoor activities here, as well as a small town for lodging and food. Try to arrive in October, when the **Autumn Glory Festival** (www.autumngloryfestival. com) celebrates the shocking fire hues of crimson and orange that paint a swathe across the local foliage. The **Garrett County Visitor Center** (☎301-387-4386; www.visitdeepcreek.com; 15 Visitor Center Dr, McHenry) is a good launching point for exploring the region.

DETOUR:
MOUNTAIN LAKE HOTEL

Start: ⑦ Fayetteville

If you're looking to have the time of your life, head two hours south of Fayetteville into the far southwestern corner of Virginia. The **Mountain Lake Hotel** (☑540-626-7172; www.mountainlakehotel.com; 115 Hotel Circle, Pembroke; r $190-500) is an old stalwart of Appalachian tourism plunked on the shores of (imagine that) Mountain Lake. It also doubled as the Catskills resort 'Kellerman's' in a little movie called *Dirty Dancing*. If you're tired of hiking, you might be interested in taking part in one of the theme weekends, where you can take dance lessons and finally learn to nail that impossible lift. Sadly, Jennifer Grey, Patrick Swayze and Jerry Orbach are not included. There are a variety of accommodations at the resort: some will prefer the massive, historic flagstone main building with traditional hotel rooms; others seeking the full *Dirty Dancing* experience might enjoy the rustic lakeside cabins (comfortably modern inside) where Baby and her family stayed. Appalachian Trail purists who just can't wait to hit the trail again will find it just north of this 2600-acre resort. The Mountain Lake Hotel offers all sorts of other entertainments as well. Got a talent for the talent show? Nobody puts Baby in a corner!

If you've succeeded in meeting your new partner through a series of impromptu, yet still intricately choreographed dirty dances, you can return home. But if for some reason you didn't connect, set off on the trail again and maybe find that mountain man or woman of your dreams.

The lake is most easily accessed via **Deep Creek Lake State Park** (☑301-387-5563; 898 State Park Road, Swanton; ⊘8am-sunset Mar-Oct, from 10am Nov-Feb; **P**🚻🎿), which sits on a large plateau known as the Tablelands. The area is carpeted in oak and hickory forest, and black-bear sightings, while uncommon, are not unheard of. Nearby is **Swallow Falls State Park** (☑301-387-6938; Swallow Falls Rd; ⊘8am-sunset Mar-Oct, from 10am Nov-Feb; **P**🚻🎿), one of the most rugged, spectacular parks in the state. Hickory and hemlock trees hug the Youghiogheny River,

which cuts a white line through wet-slate gorges. On site is the 53ft Muddy Creek Falls, the largest in the state.

The Drive » Take US 219 southbound out of Garrett County and into West Virginia. You'll be climbing though some dramatic mountain scenery on the way. Once you cross the George Washington Hwy, you're almost in West Virginia. It's about 30 miles from Deep Creek Lake to Thomas.

--- --- --- --- --- ---

⑤ Thomas

Thomas isn't more than a blip on the...where'd it go? Oh, there it is. The big business of note for travelers here is **The Purple Fiddle** (☑304-463-

4040; www.purplefiddle.com; 21 East Ave), one of those great mountain stores where bluegrass culture and artsy day-trippers from the urban South and Northeast mash up into a stomping good time. There's live music every night and it's a popular place so you may want to purchase tickets for weekend shows in advance. The artsy Fiddle is an unexpected surprise out here, and a fun one at that.

About 5 miles south of Thomas is **Blackwater Falls State Park** (☑304-259-5216; www.blackwaterfalls.com; 1584 Blackwater Lodge Road). The falls tumble into an

8-mile gorge lined by red spruce, hickory and hemlock trees. There are loads of hiking options; look for the **Pendleton Point Overlook**, which perches over the deepest, widest point of the Canaan Valley.

The Drive » From Thomas, you'll be taking the Appalachian Hwy south. The numerical and name designation of the road will switch a few times, from US 33 to WV-28 and back. After about 50 miles turn right onto US 220 and follow it for 31 miles to Warm Springs. This entire drive is particularly beautiful, all green mountains and small towns, so take your time and enjoy.

⑥ Warm Springs

There's barely a gas station in sight out here, let alone a mall. You've crossed back into Virginia, and are now in the middle of the 1.8- million-acre **George Washington & Jefferson National Forests** (📞540-839-2521; www.fs.usda.gov/gwj; 422 Forestry Road, Hot Springs; campsites around $12, primitive camping free). We have provided details for the Warm Springs Ranger District, one of eight districts managing this enormous protected area, which stretches from Virginia to Kentucky.

There are far too many trails in this area alone to list here. Note that most trails in the region are not actually in the town of Warm Springs; there is a ranger office here, and staff can direct you to the best places to explore. Some favorites include the 1-mile **Brushy Ridge Trail**, which wends past abundant blueberry and huckleberry bushes, and the 2.3-mile **Gilliam Run Trail**, which ascends to the top of Beard Mountain.

TRIP HIGHLIGHT

⑦ Fayetteville

You've crossed state lines yet again, and are back in West Virginia. Little Fayetteville serves as the gateway to the New River Gorge, a canyon cut by a river that is, rather ironically, one of the oldest rivers in North America. Some 70,000 acres of the gorge is gazetted as national park land.

Canyon Rim Visitor Center (📞304-574-2115; www.nps.gov/neri; 162 Visitor Center Road Lansing, WV; ⊙9am-5pm), just north of the impressive gorge bridge, is the only one of five National Park Service visitor centers along the river that's open year-round. It provides information on river outfitters, gorge climbing, hiking and

MYSTERY HOLE!

Oh man. We like roadside kitsch. And as such, we want to marry the **Mystery Hole** (📞304-658-9101; www.mysteryhole.com; 16724 Midland Trail, Ansted; adult/child $6/5; ⊙10:30am-6pm) and have its Mysterious Hole-y kitschy babies.

So just what is the Mystery Hole? Well, we feel like giving away the secret sort of ruins the nature of this attraction, located about 10 miles northwest of Fayetteville, but on the other hand, we know you can't bear the suspense.

So here's the skinny: the Mystery Hole is a house where everything *tilts at an angle*! And there's a great gift shop. And the laws of gravity are defied because *everything tilts at an angle*!

OK: there's not actually a whole (pun intended) lot at the Hole. And that's fine. It's still a hell of a lot of fun, if you come without taking things too seriously. What ultimately makes the Mystery Hole successful kitsch is not the Hole itself, but its promise of weirdness, as tantalizingly suggested by the billboards that proceed it and the fantastically bad art that surrounds it.

mountain biking, as well as white-water rafting to the north on the Gauley River.

If you're interested in that latter activity, also consider contacting the professionals at **Cantrell Ultimate Rafting** (☏304-574-2500, 304-663-2762; www.cantrellultimaterafting.com; 49 Cantrell Dr; packages from $60), which runs several varieties of expeditions onto the water, including rafting for beginners.

 p275

The Drive ≫ Take US 19 south for 15 miles until you can merge with I-64/77 (it eventually becomes just I-77) southbound. Take this road south for 75 miles, then get on I-81 south and follow it for 27 miles to Marion.

- - - - - - - - - - - - - - -

❽ Mt Rodgers

You'll end this trip at the highest mountain in Virginia (and yes, you've crossed state lines again!). There are plenty of trekking opportunities in the **Mt Rodgers National Recreation Area** (☏800-628-7202, 276-783-5196; www.fs.usda.gov/gwj; 3714 Hwy 16, Marion), which is part of the Washington & Jefferson National Forests. Contact the ranger office for information on summiting the peak of Rodgers, and pat yourself on the back for getting here after so many state-border hops! The local **Elk Garden Trailhead** is one of the best access points for tackling the local wilderness, and intersects the actual Appalachian Trail, making for an appropriate finish to the trip.

JOHN BROWN WAX MUSEUM

For those of you who appreciate kitsch and history, the ultimate, if overpriced, attraction to seek out in these parts is the **John Brown Wax Museum** (☏304-535-6342; www.johnbrownwaxmuseum.com; 168 High St, Harpers Ferry; adult/child $7/5; ☺9am-4:30pm, 10am-5:30pm summer).

A white abolitionist, Brown led an ill-conceived slave rebellion in Harpers Ferry that helped spark the Civil War. The uprising went wrong from the start. The first casualty was a free black man, and the raiders were soon surrounded by angry local militia in the Harpers Ferry armory. Local slaves did not rise up as Brown hoped, and the next day two of his sons were killed by the militia. Eventually, a contingent of Marines commanded by Robert E Lee captured the armory and arrested Brown. The *Albany Patriot*, a Georgia newspaper, editorialized on Brown's proposed punishment: 'An undivided South says let him hang.' In the end, that execution was Brown's fate. Northern abolitionists were convinced slavery could only be ended by war, and Southerners were convinced war was required to protect slavery.

Brown was described as eccentric at best, and perhaps mad at worst, by contemporaries, but Frederick Douglass – a leader of the abolitionist movement – held him up as a hero, and wrote: 'Had some other men made such a display of rigid virtue, I should have rejected it, as affected, false, or hypocritical, but in John Brown, I felt it to be as real as iron or granite.'

Stirring stuff, right? It is, which is why there's a cognitive disconnect when you visit the wax museum dedicated to Brown's life. The spot is sort of old-school, but well worth a visit for all that; nothing says historical accuracy like scratchy vocals, jerky animatronics and a light-and-sound show that sounds like it was recorded around the late Cretaceous.

Eating & Sleeping

Harpers Ferry

✖ Secret Six Tavern   Gastropub $

(☎304-535-1159; 186 High St; mains $7-18;
🕒11am-9pm) A fine place to grab a bite,
this convivial pub just down the hill from the
Jackson Rose hotel (p201) has friendly (if
sometimes scattered) service, delicious (if
sometimes greasy) food, and a great selection
of beer.

Shepherdstown ❷

✖ Blue Moon Cafe   Deli $

(☎304-876-1920; 200 E High St; mains
$7-10; 🕒11am-9pm Mon-Sat, noon-8pm
Sun) There's a lot to love about this deli,
with its collegiate and hippie staff, huge
outdoor patio, indoor publike dining area
and excellent menu of healthy and not-so-
healthy salads and sandwiches. The sandwich
menu is intimidatingly large, but everything
is delicious. The place is kind of scruffy, but
therein lays the Blue Moon's counter-culture
charm.

🛏 Bavarian Inn   Hotel $$

(☎304-876-2551; www.bavarianinnwv.com;
164 Shepherd Grade Rd; r from $95-180;
P🐾🛜) This place doesn't just have a cute
Germanic name; the Bavarian takes the Euro-
mountaineering theme and runs with it all the
way up the Alps. The exterior looks like a chalet,
and the rooms have an attractively severe,
clean, comfortable and efficient air that's,
forgive us the stereotype, kind of German. A
nice break from the trails.

Berkeley Springs ❸

✖ Tari's   Fusion $$

(☎304-258-1196; 33 N Washington St; lunch
$8-12, dinner $19-27; 🕒11am-9pm; 🍴) Tari's is
a very Berkeley Springs sort of spot, with fresh
local food and good vegetarian options served in
a laid-back atmosphere with all the right hints of
good karma abounding. The Thai Mahi tacos are a
delicious way to satisfy one's lunch cravings.

🛏 Highlawn Inn   B&B $$

(☎304-258-5700; www.highlawninn.com; r $98-
180, cottage $205-225; 🛜) This quaint B&B has
an excellent diversity of rooms, from cozy nooks
to full-on guest cottages that are good value for
groups. The decor is decidedly of the antique-chic
school of design, and the innkeepers are a friendly
crew.

Fayetteville ❼

✖ Cathedral Café & Bookstore   Cafe $

(☎304-574-0202; 134 S Court St; mains $5-8;
🕒7:30am-4pm; @🛜🍴) Start the day right
with breakfast and coffee under stained-glass
windows. Local staff all seem to either work in or
know someone who works in the local adventure
tourism industry, so it's a good spot to figure
out what's going on in the New River Gorge area.

🛏 River Rock Retreat Hostel   Hostel $

(☎304-574-0394; www.riverrock
retreatandhostel.com; Lansing-Edmond Rd; dm
$23; P❄) Located less than 1 mile north of
the New River Gorge Bridge, this is a well-run
hostel with basic, clean rooms and plenty of
common space. Owner Joy Marr is a wealth of
local information. The dorms are warm and dry,
and feel like heaven after camping.

Fredericksburg *Locals reenact Civil War battles*

Classic Trip

The Civil War Tour

23

Virginia and Maryland pack many of the seminal sites of America's bloodiest war into a space that includes some of the Eastern seaboard's most attractive countryside.

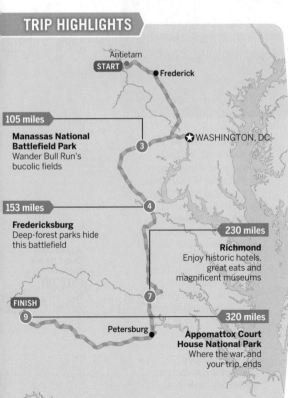

Antietam
START
● Frederick

105 miles

Manassas National Battlefield Park
Wander Bull Run's bucolic fields

3

★ WASHINGTON, DC

153 miles

4

Fredericksburg
Deep-forest parks hide this battlefield

230 miles

Richmond
Enjoy historic hotels, great eats and magnificent museums

FINISH

9

7

Petersburg ●

320 miles

Appomattox Court House National Park
Where the war, and your trip, ends

---

3 DAYS
320 MILES / 515KM

GREAT FOR...

BEST TIME TO GO

September to November for sunny skies and autumnal color shows at preserved battlefields.

ESSENTIAL PHOTO

The fences and fields of Antietam at sunset.

BEST FOR FOODIES

Lamb burgers at Richmond's Burger Bach.

Classic Trip

23 The Civil War Tour

The Civil War was fought from 1861–65 in the nation's backyards, and many of those backyards are between Washington, DC and Richmond. On this trip you will cross battlefields where over 100,000 Americans perished and are buried, foe next to foe. Amid rolling farmlands, sunny hills and deep forests, you'll discover a jarring juxtaposition of bloody legacy and bucolic scenery, and along the way, the places where America forged her identity.

1 Antietam

While most of this trip takes place in Virginia, there is Civil War ground to be covered in neighboring Maryland, a border state officially allied with the Union yet close enough to the South to have Southern sympathies. Confederate General Robert E Lee, hoping to capitalize on a friendly populace, tried to invade Maryland early in the conflict. The subsequent Battle of Antietam, fought in

Sharpsburg, MD, on September 17, 1862, has the dubious distinction of marking the bloodiest day in American history. The battle site is preserved at **Antietam National Battlefield** (☎301-432-5124; www.nps.gov/anti; 5831 Dunker Church Rd, Sharpsburg, MD; ⏱8:30am-around 6pm) in the corn-and-hill country of north-central Maryland.

As befits an engagement that claimed 22,000 casualties in the course of a single, nightmarish day, even the local geographic nomenclature has become violent. An area known as the Sunken Road turned into 'Bloody Lane' after bodies were stacked there. In the park's cemetery, many of the Union gravestones bear the names of Irish and German immigrants who died in a country they had only recently adopted.

The Drive ≫ Take MD-65 south out of Antietam to the town of Sharpsburg. From here, take MD-34 east for 6 miles, then turn right onto US 40A (eastbound). Take US 40A for 11 miles, then merge onto US 70 south, followed 3 miles later by US 270 (bypassing Frederick). Take 270 south to the Beltway (I-495); access exit 45B to get to I-66 east, which will eventually lead you to the National Mall, where the next stops are located.

❷ Washington, DC

Washington, DC, was the capital of the Union during the Civil War, just

LINK YOUR TRIP

15 Maryland's National Historic Road

For another look into the past, go east from Antietam to the picturesque and historic Frederick.

16 Along the C&O Canal

Enjoy the scenery as you head 10 miles southwest of Antietam to the bucolic Harpers Ferry.

as it is the capital of the country today. While the city was never invaded by the Confederacy, thousands of Union soldiers passed through, trained and drilled inside of the city; indeed, the official name of the North's main fighting force was the Army of the Potomac.

The **National Museum of American History** (www.americanhistory.si.edu; cnr 14th St & Constitution Ave NW; ⊙10am-5:30pm, to 7:30pm Jun-Aug; 🚶), located directly on the National Mall, has good permanent exhibitions on the Civil War. Perhaps more importantly, it provides visitors with the context for understanding why the war happened.

Following the war, a grateful nation erected many monuments to Union generals. A statue worth visiting is the **African American Civil War**

Memorial (www.afroamcivilwar.org; cnr U St & Vermont Ave NW; underground rail U St-Cardozo), next to the eastern exit of the U St metro stop, inscribed with the names of soldiers of color who served in the Union army.

The Drive ≫ From Washington, DC, it takes about an hour driving along I-66W to reach Manassas.

TRIP HIGHLIGHT

❸ Manassas National Battlefield Park (Bull Run)

The site of the first major pitched battle of the Civil War is mere minutes from the strip malls of Northern Virginia. NPS-run **Manassas National Battlefield Park** (📞703-361-1339; www.nps.gov/mana; 12521 Lee Hwy; adult/child $3/free, film $3; ⊙8:30am-5pm, tours 11:15am, 12:15pm, 2:15pm Jun-Aug) occupies the site where, in 1861, 35,000 Union soldiers and 32,500 Confederates saw the view you have today: a stretch of gorgeous countryside that has miraculously

survived the predations of the Army of Northern Virginia real-estate developers.

This is as close as many will come to 19th-century rural America; distant hills, dark, brooding tree lines, low curving fields and the soft hump of overgrown trench works.

Following the battle, both sides realized a long war was at hand. Europe watched nervously; in a matter of weeks, the largest army in the world was the Union Army of the Potomac. The second biggest was the Confederate States of America Army. A year later, at the Battle of Shiloh, 24,000 men were listed as casualties – more than all the accumulated casualties of every previous American war combined.

✖ p286

The Drive ≫ In Manassas, take US 29N for 13 miles and then turn left onto US 17S (Marsh Rd). Follow it south for about 35 miles to get to downtown Fredericksburg.

TRIP HIGHLIGHT

❹ Fredericksburg

If battlefields preserve rural America, Fredericksburg is an example of what the nation's main streets once looked like: orderly grids, touches of green and friendly storefronts. But for all its cuteness, this is the site of one of the worst blunders

---

WHAT'S IN A NAME, PART 1?

Although the Civil War is the widely accepted label for the conflict covered in this trip, you'll still hear die-hard Southern boosters refer to the period as the 'War Between the States.' What's the difference? Well, a Civil War implies an armed insurrection against a ruling power that never lost its privilege to govern, whereas the name 'War Between the States' suggests said states always had (and still have) a right to secession from the Republic.

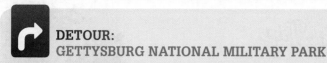

DETOUR:
GETTYSBURG NATIONAL MILITARY PARK

Start: ❶ Antietam

The Battle of Gettysburg, fought in Gettysburg, PA, in July of 1863, marked the turning point of the war and the high-water mark of the Confederacy's attempted rebellion. Lee never made a gambit as bold as this invasion of the North, and his army (arguably) never recovered from the defeat it suffered here.

Gettysburg National Military Park (📞717-334-1124; www.nps.gov/gett; for museum & visitor center, adult/child/senior $12.50/8.50/11.50; ⏲park 6am-10pm Apr-Oct, to 7pm Nov-Mar; museum 8am-6pm Apr-Oct, to 5pm Nov-Mar) does an excellent job of explaining the course and context of the combat. Look for Little Round Top Hill, where a Union unit checked a Southern flanking maneuver, and the field of Pickett's Charge, where the Confederacy suffered its most crushing defeat up to that point. Following the battle Abraham Lincoln gave his Gettysburg Address here to mark the victory and the 'new birth of the nation' on said country's birthday: July 4.

You can easily lose a day here just soaking up the scenery – a gorgeous swath of rolling hills and lush forest interspersed with hollows, rock formations and farmland. To get here, jump on US 15 northbound in Frederick, MD during the drive between Antietam and Washington, DC. Follow 15 north for 35 miles to Gettysburg.

in American military history. In 1862, when the Northern Army attempted a massed charge against an entrenched Confederate position, a Southern artilleryman looked at the bare slope that Union forces had to cross and told a commanding officer, 'A chicken could not live on that field when we open on it.' Sixteen charges resulted in an estimated 6000 to 8000 Union casualties.

Fredericksburg & Spotsylvania National Military Park (adult/child $32/10) is not as immediately compelling as Manassas because of the thick forest that still covers the battlefields, but the woods themselves are a sylvan wonder.

Again, the pretty nature of…well, nature, grows over graves; the nearby Battle of the Wilderness was named for these thick woods, which caught fire and killed hundreds of wounded soldiers after the shooting was finished.

🍴 🛏 p286

The Drive » From Fredericksburg, take US 17 south for five miles, after which 7 becomes VA-2 (also known as Sandy Lane Dr and Fredericksburg Turnpike). Follow this road for 5 more miles, then turn right onto Stonewall Jackson Rd (State Rd 606).

---

❺ Stonewall Jackson Shrine

In Chancellorsville, Robert E Lee,

outnumbered two to one, split his forces and attacked both flanks of the Union army. The audacity of the move caused the Northern force to crumble and flee across the Potomac River, but the victory was costly; in the course of the fighting, Lee's ablest general, Stonewall Jackson, had his arm shot off by a nervous Confederate sentry (the arm is buried near the Fredericksburg National Park visitor center; ask a ranger for directions there).

The wound was patched, but Jackson went on to contract a fatal dose of pneumonia. He was taken to what is now the next stop on this tour: the

WHY THIS IS A CLASSIC TRIP
ADAM KARLIN, AUTHOR

Want to see some of the finest countryside left in the Eastern seaboard, while simultaneously exploring the contradictions, struggles and triumphs at the root of the American experiment? Yeah, we thought so. The Civil War Tour allows travelers to access the formative spaces of the nation, all set against a backdrop of lush fields, dark forests, dirt-rutted country lanes and the immense weight of history.

Top: Visitors at Manassas National Battlefield Park
Left: Walking a trail at Manassas
Right: American Civil War Center, Richmond

Stonewall Jackson Shrine (☎804-633-6076; 12019 Stonewall Jackson Rd, Woodford; ☺9am-5pm) in nearby Guinea Station. In a small white cabin set against attractive Virginia horse-country, overrun with sprays of purple flowers and daisy fields, Jackson uttered a series of prolonged ramblings. Then he fell silent, whispered, 'Let us cross over the river and rest in the shade of the trees,' and died.

The Drive » You can get here via I-95, which you take to I-295S (then take exit 34A), which takes 50 minutes. Or, for a back road experience (1 hour, 10 minutes), take VA-2S south for 35 miles until it connects to VA-643/Rural Point Rd. Stay on VA-643 until it becomes VA-156/Cold Harbor Rd, which leads to the battlefield.

⑥ Cold Harbor Battlefield

By 1864, Union General Ulysses Grant was ready to take the battle into Virginia. His subsequent invasion, dubbed the Overland (or Wilderness) Campaign, was one of the bloodiest of the war. It reached a violent climax at Cold Harbor, just north of Richmond.

At the site now known as **Cold Harbor Battlefield** (☎804-226-1981; www.nps.gov/rich; 5515 Anderson-Wright Dr, Mechanicsville, VA; ☺sunrise-sunset, visitor center 9am-4:30pm), Grant threw his men into a full frontal assault; the

resultant casualties were horrendous, and a precursor to WWI trench warfare.

The area has reverted to a forest and field checkerboard overseen by the National Park Service. Ask a ranger to direct you to the third turnout, a series of Union earthworks from where you can look out at the most preserved section of the fight: the long, low field northern soldiers charged across. This landscape has essentially not changed in over 150 years.

The Drive ≫ From Cold Harbor, head north on VA-156/Cold Harbor Rd for about 3 miles until it intersects Creighton Rd. Turn left on Creighton and follow it for 6 miles into Richmond.

TRIP HIGHLIGHT

⑦ Richmond

There are two Civil War museums in the former capital of the Confederacy,

and they make for an interesting study in contrasts. The **Museum of the Confederacy** (MOC; ☎804-649-1861; www.moc. org; 1201 E Clay St; admission $8; ☺10am-5pm Mon-Sat, from noon Sun) was once a shrine to the Southern 'Lost Cause,' and still attracts a fair degree of neo-Confederate types. But the MOC has also graduated into a respected educational institution, and its collection of Confederate artifacts is probably the best in the country. The optional tour of the Confederate White House is recommended for its quirky insights (did you know the second-most powerful man in the Confederacy may have been a gay Jew?).

On the other hand, the **American Civil War Center** (☎804-780-1865; www.tredegar.org; 490 Tredegar St; adult/student/child 7-12 $8/6/2; ☺9am-5pm; ⌘), located in the old Tredegar ironworks (the main armament producer for the Confederacy), presents the war from three

perspectives: Northern, Southern and African American. Exhibits are well presented and insightful. The effect is clearly powerful and occasionally divisive, a testament to the conflict's lasting impact.

✕ ⍳ p286

The Drive ≫ Take Rte 95 southbound for about 23 miles and get on exit 52. Get onto 301 (Wythe St) and follow until it becomes Washington St, and eventually VA-35/Oaklawn Dr. Look for signs to the battlefield park from here.

⑧ Petersburg

Petersburg, just south of Richmond, is the blue-collar sibling city to the Virginia capital, its center gutted by white flight following desegregation. **Petersburg National Battlefield Park** (US 36; vehicle/pedestrian $5/3; ☺9am-5pm) marks the spot where Northern and Southern soldiers spent almost a quarter of the war in a protracted, trench-induced stand-off. The Battle of the Crater, made well-known in Charles Frazier's *Cold Mountain*, was an attempt by Union soldiers to break this stalemate by tunneling under the Confederate lines and blowing up their fortifications; the end result was Union soldiers caught in the hole wrought by their own sabotage, killed like fish in a barrel.

WHAT'S IN A NAME, PART 2?

One of the more annoying naming conventions of the war goes thus: while the North preferred to name battles for defining geographic terms (Bull Run, Antietam), Southern officers named them for nearby towns (Manassas, Sharpsburg). Although most Americans refer to battles by their Northern names, in some areas folks simply know Manassas as the Battle Of, not as the strip mall with a good Waffle House.

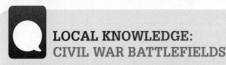

LOCAL KNOWLEDGE:
CIVIL WAR BATTLEFIELDS

What is the appeal of Civil War battlefields?

Civil War battlefields are the touchstone of the not-too-distant past. They are the physical manifestation of the great eruptive moments in American history that defined America for the last 150 years. Large events on a large landscape compel us to think in big terms about big issues.

The Civil War battlefields appeal to visitors because they allow us to walk in the virtual footsteps of great men and women who lived and died fighting for their convictions. Their actions transformed nondescript places into hallmarks of history. The Civil War converted sleepy towns and villages into national shrines based on a moment of intense belief and action. The battlefields literally focus our understanding of the American character.

I linger longest on the battlefields that are best preserved, like Antietam and Gettysburg, because they paint the best context for revealing why things happen the way they do, where they do. Walking where they walked, and seeing the ground they saw, makes these battlefields the ultimate outdoor classrooms in the world!

Why is Virginia such a hot bed for Civil War tourism?

Virginia paid a terrible price during the Civil War. Hosting the capital of the Confederacy only 100 miles from the capital of the United States made sure that the ground between and around the two opposing capitals would be a relentless nightmare of fighting and bloodshed. People can visit individual, isolated battlefields all across America – but people come to Virginia to visit several, many, if not all of them. Unlike anywhere else, Virginia offers a Civil War immersion. It gives visitors a sense of how pervasive the Civil War was – it touched every place and everyone. Around the country, people may seek out the Civil War; but in Virginia, it finds you.

– Frank O'Reilly, Historian and Interpretive Ranger with the National Park Service

The Drive » Drive south of Petersburg, then west through back roads to follow Lee's last retreat. There's an excellent map available at www.civilwartraveler.com; we prefer taking VA-460 west from Petersburg, then connecting to VA-635, which leads to Appomattox via VA-24, near Farmville.

- - - - - - - - - - - - -

TRIP HIGHLIGHT

⑨ Appomattox Court House National Park

About 92 miles west of Petersburg is **Appomattox Court House National Park** (☏434-352-8987; www.nps.gov/apco; summer $4, Sep-May $3; ⏰8:30am-5pm), where the Confederacy finally surrendered. The park itself is wide and lovely, and the ranger staff are extremely helpful.

There are several marker stones dedicated to the surrendering Confederates; the most touching one marks the spot where Robert E Lee rode back from Appomattox after surrendering to Union General Ulysses Grant. Lee's soldiers stood on either side of the field waiting for the return of their commander. When Lee rode into sight he doffed his hat; the troops surged toward him, some saying goodbye while others, too overcome to speak, passed their hands over the flanks of Lee's horse. The spot's dedicated to defeat, humility and reconciliation, and the imperfect realization of all those qualities is the character of the America you've been driving through.

🛏 p287

Eating & Sleeping

Manassas ③

✖ Tandoori Village Indian $$

(☎703-369-6526; 7607 Centreville Road; mains $8-19; ⊙11am-2:30pm & 5-10pm, Mon-Fri, 11am-10pm Sat & Sun) Tandoori Village serves up solid Punjabi cuisine, offering a welcome dash of spice and flavor complexity to an area that's pretty rife with fast food chains. No menu shockers here, but all the standards, like butter chicken, dal, paneer and the rest, are executed with competence.

Fredericksburg ④

✖ Bistro Bethem American $$$

(☎540-371-9999; 309 William St; mains $15-34; ⊙11:30am-2:30pm & 5-10pm Tues-Sat, to 9pm Sun) The New American menu, seasonal ingredients and down-to-earth but dedicated foodie vibe here all equal gastronomic bliss. On any given day duck confit and quinoa may share the table with a roasted beet salad and local clams.

✖ Foode American $$

(☎540-479-1370; 1006 C Caroline Street; mains $13-24; ⊙11am-3pm & 4:30pm-8pm Tue-Thu, to 9pm Fri, 10am-2:30pm & 4:30-9pm Sat, 10am-2pm Sun; 🖉) Foode takes all the feelgood restaurant trends of the late noughties/early teens – fresh, local, free range, organic, casual-artsy-rustic-chic decor over white tablecloths and dark lighting – and runs with the above all the way to pretty delicious results.

✖ Sammy T's American $

(☎540-371-2008; 801 Caroline St; mains $6-14; ⊙11:30am-9:30pm; 🛜🖉) Sammy T's wins points off the bat for its attractive location: a cute brick building constructed circa 1805 in the heart of historic Fredericksburg. The food isn't bad either, mainly consisting of soup and sandwich, pub-like fare, with an admirable mix of vegetarian options such as a local take on lasagna and black bean quesadillas. There's a good beer selection, too.

🛏 Richard Johnston Inn B&B $$

(☎540-899-7606; www.therichardjohnstoninn. com; 711 Caroline St; r $125-200; P ❄ 🛜) Another B&B that's pretty much as cute, friendly and historically evocative as surrounding Fredericksburg itself. There are nine rooms to pick from; the Old Town features redbrick walls and exposed beams, while the Canopy is lacy and filigreed from the floor to the ceiling.

🛏 Schooler House B&B $$

(☎540-374-5258; www.theschoolerhouse.com; 1301 Caroline St; r $160-175; P ❄) Two lacy bedrooms in a watermelon-colored house with a gorgeous patio and backyard set the scene in this excellent Victorian B&B. Owners Andi and Paul are warm and welcoming, and Andi cooks a mean breakfast to boot. Service is personalized – you feel like these folks really care about your holiday.

Richmond ⑦

✖ Burger Bach Gastropub $

(☎804-359-1305; 10 S Thompson St; mains $7-12; ⊙11am-10pm daily, to 11pm Fri & Sat; 🖉👶) We give Burger Bach credit for being the only restaurant found in the area that self-classifies as a New Zealand-inspired burger joint. And that said, why yes, they do serve excellent lamb burgers here, although the locally sourced beef (and vegetarian) options are awesome as well. You should really go crazy with the 14 different sauces available for the thick-cut fries.

✖ Croaker's Spot   Seafood $$

(📞804-269-0464; 1020 Hull St; mains $8-17;
🕐11am-9pm Mon, Tue & Thu, to midnight Wed,
to 11pm Fri, noon-11pm Sat, noon-9pm Sun;
P) Croaker's is an institution in these parts,
a backbone of the African American dining
scene. Richmond's most famous rendition of
refined soul food is comforting, delicious and
sits in your stomach like a brick. Beware the
intimidating Fish Boat: fried catfish, cornbread
and mac n' cheese.

✖ Edo's Squid   Italian $$$

(📞804-864-5488; 411 N Harrison St; mains
$12-30) One of the best Italian restaurants in
Richmond, Edo's serves up mouthwatering,
authentic cuisine such as eggplant parmesan,
spicy shrimp diavolo pasta, daily specials and,
of course, squid.

✖ Julep's   Modern American $$$

(📞804-377-3968; 1719 E Franklin St; mains
$18-32; 🕐5:30-10pm Mon-Sat; P) This is
where classy, old-school Southern aristocrats
like to meet and eat, drawn by the fresh
experimentation of an innovative kitchen.
We're a fan of the wild boar and lamb stew, but
vegetarian options abound, and the salad menu
is particularly noteworthy and creative.

🛏 Jefferson Hotel   Luxury Hotel $$$

(📞804-788-8000; www.jeffersonhotel.com;
101 W Franklin St; r from $250; P ❄ 🛜 🏊)
There's an almost imperial sense of tradition
at this most famed of Richmond hotels,
which comes off as a modern execution of
the moonlight-and-magnolia cliché. With
that said, the effect isn't put upon: service is
warm without becoming obtrusive. The grand

appearance of the place could put you in mind
of a fairy-tale castle.

🛏 Linden Row Inn   Boutique Hotel $$

(📞804-783-7000; www.lindenrowinn.com;
100 E Franklin St; r incl breakfast $120-170,
ste $250; P ❄ @ 🛜) This antebellum gem
has attractive rooms (with period Victorian
furnishings) spread among neighboring Greek
Revival townhouses in an excellent downtown
location. Friendly southern hospitality and
thoughtful extras (free passes to the YMCA, free
around-town shuttle service) sweeten the deal.

🛏 Massad House Hotel   Motel $

(📞804-648-2893; www.massadhousehotel.
com; 11 N 4th St; r $75-110) Massad's great by
any standard, but excellent rates and a supreme
location near the heart of Richmond's best
attractions give it a special place in our hearts.
The design will put you in mind of a cozy study in
Tudor-style budget bliss.

Appomattox Court House National Park ⑨

🛏 Longacre   B&B $$

(📞800-758-7730; www.longacreva.com;
1670 Church St; r from $105, ste $275; P ❄)
Longacre looks like it got lost somewhere in the
English countryside and decided to set up shop
in Virginia. Seriously, there might be rooms
here where children disappear into magical
kingdoms after slipping through wardrobes.
There are lovely grounds replete with a shady
magnolia tree, plus six elegantly furnished
rooms scattered throughout the impressive
building.

COMING TO
SCOTT THEATRE
GATE CITY, VIRGINIA
TUES. NOV. 11
CHARLIE MONROE
AND HIS
KENTUCKY PARDNERS
& OTHER STARS
Stars Of RCA Victor Records
BRING THE ENTIRE FAMILY

DIRECT FROM
GRAND OLE OPRY
IN PERSON

FLATT
EARL SCRUGGS
SHOW
SPONSORED ON RADIO AND TV BY MARTHA WHITE MILLS

BROWN COUNTY JAMBOREE
BEAN BLOSSOM, IND.
SUN. - JUNE 26
SHOWS 2:30 & 7:30 P.M.
By Popular Request
PRESENTS
IN PERSON
BILL DUDLEY
King Recording Star
PLUS
BRYANT WILSON
AND HIS
KENTUCKY PARDNERS
ALSO
BROWN CO. BOYS & GIRLS

COMING SOON!
Award Winning Bluegrass Band
PINECASTLE RECORDING ARTIST
NEW VINTAGE
WHEN FEB 27 1999 FROM 7 TO
WHERE FLOYD COUNTRY STORE

SUNSET PARK
RT. 1 Oxford, West Grove & Oxford, PA.
SUN. SEPT. 18
IN PERSON
ALEX and OLA
BELLE
FAN CLUB DAY
WITH
MAC WISEMAN
AND
CRAZY ELMER
AND MANY OTHERS

PIX THEATRE
FLOYD · VA. 8 P.M.
WED. DEC. 12 1956
IN PERSON
CHARLIE MONROE
& HIS KY. PARDNERS

HIGH SCHOOL AUDITORIUM
LUMBER CITY, PA.
FRI. - FEB. 20
MARTHA WHITE FLOUR PRESENTS
JIM & JESSE
AND THE
VIRGINIA BOYS
LOUVIN BROTHERS
SHOWTIME
8:00 P.M.
Sponsored By:
Martha White Flour
& Corn Meal

SUNSET PARK
ON ROUTE 1 betw. WEST GROVE & OXFORD, PA.
SUN. AUG. 17
DOLLY PARTON
AND THE
TRAVELING FAMILY BAND

ROXY THEATRE
MINERVA, OHIO
TUES. MAY 27
WWVA
JAMBOREE
Presents
THE BAILEY BROS
CHARLES — DANNY
ALSO FEATURING
HAPPY VALLEY BOYS
HAPPY VALLEY QUARTET
SLAP-HAPPY JAKE

BLUEGRASS
AT THE MAC
STANLEY BROWN BAND

JAN. 8. 1999 7:30
1999 CONCERT SERIES

BROWN COUNTY JAMBOREE
BEAN BLOSSOM, IND.
SUN. - JULY 17
SHOWS 2:30 & 7:30 P.M.
WSM Grand Ole Opry
Presents - In Person
BILL MONROE
AND HIS
BLUE GRASS BOYS
ALSO THE FAMOUS
BLUE GRASS QT.
PLUS
BROWN CO. BOYS & GIRLS

BROWN COUNTY JAMBOREE
BEAN BLOSSOM, IND.
SUN. - SEPT. 25
SHOWS 2:30 & 7:30 P.M.
By Popular Request
PRESENTS
DON RENO
AND THE
TENNESSEE CUTUPS
EXTRA ADDED
BRYANT WILSON
KENTUCKY RAMBLERS
A SHOW YOU DON'T WANT TO MISS

Floyd Country Store Post
advertise jamborees in
artsy town of Flo

The Crooked Road

24

On this trip, tune in to the unique music and Celtic-descended folkways of the deeply forested upcountry that lays between the Blue Ridge and Appalachian mountain ranges.

TRIP HIGHLIGHTS

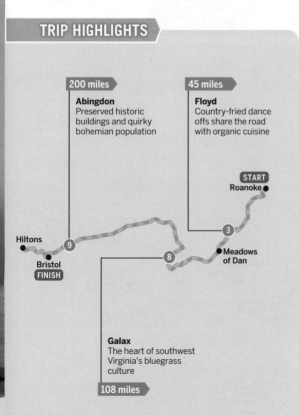

200 miles

Abingdon
Preserved historic buildings and quirky bohemian population

45 miles

Floyd
Country-fried dance offs share the road with organic cuisine

START
Roanoke ●

Hiltons
●   ⑨

Bristol
FINISH

⑧   ⑨

⑧   ● Meadows
of Dan

③

Galax
The heart of southwest Virginia's bluegrass culture

108 miles

3–4 DAYS
260 MILES / 418 KM

GREAT FOR...

BEST TIME TO GO
Visit from May to October for great weather and a packed concert schedule.

ESSENTIAL PHOTO
The Friday night bluegrass-palooza in 'downtown' Floyd.

BEST FOR NATURE LOVERS
Hiking the forested loop of the Smart View trail.

289

24 The Crooked Road

The place where Kentucky, Tennessee and Virginia kiss is a veritable hotbed of American roots music history, thanks to the vibrant cultural folkways of the Scots-Irish who settled the area in the 18th century. The state-carved Crooked Road carves a winding path through the Blue Ridge Mountains into the Appalachians and the heart of this way of life.

❶ Roanoke

This trip begins in Roanoke, the main urban hub of Southwest Virginia, and continues along the Blue Ridge Parkway, explored in Trip 25 (p299). Roanoke is steadily becoming a regional cultural center, perhaps best exemplified by the presence of the **Taubman Museum of Art** (www.taubmanmuseum. org; 110 Salem Ave SE; ⏰10am-5pm Tue-Sat, to 9pm Thu & first Fridays;). The museum is set in a futuristic glass-and-

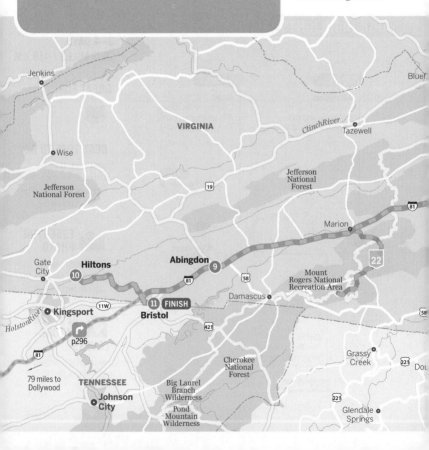

steel structure inspired by the valley's natural beauty. Inside you'll find a wonderful collection of classic and modern art. The permanent collection includes extensive galleries of American, folk and contemporary Southern art, complemented by frequently rotating guest exhibitions whose thematic content spans the globe.

Before you leave, make sure to check out one of the finest farmer's markets in the region. The **Historic City Market** (☎540-342-2028; www.downtownroanoke.org/city-market; Campbell Ave & Market St; ☺8am-5pm Mon-Sat & 10am-4pm Sun) is a sumptuous affair spread out over several city blocks, loaded with temptations even for those with no access to a kitchen.

The Drive » Get onto US 220 southbound in Roanoke and follow signs to the Blue Ridge Parkway. It's about 33.5 miles from where US 220 hits the parkway to get to the Smart View Recreational Area.

LINK YOUR TRIP

22 Across the Appalachian Trail

Head 30 miles east from Abingdon to reach Mt Rodgers and the deep Appalachian mountains.

25 Blue Ridge Parkway

From Roanoke, you can set out north to the Blue Ridge mountains.

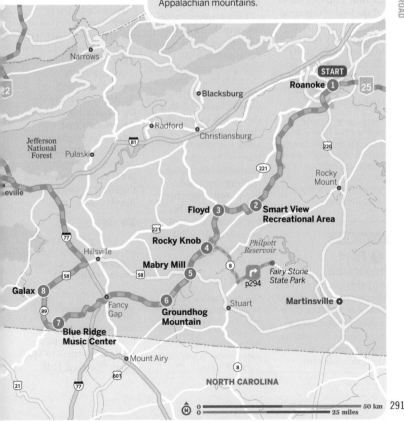

Narrows

Blacksburg

START
Roanoke ❶

25

Radford

Christiansburg

Jefferson National Forest

Pulaski

81

220

221

Rocky Mount

Floyd ❸ ❷ **Smart View Recreational Area**

221

Rocky Knob ❹

Philpott Reservoir

8

Mabry Mill ❺

58

58

p294

Fairy Stone State Park

Galax 8

77

Hillsville

89

Fancy Gap

❻

Groundhog Mountain

Stuart

Martinsville ○

Blue Ridge Music Center ❼

601

Mount Airy

8

21

77

NORTH CAROLINA

Ⓝ 0 ⊢——————⊣ 50 km
0 ⊢——————⊣ 25 miles

❷ Smart View Recreational Area

The aptly named Smart View Recreational Area sits at an elevation of 2500ft with commanding vistas of the surrounding valleys. The area is a birder's parade, rife with trails that cut into hardwood, broadleaf forest that teem with brown thrashers, great-crested flycatchers and Kentucky warblers, among many, many other species.

The **Smart View Trail** is a moderately difficult 2.6-mile loop that shows off the best of this area. If you're not in the mood (or don't have the time) to complete the entire circuit, the paths near the main parking pull-off for this area offer similar landscapes.

The Drive » Continue along the Blue Ridge Parkway for 4 miles, then turn right onto State Route 860/Shooting Creek Rd. After about a mile, turn left onto State Route 681/Franklin Pike. Follow it for 2 miles, then turn left on Floyd Hwy.

TRIP HIGHLIGHT

❸ Floyd

Tiny Floyd is a surprising blend of rural conservatives and slightly New Age artisans. Grab a double espresso from a bohemian coffeehouse, then peruse farm tools in the hardware store.

The highlight of this curious town is the jamboree at the **Floyd Country Store** (📞540-745-4563; www. floydcountrystore.com; 206 S Locust St; ⏰11am-5pm Tue-Thu, 11am-11pm Fri, to 5pm Sat, noon-5pm Sun). Every Friday night, this little store in a clapboard building clears out its inventory and lines up rows of chairs around a dance floor. Around 6:30pm the first musicians on the bill play their hearts out on the stage. Pretty soon the room's filled with locals and visitors hootin' and hollerin' along with the fiddles and banjos.

Then the music spills out onto the streets. Several jam bands twiddle their fiddles in little groups up and down the main road. Listeners cluster round their favorite bands, parking themselves in lawn chairs right on the sidewalk or along the curb. Motorists stare at the scene in bewilderment. There's really nothing else like it. Just remember: this tradition has been maintained as a family-friendly affair. Drinking, smoking and swearing are frowned upon.

🍴 🛏 p297

The Drive » Take VA-8/Locust St southbound for 6 miles back to the Blue Ridge Parkway. Then it's a little over 1.5 miles to Rocky Knob. If you follow VA-8, you can detour to Fairy Stone State Park (p294).

❹ Rocky Knob

At Rocky Knob, almost 1000ft higher than Smart View, rangers have carved out a 4800 acre area that blends natural beauty with landscaped amenities, including picnic areas and comfortable cabins.

If you're really looking to punish yourself and simultaneously soak up the best the Blue Ridge mountains have to offer, set out on the **Rock Castle Gorge Trail**, a hard-going 10.8-mile trail that descends deep into the shadowed buttresses of Rock Castle Gorge before clambering out of the dark woods back into the sunlit slopes of Rocky Knob.

A much easier option is covering a small portion of the above via the 0.8-mile **Hardwood Cove Nature Trail**, which follows the beginning of the Rock Castle Gorge Trail and cuts under the dense canopies of some of the oldest forests in the Appalachians.

🛏 p297

The Drive » Mabry Mill is only a little over 3 miles south of Rocky Knob via the Blue Ridge Parkway, at milepost 176.

❺ Mabry Mill

Here's where things go from picturesque Blue Ridge bucolicness to 'Oh, c'mon. Too cute.' Built

Wooden mill with autumn leaves

in 1910, Mabry Mill is a working water-wheel-driven grist mill. Its wooden construction has distressed over the years to a state of wonderful entropy; the structure looks like it just fell out of a historical romance novel, except you won't find a strapping young couple in a state of dramatic embrace in

front of this building. The mill is managed by **Mabry Mill Restaurant** (☎276-952-2947; www. mabrymillrestaurant.com; 266 Mabry Mill SE, Meadows of Dan; mains $5-8; ◷8am-6pm May-Oct), which happens to whip up some of the better breakfasts along the Blue Ridge Parkway. They've got three kinds of specialty pancakes –

cornmeal, buckwheat and sweet potato. Throw in a biscuit with some Virginia ham and that's a perfect way to start your day.

Three miles down the road, at milepost 179, the half-mile **Round Meadow Creek Loop Trail** leads trekkers through a lovely forest cut through by

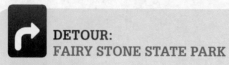

DETOUR:
FAIRY STONE STATE PARK

Start: ❹ Rocky Knob

From the Rocky Knob portion of the Blue Ridge Parkway, head east for about 30 miles. You'll be passing through the upcountry region of Virginia that blends between the Blue Ridge mountains and the Southside, one of the most rural, least developed parts of the Commonwealth. Marking the border between these regions is **Fairy Stone State Park** (☎276-930-2424; www.dcr.virginia.gov/state_parks/fai.shtml; 967 Fairystone Lake Dr, Stuart; weekdays/weekends $3/4).

What's in a name? Well, the park grounds contain a silly amount of staurolite, a mineral that crystallizes at 60- or 90-degree angles, giving it a cross-like structure. Legend has it the cruciform rocks are the tears shed by faeries who learned of the death of Christ.

What else is here? Most folks come for 2,880 acre **Philpott Lake**, created as a byproduct reservoir after the Army Corps of Engineers completed the Philpott Dam back in 1952. The mountain waters of the lake are a popular spot for swimming and fishing for smallmouth and largemouth bass. Some 10 miles of multiuse trails wend their way around the dark blue waters. There's also camping and cabins if you want to spend the night.

Get here by taking SR-758 south to US58 eastbound; follow for 11 miles to VA-8. Take VA-8 to VA-57 and follow that road eastbound to Fairy Stone State Park.

an achingly attractive stream.

The Drive ❯❯ Groundhog Mountain is 12 miles south of Mabry Mill on the parkway at milepost 188.

❻ Groundhog Mountain

A split-rail fence and a rickety wooden observation tower overlook the lip of a grassy field that curves over a sky blue vista onto the Blue Ridge Mountains and Piedmont plateau. Flowering laurel and galax flurry over the greenery in white bursts, framing a picture-perfect picnic spot.

This, in any case, is the immediate impression one gets upon arriving at **Groundhog Mountain**, one of the more attractive parking overlooks in this stretch of the Blue Ridge Parkway. Note that the aforementioned observation tower is built in the style of local historical tobacco barns.

A mile down the road is the log-and-daube **Puckett Cabin** (☎276-730-3100, 828-298-0398; Milepost 189.9, Blue Ruarkway; ◷8am-8pm), last home of local midwife Orleana Hawks Puckett (1844–1939). The site of the property is dotted with exhibitions on the folkways and traditions

of local mountain and valley folk.

The Drive ❯❯ Continue along the parkway for about 23 miles to the Blue Ridge Music Center, at milepost 213.

❼ Blue Ridge Music Center

As you come closer to the Tennessee border, you'll come across a large, grassy outdoor amphitheater. This is the **Blue Ridge Music Center** (☎276-236-5309; www.blueridgemusiccenter. net; Milepost 213 Blue Ridge Pkwy; ◷weekend shows May-Oct), an arts and music hub for the region that offers programming that focuses on local musicians carrying on the traditions of Appalachian music. Performances are mostly on weekends and occasionally during the week. Bring a lawn chair and sit yourself down for an afternoon or evening performance. At night you can watch the fireflies glimmer in the darkness.

There's two trails in the vicinity as well – the easy, flat **High Creek** (1.35 miles) and moderate **Fisher Peak** (2.24 miles), which slopes up a small mountain peak.

The Drive >> Take VA-89 north for about 7 miles to reach downtown Galax. You'll pass working farms, some of which have quite the hardscrabble aesthetic – very different from the estate farms and stables of northern Virginia and the Shenandoah Valley.

TRIP HIGHLIGHT

8 Galax

In Galax's historic downtown, look for the neon marquee of the **Rex Theater** (☎276-236-0329; www.rextheatergalax.com; 113 E Grayson St). This is a big old grande dame theater, with a Friday night show called Blue Ridge Backroads. Even if you can't make it to the theater at 8pm, you can listen to the two-hour show broadcast live to surrounding counties on 89.1 FM.

Galax hosts the Smoke on the

Mountain Barbecue Championship (www. smokeonthemountainva. com) on the second weekend in July. Teams from all over crowd the streets of downtown with their tricked-out mobile BBQ units.

If you think you've got what it takes to play, poke your head into **Barr's Fiddle Shop** (☎276-236-2411; http:// barrsfiddleshop.com; 105 S Main St; ⊙9am-5pm Mon-Sat). This little music shop has a big selection of homemade and vintage fiddles and banjos along with mandolins, autoharps and harmonicas. You can get a lesson if you have time to hang around, or just admire the fine instruments that hang all over the walls.

✖ ⊨ p297

The Drive >> Take US 221/ US 58 east for 11 miles and hop on I-77 northbound. Take I-77 for 17 miles, then follow I-81 southbound for 65 miles to Abingdon.

TRIP HIGHLIGHT

9 Abingdon

The gorgeous town of Abingdon anchors Virginia's southwesterly corner. Here, like a mirage in the desert, is the best hotel for hundreds of miles in any direction. The Martha Washington Inn (p297) resides inside of a regal, gigantic brick mansion built for General Francis Preston in 1832. Pulling up after a long day's drive is like arriving at heaven's gates. You can almost hear the angels sing as you climb the grand stairs to the huge porch with views framed by columns.

FIDDLE-DEE-DEE

Every second weekend in August for the last 70-odd years, Galax has hosted the **Old Fiddler's Convention** (www.oldfiddlersconvention.com), which now lasts for six days. Hosted by the local Loyal Order of the Moose Lodge, musicians come from all over to compete as well as to play. And for the record, this isn't just a fiddling competition; almost all of the instruments of the American roots music of the mountains are represented, including banjos, autoharp, dulcimer and dobro. Plus: there's clog dancing competitions. This fascinating local form of dance has roots that can be traced all the way back to the British Isles, and represents a relatively unbroken cultural thread that links the people of this region to their Scots-Irish ancestors.

DETOUR: DOLLYWOOD

Start: ⑪ Bristol

Across the Tennessee border, about two hours southwest of Bristol, is the legendary Dolly Parton's personal theme park **Dollywood** (☏865-428-9488; www.dollywood.com; 2700 Dollywood Parks Blvd; adult/child $57/45; ⊙Apr-Dec). The Smoky Mountains come alive with lots of music and roller coasters. Fans will enjoy the daily Kinfolk Show starring Dolly's relatives or touring the two-story museum that houses her wigs, costumes and awards. You can buy your own coat of many colors in Dolly's Closet. To take this detour, take I-81 southbound for 75 miles, then take exit 407 and follow signs to Dollywood.

The **Barter Theatre** (☏276-628-3991; www.bartertheatre.com; 133 W Main St; performances from $20), across the street, is the big man on Main St in its historic red-brick building. This regional theater company puts on its own productions of brand-name plays.

Just outside of town is a relic from a more recent age, the **MoonLite Drive-In** (☏276-628-7881; www.facebook.com/abingdonmoonlite; 17555 Lee Hwy; adult/child $7/2; ⊙double feature from 9pm). Bring some beers or grab a Coke from the concession stand and settle in for a double feature picture show. The presence of local teenagers smoking cigarettes and having makeout sessions in the back of their pickup trucks is as American as apple pie.

✕ 🛏 p297

The Drive ≫ Take I-81 south from Abingdon for about 16 miles, then turn onto US 421 north/US 58 west. Follow the road for about 20 miles to reach Hiltons.

⑩ Hiltons

Another star attraction on the Crooked Road is about 30 miles and a rural world away from Abingdon in the microscopic town of Hiltons. Here at Clinch Mountain, subject of countless bluegrass and country ballads, you will find the **Carter Family Fold** (☏276-386-6054; www.carterfamilyfold.org; 3449 A P Carter Hwy; adult/child $8/1; ⊙7:30pm Sat), which has live music every Saturday night. At the time of research, the Fold was overseen by Janette Carter, the youngest daughter of AP and Sara Carter, who, along with sister-in-law Maybelle, formed the core Carter group, a bedrock lineage of American country music (June Carter Cash was Maybelle's daughter). The music starts at 7:30pm in the big wooden music hall. In the summer there is outdoor seating too. The hall has replaced the original locale, AP's store, which now houses a museum dedicated to Carter family history. Also: there's amateur clog dancing!

The Drive ≫ Come back the way you came on US 421/US 58 and drive about 20 miles to reach the Tennessee border and the town of Bristol.

⑪ Bristol

Vrrrrooom! In nearby Bristol you can attend the **Bristol Motor Speedway** (☏423-989-6933; www.bristolmotorspeedway.com; 151 Speedway Blvd; ⊙showtimes vary), which runs lots of NASCAR events. If they're not racing, you can still tour the 'world's fastest half-mile' and check out the 'The Bristol Experience' in the adjacent museum.

Ready to head back home? Pop on one of the CDs you picked up along the way and thrill to old-time music one last time as you ease back to modern life, keeping the wistful memories of banjos and bluegrass tucked safely inside your heart so nobody don't break it again.

Eating & Sleeping

Floyd ❸

✖ Oddfella's   Fusion $
(📞540-745-3463; 110 N Locust St; lunch mains
$7-14, dinner $8-21; 🕙11am-2:30pm Wed-Sat,
5-9pm Thu-Sun, 10am-3pm Sun; P 🖊) This
woodsy, organic eatery touts its menu as
'conscious comfort food with an Appalachian
Latino twist.' Que? Think jumbo chimichangas,
goats cheese tostadas and grilled veggie
platters, including some vegan options. Plus
there's a great beer and wine menu.

✖ Pine Tavern   American $
(📞540-745-4482; 611 Floyd Hwy; mains $7-13;
🕙4:30-9pm Thu-Sat, 11am-8pm Sun; P 🖊)
One taste of the buttermilk biscuits, fried
chicken and country ham at this all-you-can-eat
restaurant and your mouth won't stop salivating.
They pile on dumplings, pinto beans, green
beans and mashed potatoes, because why not?

🛏 Hotel Floyd   Hotel $$
(📞540-745-6080; www.hotelfloyd.com; 120
Wilson St; r $85-146; P 🖾 🛜 🖼) Built in 2007
with ecofriendly materials and furnishings,
Hotel Floyd is one of the 'greenest' hotels in
Virginia and a model of sustainability. Each of
the 14 rooms were decorated by local artisans
and exude a rustic, warm charm.

🛏 Oak Haven Lodge   Hotel $
(📞540-745-5716; www.oakhavenlodge.com;
323 Webb's Mill Rd; r $75-90; P 🖊) This
comfortable lodge is just a few minutes outside
downtown Floyd and is good value for money.
It's located in a fairly new building and features
big decks and comfortable beds. Some rooms
have their own Jacuzzi.

Rocky Knob ❹

🛏 Rocky Knob Cabins   Cabins $
(📞540-593-3503; www.rockyknobcabins.com;
266 Mabry Mill Rd; cabin with shared bath $75;

🕙May-Oct; P 🖼) These low-fi cabins are set
in a secluded stretch of forest. Bring food, as
eating options are limited along this stretch of
the parkway.

Galax ❽

✖ Galax Smokehouse   Barbecue $
(📞276-236-1000; 101 N Main St; mains $7-18;
🕙11am-9pm Mon-Sat, to 3pm Sun) This popular
restaurant has loads of fans, chipper staff and
stupidly good barbecue (and chili. Man, that
chili).

🛏 Fiddlers Roost   Cabins $$
(📞276-236-1212; http://fiddlersroostcabins.
com; 485 Fishers Peak Rd; cabins $120-160;
P 🖊) We love these eight cabins, which
resemble Lincoln Logs playsets. The interiors
are decorated in 'quilt' chic; they may not win a
place in Wallpaper magazine, but they're cozy
and have gas fireplaces, kitchens, TVs and DVD
players.

Abingdon ❾

✖ Rain   American $$$
(📞276-739-2331; 283 E Main St; mains
$18-27; 🕙11am-2pm & 5-9pm Tue-Sat; P)
Excellent New American cuisine inspired by the
Appalachians. The mains, like seared salmon
and sweet mustard pork chops, are executed
wonderfully, with great consistency – this is the
best splurge around.

🛏 Martha Washington Inn   Hotel $$
(📞276-628-3161; www.marthawashingtoninn.
com; 150 W Main St; r from $173; P 🖾 @ 🛜 🖼)
This super glamorous hotel sits in a huge 1832
mansion estate. Breakfast is great. Bonus
points if you dare to wear your cuddly robe
downstairs.

Blue Ridge Parkway
*Aerial view through
the Appalachian Mountains*

Blue Ridge Parkway

25

Dark laurel, fragrant galax, white waterfalls and blooms of dogwood, mayapple, foamflower and redbud line this road that runs through the heart of the Appalachians.

TRIP HIGHLIGHTS

1 mile

Staunton
Historic mountain town and center for the arts

START 1

3

73 miles

Lexington
College students, cafe culture, great eats and trekking adventures

Natural Bridge

6

Bedford

Roanoke
FINISH

8

Smith Mountain Lake
Woods, water and wine tastings

160 miles

Peaks of Otter
Three mountains dominate the wooded valleys

127 miles

3 DAYS
185 MILES / 300 KM

GREAT FOR...

BEST TIME TO GO

Visit June through October for great weather and open amenities.

 ESSENTIAL PHOTO

A panorama of the Blue Ridge Mountains from Sharp Top, Peaks of Otter.

 BEST FOR CULTURE

Staunton is an arts oasis.

Classic Trip

25 Blue Ridge Parkway

Running through Virginia and North Carolina, the Blue Ridge National Scenic Byway – 'America's Favorite Drive' – is the most visited area of national parkland in the USA, attracting almost 20 million roadtrippers a year. The parkway meanders through quintessentially bucolic pasturelands and imposing Appalachian vistas, past college towns and mountain hamlets. On this trip we'll thread into and off the parkway, exploring all of the above and some back roads in between.

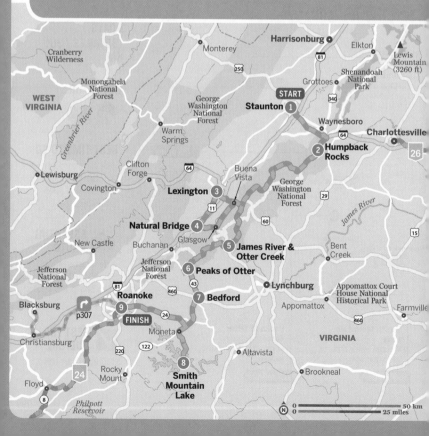

1 Staunton

Our trip starts in a place we'd like to end. End up retiring, that is. There are some towns in the USA that just *nail it*, and Staunton is one of them. Luckily, it can serve as a good base for exploring the upper parkway.

So what's here? A pedestrian-friendly, sigh-inducingly handsome center; more than 200 of the town's buildings were designed by noted Victorian architect T J Collins, hence Staunton's attractive uniformity. There's an artsy yet unpretentious bohemian vibe thanks to the presence of two things: Mary Baldwin, a small women's liberal arts college, and the gem of the Shenandoah mountains:

LINK YOUR TRIP

24 The Crooked Road

In Roanoke, slip on dancing clogs and explore regional folkways and backroads.

26 Peninsula to the Piedmont

Head east to Charlottesville and the green hills of the Piedmont.

Blackfriars Playhouse

(☎540-851-1733; www.americanshakespearecenter.com; 10 S Market St; tickets $20-42). This is the world's only re-creation of Shakespeare's original indoor theater. The facility hosts the immensely talented American Shakespeare Center company, which puts on performances throughout the year. See a show here. It will do you good.

History buffs should check out the **Woodrow Wilson Presidential Library** (www.woodrowwilson.org; 18-24 N Coalter St; adult/student/child $14/7/5; ⏰9am-5pm Mon-Sat, from noon Sun) across town. Stop by and tour the hilltop Greek Revival house where Wilson grew up, which has been faithfully restored to its original 1856 appearance.

By this point you'll probably be dreaming of ditching your nine-to-five job and moving to the country. A good way to snap yourself out of this fantasy is by visiting the **Frontier Culture Museum** (☎540-332-7850; overlooking I-81 exit 222; adult/student/child $10/9/6; ⏰9am-5pm mid-Mar–Nov, 10am-4pm Dec–mid-Mar). The hard work of farming comes to life via the familiar Virginia trope of employing historically costumed interpreters. The museum has Irish, German and English farms to explore.

✕ 🛏 p310

The Drive ≫ From Staunton, take I-64E towards Richmond for about 15 miles. Take exit 99 to merge onto US 250/Three Notched Mountain Hwy heading east toward Afton, then follow the signs onto the Blue Ridge Pkwy. Humpback Rocks is at milepost 5.8.

2 Humpback Rocks

Had enough great culture and small-town hospitality? No? Tough, because we're moving on to the main event: the **Blue Ridge Parkway** (☎828-298-0398; http://www.nps.gov/blri; Milepost 384, Asheville, NC). Now, we need to be honest with you: this is a weird trip. We're asking you to drive along the parkway, which slowly snakes across the peaks of the Appalachians, but every now and then we're going to ask you to detour off this scenic mountain road to, well, other scenic roads.

Anyways, we start at **Humpback Rocks** (Mile 5.8), the entrance to the Virginia portion of the parkway (252 miles of the 469-mile parkway are in NC). You can tour 19th-century farm buildings or take the steep trail to the namesake Humpback Rocks, which offer spectacular 360-degree views across the mountains. The onsite visitor center is a good primer for the rest of your parkway experience.

The Drive » The next stretch of the trip is 39 miles on the parkway. Follow signs for US 60, then follow that road west for 10 miles to Lexington.

TRIP HIGHLIGHT

❸ Lexington

What? Another attractive university town set amid the forested mountains of the lower Shenandoah Valley? Well, why not.

In fact, while Staunton moderately revolves around Mary Baldwin, Lexington positively centers, geographically

and culturally, around two schools: the **Virginia Military Institute** (VMI; Letcher Ave; ⊙9am-5pm when campus & museums open) and **Washington & Lee University**. VMI is the oldest state-supported military academy in the country, dedicated to producing the Classical ideal of citizen-soldiers; the ideals of this institution, and the history of its cadet-students, is explored at the **VMI Museum** (☎540-464-7334; ⊙9am-5pm). While graduates do not have to become enlisted officers within the US military, the vast majority do so. In addition, the school's **George**

C Marshall Museum (☎540-463-7103; http://www.marshallfoundation.org/museum; adult/student $5/2; ⊙9am-5pm Tue-Sat, from 1pm Sun) honors the creator of the Marshall Plan for post-WWII European reconstruction.

VMI cadets can often be seen jogging around Lexington, perhaps casting a glance at the students at Washington & Lee, a decidedly less structured but no less academically respected school. The W&L campus includes the **Lee Chapel & Museum** (☎540-458-8768; ⊙9am-4pm, from 1pm Sun), where the school's namesake, patron and Confederate

LOCAL KNOWLEDGE:
FOAMHENGE

An aside: ever heard of the mad professor Mark Cline? No? He used to create monsters for haunted house attractions in Virginia Beach. Then the spirit seized him and he moved a menagerie of weirdness – an army of 1950s-era movie matinee monster models – to the woods around Natural Bridge. Cline's attractions included Escape From Dinosaur Kingdom, which featured Civil War soldiers getting devoured by velociraptors, a haunted mansion and a 'Hunt Bigfoot with a Redneck' tour that was quite possibly the best tourism outing ever devised in the Commonwealth of Virginia (not to spoil anything, but this particular activity involved a missing talking fish, a shotgun, a UFO filled with beer and an exploding outhouse).

Sadly, a major fire closed all of the above during the time of research. Fingers crossed, the attractions will be reopened when you read this; check www.monstersanddinosaurs.com for updates. In the meantime, the first of Cline's Natural Bridge–area oddities – and, some may say, the greatest – remains: the outrageously out-of-place and utterly ingenious Foamhenge, located a mile south of Natural Bridge on US 11. What's that, you say? You mean a life-sized replica of England's most famous mystery site built entirely out of styrofoam? Yes, and this crown jewel of the Blue Ridge foothills is one of the most ridiculous and incredible sights in the state of Virginia. The utter ludicrousness of Foamhenge is its sole reward. Bring your druid/pagan claptrap and see if anything happens at sundown on the solstice.

– Adam Karlin

PARKWAY PRACTICALITIES

Most facilities along the the Blue Ridge Parkway (p301), including picnic areas, visitor centers and museum-style exhibits, such as the historic farms at Humpback Rocks, officially open on Memorial Day weekend (the last weekend in May). With that said, some facilities are open year-round and private concessionaires along the parkway maintain their own hours; we have listed these where applicable, and you can also check on updated opening hours and facility renovations at www.nps.gov/blri/planyourvisit (click on Operating Hours & Seasons). During winter, portions of the parkway may be snowed out; check the aforementioned website for updates.

Distances in the park are delineated by mileposts (MPs). The countdown starts around MP 1 in Virginia, near Waynesboro, and continues all the way to MP 469 near Cherokee, North Carolina.

The Blue Ridge Parkway can feel crowded in spring and summer, when thousands of motorists crowd the road, but there are so many pull-offs and picnic areas you rarely feel too hemmed in. Just remember this is a scenic route; don't be the jerk who tailgates on the parkway. Expect people to drive slowly up here. Honestly, it's a good idea to follow suit; this road has lots of narrow twists and turns.

You can take your RV on the parkway. The lowest tunnel clearance is 10ft 6in near the park's terminus in Cherokee, NC.

General Robert E. Lee is buried. One of the four Confederate banners surrounding Lee's tomb is set in an original flagpole, a branch a rebel soldier turned into a makeshift standard. Lee's beloved horse, Traveler, is buried outside.

Just a few miles north on Rte 11 is **Hull's Drive-In Movie Theater** (☎540-463-2621; http://hullsdrivein.com; 2367 N Lee Hwy/US 11; per person $6; ☺7pm Thu-Sun May-Oct). This totally hardcore artifact of the golden age of automobiles is a living museum to the road trips your parents remember.

✕ ⎸ p311

The Drive ≫ Take US 11 southbound for about 12 miles to get to Natural Bridge (you can take I-81 as well, but it's not nearly as scenic and takes just as long).

- - - - - - - - - - -

④ Natural Bridge

Before we send you back to the Blue Ridge Parkway, stop by the gorgeous **Natural Bridge** (www.naturalbridgeva.com; bridge adult/child $21/12, bridge & caverns $29/17; ☺9am-dusk) and its wonderful potpourri of amusements. Natural Bridge is a legitimate natural wonder – and is even claimed to be one of the Seven Natural Wonders of the World, though just who put that list together remains unclear. Soaring 200ft in the air, this centuries-old rock formation lives up to the hype. Those who aren't afraid of a little religion should hang around for the 'Drama of Creation' light show that plays nightly underneath and around the bridge.

A *lot* of other attractions have been built into the Natural Bridge experience, including a butterfly garden, a wax museum, a living history Native American village-cum-museum, a horribly garish children's play area and a series of caverns; visiting this last attraction adds a little to the cost of your ticket. It's worth it, if you're into caves.

The Drive ≫ Head back to the Blue Ridge Parkway using US 60 and get on at Buena Vista. Drive about 13 miles south to the James River area near milepost 63.

Classic Trip

WHY THIS IS A CLASSIC TRIP
ADAM KARLIN, AUTHOR

The Blue Ridge separates the East Coast from the beginning of the Midwest, the Mid-Atlantic from the South and the cities of the coastal plain from the rural villages of the mountains. As a result, this is a fascinating transition space between several different cultures, with distinct folkways all of its own. And incidentally, the Blue Ridge Parkway is a beautiful byway, with jaw-dropping views greeting travelers at every curve.

Top: Views of the Appalachians
Left: Scallops, Zynodoa, Staunton
Right: Natural Bridge

⑤ James River & Otter Creek

The next portion of the Blue Ridge Parkway overlooks the road that leads to Lynchburg. Part of the reason for that town's proximity is the James River, which marks the parkway's lowest elevation (650ft above sea level); the course of the river was the original transportation route through the mountains.

This area is rife with hiking and sightseeing opportunities. The **Otter Creek Trail** begins at a local campsite and runs for a moderately strenuous 3.5 miles; you can access it at different points from overlooks at mileposts 61.4, 62.5 and 63.1.

If you're in the mood for a really easy jaunt, head to the **James River Visitor Center** at milepost 63.6 and take the 0.2-mile **James River Trail** to the restored James River and Kanawha Canal lock, built between 1845–51. The visitor center has information on the history of the canal and its importance to local transportation. From here you can follow the **Trail of Trees**, which goes a half mile to a wonderful overlook on the James River.

The Drive ≫ It's about 20 miles from here to Peaks of Otter along the Blue Ridge Parkway.

At milepost 74.7, the very easy, 0.1-mile Thunder Ridge trail leads to a pretty valley view. The tough 1.2-mile Apple Orchard Falls trail leads can be accessed at milepost 78.4.

TRIP HIGHLIGHT

6 Peaks Of Otter

The three **Peaks of Otter** – Sharp Top, Flat Top and Harkening Hill – were once dubbed the highest mountains in North America by Thomas Jefferson. He was decidedly wrong in that assessment, but the peaks are undeniably dramatic, dominating the landscape for miles around.

There's a visitor center at milepost 86; from here you can take the steep 1.5 mile **Sharp Top Trail**, which summits the eponymous mountain (3875ft). The **Flat Top Trail** goes higher and further (4.4 miles), but at a considerably less demanding incline. You'll end at the Peaks Picnic area (say that three times fast). If you're pressed for time, the 0.8-mile **Elk Run Trail** is an easy self-guided nature tour.

At milepost 83.1, just before the visitor center, the **Fallingwater Cascades Trail** is a 1.5 mile loop that wanders past deep-carved ravines to a snowy-white waterfall.

Although closed at the time of research, this is the location of the Peaks of Otter Lodge.

The Drive » Get on VA-43 south, also known as Peaks Rd, from the Blue Ridge Parkway. It's about an 11 mile drive along this road to Bedford.

----

7 Bedford

Tiny Bedford suffered the most casualties per capita during WWII, and hence was chosen to host the **National D-Day Memorial** (📞540-586-3329; US 460

LOCAL KNOWLEDGE:
CAMPING & CABINS ALONG THE BLUE RIDGE PARKWAY

There are numerous private camping sites, and four public **campgrounds** (📞877-444-6777; www.recreation.gov; campsites $19; ⊙May-Oct) located at mileposts 60.8, 85.6, 120.4 and 161.1, on the Virginia side of the Blue Ridge Parkway.

Campgrounds along the parkway are open from May to October, with a per-night charge. Use the aforementioned reservations website to book these sites. Demand is higher on weekends and holidays. While there are no electrical hookups at parkway campsites, you will find restrooms, potable water and picnic tables. You're often at a pretty high elevation (over 2500-ft high), so even during summer you may want to bring some extra layers, as it can get chilly up here.

You can also stay in two cabin-style accommodations options, although only one was open during our research. **Rocky Knob Cabins** (📞540-593-3503; www.rockyknobcabins.com; 266 Mabry Mill Rd; cabin with shared bath $75; ⊙May-Oct; P 🐾), in the wonderfully named Meadows of Dan, are pretty rustic, but comfortable and cozy as well. Each cabin comes with two full-sized beds, but bath facilities are shared. Bring food, as eating options are limited along the parkway.

Peaks of Otter Lodge (📞540-586-1081; www.peaksofotter.com; Mile 86, 85554 Blue Ridge Pkwy; r from $130; ❄), about 20 miles from Roanoke, is a pretty, split-rail-surrounded lodge on a small lake nestled between two of its namesake mountains. The lodge had recently been sold to new ownership at the time of research. There's a restaurant, but no public phones and no cellphone reception.

DETOUR:
BLACKSBURG

Start: ⑨ Roanoke

Located about 42 miles west of Roanoke, Blacksburg is another higher education-centered community in the mountains of highland Virginia. But this is no small, liberal arts college town. Blacksburg is the home of the largest university in Virginia: the Virginia Polytechnic Institute, better known as **Virginia Tech**, V-Tech or just Tech. The local, odd mascot? That would be 'Hokies,' also known as the Hokie Bird. It's basically a turkey. Sort of. Well...

OK, here's the skinny: the world 'hokie' comes from VT's nonsensical fight song, chanted at all university athletic events and many a Blacksburg bar. It has nothing to do with turkeys, but a wild turkey was the team's mascot for much of the 20th century. Said turkeys were the reason the team was nicknamed the 'Fighting Gobblers': 'Gobbler' is North American slang for a turkey, but it has some, well, pejorative connotations, so the university amended the name to 'Hokie Bird,' invoking the school's fight song. Now, go enjoy pub trivia, or feel free to look around the green 2600-acre campus; a good place to start is the **visitor center** (☎540-231-3548; www.visit.vt.edu; 925 Prices Fork Rd, Blacksburg; ⊗7:30am-6pm Mon-Fri, 8:30am-2:30pm Sat, 1-5pm Sun).

Blacksburg as a town basically revolves around Tech. The nearby **Smithfield Plantation** (☎540-231-3947; www.smithfieldplantation.org; 1000 Smithfield Plantation Rd; adult/child $8/3; ⊗10am-5pm Mon-Sat, 1-5pm Sun), built in 1774, is an excellent example of late-colonial architecture. We highly recommend a drive on **Catawba Rd** (Virginia Rte 785), which rolls past stunning murals of farmland, streams and forestscape.

To take this detour, take I-81 westbound, then exit at 118B to get on US 460; follow this road westbound to Blacksburg.

& Hwy 122; adult/child $7/5; ⊗10am-5pm). Among its towering arch and flower garden is a cast of bronze figures re-enacting the storming of the beach, complete with bursts of water symbolizing the hail of bullets the soldiers faced.

The surrounding countryside is speckled with vineyards, including an outfit that specializes in the juice of apples, pears, peaches and chili peppers. **Peaks of Otter Winery** (☎540-586-3707; www.peaksofotterwinery.com; 2122 Sheep Creek Rd, Bedford; ⊗noon-5pm daily Apr-Dec, weekends only Jan-Mar) stands out from other viticulture tourism spots with its focus on producing fruit wines (the chili pepper wine is, by the way, 'better for basting than tasting' according to management).

White Rock Vineyards (☎540-890-3359; http://www.whiterockwines.com; 2117 Bruno Dr, Goodview; ⊗noon-5pm Thu-Mon), on the other hand, is a more traditional winery. A few acres of green grapevines (well, green in the right season anyway) seem to erupt around a pretty house; if you head in for a tasting, we're fans of the White Mojo Pinot Gris.

Learn more about the many vineyards here via the **Bedford Wine Trail** (www.bedfordwinetrail.com).

The Drive » Take VA-122 (Burks Hill Rd) southbound for about 13.5 miles. In Moneta, take a left onto State Route 608 and drive for 6 miles, then turn right onto Smith Mountain Lake Pkwy. Go 2 miles and you're at the park.

Classic Trip

MICHAEL RUNKEL, APPALACHEANS/ALAMY ©

8 Smith Mountain Lake

This enormous, 32-sq-mile reservoir is one of the most popular recreation spots in Southwestern Virginia and the largest lake contained entirely within the borders of the commonwealth. Vacation rentals and water activities abound, as does development, and there are portions of this picturesque dollop that have been overwhelmed with rental units. Most lake access is via private property only.

This isn't the case at **Smith Mountain State Park** (☎540-297-6066; http://www.dcr.virginia.gov/state_parks/smi.shtml; 1235 State Park Rd, Huddleston; weekdays/weekends $2/3), located on the north shore of the lake. Don't get us wrong – there's lots of facilities here if you need them, including a boat ramp, picnic tables, fishing piers, an amphitheater, camping sites and cabin rentals, but in general, the area within the state park preserves the natural beauty of this area. Thirteen hiking trails wind through the surrounding forests.

The nearby **Hickory Hill Winery** (☎540-296-1393; www.smlwine.com; 1722 Hickory Cove Lane, Moneta; ◷noon-6pm Apr-Oct, to 5pm Nov-Mar), anchored by a charming 1923 farmhouse, is a lovely spot to lounge about sipping Merlot either before or after your adventures on the lake.

The Drive » Head back toward Bedford on VA-122 and go left on State Route 801/Stony Fork Rd. Follow this to VA-24/Stewartsville Rd; take that road west about 20 miles to Roanoke.

9 Roanoke

Roanoke is the largest city and commercial hub of Southwest Virginia.

Lexington Washington & Lee University campus

It's not as picturesque as other towns, but its a good logistical base. The site of the **Harrison Museum of African American Culture** (www.harrisonmuseum.com) was the first public high school for African Americans in America. It has displays on local African American culture and traditional and contemporary African art. Nearby, **Center in the Square** (☎540-342-5700; www.centerinthesquare.org; 1 Market Sq; ☉10am-5pm Tue-Sat, from 1pm Sun) is the city's cultural heartbeat, with a science museum and planetarium (adult/child $8/6), local history museum (adult/child $3/2) and theater.

✕ 🛏 p311

The Drive ❱❱ From Roanoke, you can hop back on the parkway and continue on into the Meadows of Dan portion of the park, covered in Trip 24: The Crooked Road (p289).

Classic Trip

Eating & Sleeping

VIRGINIA TRIPS **25** BLUE RIDGE PARKWAY

Staunton ❶

✖ AVA Restaurant & Wine Bar   American $$

(📞540-886-2851; 103 W Beverley St; mains $10-30; 🕒4-9:30pm Wed-Thu, noon-10pm Fri & Sat, 10:30am-2:30pm Sun; 🍴) AVA offers fine dining in the heart of historic Staunton. Creole-style catfish and roasted duck breast share space with the best vegetarian food in town – the vegetarian 'Beef' Wellington uses beets in place of beef. There's plenty of vegan options as well, and a long wine menu adds a nice buzz to your meal.

✖ Beverly Restaurant   Diner $

(12 E Beverley St; mains under $10; 🍴) The Beverly is a tried-and-true diner and a cornerstone of downtown Staunton. It may not possess the most imaginative menu – we're talking meat and potatoes, and the potatoes are usually baked – but the food is both tasty and damn good value.

✖ Downtown 27 at the Clocktower   American $$

(📞540-213-0665; 27 W Beverly St; mains $13-23; 🕒11am-10pm Mon-Thu, til 11:30pm Fri & Sat; 🍴) More often just known as the Clocktower, this spot is as central to Staunton as the Blackfriars Playhouse. The menu swings between Italian specialties (pasta and lasagna) and pub grub fare (roast beef and burgers). Live music usually livens up this spot on weekends.

✖ Mugshots   Cafe $

(📞540-887-0005; 32 S New St; pastries under $5; 🕒7am-5:30pm Mon-Fri, 8am-5pm Sat, 8am-4pm Sun; 📶) This simple cafe is a prime spot to sit down, catch up on your emails, sip a coffee and enjoy a bagel or a muffin.

✖ Pompeii Lounge   Italian $

(📞540-885-5553; 23 East Beverley St; snacks $4-9; 🕒5pm-1am Tue-Thu, til 2am Fri & Sat; 🍴) The Pompeii is a three-story Italian restaurant that doubles as the nicest spot in Staunton to grab a drink. The jewel in the crown is the top-floor deck, from where you can stare out over the Staunton skyline and enjoy live music, antipasto-style small plates and some fine locally crafted cocktails.

✖ Zynodoa   Southern $$$

(📞540-885-7775; 115 E Beverley St; mains $21-28; 🕒5-9:30pm Sun-Tue, til 10pm Wed-Sat; 🍴) Local farms and wineries are the backbone of Zynodoa's larder (and, of course, your table). This place puts together fine dishes in the vein of Shenandoah-sourced chicken cassoulet (crunchy, warm, inviting) and Chesapeake-caught Rockfish.

🛏 Anne Hathaway's Cottage   B&B $$

(📞540-885-8885; www.anne-hathaways-cottage.com; 950 West Beverley St; r $150-170; 🅿❄📶) We showed up hoping to meet Catwoman from *The Dark Knight Rises*, but as you may guess in Staunton, this inn's namesake is Shakespeare's wife. And we imagine the Elizabethan Anne Hathaway would have thoroughly enjoyed a night in one of the three rooms in this ridiculously romantic Tudor-style, thatched-roof cottage. Rates drop on weekdays and for last-minute bookings.

🛏 Frederick House   B&B $$

(📞540-885-4220; www.frederickhouse.com; 28 N New St; r incl breakfast $130-240; 🅿❄📶) Right downtown, the thoroughly mauve and immensely welcoming Frederick House consists of five historical residences with a combination of rooms and suites, all with private bathrooms and some with fireplaces and decks.

🛏 Stonewall Jackson Hotel   Hotel $$

(☎540-885-4848; www.stonewalljacksonhotel.
com; 24 S Market St; r $112-300; P✳🎧🏊)
A restored and renovated Staunton classic,
the Stonewall oozes class and the restrained
Southern style of the classical commonwealth.
The central lobby could be plucked from a
chapter of *The Great Gatsby* (if *Gatsby* was set
in old Virginia). Rooms are comfortable and
retain the classic atmosphere promised by the
entrance, and amenities are extensive.

Lexington ❸

✖ Red Hen   Southern $$

(☎540-464-4401; 11 E Washington St; mains
$17-26; ⏱5:30-9pm Tue-Sat; 🍴) It looks like
plenty of VMI cadets take their Washington &
Lee undergrad dates out to the Red Hen, and
with good reason. Besides serving fine farm-to-
table Southern cuisine that's been written up by
the national food press, the setting is intimate
and romantic. Try the herb-roasted quail on
polenta – woo! Excuse our drool.

✖ Macado's   Sandwiches $

(☎540-464-8200; 30 N Main St; mains $6-12;
⏱8am-12:30am) Overstuffed sandwiches are
the name of the game at this immensely popular
eatery. The long beer menu ensure Macado's
doubles as the closest thing to nightlife in
Lexington.

🛏 Applewood Inn &
Llama Trekking   Inn $$

(☎800-463-1902; www.applewoodbb.com;
242 Tarn Beck Lane; r $155-165; P✳) The
charming, ecominded Applewood Inn & Llama
Trekking offers a slew of outdoorsy activities
(including, yes, llama trekking) on a farm a
10-minute drive away from downtown Lexington
in a positively bucolic valley.

🛏 Brierley Hill B&B   B&B $$$

(☎540-464-8421, 800-422-4925; www.
brierleyhill.com; 985 Borden Rd; r $190-270,
cottage $380; P✳🎧) The namesake hill that
Brierley is situated on overlooks a lovely stretch
of the Shenandoah valley. Inside this charming
home you'll find handsome, well-appointed rooms
and a lovely, fresh breakfast. Rates plummet
precipitously from December to March.

Roanoke ❾

✖ Wildflour Restaurant
& Bakery   Fusion $$

(☎540-343-4543; 1212 4th Street Southwest;
sandwiches under $10, dinner mains $15-24;
⏱11am-9pm Mon-Sat; P) Give us our daily
bread, Wildlflour. We mean that – give us
your daily bread selection, especially French
cornmeal on Mondays. Then there's the
wonderful homemade sandwiches and rustic
fusion-meets-New-American menu, with
entrees like maple soy-glazed salmon and a
hearty as hell meatloaf.

🛏 Hotel Roanoke   Hotel $$$

(☎540-985-5900; www.hotelroanoke.com; 110
Shenandoah Ave; r $150-300) Check in to the
Tudor-style Hotel Roanoke after a long day's
drive. This grand dame has presided over this
city at the base of the Blue Ridge Mountains
for the better part of a century and provides a
welcome respite. Downstairs is the Pine Room
for those requiring a stiff drink.

Charlottesville Hills covered in vineyards in the Piedmont

Peninsula to the Piedmont

26

Explore fair Virginia tip to toe, from forested, highland horse country and vineyards to riverside plantations and battlefields where the nation was born.

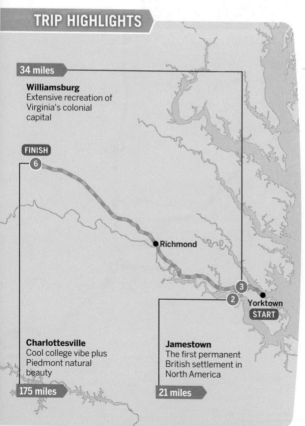

34 miles

Williamsburg
Extensive recreation of Virginia's colonial capital

FINISH
6

Richmond

3
2
Yorktown
START

Charlottesville
Cool college vibe plus Piedmont natural beauty

175 miles

Jamestown
The first permanent British settlement in North America

21 miles

2 DAYS
158 MILES / 254KM

GREAT FOR ...

BEST TIME TO GO
April to July, to soak up sun and American patriotism.

ESSENTIAL PHOTO
Monticello set against the sunset.

BEST FOR FAMILIES
A day exploring Colonial WIlliamsburg.

ANDRE JENNY/ALAMY ©

26 Peninsula to the Piedmont

You stand on the cusp of Monticello and look out. There: the Blue Ridge mountains, and there: the Piedmont plateau meandering off to a topographic pancake intercut by the squiggly blue waters of the Elizabeth and James Rivers. And spread over all of this: the place where America was founded (well, by the British). Where America governed herself. And where she won her independence.

1 Yorktown

Virginia's Historic Triangle consists of the towns of Yorktown, Jamestown and Williamsburg, all arranged in a rough triangular shape on the wooded Virginia peninsula, a geographic appendage known for tidal inlets and marshes, if not the originality of its name.

Yorktown was the site of the American victory of George Washington over the British Lord Cornwalllis. The event

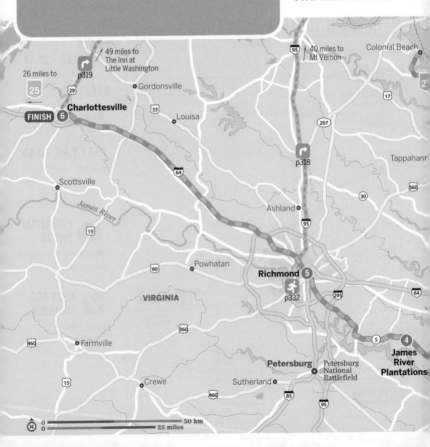

was more of a whimper than a bang; Cornwallis' forces had endured weeks of siege and faulty supply lines in the fight against the Americans, and Chesapeake Bay, their source of resupply, was blockaded by the French Navy.

There's two ways of experiencing Yorktown's charms. One is the **Yorktown Victory Center** (📞757-887-1776; www. historyisfun.org; 200 Water St; adult/child $9.75/5.50; ⏰9am-5pm; P ✦). The state-run park is an interactive, living-history

museum that focuses on reconstruction, reenactment and the Revolution's impact on the people who lived through it. It caters a little more to kids, but its cuteness is certainly balanced out by an effort to have a candid conversation about the course of the battle and the motivations of the revolutionaries.

Yorktown Battlefield (📞757-898-3400; 1000 Colonial Pkwy; incl Historic Jamestowne adult/child $10/ free; ⏰9am-5pm; P ✦), run by the National Park Service (NPS), is the actual site of the last major battle of the American Revolution. Start your tour at the visitor center and check out the orientation film and the display of Washington's original tent. The 7-mile Battlefield Rd Tour takes you past the major highlights. Don't miss a walk through the last British defensive sites, Redoubts 9 and 10.

The Drive » Get on Colonial National Historic Pkwy and take it 7 miles west. Turn onto SR-641, which becomes VA-199, and follow it for 6 miles, then turn left onto Jamestown Rd. Drive on this for 5 miles and keep an eye out for signs to Jamestown.

- - - - - - - - - -

TRIP HIGHLIGHT

② Jamestown

Jamestown was the first permanent English settlement in North America, although permanent is a relative term. The colony was founded in 1607 on a marshy spit of malaria-stricken wetlands; the settlers included aristocrats and tradesmen, but no farmers. During the 'starving times' of 1609–10, only 61 out of 500 colonists survived; forensic evidence indicates some settlers resorted to cannibalism. Future waves of colonists proved more competent, and turned to tobacco as a profitable cash crop.

LINK YOUR TRIP

25 Blue Ridge Parkway

In Charlottesville, head west for 40 miles to reach Staunton and the mountains of the Blue Ridge.

27 Bracketing the Bay

From Williamsburg, head southeast for 20 miles to Newport News, Hampton Roads and shores of Chesapeake Bay.

Again, there are two areas to explore here. More child-friendly and entertaining, the state-run **Jamestown Settlement** (📞757-253-4838; www.historyisfun.org; 2110 Jamestown Rd; adult/child $16/7.50, incl Yorktown Victory Center $20.50/10.25; ⊙9am-5pm; 🅿🚻) reconstructs the 1607 James Fort, a Native American village and full-scale replicas of the first ships that brought the settlers to Jamestown, along with living-history fun.

Located on the former site of the actual Jamestown colony, **Historic Jamestowne** (📞757-856-1200; www.historicjamestowne.org; 1368 Colonial Pkwy; adult/child $14/free; ⊙8:30am-4:30pm) is less flashy and far more reflective; if the settlement feels like a living history park, this comes off as an engaging, quiet archaeology lecture. You're welcome to wander the grassy ruins of the original city of Jamestown, which was abandoned in 1699 as Williamsburg's star ascended, and spend time by the interpretive signage.

The Drive ›› Return to the Colonial National Historic Pkwy, then turn right onto Jamestown Rd and follow for 5.5 miles to downtown Williamsburg.

TRIP HIGHLIGHT

❸ Williamsburg

The restored capital of England's largest colony

in the New World is a must-see attraction for visitors of all ages. This is not some cheesy, fenced-in theme park; **Colonial Williamsburg** (www.colonialwilliamsburg.org; adult/child $42/21; ⊙9am-5pm; 🅿) is a living, breathing, working history museum that transports visitors back to the 1700s.

The 301-acre historic area contains 88 original 18th-century buildings and several hundred faithful reproductions. Costumed townsfolk and 'interpreters' in period dress go about their colonial jobs as blacksmiths, apothecaries, printers, barmaids, soldiers and patriots, breaking character only long enough to pose for a snapshot.

Costumed patriots like Patrick Henry and Thomas Jefferson still deliver impassioned speeches for freedom, but to its credit, Colonial Williamsburg has grown up a little. Where once it was all about projecting a rah-rah version of American-heck-yeah in a powdered wig, today reenactors debate and question slavery, women's suffrage, the rights of indigenous Americans and the very moral right of revolution.

Walking around the historic district and patronizing the shops and taverns is free,

PETER PTSCHELINZEW/GETTY IMAGES ©

but entry to building tours and most exhibits is restricted to ticket holders. To park and purchase tickets, follow signs to the visitor center, north of the historic district between Hwy 132 and Colonial Pkwy, where kids can hire out period costumes. Most day activities are included with the admission price. Evening events

Williamsburg Restored buildings and costumed actors create a sense of history

(ghost walks, witch trials, chamber recitals) cost extra.

Parking is free; shuttle buses run frequently to and from the historic district, or walk along the tree-lined footpath.

Colonial Williamsburg isn't the only sight to see in Williamsburg. Chartered in 1693, the **College of William & Mary** (www.wm.edu; 200 Stadium Dr) is the second-oldest college in the country and retains the oldest academic building in continued use in the USA, the Sir Christopher Wren Building. The school's alumni include Thomas Jefferson, James Monroe and comedian Jon Stewart. The campus is green, attractive, filled with historic buildings and worth a wander.

🍴 🛏 p321

The Drive » Take the Jamestown Rd out of Williamsburg to VA-199, then turn right. Follow for about 2 miles, then turn left on VA-5 and follow it west for about 18 miles to reach Sherwood Forest plantation.

④ James River Plantations

The grand homes of Virginia's slaveholding aristocracy were a clear sign of the era's class

DETOUR:
MT VERNON

Start: ❺ Richmond

Well, we hit the homes of two Founding Fathers on this trip – why not shoot for a threesome? So drive to the outskirts of Washington, DC, and the home of George and Martha Washington: **Mt Vernon** (📞703-780-2000, 800-429-1520; www.mountvernon. org; 3200 Mount Vernon Memorial Hwy, Mount Vernon; adult/child $17/8; ⏱8am-5pm Apr-Aug, 9am-4pm Nov-Feb, 9am-5pm all other months).

A visit here is an easy escape from the city – one that the president himself enjoyed. It's also a journey through history: the country estate of this quintessential gentleman has been meticulously restored and affords a glimpse of rural gentility from a time long gone. On the Potomac banks, the 19-room mansion displays George and Martha's colonial tastes, while the outbuildings and slave quarters show what was needed for the functioning of the estate.

George and Martha are both buried here, as requested by the first president in his will. The modern **Ford Orientation Center**, also on the grounds, is a must-see. It features a 20-minute film that shows Washington's courage under fire, including his pivotal crossing of the Delaware River (the do-or-die moment of the Revolutionary War). Another highlight is the sleek **Reynolds Museum and Education Center**. Home to galleries and theaters, it gives more insight into Washington's life using interactive displays, short films produced by the cable TV History Channel and three life-size models of Washington himself. The museum also features period furnishings, clothing and jewelry (Martha was quite taken with finery) and George's unusual dentures.

To visit, take I-95 northbound for 85 miles, then take exit 161 and follow US 1 northbound. Drive for about 9 miles, then follow signs to Mt Vernon.

---

divisions. A string of them line scenic Hwy 5 on the north side of the river. The ones listed here run from east to west.

Sherwood Forest (📞804-829-5377; www. sherwoodforest.org; 14501 John Tyler Memorial Hwy; tours by appointment $35 per person), the longest frame house in the country, was the home of 10th US president John Tyler. The grounds (and a touching pet cemetery) are open to self-guided tours.

Berkeley (📞804-829-6018; www.berkeleyplantation. com; 12602 Harrison Landing Rd; adult/child $11/7.50; ⏱9:30am-4:30pm) was the site of the first official Thanksgiving in 1619. It was the birthplace and home of Benjamin Harrison V, a signer of the Declaration of Independence, and his son William Henry Harrison, ninth US president.

Shirley (📞800-232-1613; www.shirleyplantation.com; 501 Shirley Plantation Rd; adult/child $11/7.50; ⏱9am-5pm), situated picturesquely on the river, is Virginia's oldest plantation (1613) and perhaps the best example of how a British-model plantation actually appeared, with its tidy row of brick service and trade houses (tool barn, ice house, laundry etc) leading up to the big house.

The Drive »» Continue west on VA-5 for about 31 miles – you'll follow this road right into downtown Richmond. Alternatively, you may want to take VA-5 for 27 miles to I-895; head along that road westbound, then take I-95 northbound. Take exit 74A to reach Richmond.

❺ Richmond

Virginia's capital is a handsome town,

full of red-brick and brownstone row houses that leave a softer impression than their sometimes staid Northeastern counterparts. History is ubiquitous and sometimes uncomfortable; this was where patriot Patrick Henry gave his famous 'Give me Liberty, or give me Death!' speech, and where the slave-holding Southern Confederate States placed their capital.

Monument Avenue, a tree-lined boulevard in northeast Richmond, holds statues of such revered Southern heroes as JEB Stuart, Robert E Lee, Matthew Fontaine Maury, Jefferson Davis, Stonewall Jackson and, in a nod to diversity, African American tennis champion Arthur Ashe.

Designed by Thomas Jefferson, the Virginia State Capitol (p332) was completed in 1788. Free tours are offered throughout the week.

The **Virginia Museum of Fine Arts** (VMFA; ☑804-340-1400; www.vmfa. state.va.us; 2800 Grove Ave; ⊙10am-5pm Sat-Wed, to 9pm Thu & Fri) has a remarkable collection of European works, sacred Himalayan art and one of the largest Fabergé egg collections on display outside Russia. It also hosts excellent temporary exhibitions (admission free to $20).

The Drive » Take I-64 westbound for 63 miles, then take exit 124 to follow US 250 westbound. Follow 250 for 2 miles, then turn left onto High St to reach downtown Charlottesville.

- - - - - - - - - - - - - -

6 Charlottesville

Set in the shadow of the Blue Ridge Mountains, Charlottesville is

DETOUR:
THE INN AT LITTLE WASHINGTON

Start: 6 Charlottesville

Feeling hungry? Not just 'I could use a sandwich' hungry but 'In the mood for a rustic five-star gastronomic head-explosion' hungry? Then head 60 miles northeast towards Washington (the town, not the capital) and settle in at the **Inn at Little Washington** (☑540-675-3800; www.theinnatlittlewashington.com; cnr Middle & Main Sts, Washington, VA; dinner prix fixe $148-165; ⊙5:30-11pm), a sacred destination on the epicurean trail. Founded more than 30 years ago by Patrick O'Connell and his partner, it has been named one of the '10 Best Restaurants in the World' by the *International Herald Tribune*. But the inn's pleasures come at a price so beware – the dinner prix fixe started at $148 on a recent visit and goes higher on weekends.

It is worth every penny.

First of all the service is, unsurprisingly, impeccable, and the food hits all the grace notes. For the first course you might try the beet fantasia or the eggs in an egg (once prepared for the Queen of England on her visit to American shores). Next, you could try the pecan-crusted soft-shell crab tempura with Italian mustard fruit. The 'pepper crusted tuna pretending to be a filet mignon capped with seared duck fois gras on charred onions with a burgundy butter sauce' is a good example of what's happening in the kitchen; namely, taking the finest ingredients and turning them into a global medley, a sort of international gastronomic carnival.

So, yeah, any questions? Go. Toss your credit score to the wind and just go. To really make the evening count, reserve one of the achingly perfect rooms at the adjacent inn from which the restaurant gets its name.

regularly ranked as one of the country's best places to live. This culturally rich town of 45,000 is home to the University of Virginia (UVA), which attracts Southern aristocracy and artsy bohemians in equal proportion. The UVA's centerpiece is the Thomas Jefferson-designed **Rotunda** (📞434-924-7969; 1826 University Ave), a scale replica of Rome's Pantheon. Free, student-led tours of the Rotunda meet inside the main entrance daily at 10am, 11am, 2pm, 3pm and 4pm. UVA's **Fralin Art Museum** (📞434-924-3592; 155 Rugby Rd; ⊙noon-5pm Tue-Sun) has an eclectic and interesting collection of American, European and Asian arts.

The main attraction is just outside of 'C-ville': **Monticello** (📞434-984-9800; www.monticello.org; 931 Thomas Jefferson Pkwy; adult/child $24/16; ⊙9am-6pm Mar-Oct, 10am-5pm Nov-Feb), an architectural masterpiece designed and inhabited by Thomas Jefferson, Founding Father and third US president. Today it is the only home in America designated a Unesco World Heritage site. Built in Roman neoclassical style, the house was the centerpiece of a 5000-acre plantation tended by 150 slaves. Monticello today does not gloss over the complicated past of the man who declared that 'all men are created equal' in the Declaration of Independence. Jefferson, a slave owner, is thought to have fathered children with slave Sally Hemings. Jefferson and his family are buried in a small wooded plot near the home.

✕ 🛏 p321

BREWERIES AND WINERIES OF THE PIEDMONT

Small- and medium-scale wine making and beer brewing is rapidly growing in the Piedmont. The following are all in Charlottesville or the surrounding vicinity.

Blenheim Vineyards (📞434-293-5366; http://blenheimvineyards.com; 31 Blenheim Farm, Charlottesville; tastings $5; ⊙11am-5:30pm) Blenheim is owned by musician Dave Matthews (of the Dave Matthews band), who in some ways – what with his folkie-preppie vibe and eternal gap-year sunniness and sense of discovery and the fact that he owns a vineyard – is the Platonic ideal of a University of Virginia student. Trust us, the album *Crash* is as popular on campus as it was in 1998. Anyway, the wines are great and the setting is sheer bucolic joy.

Blue Mountain Brewery (📞540-456-8020; www.bluemountainbrewery.com; 9519 Critzer's Shop Rd, Afton; ⊙11am-10pm Mon-Sat, to 9pm Sun) Located 20 miles from Charlottesville near the high slopes of Skyline Dr, Blue Mountain Brewery is some kind of wonderful. These guys are dedicated to their craft and their craft beers, which includes a crisp Bavarian-style wheat beer that is all kinds of good in the hot summer swelter, and the muscular Full Nelson, brewed with local hops.

Pippin Hill (📞434-202-8063; www.pippinhillfarm.com; 5022 Plank Rd, North Garden; tastings $6; ⊙11am-5pm Tue-Sun) Wonderful views over the rolling plateau of the Piedmont greet you at Pippin Hill, which is located in a bar that just about screams rustic hipster paradise. Pippin Hill leads the way in practicing sustainable viticuture.

Champion Brewing Company (📞434-295-2739; www.championbrewingcompany.com; 324 6th St, SE Charlottesville; ⊙5-9pm Wed, 4-11pm Thu-Sat, 1-6pm Sun) The Champion is in Charlottesville proper, so there's no need to worry about calling that cab after your brewery-bound tasting test. More importantly, these guys know their stuff, as evidenced by their heavy porters and flavorful kolsches.

Eating & Sleeping

Williamsburg ❶

✖ Fat Canary   American $$$

(☎757-229-3333; 410 Duke of Gloucester St, Merchants Sq; mains $28-39; ⏱5-10pm) For a splurge, there's no better place in the Historic Triangle. Top-notch service, excellent wines and heavenly desserts are only slightly upstaged by the magnificent seasonal cuisine (recent favorites: pan-seared sea scallops with oyster pork belly; wild rice stuffed quail; and seared foie gras and hazelnut toast).

🛏 Governor's Inn   Hotel $

(☎757-253-2277; www.colonialwilliamsburg resorts.com; 506 N Henry St; r $70-120; P 🛜 🖳) Williamsburg's official 'economy' choice is a big box by any other name, but rooms are clean, and guests can use the pool and facilities of the nearby Woodlands Hotel. It's in a great location three blocks from the historic district.

🛏 Williamsburg White House   B&B $$

(☎757-229-8580; www. awilliamsburgwhitehouse.com; 718 Jamestown Rd; r $160-200, ste $375; P 🛜) This romantic B&B, decorated with red- white- and blue-bunting, is located across from the campus of William & Mary, just a few blocks' walk from Colonial Williamsburg. It's a favorite spot of visiting politicos and bigwigs, but the atmosphere and amicable management exudes more stateliness than stuffiness.

Charlottesville ❻

✖ Continental Divide   Mexican $$

(☎434-984-0143; 811 W Main St; mains $10-15; ⏱5-10:15pm, to 10:45pm Fri & Sat, to 9:45pm Sun) This fun, easy-going spot has no sign (look for the neon 'Get in Here' in the window) but is well worth seeking out for its Mexican fusion fare – tacos with slow-cooked pork, tuna tostadas, nachos with bison chili – and Charlotteville's best margaritas.

✖ The Whiskey Jar   Southern $

(☎434-202-1549; 227 West Main St; mains $9-16; 🍴) The Whiskey Jar does neo-Southern comfort food in an affected rustic setting, all wooden furniture and wait staff wearing plaid, and drinks served out of mason jars. We're tempted to say it's a little too cute, but honestly, the Jar nails it – the simple, fresh food like mustard-braised rabbit is delicious and exceedingly good value.

🛏 Inn at Monticello   B&B $$$

(☎877-735-2982, 434-979-3593; www. innatmonticello.com; 1188 Scottsville Rd; r $210-250; P ❄ 🛜) Located across from Monticello, this Victorian B&B is set off against the Piedmont's rolling hillscape. Every one of the lodge's five rooms are cozy little testaments to colonial grandeur. The friendly, knowledgeable innkeepers are a good travel resource, and provide excellent cooked breakfasts as well.

🛏 South Street Inn   B&B $$$

(☎434-979-0200; www.southstreetinn.com; 200 South St; r incl breakfast $150-255; P ❄) In the heart of downtown, this elegant 1856 building went through previous incarnations as a girl's finishing school, boarding house and brothel. Now it houses heritage-style rooms – a total of two dozen – some with antiques and working fireplaces. There's wine and cheese in the evenings.

Virginia Beach
Striking attractions include the
Cape Henry lighthouse

Bracketing the Bay

27

From presidential residences to surfer boy beaches to burgeoning naval bases, Virginia offers drastically different experiences on either side of Chesapeake Bay.

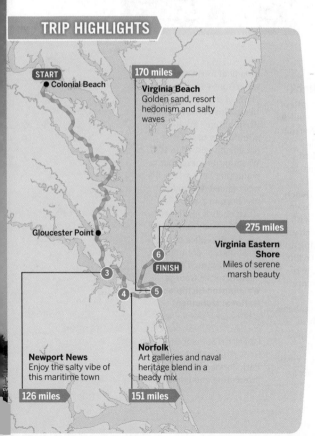

TRIP HIGHLIGHTS

START
● Colonial Beach

170 miles

Virginia Beach
Golden sand, resort hedonism and salty waves

275 miles

Virginia Eastern Shore
Miles of serene marsh beauty

Gloucester Point ●

6
FINISH

3

4 **5**

Newport News
Enjoy the salty vibe of this maritime town

126 miles

Norfolk
Art galleries and naval heritage blend in a heady mix

151 miles

2 DAYS
275 MILES / 442KM

GREAT FOR ...

BEST TIME TO GO
Visit from June to September to enjoy the best of the beaches.

ESSENTIAL PHOTO
George Washington's birthplace set against woods and water.

BEST FOR FOODIES
A deli sandwich at Jewish Mother in Virginia Beach

323

27 Bracketing the Bay

Virginia is blessed with three coasts, and you'll experience them all on this trip. From the golden sands of Virginia Beach to the quiet forests that line the rivers of the Northern Neck, to the gentle marsh country lining Chesapeake Bay and the skinny Virginia Eastern Shore, there's always water at your fingertips, and all the leisure and seafood that watery geography promises.

1 Northern Neck

About 85 miles south of Washington, DC via I-95 and VA-3 is the Northern Neck, a peninsula of land sandwiched between the Potomac and Rappahannock Rivers. **Colonial Beach** is a small resort town on the Potomac, with a pretty public beach and some decent dining and lodging options (p330). But the main draw to this area is of a more historical bent.

Eleven miles southeast of Colonial Beach, at the point where Pope's Creek flows into the Potomac River, is a rustic patchwork of tobacco fields, wheat plots,

broadleaf forest and waterfront views over the bluffs of the Northern Neck. This is where John Washington – great-grandfather of the first president – settled in 1657. Washington carved out a plantation here, where his most famed descendant was born in 1732.

An obelisk fashioned from Vermont marble, a one-tenth replica of the Washington Monument in Washington, DC greets visitors to the **George Washington Birthplace National Monument** (☎804-224-1732; www.nps.gov/gewa; 1732 Popes Creek Rd, Colonial Beach; ☺9am-5pm), run by the National Park Service. The site is interesting enough as

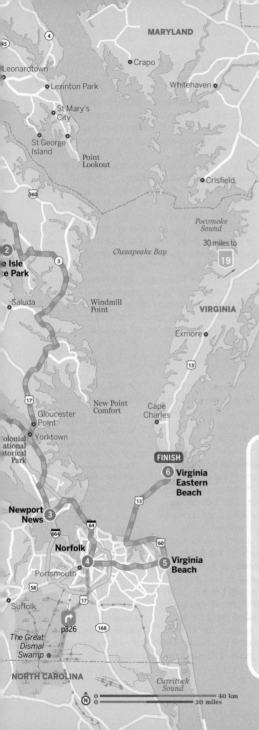

Washington's birthplace, but it's more engaging as a peek into the lifestyle of the plantation owners who formed Virginia's original aristocracy – a class of essentially large-land-owning gentry, which stood in contrast to the small plot farmers and mercantile class of Northern colonies like New York and Massachusetts.

✕ 🛏 p330

The Drive » Take VA-205E out of Colonial Beach for 6 miles to VA-3. Head east on VA-3 for about 41 miles, then turn right onto VA-354 (River Rd). Follow signs to State Rd 683/Belle Isle Rd, which leads to Belle Isle State Park.

- - - - - - - - - -

➋ Belle Isle State Park

Belle Isle State Park
(www.dcr.virginia.gov/state_parks/bel.shtml; 1632 Belle

LINK YOUR TRIP

19 **Delmarva**
From Chincoteague Island, head north into the marshes and beaches fronting the Atlantic Ocean.

26 **Peninsula to the Piedmont**
Go west from Hampton Roads into the rolling farmland and living history museums of Virginia's Historic Triangle.

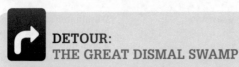

DETOUR:
THE GREAT DISMAL SWAMP

Start: ❹ Norfolk

About 30 miles southwest of Norfolk, straddling the Virginia and North Carolina border, is over 1 million acres of morass, rivers, lakes, flooded forests and mud flats. Here, the water runs red, brown and black as it leaches highly concentrated tannins from a veritable jungle's worth of vegetation, including bald cypress, tupelo and pine trees.

This is the **Great Dismal Swamp**, and here on the Virginia side of the border one can find the **Great Dismal Swamp National Wildlife Refuge** (☎757-986-3705; www.fws.gov/refuge/great_dismal_swamp/; 3100 Desert Rd, Suffolk; ☼sunrise-sunset; 🐾). There are some 112,000 acres of protected land here, a wet home for bobcats, black bears, red foxes, coyotes and over 200 species of birds. In late April, the refuge hosts an annual birding festival (see website for details) that coincides with the biggest migratory period of the year; during past festivals, birders have seen the extremely secretive Wayne's warbler. Disclosure: we're not sure how big a deal this is, but when we told a birding friend, they practically cried.

The Great Dismal Swamp is not just a home for animals. Native Americans may have first settled here a full 13,000 years ago, and for centuries, escaped African slaves known as maroons hid in the swamp's shadowy depths.

There are miles of hiking trails within the swamp, almost all of which are quite flat. Contact the park headquarters to speak with rangers about local fishing and hunting opportunities.

Isle Rd, Lancaster; weekdays/weekends $2/3; ☼sunrise to sunset) beckons travelers who want a full menu of outdoor activities to pick from. This is a small state park, yet it boasts picnic areas, boat launches, hiking and biking trails and a host of other well-maintained amenities. Keep an eye out for numerous bald eagles patrolling this marsh and forest habitat.

The entire park is built around a Georgian mansion – the **Belle Isle Mansion** – that feels like a dictionary illustration that hangs next to the word 'mansion.' It was built around 1760 by Raleigh Downman and restored in the 1940s by Thomas Tileston Waterman, the first director of the Historic American Buildings Survey; today the mansion can be admired from afar, but the big building itself is owned by a private family.

Another onsite historic property, the **Bel Air House** (no fresh princes, sadly), is available for overnight rentals ($284 to $316). It's almost always booked every weekend in summer for weddings months in advance, but if you're interested, call ☎800-933-7275, or go to www.reserveamerica.com.

The Drive ≫ Take Belle Isle Rd (VA-354S) for 3 miles to VA-201. Turn left onto 201 and take it to VA-3E. Follow VA-3E through hills and woodlands for 42 miles until it runs into US 17 S. Take US 17 south for 25 miles to reach Newport News.

- - - - - - - - - -

TRIP HIGHLIGHT

❸ Newport News

Newport News is the first town you'll come across in the Hampton Roads. Almost everything you encounter in these parts is either tied to the water or the military in some way (and often, both). So why is the area called Hampton 'Roads'? The term roads comes from roadstead, an old nautical term for an area where a ship can be at anchor that is not as sheltered as a harbor – other examples include Castle Roads in Bermuda and Brest Roads in France.

What about Newport News? That's up for a lot more debate. What seems most probable is 'News' derives from 'Ness,' an old mariner's term for 'point.'

The area's connection to the water and the military is exemplified by the **Mariners' Museum** (☎757-596-2222; www.marinersmuseum. org; 100 Museum Dr; adult/child $12/7; ⊗9am-5pm Wed-Sat, from 11am Sun), one of the largest maritime museums in the country. Exhibits include an intimidatingly comprehensive collection of miniature boats depicting the evolution of shipbuilding from the ancient world to modern navies; displays on Chesapeake Bay; and the USS *Monitor* exhibit, which contains the remains of one of the world's first ironclad warships, dredged from the waters of Hampton Roads.

The **Virginia Living Museum** (☎757-595-1900; www.thevlm.org; 524 J Clyde Morris Blvd; adult/child $17/13; ⊗9am-5pm, from noon Sun; P ♿) is an educational extravaganza that comprises a petting zoo, planetarium and other interactive science-y stuff. The best exhibits feature native wildlife in their natural habitats, including three beautiful, extremely rare red wolves.

The Drive ≫ Take I-64E for about 19 miles across the Elizabeth River. Get off in Norfolk on Exit 277 onto Tidewater Blvd.

A PENINSULA APART

Delmarva – the Eastern Shore of Maryland (made up of the nine counties in the state that lie on the east side of Chesapeake Bay), the Eastern Shore of Virginia (which consists of Accomack and Northampton counties) and the entire state of Delaware – is decidedly off the radar. Not just the tourist radar either; Delmarva residents have a sense of separation from the rest of the country that is both a source of pride and sporadic resentment.

The former derives from a cultural legacy passed through generations of small town traditions and connection to a unique geography; the latter manifests in occasional insularity, although the growth of the tourism industry discourages this sort of behavior.

So why is this region so distinct, when it seems so close to some of the nation's biggest metropolitan areas? The answer lays in the question, because said cities and their culture were historically cut off from America by Chesapeake Bay. The Bay Bridge wasn't built until 1952; the Hampton Roads Bridge–Tunnel wasn't completed until 1957 (and traffic wasn't flowing in both directions until 1976). Until then, the only way out here was by boat or twisting back roads.

While the highway, the internet and the shrinking small-scale commercial fishing industry have contributed to the homogenization of the region, this area still feels set apart from the rest of the Eastern seaboard. It's a flatland that's not quite Mid-Atlantic, not quite Southern yet also all of the above, where Philly pizza shares space on a menu with Maryland fried chicken and Virginia ham. Southern Delaware, Maryland's Eastern Shore and Virginia's Eastern Shore – the 'Del', 'Mar' and 'Va' of DelMarVa – may be divided between three states east of Chesapeake Bay, but in practice they form one cohesive cultural unit.

TRIP HIGHLIGHT

④ Norfolk

Norfolk is the home of **Naval Station Norfolk** (☎757-444-7955; www.cnic. navy.mil/norfolksta; 9079 Hampton Blvd; adult/child $10/5), the largest naval base in the world. Even if you're not into boats, it's hard not to be awed at the sight of the stunningly enormous warships at berth here. Depending on which ships are in, you might see aircraft carriers, destroyers, frigates, amphibious assault ships and submarines. The 45-minute bus tours are conducted by naval personnel and *must* be booked in advance (hours vary).

Nauticus (☎757-664-1000; www.nauticus.org; 1 Waterside Dr; adult/child $16/11.50; ☺10am-5pm, Tue-Sun) is a massive interactive maritime-themed museum that has exhibits on undersea exploration, the aquatic life of Chesapeake Bay and US Naval lore. Clambering around the decks and inner corridors of the USS *Wisconsin* is a definite highlight.

Although closed at the time of research, Norfolk's excellent **Chrysler Museum of Art** (☎757-664-6200; www. chrysler.org; 245 W Olney Rd; ☺10am-9pm Wed, to 5pm Thu-Sat, noon-5pm Sun) is set to reopen with a brand

new facade and interior in April 2014.

 p330

The Drive » In Norfolk, hop on I-264E and follow the highway about 16 miles east to downtown Virginia Beach.

TRIP HIGHLIGHT

⑤ Virginia Beach

The largest city in Virginia. The longest pleasure beach in the world. A location along the Chesapeake Bay bridge-tunnel, the longest bridge-tunnel complex in the world.

There's a lot of superlatives going on in Virginia Beach, which sprawls in several directions and consists of several distinct areas. The **resort beach** is the main strip of golden sand, with a 3-mile boardwalk and loads of beach games, greasy food and amusement park tat.

The **Chesapeake Bay Beaches** line Shore Dr on the northern side of the city. These are calmer, more nature-oriented beaches, for those who prefer waterfront forest to sandy coast. South of the resort beaches, along Sandbridge Rd, is **Sandbridge Beach**. This is a more upscale area of vacation rentals and seasonal condos.

Just north of Sandbridge is the

Virginia Aquarium & Marine Science Center (☎757-385-3474; www. virginiaaquarium.com; 717 General Booth Blvd; adult/child $22/15; ☺9am-5pm). If you want to see an aquarium done right, head here. The harbor seals and komodo dragons are a lot of fun, and there's an IMAX cinema on site.

p330

The Drive » Follow signs north to US 13 N and the Chesapeake Bay bridge-tunnel. You'll pay a $12 toll to cross 23 miles of bridge and tunnel, one of the most impressive engineering feats anywhere. US 13 runs the length of the Virginia Eastern Shore.

TRIP HIGHLIGHT

⑥ Virginia Eastern Shore

This long, flat peninsula is separated from Virginia by Chesapeake Bay, culture and history. The main town for eating and lodging (p331) is Chincoteague Island, at the other end of the peninsula, some 68 miles north by the Maryland border, covered in Trip 19: Delmarva (p227).

Wild dunescapes are a disappearing feature of the American landscape – they're often swallowed by developments or erosion. The 300-acre **Savage Neck Dunes Natural Area Preserve** (☎757-787-5989; Savage Neck Dr; ☺sunrise-sunset) protects a small patch of dusty

Northern Neck Kitchen at George Washington Birthplace National Monument

headland, all windblown umbrella sedge and tiny dwarf burhead.

The main pleasure on the Shore is just poking around back roads out to the waterfront(s) – either the rough Atlantic or placid Chesapeake Bay. The best way to access

the water is by small craft like kayaks, and if you're gonna get in a kayak, you might as well have a buzz, right? So hook up with **Southeast Expeditions** (☎757-525-2925; www. southeastexpeditions.net; 6631 Maddox Blvd, Chincoteague Island; kayak winery

tour $85), which leads a **Paddle Your Glass Off** kayak winery tour to some local vineyards. It's a *lot* of fun. Southeast offers plenty of sober, nature-oriented kayak tours as well.

🛏 p331

329

Eating & Sleeping

Colonial Beach

✗ Seaside Thai & French
Thai, French $$

(📞804-224-2410; 201 Wilder Ave; mains $12-23; ⏱11am-9pm Tue-Thu & Sun, til 10pm Fri & Sat) You read that right: two disparate cuisines – Thai and French – link up on the menu of this Colonial Beach restaurant, which is one of the most popular places in town. It's brilliant actually; this kitchen cranks out some stupendous Thai cuisine and very good French food. *Bon appetit* and *gin khao*.

🛏 Bell House B&B
B&B $$

(📞804-224-7000; www.thebellhouse.com/; 821 Irving Ave; s/d $125/142) As you explore historical homes and the residences of famous Americans in coastal Virginia, why not consider staying in one of their houses? The Bell House is the former digs of inventor Alexander Graham Bell, most famously the inventor of the telephone. His former mansion consists of four elegantly decked out rooms.

Norfolk ❹

✗ Todd Jurich's Bistro
American $$$

(📞757-622-3210; 150 W Main St #100; mains $20-37; ⏱11:30am-2pm Mon-Fri, 5:30-10pm Mon-Sat) This award-winning bistro serves innovative regional fare, like lump crab cakes and buttermilk cornbread pudding. The land options are nice as well; we dig the ribeye with (oh yes) duck-fat fries. The wine menu is wonderful and possesses a ton of depth and diversity. Your best romantic night option in town.

🛏 Residence Inn
Hotel $$

(📞757-842-6216; www.marriott.com; 227 W Brambleton Ave; r $140, ste $210; P 🛜 🏊 👪) A short stroll to a lot of the action on Granby St, one of Norfolk's main drags, this friendly chain hotel has a boutique feel, with stylish, spacious rooms with small kitchenettes and excellent

amenities. Book ahead or online for significantly reduced rates.

Virginia Beach ❺

✗ Jewish Mother
Deli $

(📞757-428-1515; 600 Nevan Rd; mains $5-14; ⏱10am-9pm Mon-Thu, 8am-2am Fri & Sat, 8am-9pm Sun) Get your nosh on with packed deli sandwiches, 'penicillin soup' (chicken and matzo ball) and monster-sized pie. The Reubens make a great lunch. Excellent live music is staged nightly; this is as much a gathering space for Virginia Beach youth as it is a great deli.

✗ Mahi Mah's
Seafood $$$

(📞757-437-8030; www.mahimahs.com; 615 Atlantic Ave; mains $18-33; ⏱5pm-late Mon-Fri, 7am-2pm Sat & Sun; 👪) This oceanfront local has some fantastic sushi, which makes up for the snail-paced service. By day, it's a bouncy restaurant that is a good option for families who want a nice meal out. After dark, this is one of the most popular nightspots on the beach.

🛏 First Landing State Park
Campground $

(📞800-933-7275; http://dcr.virginia.gov; Cape Henry; campsites $24-30, cabins from $75; P) You couldn't ask for a prettier campground than the one at this bayfront state park, although the cabins do not have a view of the water.

🛏 Hilton Virginia Beach Oceanfront
Hotel $$$

(📞757-213-3000; www.hiltonvb.com; 3001 Atlantic Ave; r $180-250, ste from $290; P 🛜 🏊) The premier place to stay on the beach is this super-luxurious 21-story hotel. The oceanfront rooms are spacious, comfortable and packed with amenities like huge flat-screen TVs, dreamy bedding and large balconies that open out to views of the beach and Neptune Park below. Check the website for information on the many spa treats and packages you can indulge in.

Virginia Eastern Shore ⑥

🛏 Bay View Waterfront　　　B&B $$

(📞757-442-6963, 800-442-6966; www.bayview
waterfrontbedandbreakfast.com; Copes Dr, Belle
Haven; r $140; 🅿🛜) You'll find Bay View at the
end of a pretty, isolated coastal country road
in Belle Haven, on the Bay side of the middle
of the Virginia Eastern Shore. There's three
rooms, friendly service, waterfront views and a
screened-in porch.

🛏 Cape Charles B&B　　　B&B $$

(📞757-331-4920; www.capecharleshouse.com;
645 Tazewell Ave, Cape Charles; r $140-200)
If you want to stay in Cape Charles, on the
southern end of Virginia's Eastern Shore, this
B&B is a good bet. Five individually appointed
rooms are done up in different colors, with
different historical accents; the Thomas
Dixon room, for example, features silk purses
recycled from hats worn to Woodrow Wilson's
inauguration.

Chincoteague Island

✕ Etta's Channel
Side Restaurant　　　Seafood $$

(📞757-336-5644; 7452 East Side Rd; mains
$17-23; 🕙5-9pm, til 9:30pm Fri & Sat; 🅿) As
the name implies, Etta's has a waterfront view. A
really superb waterfront view, when it comes to
it, but that's not the best feature of this standby.
We'd say our favorite element is having the

excellent coconut shrimp washed down with a
cold beer as the sun sets ... so OK, maybe the
view is kinda crucial.

✕ Mr Baldy's
Family Restaurant　　　American $$

(📞757-336-1198; 3441 Ridge Rd; mains $8-19;
🕙5:30am-9pm, til 10pm Fri & Sat; 🅿👶) An
old school Chincoteage institution, Mr Baldy's
offers delicious, great value food and, as
promised by the name, is family friendly. We're
not afraid to say this is the best breakfast on
the island, but the rest of the menu is great too.
We recommend sticking to the seafood: the
soft-shell crabs and oysters are a particular
strong point.

✕ Village Restaurant　　　Seafood $$$

(📞757-336-5120; 6576 Maddox Blvd; mains $12-
29; 🕙5-9pm) Perched on a romantic creekside
that provides plenty of birdsong and outdoor
insect buzz to accompany your meal, the
Village is a fine upscale seafood option for those
seeking a little romance and local flavor. Oyster
stew is a nice start; follow it up with broiled local
fish and a cold beer.

🛏 Island Manor House　　　B&B $$

(📞800-852-1505; http://islandmanor.com;
4160 Main St; r $125-185; 🛜) There's lots to love
about this bright and cheerful B&B. One of our
favorite qualities is the diversity – where many
B&Bs only offer two or three rooms, there are
nine to pick from here, and none of them are
overwhelmingly lacy.

STRETCH YOUR LEGS
RICHMOND

Start/Finish: Capitol Square

Distance: 2.7 miles

Duration: 3 hours

Stroll along the James River and experience the best Richmond has to offer: magnificent river views, historic architecture, the quiet dignity of the state capitol complex, red-brick buildings and plentiful park space.

Take this walk on Trips

Capitol Square

We start at the Virginia state **Capitol Square** (www.virginiacapitol.gov; cnr 9th & Grace Sts, Capitol Sq; ⊕9am-5pm Mon-Sat, 1-4pm Sun), one of the oldest state capitol complexes in the country. Designed by Thomas Jefferson, the main building was completed in 1788 and houses the oldest legislative body in the western hemisphere, the Virginia General Assembly, which was established in 1619. The free docent-led tours are excellent and highly informative.

The Walk >> Head down 10th St for about 2000ft toward the James River. Once you reach the river, turn right toward Brown's Island, which will then be directly ahead of you.

Brown's Island

Sitting in the James River, artificial **Brown's Island** (www.brownsisland.com) has been a major landmark since 1789 and the construction of the Haxall Canal. Back in the day the island hosted a coal factory and a hydroelectric plant; it has been a park since 1987. Trails crisscross the green and concerts are held regularly in warm months, including the Friday Cheers series which occurs ever Friday night in May and June from 6:30pm to 9pm.

The Walk >> Cross over the James River in front of the American Civil War Center. Turn left on Tredegar St; after 2000ft, turn right onto the 2nd St Corridor. At the end of the street cross the lawn to reach the Virginia War Memorial.

Virginia War Memorial

The **Virginia War Memorial** (☎804-786-2060; www.vawarmemorial.org; 621 S Belvidere Street; ⊕tours 9am-2:30pm), dedicated to all branches of service who served in all theaters of American combat since WWII, is an impressive structure. A large glass fronting overlooks the James River, and behind you, the Shrine of Memory is inscribed with the names of Virginia war dead. Names are arranged by county, city and then alphabetically.

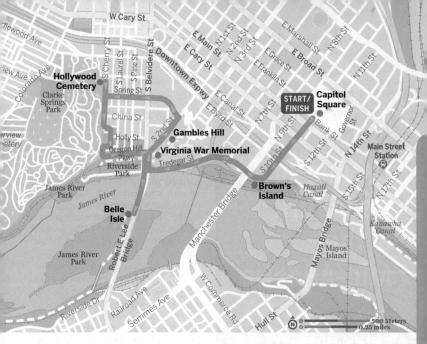

The Walk >> This walk is easy – you're already on Gambles Hill.

Gambles Hill

Gambles Hill is the park area immediately surrounding the Virginia War Memorial. There are great views over both the James River and downtown Richmond, depending on where on the hill you're standing. The west side of the hill towards Belvidere St is a pretty residential neighborhood of brightly colored townhouses.

The Walk >> Take Spring St to Cherry St, then turn right and walk a block to the cemetery entrance.

Hollywood Cemetery

Tranquil **Hollywood Cemetery** (hollywoodcemetery.org; entrance cnr Albemarle & Cherry Sts; ⏲8am-5pm, to 6pm summer), perched above the James River rapids, contains the gravesites of two US presidents (James Monroe and John Tyler), the only Confederate president (Jefferson Davis) and 18,000

Confederate soldiers. Free walking tours are given at 10am, Monday through Saturday.

The Walk >> Head towards James River (turn right out of the cemetery entrance you came in at) and walk towards Oregon Hill Parkway. Take the Parkway back toward the war memorial, then take one of the paths down the hill to Tredegar St, from where you can access a bridge to Belle Isle.

Belle Isle

A cute pedestrian bridge opens up **Belle Isle** (☎804-646-8911; www.jamesriverpark. org) to exploration. Once a quarry, power plant and POW camp during the Civil War (though never all at once), today this is one of Richmond's finest city parks. Big flat rocks are lovely for sunbathing, and hiking and biking trails abound. That said – don't swim in the James River. It's polluted and the currents are treacherous.

The Walk >> From Belle Isle, cross back over the pedestrian bridge and walk back along the James River on Tredegar St toward Brown's Island; turn left on S 10th St to reach Capitol Square.

Driving in New York & the Mid-Atlantic

A combination of scenic rural roadways and a dense network of highways – allowing you to leapfrog large distances – makes this a great road-tripping region.

Driving Fast Facts

→ **Right or left?** Drive on the right.

→ **Legal driving age** 16

→ **Top speed limit** 65mph (70mph on some Virgina hwys)

→ **Best Bumper Sticker** What if the Hokey Pokey IS What It's All About?

DRIVER'S LICENSE & DOCUMENTS

All drivers must carry a driver's license, the car registration and proof of insurance. If your license is not in English, you will need an official translation or an International Driving Permit (IDP). You will also need a credit card to rent a car.

INSURANCE

Liability All drivers are required to obtain a minimum amount of liability insurance, which would cover the damage that you might cause to other people and property in case of an accident. Liability insurance can be purchased from rental-car companies for about $12 per day.

Collision For damage to the rental vehicle, a collision damage waiver (CDW) is available from the rental company for about $18 a day.

Alternative sources Your personal auto insurance may extend to rental cars, so it's worth investigating before purchasing liability or collision from the rental company. Additionally, some credit cards offer reimbursement coverage for collision damages if you rent the car with that credit card; again, check before departing. Most credit-card coverage isn't valid for rentals of more than 15 days or for exotic models, SUVs, vans and 4WD vehicles.

RENTING A CAR

Rental cars are readily available at regional airports and in major towns. Rates usually include unlimited mileage. Dropping the car off at a different location from where you picked it up generally incurs a substantially higher fee. Of course, shop around on price-comparison websites. Renting a car without a major credit card is difficult, if not impossible. Most agencies rent child safety seats but you should reserve in advance.

Every major car-rental company operates in the area including:

Alamo (www.goalamo.com)

Avis (www.avis.com)

Budget (www.budget.com)

Dollar (www.dollar.com)

BORDER CROSSING

Crossing the US–Canada border at Niagara Falls, the St Lawrence Seaway (Wellesley Island State Park, Ogdensburg or Massena) or on Hwy 87 north of Champlain, NY on the way to Montreal is generally straightforward, though lines can be a hassle. All travelers entering the USA are required to carry passports, including citizens of Canada and the USA. If you're driving a rental car from Canada or Mexico you'll need documentation from your rental car company showing permission to bring the car to another country (check the policy before making the trip). Otherwise, you'll simply need documentation proving you're the owner of the vehicle.

MAPS

Detailed state-highway maps are distributed free by state governments. You can call or write to state tourism offices to request maps, or they can be picked up at tourism offices.

Another excellent map resource is **DeLorme Mapping Company** (www. delorme.com), which publishes individual state maps – atlas-style books with detailed coverage of backcountry roads. The scales range from 1:65,000 to 1:135,000.

The Mid-Atlantic box set includes Delaware, Maryland, New York, Pennsylvania, Virginia and West Virginia for $75.

ROADS & CONDITIONS

The quality of roadways varies widely, from potholed, suspension-killing sections of 'expressways' to smooth-as-glass highways, to sandy, rocky and everything-in-between rural byways. Rush-hour traffic around major cities could test the patience of Buddha. In the DC area, each lasts as long as three to four hours, and tunnels and bridges into and out of NYC can be backed up for miles. Northern Virginia is a nightmare of exits and fast interchanges between major roads.

➡ Road signage is not always well-placed or easy to interpret.

➡ One-way streets can make navigation in some cities and towns difficult.

➡ Roads to the region's beaches and shore areas are best avoided on Friday afternoons and Sunday evenings. Tune into local radio stations for traffic updates, especially at these times.

Tolls

The shortest and fastest route between two points often means taking a toll road. Most bridge and tunnels, in urban areas

Driving Problem Buster

What should I do if my car breaks down? Call the service number of your car-hire company and a local garage will be contacted. If you're driving your own car, it's a good idea to join AAA, who can be called out to breakdowns at any time. Many car insurance companies also offer roadside assistance.

What if I have an accident? If there are no serious injuries and your car is operational, move over to the side of the road. If there are serious injuries, call 911 for an ambulance. Exchange information with the other driver, including names, contact and insurance info, and license tag numbers. Then file an accident report with the police or Department of Motor Vehicles.

What should I do if I get stopped by the police? Stay in your car and keep your hands visible. The police will want to see your driver's license and proof of liability insurance. As long as you're not a serious threat, you probably won't end up in the pokey, although you'll probably get either a ticket or a warning if you've broken a road rule.

Will my E-Z Pass work in every state in the region? Yes, E-Z Pass, the electronic toll collecting system used in the northeastern US, is integrated so that you can pay tolls everywhere regardless of the state agency you are registered with.

Road Trip Websites

American Automobile Association (AAA; www.aaa.com) Provides maps and other information, as well as travel discounts and emergency assistance for members.

Cost of Tolls (www.costoftolls. com) Latest prices for all bridges, tunnels and roadways in the area.

Gas Buddy (www.gasbuddy.com) Find the cheapest places to gas up nearby.

Traffic.com (www.traffic.com) Real-time traffic reports, with details about accidents and traffic jams.

as well, call for a toll though usually not in both directions. Consider paying for an E-Z Pass account in advance to speed things up, avoid having to scrounge around for bills and change, and for reduced rates. Otherwise, tolls can be hefty (for example, bridge and tunnel tolls into New York City are about $13 one way). The following is only a short list:

➡ Atlantic City Expressway (connects Philly and AC)

➡ Garden State Parkway, New Jersey (from Cape May to Paterson)

➡ Gov Thomas E Dewey Thruway, New York (I-90)

➡ New Jersey Turnpike and John F Kennedy Memorial Highway (I-95)

➡ Pennsylvania Turnpike (I-76)

➡ Delaware Rte 1 (103-mile long highway from Maryland border to I-95)

➡ Dulles Toll Road (Rte 267) Northern Virginia

➡ Chesapeake Bay Bridge Tunnel (Virginia's Eastern Shore to Virginia Beach)

ROAD RULES

The maximum speed limit on most freeways is 65mph; Virginia has some sections where it is 70mph. Police in cruisers and unmarked cars enforce speed limits with varying degrees of intensity. Some stretches, like the Palisades Parkway in New York and New Jersey, are known hot spots for speed traps.

Other road rules:

➡ Driving laws are different in each state, but most require the use of safety belts. Texting while driving is prohibited.

➡ Unless otherwise indicated, making a right turn on a red light is allowed. The exception is NYC, where it is prohibited unless otherwise indicated.

➡ Children under four years of age must be placed in a child safety seat secured by a seat belt.

➡ Most states require motorcycle riders to wear helmets whenever they ride. In any case, the use of a helmet is highly recommended.

PARKING

Public parking in cities like NYC can be extremely challenging. Private lots tend to be very expensive, and metered parking rules confusing. In rural areas, it's generally free and easy to find. See p26 for more information about parking in New York City, Philadelphia and Washington, DC.

FUEL

Self-service gas stations in New Jersey are illegal. All are full-service; no tip is expected. Most in NYC are self-service. Otherwise, it varies, though the majority are self-service. Most pumps have credit-/debit card terminals built into them, so you can pay with plastic without interacting with a cashier. Fuel prices change frequently and vary according to location; on average, expect to pay $3.50 to $3.90 per gallon.

Loyalists swear by their favorite service stations which include gas and convenience stores: two behemoths in the area are Wawa, in New Jersey, eastern Pennsylvania and urban areas to the south; and Sheetz, found mostly in rural Pennsylvania, Maryland and Virginia.

SAFETY

The area in general might present a few more hazards than elsewhere, if only because it includes the most densely populated corridor in the country. So traffic around urban areas is thick; and drivers, especially in New Jersey and New York, are known for for being aggressive, if not just plain bad. Construction is virtually non-stop so sudden changes in traffic patterns and obstacles can arise without too much warning.

In urban areas especially, travelers are advised to always remove valuables and lock all car doors. Be extra cautious driving at night on rural roads, which might not be well lit and may be populated by deer and other creatures that can total your car if you hit them the wrong way.

FERRY CROSSINGS

Cape May – Lewes Ferry (www.capemaylewesferry.com; round-trip vehicle and driver $44, additional adult/child $10/5) Connects Delaware and Cape May on the southern tip of the New Jersey shore.

Lake Champlain (www.ferries.com; round-trip vehicle and driver $19, each additional adult/child $3.75/1.50) Plattsburgh, Port Kent and Essex, NY to Grand Isle, Burlington and Charlotte, VT.

White's Ferry (☎301-349-5200; one-way car/bicycle/pedestrian $5/2/1) Small car and passenger ferry that crosses the Potomac River between Leesburg, VA and Poolesville, MD.

RADIO

DC WAMU (88.5FM) for NPR; WKYS (93.9FM) is good for hip-hop and R&B.

Maryland WTMD (87.9FM) Great college station in Baltimore; WRNR (103.1FM) does good rock out of Annapolis.

Road Distances (miles)

	Albany, NY	Atlantic City, NJ	Baltimore, MD	Buffalo, NY	Charlottesville, VA	Dover, DE	East Hampton, NY	Ithaca, NY	Lake Placid, NY	Lancaster, PA	New York City, NY	Norfolk, VA	Philadelphia, PA	Pittsburgh, PA	Plattsburgh, NY	Princeton, NJ	Richmond, VA	Roanoke, VA	Washington, DC
Atlantic City, NJ	270																		
Baltimore, MD	330	150																	
Buffalo, NY	290	445	370																
Charlottesville, VA	480	305	155	460															
Dover, DE	310	130	105	450	210														
East Hampton, NY	250	230	290	480	450	270													
Ithaca, NY	165	290	305	155	455	300	330												
Lake Placid, NY	140	405	475	340	625	445	380	255											
Lancaster, PA	280	140	80	320	235	100	270	240	420										
New York City, NY	155	125	190	375	340	165	105	225	290	165									
Norfolk, VA	500	330	235	570	165	190	465	490	640	315	360								
Philadelphia, PA	240	60	100	380	255	80	200	230	375	80	100	275							
Pittsburgh, PA	460	365	250	215	320	330	480	315	550	240	370	435	305						
Plattsburgh, NY	160	430	495	375	645	470	400	320	50	440	310	660	395	590					
Princeton, NJ	185	90	145	370	300	125	155	255	320	110	50	315	45	340	345				
Richmond, VA	480	300	150	485	70	205	440	430	620	230	335	95	250	345	340	295			
Roanoke, VA	580	430	280	510	120	340	565	500	720	330	460	285	380	345	745	420	190		
Washington, DC	370	190	40	385	120	95	335	330	510	120	230	195	145	245	530	185	110	240	
Watertown, NY	175	385	400	215	560	390	420	130	125	335	320	585	325	425	160	315	540	610	450

New York & the Mid-Atlantic's Playlist

Take the 'A' Train Ella Fitzgerald with the Duke Ellington Orchestra

Autumn in New York Frank Sinatra

New York State of Mind Billy Joel

Jersey Girl Tom Waits

4th of July, Asbury Park (Sandy) Bruce Springsteen

My Old School Steely Dan

Take me Home Country Roads John Denver

My Blue Ridge Mountain Boy Dolly Parton

Gonna Fly Now (Theme from Rocky) Nelson Pigford & DeEtta Little

In the Jailhouse Now Jimmie Rodgers

East Virginia Blues Ralph Stanley & The Clinch Mountain Boys

Turkey in the Straw Dock Boggs

Mule Skinner Blues Dolly Parton

Hey, Good Lookin' Tennessee Ernie Ford

Keep on the Sunny Side Carter Family

My Clinch Mountain Home Carter Family

Blue Eyes Crying in the Rain Willie Nelson

New York WQXR (105.9FM) Classical music in NYC to calm gridlock-frayed nerves.

New Jersey WFMU (91.1FM) DJs have free rein to indulge their idiosyncratic interests.

Pennsylvania WXPN (88.5FM) Public radio station broadcasting from UPenn.

Virginia WBRF (98.1FM) Does classic country and bluegrass in southwestern Virginia.

BEHIND THE SCENES

SEND US YOUR FEEDBACK

We love to hear from travelers – your comments help make our books better. We read every word, and we guarantee that your feedback goes straight to the authors. Visit **lonelyplanet. com/contact** to submit your updates and suggestions.

Note: We may edit, reproduce and incorporate your comments in Lonely Planet products such as guidebooks, websites and digital products, so let us know if you don't want your comments reproduced or your name acknowledged. For a copy of our privacy policy visit lonelyplanet.com/privacy.

OUR READERS

Many thanks to the travelers who used the last edition and wrote to us with helpful hints, useful advice and interesting anecdotes: Dave Connelly, Mark Sauerhoff.

AUTHOR THANKS

MICHAEL GROSBERG

Special thanks to Carly Neidorf, my sometime trip and otherwise companion; my parents, Sheldon and Judy, for advice; to Kristin Mitchell and Claire Shubik on Pittsburgh; Darrah Feldman re Milford; Rebbecca Steffan for Adirondacks help; Gregory Henderson in the Catskills; Julie Donovan in the Laurel Highlands; Nina Kelly in the Brandywine Valley; and Terri Dennison for Route 6 insight.

ADAM KARLIN

Thank you to the Lonely Planet crew: Michael Grosberg, an understanding, gracious and ever-helpful coordinating author, the fabulous editorial team of Suki Gear, Bruce Evans, Alison Lyall and Jennye Garibaldi; mom and dad for raising me here; and Rachel Houge, whom I married right after I turned this book in.

PUBLISHER THANKS

Climate map data adapted from Peel MC, Finlayson BL & McMahon TA (2007) 'Updated World Map of the Köppen-Geiger Climate Classification,' *Hydrology and Earth System Sciences*, 11, 1633–44. Cover photographs: Front (clockwise from top): Adirondack State Park, Lake Flower/4Corners; Sugarloaf Mountain Winery, Comus, Maryland/Alamy; Red Truck on rural road, Maryland/Corbis. Back: Autumn in Shenandoah Valley, Virginia/Getty Images.

THIS BOOK

This 2nd edition of Lonely Planet's New York & the Mid-Atlantic's Best Trips guidebook was researched and written by Michael Grosberg and Adam Karlin. This guidebook was commissioned in Lonely Planet's Oakland office, and produced by the following:

Commissioning Editors Jennye Garibaldi, Suki Gear and Clifton Wilkinson

Coordinating Editors Luna Soo, Tasmin Waby

Senior Cartographer Alison Lyall

Coordinating Cartographer Gabriel Lindquist

Coordinating Layout Designer Katherine Marsh

Managing Editors Bruce Evans, Angela Tinson

Managing Layout Designer Jane Hart

Assisting Editors Tali Budlender, Trent Holden

Assisting Cartographer Fatima Basic

Cover Research Naomi Parker

Internal Image Research Aude Vauconsant

Thanks to Anita Banh, Laura Crawford, Ryan Evans, Larissa Frost, Chris Girdler, Andi Jones, Dan 'Spider-Dan' Moore, Trent Paton, Alison Ridgway, Dianne Schallmeiner, James Smart, Gerard Walker

INDEX

OUR WRITERS

OUR STORY

A beat-up old car, a few dollars in the pocket and a sense of adventure. In 1972 that's all Tony and Maureen Wheeler needed for the trip of a lifetime – across Europe and Asia overland to Australia. It took several months, and at the end – broke but inspired – they sat at their kitchen table writing and stapling together their first travel guide, *Across Asia on the Cheap*. Within a week they'd sold 1500 copies. Lonely Planet was born.

Today, Lonely Planet has offices in Melbourne, London and Oakland, with more than 600 staff and writers. We share Tony's belief that 'a great guidebook should do three things: inform, educate and amuse'.

Michael Grosberg Thanks to an uncle and aunt's house upstate on the Delaware River in the southern Catskills, Michael has had a base to explore the region for two decades– that is, when he's not home in Brooklyn, NYC. No matter his love for the city, getaways are necessary and he's taken every opportunity to travel far and wide in New York, New Jersey and Pennsylvania, from cross-country skiing in the Adirondacks, pitching a tent on an island in the St Lawrence River, chowing down on ballpark food at a Pirates game in Pittsburgh and finding a classic diner in Jersey's Pine Barrens.

My Favorite Trip 5 **Adirondack Peaks & Valleys** for wilderness forests, high peaks, glacial lakes and rustic camps.

Adam Karlin Adam was born in Washington, DC and raised in rural Maryland. His love of travel stems from a love of place that was engendered by the tidal wetlands of the Mid-Atlantic. That need for wandering has pushed him overseas and across the world, and in the process he has written close to 40 guidebooks for Lonely Planet, from the Andaman Islands to the Zimbabwe border.

My Favorite Trip 17 **Maritime Maryland** for its sheer pleasantness: a trek across preserved countryside, wild wetlands and postcard-perfect small towns.

Published by Lonely Planet Publications Pty Ltd

ABN 36 005 607 983

2nd edition – Feb 2014

ISBN 978 1 74179 8142

© Lonely Planet 2014   Photographs © as indicated 2014

10 9 8 7 6 5 4 3 2 1

Printed in China

MIX
Paper from responsible sources
FSC™ C021741

Paper in this book is certified against the Forest Stewardship Council™ standards. FSC™ promotes environmentally responsible, socially beneficial and economically viable management of the world's forests.